JONATHAN SWIFT
Political Writer

JONATHAN SWIFT

Political Writer

J. A. Downie

Senior Lecturer in English
University of London Goldsmiths' College

Routledge & Kegan Paul

London, Boston, and Henley

First published in 1984
Reprinted and first published as a paperback in 1985
by Routledge & Kegan Paul plc
14 Leicester Square, London WC2H 7PH
9 Park Street, Boston, Mass. 02108, USA and
Broadway House, Newtown Road,
Henley-on-Thames, Oxon RG9 1EN, England

Set in Baskerville by
Ann Buchan (Typesetters)
and printed in Great Britain by
Redwood Burn Ltd, Trowbridge

Library of Congress Cataloging in Publication Data

Downie, J. A. (James Alan), 1951–

Jonathan Swift, political writer.
Includes bibliographical references and index.
1. Swift, Jonathan, 1667-1745 – Political and social views.
2. Swift, Jonathan, 1667-1745.
3. Authors, Irish – 18th century – Biography.
4. Ireland – Politics and government – 18th century.
I. Title.
PR3728.P6D6   1984   828'.509[B]   83-19194

ISBN 0–7100–9645–3 (c)
ISBN 0–7102–0769–7 (p)

In Memory of
Henry Vaughan Jobling
(1924 - 1983)

'I have lived, and by the grace of God will die, an enemy to servitude and slavery of all kinds.'

Swift to Archbishop King, 18 May 1727

Our century —

Contents

Contents

Preface

In writing a new biography of Swift, I have tried to do four things: to present such facts as we have about his life, rather than to indulge in hypothesis or conjecture; to offer an account of his political ideas which is neither anachronistic nor unduly influenced by the (clearly) distorted views of his enemies; to provide a critical commentary on his major works which might form the basis for further study; and to present all these within the framework of a single volume which is neither unwieldy nor unintelligible to that inexorable arbiter of public taste, 'the general reader'.

Because of these ambitious aims, I realise that I have offered several hostages to fortune. Let it be said, then, that the most original part of the biography is the proposed revision of the prevailing view of Swift's politics. In the terms of the reign of Queen Anne, I argue, he is neither Whig nor Tory. To the best of my knowledge, he never called himself a Tory. Whenever he felt the inclination to label himself politically at all – which was not often – he consistently claimed to be a Whig. Usually he adopted the standpoint of a disinterested spectator witnessing the ridiculous affectation of Whig and Tory alike. 'I tell you what comes into my head', he wrote to Hester Johnson and Rebecca Dingley as late as 15 January 1713, 'that I never knew whether [you] were Whigs or Toryes; and I value our Conversation the more, that it never turned on that Subject.'

Clearly the ladies enlightened their friend, for on 7 March he noted that he 'never knew [Md's] Politicks before'. 'I avoid all Conversation with the oth^r Party,' he observed, 'it is not to be born, & I am sorry for it.' Presumably the ladies had revealed that, in the political hotbed which was the reign of Queen Anne, they were Tory in inclination. But we will look in vain for such a statement from Swift about his own politics, for he was 'of the old Whig principles, without the modern articles and refinements.' I feel it unwise to ignore this sort of profession. Perhaps as a type of shorthand it might be permissible to call Swift a Tory, because his attitudes are those which by Dr Johnson's day were embraced under the general banner of Toryism. But we must be careful. Better, I think, to try to come to terms with Swift's anachronistic political outlook, and to attempt to understand just what he meant by being 'of the old Whig principles, without the modern articles and refinements.' Otherwise, if we simply label him a Tory, we are distorting, quite wilfully, his ideas, and failing to identify the tradition in which he was writing.

Swift's Old Whiggery was not so much a political dogma as a view of the way life should be lived. Thus it affected more than merely his reaction to the politics of party, it informed his world view *tout court*. And as his views on morality, religion and politics are so closely interlinked, failure to comprehend his political ideas can lead to the misinterpretation of his writings. Even *A Tale of a Tub* is political, in that it refers back to a coherent picture of an ideal society. True, it is not *party* political, but its exposure of abuses in religion and learning serves, through metonymy, to make a political point about the manner in which society is deviating from an ideal. Swift's concept of the ideal is what I have chosen to call the Golden Age which, although it sometimes approximates to a pastoral golden age, is much more than a simple picture of rural innocence and benevolence. The Golden Age is, to Swift, a state in which human nature and human institutions, both ecclesiastical and political, are in pristine condition. They have since degenerated from this ideal situation and have become *corrupted* – a key word as far as the understanding of Swift's ideas is concerned. In his various writings, Swift implicitly but consistently refers back to this state of purity to show how great a discrepancy exists between actual and ideal. This is the constant thrust of his satire.

A considerable amount of space, therefore, is taken up in

the explanation of Swift's world view. Compensation has had to be found elsewhere. In presenting the facts of his life, I have elected to ignore, almost entirely, old, unproven traditions with which I disagree, instead of rehearsing them merely in order to dismiss them. Only when they constitute a genuine problem of interpretation have I devoted space to them. In the same way, other facets of Swift's career have been severely curtailed in the telling, or even omitted altogether. The problem of selection is particularly acute when it comes to balancing the account between years when we have been left very little information about his life, and others, such as those of the *Journal to Stella*, when we know his day-to-day activities. In being selective, I have of course borne in mind the political orientation of the biography. Those who want detailed information on the polite society in which Swift moved or on Swift's Irish friends, for instance, will inevitably be disappointed, and will be forced to look elsewhere. Similarly the critical sections are not meant to be comprehensive, much less exhaustive. They attempt to answer questions most commonly asked about the text by the student, and to suggest further lines of enquiry.

It is a pleasure to be able to thank those friends and colleagues who assisted me in the course of writing this book. I was especially fortunate to meet David Woolley almost as soon as I began work on Swift's biography, and his unmatched knowledge of the man and his writings was constantly available to me. I am grateful to David for many kindnesses, for comments on successive drafts of the manuscript, and for correcting Swift's correspondence and the *Journal to Stella* from the holographs. Michael Bruce, Bill Speck and Mary Wedd were also good enough to read the book in manuscript and make many pertinent suggestions. Irvin Ehrenpreis discussed Swift with me, and I benefited greatly not only from his conversation, but from the two published volumes of his monumental *Swift: The Man, His Works, and the Age*. I look forward to the appearance of the final volume, and am only sorry that I was unable to make use of it here.

Preface

Similarly, Pat Rogers's Penguin edition of Swift's *Poems* appeared too late for me to refer to it, though Pat was as encouraging and helpful as ever with regard to my own studies. Joan Mayhew generously lent me the manuscript of Professor George P. Mayhew's study of Swift's early life. Bill McCormack, Renny and Vicki McLeod, David Nokes and James Woolley assisted me in ways that were by no means confined to matters of scholarship. Without the friendship of such people over the years, this book would not have been written.

Finally acknowledgments of a pecuniary nature must be made. I was fortunate to spend several months in California in the summer of 1980 where I was, consecutively, a postdoctoral fellow at the William Andrews Clark Memorial Library, Los Angeles, and a visiting fellow at the Huntington Library, San Marino. The former fellowship allowed me to investigate Swift's polemical strategies in congenial company, and to attend seminars chaired by Professor William Frost. The latter made it possible for me to examine the Swift manuscripts at the Huntington. A travel grant from the Friends of London House Foundation enabled me to cross the Atlantic in the first place. I have also benefited from various grants from Goldsmiths' College research funds.

Cuxton, Kent, March 1983

Chronological Table

1667	Jonathan Swift was born on 30 November in Dublin
1668?	Taken by his nurse to Whitehaven in Cumberland?
1673	Began his education at Kilkenny College
1682	Entered Trinity College, Dublin on 24 April
1686	Graduated BA, February, *speciali gratia*
1688	William of Orange invaded England
1689	Swift left Ireland; went to his mother at Leicester; on her advice, he travelled to seek the patronage of Sir William Temple; in November he accompanied Temple from Sheen to Moor Park
1690	Returned to Ireland on the advice of physicians
1691	Returned to England; visited Oxford; arrived back at Moor Park around Christmas; composed his first, extant poem
1692	Took his MA from Hart Hall, Oxford; published *An Ode to the Athenian Society*, his first published work (?)
1693	Published his first prose work, *An Answer to a Scurrilous Pamphlet* (?)
1694	Left Temple's household and went to Ireland to take holy orders; ordained deacon on 25 October
1695	Ordained priest on 13 January; presented to the Prebend of Kilroot on 28 January; arrived in Ulster in March; became involved with Jane Waring
1696	Left Ulster; rejoined Temple at Moor Park; began work on *A Tale of a Tub* (?)
1698	Resigned Kilroot
1699	Death of Temple on 27 January; Swift left for

	London; travelled to Ireland in August as chaplain to the Earl of Berkeley
1700	Instituted Vicar of Laracor on 22 March; presented to the Prebend of Dunlavin in St Patrick's Cathedral in September
1701	Travelled to London; Hester Johnson and Rebecca Dingley left England to live in Ireland; Swift published the *Discourse*, his first political pamphlet, supporting the Whigs against the Tories; returned to Ireland
1702	Once again in England; met a number of leading Whigs; awarded degree of Doctor of Divinity from Trinity College, Dublin
1703	Again in England, arranging the publication of *A Tale of a Tub*
1704	Returned to Ireland in May; publication of *A Tale of a Tub*
1707	Returned to England to solicit the gift of Queen Anne's Bounty to the Irish clergy; met Esther Vanhomrigh (?)
1708	Met Addison and Steele; published *Bickerstaff Papers*; wrote *An Argument against Abolishing Christianity*
1709	Involved in the early *Tatler*; returned to Ireland at the end of June
1710	Trial of Dr Sacheverell; fall of the Whigs; Harley returned to power at the head of a predominantly Tory ministry; Swift returned to London at the beginning of September to solicit Queen Anne's Bounty from the new Prime Minister; met Harley; began writing *The Examiner* on Harley's behalf; fell out with the Whigs; began the *Journal to Stella*; visited the Vanhomrighs
1711	Friendship with the ministers growing; published *Miscellanies in Prose and Verse* (March); ended contributions to *The Examiner* (June); published *The Conduct of the Allies* (27 November)
1712	Published *Remarks on the Barrier-Treaty* (February); acted as ministerial *chef de propagande*; started work on a history of the peace-making; wrote *Cadenus and Vanessa* (?)

1713	Appointed to the Deanery of St Patrick's (April); installed (June); returned to England (October); wrote against Steele and Burnet
1714	Published *The Publick Spirit of the Whigs* (February); threatened with prosecution (March); the Scriblerus Club met; Swift left for Letcombe Bassett (31 May); fall of Harley (27 July); death of Queen Anne (1 August); succession of George I; fall of the Tories; Swift returned to Ireland, followed by Esther Vanhomrigh
1720	Published his first pamphlet since 1714, *A Proposal for the universal Use of Irish Manufacture*; began to write *Gulliver's Travels* (?)
1723	Death of Esther Vanhomrigh
1724	Published *Drapier's Letters*
1725	Wood's halfpence defeated; *Gulliver's Travels* completed
1726	Returned to England (March); interview with Walpole (April); arranged for publication of *Gulliver's Travels*; returned to Ireland (August); publication of *Gulliver's Travels* (28 October)
1727	Last visit to England; death of George I; Walpole still in power
1728	Death of Hester Johnson (28 January); visited Market Hill
1729	Returned to Market Hill; published *A Modest Proposal* (October)
1730	Last visit to Market Hill; published *A Libel on D— D—*
1731	Wrote many poems including the scatological verses; began work on *Verses on the Death of Dr. Swift*
1733	Published *An Epistle to a Lady* and *On Poetry: A Rapsody*
1735	Publication of the first volumes of Faulkner's edition of Swift's *Works*; Swift's memory deteriorated
1738	Onset of senile decay; published *Polite Conversation*
1742	Commission *de lunatico inquirendo* found Swift incapable
1745	Death of Swift (19 October)

'Whatever Reader desires to have a thorow Comprehension of an Author's Thoughts, cannot take a better Method, than by putting himself into the Circumstances and Postures of Life, that the Writer was in, upon every important Passage as it flow'd from his Pen.'

A Tale of a Tub

Granted, there is always much that is hidden, and we must not forget that the writing of history – however dryly it is done and however sincere the desire for objectivity – remains literature. History's third dimension is always fiction.

Hermann Hesse, *The Glass Bead Game*

Part One
Days of Deference, 1667–1700

1
Infancy

Men do not usually invent stories to explain the circumstances of their birth. Jonathan Swift was born in Dublin on 30 November 1667. And yet, complaining that 'all persons born in *Ireland* are called and treated as *Irishmen*, although their fathers and grandfathers were born in *England*,'[1] he would often deny that he was an Irishman. His friends were encouraged to think of him as an Englishman to such an extent that many of them, including Pope, 'imagined him a native.'[2] But on occasion Swift would go further. 'Sometimes he would declare that he was not born in Ireland at all, and seem to lament his condition, that he should be looked upon as a native of that country; and would insist, that he was stolen from England when a child, and brought over to Ireland in a band-box.'[3]

Swift made many claims about his birth and childhood which were only half true, or not true at all. He had been born in Ireland of an English father, thus it was, in his own view, 'a perfect accident' which led to his life-long association with Ireland,[4] and he took great care to emphasise his English background, down to spinning romantic stories minimising his contact in his infancy with the land of his birth. Swift was a posthumous child, named after his father. The elder Jonathan Swift had emigrated to Ireland soon after the death of his own father, Thomas, vicar of Goodrich and rector of Bridstow in Herefordshire, in 1658. The country was 'at this Time almost without Lawyers', and so he took up a career in law.[5] He married Abigail Errick in the summer of 1664, and a daughter, Jane, was baptised on 1 May 1666.[6] And then he died, quite unexpectedly, some months before the birth of his second child.

According to Swift, his father was 'much lamented on account of his reputation for integrity with a tolerable good understanding',[7] but this did little to ensure his mother's immediate security. For financial support, Abigail Swift was thrust upon the charity of her late husband's family. The elder Jonathan Swift had five brothers, three of whom – Godwin, William and Adam – lived in Ireland. Godwin Swift apparently received his brother's widow into his family 'with great affection.'[8] But Swift's early reliance on the kindness of his closest relations created a deep and powerful impression which coloured his adult outlook, and he regarded his parents' marriage as particularly irresponsible, as it was

> on both sides very indiscreet, for his wife brought her
> husband little or no fortune, and his death happening so
> suddenly before he could make a sufficient establishment
> for his family: And his son (not then born) hath often been
> heard to say that he felt the consequences of that marriage
> not onely through the whole course of his education, but
> during the greatest part of his life.[9]

Neither the Swifts nor the Erricks were native Irish families. Although, in the marriage register, Abigail Errick was described as a spinster of the city of Dublin, 'about two Years after her Husband's Death, [she] quitted the Family of Mr. *Godwin Swift*, in *Ireland*, and retired to *Leicester*.' We are unable to verify the assertion that this was 'the Place of her Nativity', but the Errick family certainly hailed from that area, her parents emigrating to Ireland in or around 1634.[10] However, Swift did not accompany his mother to England. As a baby, he had a wet nurse. Her presence was urgently required in Cumberland when he was about a year old, and so, instead of consulting his relations, she 'stole him on shipboard unknown to his Mother and Uncle, and carryed him with her to Whitehaven, where he continued for almost [two *erased*] three years.' When the abduction was discovered, Swift's mother 'sent orders by all means not to hazard a second voyage, till he could be better able to bear it.'[11]

And so, if we accept the tradition of Swift's kidnapping to be true, he was separated from his mother in his infancy, and it is uncertain when next he saw her. After about three years, he was 'brought into *Ireland* by his nurse', and 'replaced under the Protection of his Uncle *Godwin*.' Subsequently, 'he was sent at six years old to the School of Kilkenny.'[12] If this is true, then Swift spent virtually the whole of his childhood away from his mother. While he was in Kilkenny, she was on the other side of the Irish Sea. Swift is at pains to show that he was not neglected by his nurse. She was 'so carefull of him that before he returned [to Ireland] he had learnt to spell, and by the time that he was three years old he could read any chapter in the Bible.'[13] In the normal course of things, when children were brought up in the custody of nurses, even a mother's personal concern in her child's welfare could be quite limited. 'The behaviour did not appear odd, as no early biographer of Swift picked it out for special comment,' Irvin Ehrenpreis pertinently remarks. 'He himself implies that his mother's conduct seemed normal to him.'[14] But he did call the circumstances of his abduction 'very unusuall',[15] and whether or not Swift regarded as normal his relationship with his mother, the modern reader will hardly fail to be conscious of its peculiarities.

Perhaps the story of his kidnapping was merely one more elaborate fiction of Swift's old age to extenuate the fact of his Irish birth. True, he was peculiarly fond of merchants from Whitehaven, whom he regaled when they visited Dublin.[16] And yet he was inconsistent in the telling of his own story, for on another occasion he hinted that he had been *sent* to England when a year old.[17] Orrery suggests that the 'extraordinary event' of Swift's sojourn in England 'made his return seem as if he had been transplanted to *Ireland*, rather than that he had owed his original existence to that soil'.[18] This is a reasonable assessment of the probable effect of Swift's alleged kidnapping on his infant mind. But he had a happy knack of altering his recollection of the past to fit in with his current prospect of things. As he was content to stress on many occasions in his adult life, Swift's genius was not that of the infant prodigy, and yet here he is reading any chapter in the Bible when no more than three years old. Age plays tricks with memory, and Swift appears, at the last, to have had difficulty distinguishing the facts of his early years from the fictions he assiduously cultivated in his correspondence and conversation, and this may well have been the case with the strange tales he told about his birth and childhood.

The England into which Swift sometimes claimed to have been born had experienced seven years of the rule of the restored Charles II. It is far from clear exactly what had been restored in 1660, but the effect of the Great Rebellion on Swift's mind must not be underestimated. He preached remembrance 'of that excellent Kind and blessed Martyr CHARLES I. who rather chose to die on a scaffold than betray the religion and liberties of his people, wherewith GOD and the laws had entrusted him',[19] and his controlling ideas are clearly indicated in his insistence on religion and law as the safeguards of the 'common Rights and Privileges of Brethren, Fellow-Subjects, and even of Mankind'.[20] Without the security of liberty and property, in Swift's view, men were reduced to slavery, and he recognised, 'from [his] Youth upwards',[21] the threat posed by an encroaching executive. Not only could 'the rise and progress of Atheism among us' be traced back to the consequences of the Great Rebellion, but the decline in the virility of the nation's natural leaders, the aristocracy, was in large part a result of the shedding of the 'noblest Blood of *England*' in the king's defence. Thus their progeny 'either received too much Tincture of bad Principles from those fanatick Times; or coming to Age at the Restoration, fell into the Vices of that dissolute Reign'.[22]

The consequences of the Great Rebellion, then, were, in Swift's opinion, tremendously far-reaching, tending to the overthrow of all moral rectitude, and the destruction of the mixed monarchy of King, Lords, and Commons. As Algernon Sydney put it, 'Liberty cannot be preserved, if the manners of the people are corrupted,'[23] and in the loss of religion and the degeneration of the natural aristocracy, Swift saw ample reason to fear for the safety of the 'ancient constitution' in Church and State. He believed implicitly in a Golden Age, and decried the 'vile and false moral' that it was 'but a Dream'.[24] True, he felt that there was 'not virtue enough left among mankind';[25] that was the problem. His response was the traditional response to the satirist who is always looking over his shoulder to halcyon times when an idyllic, paternalistic society existed under the auspices of a morally upright land-based nobility. In explaining the causes of the Great Rebellion, Swift observed that 'power, which always follows property, grew to lean to the side of the people, by whom even the just rights of the crown were often disputed.'[26] The resulting imbalance of power between the three components of the body politic – King, Lords and Commons – led to the outbreak of hostilities in 1642.

But the Restoration of Charles II indicated, at the very least, that the political nation had reached a consensus of opinion on the question of the structure of society. Prior to the civil wars, and after a measure of stability had been achieved under Cromwell, society had been hierarchical – and hierarchical it was to remain. This meant monarchy, for even this basic assumption had been threatened during the hostilities, and a figure-head was needed at the social apex. Sir William Temple observed, in his *Essay upon the Original and Nature of Government,* that the pyramid was the 'firmest' social model. Swift agreed. The narrowing of the base of society only led to trouble, and in 1660 the 'usurped powers' had enjoyed no broad foundation in the affections of the nation.[27]

This was one popular view of the Restoration. In the 1640s the heterogeneous Levellers had brought the rights of the less well-off – those whose property did not consist solely of land – to the forefront of affairs, whilst the Diggers or True Levellers, through the writings of Gerrard Winstanley, had put forward a radical if totally ineffectual manifesto which was communist or even anarchist in spirit. Indeed the unspoken assumption that only the propertied had a voice in the nation's affairs had had to be enunciated at times by confused and frightened men – a signal illustration of the various pressures being exerted on the social fabric. 'When we speak of the people', Marchamont Needham explained, 'we do not mean the confused promiscuous body of the people.'[28] It would be worthwhile to reflect that, as we have seen, when Swift refers to the 'people' in his writings, he almost certainly had this sort of unspoken distinction in mind.[29]

The electoral system provides a practical view of the hierarchical concept at work. Out of a population of around

5½ million in England and Wales, no more than 300,000 had the right to vote – perhaps one adult male in four had a say of any sort in the affairs of the kingdom. The deciding factor was one of property. It should be stressed that while social divisions were quite clear and well-defined, there was none the less a healthy degree of social mobility. Writing of the century after 1688, Geoffrey Holmes notes that British society 'enjoyed the advantages of rock-like solidity without the disadvantages of petrifaction'.[30] Even so, the hierarchical model which had been confirmed by the Restoration was jealously guarded by the political nation under the banner of 'Liberty and Property'. The lesson of the Great Rebellion – 'he who practiseth disobedience to his superiors, teacheth it to his inferiors' – had been learnt, and learnt well. The bloodless character of the 'Palace Revolution' of 1688 is indicative of this new circumspection. A monarch was necessary, but he could be replaced without jeopardising the very fabric of society.

Swift approved of this new-found wisdom, appreciating the dangers of instability. And yet, however imperceptibly, and however loath contemporaries were to admit it, the balance of power had changed in 1660; not, indeed, between propertied and unpropertied, but between King and Parliament, and this is what perturbed Swift. True, monarchy had been restored, but its powers had been imprecisely yet indelibly redefined. The Triennial Act of 1664 encouraged the calling of a new Parliament every three years. It points to a new attitude towards this hallowed institution. It was emerging from the Middle Ages, when it had been dependent on the whim of the King, and was beginning to wield its own very considerable authority. The religious settlement, for instance, was dictated by Parliament. The Act of Uniformity of May 1662, which established the Church of England by law, also defined the precise nature of the Establishment. The King no longer decided the character of the national faith. By the 1670s Parliament was demanding the exclusion of the Roman Catholic, James, Duke of York, from the line of succession to the throne. With the Glorious Revolution, the monarchy became **Parliamentary** in name as in fact, and an Act of Parliament settled the Crown in the Protestant line.

Hereditary title had ceased to be sufficient recommendation. Although the relative position of King and 'people' had been largely undefined in 1660, the Great Rebellion had undoubtedly left its mark. Things could never be quite the same again.

Although Swift's adherence to the concept of not only a hierarchical society, but also an Established Church, was beyond dispute, the balance of the mixed monarchy of King, Lords, and Commons was of great concern to him. He never denied the right of the people to settle the succession by law. But he was worried lest the weakening of the power of the Crown would unsettle the delicate balance which was so crucial to the well-being of the ancient constitution. This was the line of argument he pursued against the House of Commons in his first political tract, *A Discourse of the Contests and Dissensions between the Nobles and Commons in Athens and Rome, with the Consequences they had upon both those States,* in 1701. For the state to avoid corruption, no one element could be allowed to predominate. For this reason it was imperative that, as in 'all well-instituted States', the executive and legislative powers were 'placed ... in different Hands'.[31] But with the curtailing of the powers of the Crown, it was a question how long this vital check on the power of the executive would remain viable, and Swift loudly lamented the Court's frequent interference in the free proceedings of Parliament.

Most of these principles seem to have been derived from his family background. In the Great Rebellion, Thomas Swift's house at Goodrich on the banks of the Wye was, from the beginning of the fighting, under almost constant threat from Parliamentarian forces. 'My Grandfather was so persecuted and plundered two and fifty Times by the Barbarity of Cromwell's Hellish Crew', Swift noted in 1739, 'that the poor old Gentleman was forced to sell the better half of his Estate to support his Family.'[32] His death in 1658, two years before the Restoration, deprived him of any chance of reparation under the terms of the land settlement. It was, no doubt, the impoverishment of the family estate which induced four of his sons (including the eldest) to try their luck in Ireland.

Thomas Swift was not the first of his line to pursue a career in the Church. Both his father, William, and his grandfather, Thomas, had been rectors of St Andrew's, Canterbury. On his mother's side, Swift's grandfather was descended from members of the Episcopal Bench. If we go back five generations, then, Jonathan Swift's ancestors were bishops. The family's loyalty to the Church of England had been tried and tested, and the Swifts did not take kindly to nonconformity. Deane Swift remarks that Swift's paternal grandfather was 'bred up ... with an abhorrence and contempt for all *sectaries*'.[33] This was the tradition into which Jonathan Swift was born in 1667, and his own strong opinions on nonconformity can be imputed, with confidence, to his upbringing. 'Pox on the Dissenters and Independents!' he wrote in 1704, 'I would as soon trouble my head to write against a louse or a flea.'[34] Clearly Thomas Swift's contempt for Protestant Dissenters from the Church of England was mirrored in his grandson's attitudes, and Swift's equal abhorrence of Atheists, Socinians and Deists led him, on many occasions, to break his silence, and to attack the Dissenters in print with unbated ferocity.

One aspect of Swift's future, therefore, can be attributed to the influence of family tradition, and literary leanings can also be discerned among his widespread relatives. Swift's maternal grandmother was a Dryden. John Dryden's grandfather was Swift's father's great-uncle; the author of *Absalom and Achitophel* and the author of *Gulliver's Travels* were second cousins once removed.[35] Swift was related by marriage to Sir William Davenant, too, and the author of *Gondibert* was a widely respected figure in the seventeenth century. Swift's uncle Thomas married Davenant's daughter Mary. Thus Sir William's son, Charles Davenant, whose 'Tom Double' pamphlets were to be so popular in the first decade of the eighteenth century, was the uncle of Swift's cousin Thomas – his companion at Kilkenny and Trinity College, and the reputed co-author of *A Tale of a Tub*.[36] Swift's literary connexions were surprisingly extensive.

While some traits can be seen to have their origins in Swift's family background, others can be attributed to the circumstances of his infancy. Certainly his adult tendency to look after and account for every farthing can be seen as a natural legacy of his childhood. It was not simply that he was mean. He asked to be 'represented as a man of thrift onely as it produceth liberty and Independence, without any thoughts of hoarding; and as one who bestows every year at least one third of his income.'[37] His generosity was proverbial in Dublin. But for much of his life he had had to make do, and so financial security was high on his list of priorities.

A second consequence of his infancy was a profound reluctance to become too closely involved with individuals, however much he responded to the needs of the community as a whole. His own words on the subject are often quoted:

> I have ever hated all Nations professions and Communityes and all my love is towards individualls for instance I hate the tribe of Lawyers, but I love Councellor such a one, Judge such a one for so with Physicians (I will not speak of my own Trade) Soldiers, English, Scotch, French; and the rest but principally I hate and detest that animal called man, although I hartily love John, Peter, Thomas and so forth. this is the system upon which I have governed my self many years (but do not tell) and so I shall go on till I have done with them ...[38]

And yet they should not be taken too seriously. True, Swift attacked those habitual butts of satire, lawyers, judges, physicians, but he was quickly moved to anger *on behalf of* nations and communities. We only have to think of his defence of the Irish, and the Irish weaving community in particular. Similarly, although he satirised clergymen, he was a staunch supporter of their rights. His bantering tone can be detected in his reference to his own calling as a 'Trade'.

Swift undoubtedly did make close friends, and he valued friendship more highly than virtually anything else. But he found intimate relationships very painful, and often regretted his own involvement in them. 'I think there is not a greater folly than that of entering into too strict and particular a friendship', he wrote, because the loss of such friends meant that 'a man must be absolutely miserable.'[39] It would seem reasonable to assume that his ability to relate to people was inevitably affected by his upbringing. Separated from his mother and sister, and dependent on a surrogate father, his

11

early relationships were surely brief. True, he had a surrogate mother in his wet nurse. It was, after all, a fondness for the child at her breast which, apparently, incited her to abduct her charge. But presumably he was separated from her, too, on his return to Ireland sometime around his fourth birthday. Not even her name has been handed down to posterity. And then, at the age of six, he was sent away to school, probably never to see his mother again until he was quite grown up.

The effect of these disruptions on Swift can only be conjectured, not accurately assessed. His antipathy to Godwin Swift in later life was marked. Swift tended to look up to older men, however, as if trying to see in them an example, a pattern worthy of emulation. It was perhaps the want of a father which provoked such a response. Similarly his abnormal attitude to women might be explained by his lack of sustained involvement with the sex from his infancy. Women had had a disconcerting tendency to fade out of his early life without the slightest reason, or so it might have seemed. They were unreliable. To set one's heart on such unaccountable objects was rather imprudent. Of marriage, he wrote thus in 1692:

> among all the young gentlemen that I have known to have Ruind them selves by marrying (which I assure you is a great number) I have made this general Rule that they are ... young, raw & ignorant Scholars, who for want of knowing company, believe every silk petticoat includes an angell...

Profound sentiments from a worldly-wise young man of twenty-four who had experienced life, and who acknowledged himself to be 'so hard to please, that I suppose I shall put it off to the other world'![40]

Swift had what he took to be the bad example of his own parents' marriage as a model. He had never known his father. It is questionable how much he knew his mother. Very little is known about Abigail Swift, or about Swift's frequent adult visits to Leicester. He saw her every time he crossed over to England, both on his way to London, and on his way back to Ireland. By 1704 he had, by his own calculation, made sixteen

12

voyages.[41] But Leicester was never his home. Usually he was just passing through. On only one occasion does Abigail Swift appear to have returned to Ireland.[42] 'If the way to Heaven be through piety, truth, justice, and charity', he wrote on her death in 1710, 'she is there.'[43] There are no real grounds for questioning the sincerity of Swift's apostrophe, but it is conspicuous that, in his enumeration of his mother's virtues, he fails to mention the quality of love.

Jane Swift, his sister, hardly appears to have entered Swift's life at all. She seems to have travelled to Leicester with her mother within a very few years of her father's death, and so she would not have seen her brother during by far the greatest part of his childhood. She fails to command much attention in Swift's extant correspondence, and he shunned her company after her marriage in 1699, apparently on account of her choice of husband. His strict sense of marital rectitude would not allow him to condone the ill-considered match. But what his firm view of the right way of behaving denied, his generosity supplied. He paid his sister an annuity of around £15 until her death.[44]

Swift's knowledge of women, then, appears to have been limited. And yet, perhaps because of their strangeness, he was obsessed by them. Women fascinated him to such an extent that some contemporaries thought they were his greatest weakness.[45] Certainly he loved to be surrounded by admiring women, and he responded to their flattery with a gallantry peculiar to his own 'unconfin'd humour'.[46] But they were not to come too close, for he observed that 'the satyrical Part of Mankind will needs believe, that it is not impossible, to be very fine and very filthy.' Swift was of this camp. His motto would seem to have been *noli me tangere*.

Swift was preoccupied with female cleanliness. In *A Letter to a Young Lady on her Marriage,* he recommended 'a suitable Addition of Care in the Cleanliness and Sweetness of their Persons'. This merely echoed his advice to a woman to whom he offered his hand in marriage. It was of no matter to him, he wrote, 'whether your person be beautiful' – 'Cleanliness ... is all I look for'![47] True, by the time he offered this kind counsel, his feelings for Jane Waring had considerably abated. But Swift was a strange suitor for any woman to have, for he was

13

never able to come to terms with the fact that 'Love has pitched his mansion in/The place of excrement.' It was not so much that this was the 'excremental vision' it has been labelled. Satire traditionally dealt in the cloacal.[48] Swift's own personal concern for the scatological may have given an edge to his satire. But, for whatever reason, he was unable to contemplate sexual intimacy. The nineteenth century, with its own obsession with masturbation, liked to lay the blame for Swift's 'perversion' on over-indulgence in adolescence leading to impotence in adulthood.[49] There is no evidence for this. To all appearances, Swift was perfectly capable of initiating sexual relations, but he chose to remain celibate. Marriage, in his opinion, was one of the two 'points of the greatest moment' when the passions were intended 'to prevail over reason', 'since', as he put it, 'no wise man ever married from the dictates of reason.'[50]

It is, then, significant that the woman to whom Swift was constant, and with whom he felt completely confident, he had known since he was a young man of about twenty-one, and she a girl of six. Hester or Esther Johnson – 'Stella' – was another in Swift's long line of surrogates. She was a little sister. He played with her, taught her to write, and advised her what to read. In consequence, he took great delight in her achievements, and recorded her merits and her bon mots 'for [his] own satisfaction'.[51] And so, as England was seeking political stability after the shocks of civil war, plague and fire, Jonathan Swift, a child of the Restoration, embarked on a life-long search for emotional stability, after the trauma of infancy. 'I will ... tell you', he wrote to Bolingbroke and Pope when he was sixty-one:

> all my endeavours from a boy to distinguish my self, were only for want of a great Title and Fortune, that I might be used like a Lord by those who have an opinion of my parts; whether right or wrong, it is no great matter; and so the reputation of wit or great learning does the office of a blue riband, or of a coach and six horses.[52]

It would be unwise to take Swift too seriously, but there are cases in which the pursuit of fame, 'That last infirmity of noble mind', serves as a form of therapy.

14

2
Education

When he was six years old, Swift started his formal education at Kilkenny College, 'the finest institution of its kind in Ireland'.[1] Founded in the previous century by the eighth Earl of Ormond, it had a distinguished tradition and enjoyed a considerable reputation. If he did nothing else, Godwin Swift gave his nephew a sound start in life.

The school's rigorous curriculum was outlined in new statutes drawn up in 1684, when it transferred to its present site in the city. Although Swift was no longer at Kilkenny at the time, some details of his school-life may perhaps be taken from this source. The day began with prayers at six o'clock in spring and summer, and the first session of lessons lasted until ten, with a second session of four hours from noon onwards. In autumn and winter the routine was put back a whole hour. Thursdays and Saturdays were half-days on which, after the catechism, which took up the half-hour immediately after ten o'clock, the pupils were free for the rest of the day until evening prayers. Sundays were given over to worship. Short holidays at Easter, Whitsuntide and Christmas punctuated the calendar.[2]

Looking back on his schooldays, Swift remarked upon the tendency to dwell only on the good times. 'I formerly used to envy my own Happiness when I was a Schoolboy, the delicious Holidays, the Saterday afternoon, and the charming Custards in a blind Alley', he wrote to Charles Ford, 'I never considered the Confinement ten hours a day, to nouns and Verbs, the Terror of the Rod, the bloddy Noses, and broken Shins.'[3] Swift's suspect memory none the less suggests similarities between the regimes that obtained at Kilkenny before

15

and after 1684: the Saturday half-day, and the long classroom hours. The study of Latin and Greek grammar was a prominent part of contemporary educational practice. It is perhaps no coincidence that the classical languages were Swift's best subject at Trinity College.

But really we know very little about Swift's schooldays. A few stories survive, deriving, unfortunately, from sources of dubious reliability. 'When I was a little boy', Swift recalled in later life, 'I felt a great fish at the end of my line which I drew up almost on the ground, but it dropt in, and the disappointment vexeth me to this very day, and I believe it was the type of all my future disappointments.'[4] Perhaps this is of more interest for the light it throws on his adult outlook on life than as an authentic picture of his childhood. However, Lyon notes that 'soon after he entered the school', Swift came up with 'these words whch he term'd *Latino-Anglice, Mi dux et amasti cum*' (My duck's ate [i.e. eaten] a masticum). Here, perhaps, is the prototype of the more complicated Anglo-Latin word-games he was to play in the 1730s in particular with Thomas Sheridan.[5] Otherwise, his schooldays elude us.

It is doubtful if Swift even so much as saw his mother throughout his time at Kilkenny. There is no indication that she visited him, and the school vacations were almost certainly too short for a journey to England.[6] For companionship, Swift apparently learned to rely on his cousin and fellow-pupil, Thomas Swift, whose straitened circumstances were very similar to his own, and who was a year or so the elder. Out of the other fifty or sixty boys at Kilkenny, very few are mentioned by Swift in his later life. Two exceptions are William Congreve the poet and playwright, whom Swift can have known but briefly at the school, as he began his studies only a few months before Swift left for Trinity College, and the merchant adventurer, Francis Stratford, who is mentioned in the *Journal to Stella*.[7]

The town of Kilkenny is situated some sixty miles southwest of Dublin. In 1682 Swift retraced his steps to his native city where, on 24 April, he was admitted as a pensioner into Trinity College at the age of fourteen.[8] He was one of the youngest undergraduates – if not the youngest – and he lived in the College as a paying boarder. His time at TCD does not appear to have been an unduly happy one, nor was Swift inclined, in his later years, to look back upon the good times. He expressed his feelings thus:

> at fourteen he was admitted into the University at Dublin, where by the ill Treatment of his nearest Relations, he was so discouraged and sunk in his Spirits, that he too much neglected some parts of his Academical Studyes, for which he had no great relish by Nature, and turned himself to reading History and Poetry.[9]

When he was at Oxford in 1692, he wrote that he felt 'more obliged in a few weeks to strangers, than ever I was in seven years to Dublin College'.[10]

It would be worthwhile to deal in turn with these aspects of Swift's undergraduate career. The precise nature of the 'ill Treatment of his nearest Relations' is uncertain. Does this refer to his mother, or to Godwin Swift? Orrery notes that Godwin Swift 'voluntarily became [Swift's] guardian',[11] but, as Irvin Ehrenpreis notes, 'there is no conclusive proof that Godwin *was* the boy's mainstay through school and university.'[12] Our main source for involving Godwin Swift at all is Swift's own keen, long-lasting dislike of his uncle, perhaps best seen in his cutting comments on Swandlingbar, 'a famous town, where the worst iron in the kingdom is made':

> It was a most witty conceit of four gentlemen, who ruined themselves with this iron project. *Sw.* stands for *Swift*, *And.* for *Sanders*, *Ling.* for *Darling*, and *Bar.* for *Barry*. Methinks I see the four loggerheads sitting in consult, like Smectimnius [*sic*], each gravely contributing a part of his own name to make up one for their place in the iron-work; and could wish they had been hanged, as well as undone, for their wit.[13]

Swift's charity rarely extended to the forgiveness of what he took to be slights or insults. His 'old Maxim', as Lady Betty Germain reminded him in 1732, was 'you must have offended them because you dont forgive.'[14] Swift's disrespect for

17

Godwin Swift was profound, but whether or not he had offended his guardian, indeed whether or not his guardian had ill-treated him, we simply do not know.

When we consider that the Swifts in Ireland had two fatherless relations, Jonathan and Thomas, to take care of almost from birth, that both went to Kilkenny School and to Trinity College, that both took degrees and went on to take holy orders, there seems little basis for Swift's overwhelming ingratitude. But whatever were Swift's feelings for his Uncle Godwin, he displayed no such irreverence to William Swift. 'My sister told me, you was pleased to ... wonder, I did so seldom write to you', he explained to him on 29 November 1692, 'I [hope you have] been so kind, to impute it neither to ill mann[ers or want of] respect. I always [have] thought that sufficient from one, who has always been but too troublesome to you.'[15] And Swift appears to have been on friendly relations with Godwin Swift's sons, Willoughby and Deane, even after their father's death. Lyon notes that Swift 'received frequent Remittances from his Uncle *William* and his Cousin *Willoughby Swift whilst he was at Moorpark*', while his mother always retained 'a grateful remembrance of all the kindness [Willoughby] was pleased to shew to [her] son'.[16]

If these instances of the charity of his relations are set against Swift's allegations of ill-treatment while at TCD, we can recognise the symptoms of his insecurity. For Swift, it took very little for indifference to become hatred, or neglect to be transformed by his fervent imagination into studied contempt. This, at least, would explain his resentment towards his 'nearest Relations' on the account of his student days. No doubt the adolescent Swift was far from well-off, but we should take into account the financial circumstances of the family before joining in his cries of injustice. Unless, that is, Swift's complaint refers not to matters financial, but emotional. With his mother in England, it is quite possible that during his adolescence Swift felt unloved, for where would he go to find affection?

Swift, then, on his own admission, was in low spirits at TCD. It is impossible to say how much this detracted from his academic performance. It is clear, however, that he nourished an active dislike for certain parts of the undergraduate curriculum. The studies for the degree of Bachelor of Arts included Latin, Greek, Hebrew, and Aristotelian philosophy. There was an emphasis on logic – on syllogistic disputation – – which was not at all to Swift's taste. His feelings are vividly recorded in a letter of 3 May 1692 to his cousin, Thomas Swift, when Swift was preparing to take his MA degree at Oxford: 'to enter upon causes of Philosophy', he wrote, 'is what I protest I will rather dy in a ditch than go about.'[17] 'He held logic and metaphysics in the utmost contempt', Orrery recalled, 'and he scarce considered mathematics and natural philosophy, unless to turn them into ridicule.'[18]

The natural consequence of this antipathy, of course, is to be seen in both *A Tale of a Tub* and the Laputian episodes of *Gulliver's Travels*. But a more immediate result was his poor performance in the relevant subjects at university. Only the terminal examination marks for Easter 1685 survive, but they reveal Swift's lack of application in those studies he disliked. While, as one might expect, he received *bene*, the top grade, for Greek and Latin, his mark for Aristotelian physics was *male*. This was not the worst category. In descending order, the five grades used were *bene, mediocriter, negligenter, male,* and *pessime.* For the 'thema', or Latin essay on a set theme, he received *negligenter*.[19]

These are not distinguished marks, of course, but they endorse Swift's claim that he concentrated on more congenial studies at the expense of the rest. Nor was *male* a failure. Only seven students in the examinations (including Swift) were awarded *bene* in Greek and Latin, and only eight achieved that mark in more than one subject. Thomas Swift was given *mediocriter* on each of his three papers. Jonathan Swift was not an average student. His grades fluctuated, but the potential for first-class results was there. The relevance of Swift's performance at the Easter 1685 examinations can be understood when we turn to his actual degree. He took his BA in February 1686, at the age of eighteen, *speciali gratia.* Instead of simply being admitted to his degree in the regular way, Swift graduated by special dispensation.

The term, *speciali gratia,* has bedevilled Swift scholarship. Swift himself noted that the result of his neglecting his 'Academical Studyes' was that when the time came for taking his degree of Batchlor, although he had lived with great Regularity and due Observance of the Statutes, he was stopped of his Degree, for Dullness and Insufficiency, and at last hardly admitted in a manner little to his Credit, which is called in that Colle[*d*]ge *Speciali gratia*, [which *erased and in the margin:* And this discreditable mark] as I am told, stands upon record in their Colle[*d*]ge Registry.[20]

To put this 'disgrace' into perspective, it is necessary to realise its implications. Each year, several students graduated by special grace; far from being unique, it was not even an unusual procedure. Swift was 'stopped of his Degree, for Dullness and Insufficiency'. What does this phrase mean? During the statutory twelve terms of residence, the undergraduate had to pass examinations at the beginning of each term, relating to the previous term's studies. To reach this point in his career, therefore, Swift must have passed examinations in all of his subjects, including logic.[21] What went wrong?

Before qualifying for his degree, the undergraduate had to perform a scholastic disputation. Perhaps Swift stumbled at the final hurdle. As we have seen, he had no great liking for logic. Failure at this 'final and perfunctory ritual' might have been sufficient to prevent him being awarded the degree other than *speciali gratia*.[22] Swift emphasised that it was not withheld for bad behaviour. One final consideration may be the use of the term 'insufficiency'. Does this refer simply to academic inadequacy, or to a lack of funds? If, for some reason, Swift took his BA *speciali gratia* because of a combination of circumstances, including financial ones, then it might substantiate his grievances against the 'ill Treatment of his near Relations'. In any event, Swift's undergraduate career was hardly a distinguished one, and, without doubt, embarrassing to the future Dean of St Patrick's, Dublin. But it was not a disgraceful performance either, and he was in the company of four older students who also received their degrees by special grace in February 1686.

Despite his problems, Swift stayed on at TCD, studying for

his master's degree. To the undergraduate curriculum were added mathematics and politics. But whether or not Swift, as an undergraduate, lived 'with great Regularity and due Observance of the Statutes' (we have no evidence on which to judge), his postgraduate years were fraught with insubordination. 'During one week in the summer of 1686', writes Irvin Ehrenpreis, 'only a single other student was fined as heavily as Swift for missing chapel.'[23] While such fines were relatively commonplace, Swift's admonishment for 'neglect of duties and frequenting the town' in March 1687 appears more serious. Clearly he was kicking at the traces, perhaps a reflection of his situation within the College.[24] He may even have been involved in the notorious *tripos* of John Jones, which, in 1688, abused members of the faculty with so much freedom that the *terrae filius* was suspended. Swift was not the secret author of the whole of Jones's heavy-handed satire, but the better sections of dog-latin bear comparison with his own Anglo-Latin word-games, and may indicate his collaboration.[25]

The culmination of this outburst of juvenile delinquency occurred, appropriately enough, on Swift's twenty-first birthday. On 30 November 1688 he was found guilty of starting a tumult in the College, during the course of which he had insulted the Junior Dean. Clearly Swift was one of the ringleaders, and, with another student, he was ordered to beg the Junior Dean's pardon in public, on bended knees. He was also suspended for a month from his degree.[26] But Swift's 'seven-year' association with TCD ended soon after this disgrace. On 19 February 1689 a permissive was issued by the Board of the College for all to act 'for their better security'. In all probability, Swift was already in England. According to Sir William Temple, he was 'neer seven years in the Colledge of Dublyn, and ready to take his degree of Master of Arts, when he was forced away by the desertion of that Colledge upon the calamitys of the Country.' [27]

Our immediate task is to give some account of the 'calamitys' of Ireland, and to relate them to the wider implications for the three kingdoms. Only then will we be in a position to understand the issues which informed Swift's mature political ideas, and to interpret correctly the events in which he was concerned. Ireland's dependency on England had been enshrined in Poynings' Law. In 1494 the Irish Parliament agreed to submit all legislation to the King and Privy Council in England for scrutiny. Only then could those bills which had been approved be accepted or rejected. Should the Irish Parliament choose to amend them, then the process had to be repeated. In this way, the Irish Parliament was reduced to a mere cipher or rubber stamp, and Ireland's colonial status was confirmed.

At the same time, encroachments had been made on the estates of Catholics in Ireland, and the resulting confiscations granted to English Protestant settlers, strengthening the grip of the 'colonials' at the expense of the native Gaelic population. But until the Great Rebellion, a distinction had been made between the Gaelic Irish Catholics, and the 'Old English' who had settled in the country prior to the Reformation, and who had retained their Catholic faith. The deciding factor hitherto had been one not of religion, but of national character. A common sense of identity existed between the Old English landowner and the new English settler which unmistakably separated them from the native Irishman. Their English nationality was forcibly imposed upon the Gaelic civilisation of Ireland.

With the Cromwellian Settlement, however, a new trend began to emerge. The question of religion gained relevance, to dominate Irish affairs down to the present day. In accordance with the prevailing practice, the Old English Catholics expected to have their estates restored to them in full upon the Restoration of Charles II, but many failed either in whole or in part to recover the land they had held on the outbreak of hostilities. On the other hand, Cromwellian settlers who had benefited from the confiscation of Catholic land in the 1650s were reluctant to hand over their newly acquired possessions. Those who were forced to do so showed keen resentment against the Catholic 'usurpers' whom they regarded without compunction as conquered rebels. Catholics were disappointed at failing to recover their estates in full; Protestants were aggrieved at having to surrender any land whatsoever to returning Catholics.

At the time of Swift's birth, therefore, growing dissatisfaction with the consequences of Irish dependency was exacerbated by discontent with the position created by the Restoration Settlement. Irish fears were scarcely allayed when England proceeded to impose restrictions on Irish trade. Prohibitions were placed on the importation of cattle into England from Ireland, which at a stroke destroyed by far the biggest market for Irish trade. It was the first indication of increased English awareness of the potential threat posed by Ireland to the English economy. 'Charles II's reign was a time of great economic expansion in Ireland,'[28] and trade with France and the English colonies soon made up for the loss of markets in England. The religious question, however, was gaining in relevance with the prospect of a Catholic king in the person of the heir-apparent, James, Duke of York, and on his accession in 1685, Protestant anxiety over the security of the status quo was speedily aroused.

Although James II began his reign by governing along the traditional lines that had been laid down before 1641, maintaining English, rather than Catholic, interests in Ireland – granted he was a Papist, but he was also an Englishman – his policies were increasingly influenced by the Irish Catholic Earl of Tyrconnell. Early in 1687 Tyrconnell replaced Clarendon as Lord Deputy in Ireland, and a strong resurgence of Catholic feeling could be felt in the country. This was the background to Swift's educational years, and his awareness of the vulnerability of the Anglican Establishment, particularly in Ireland, can with confidence be attributed to his first-hand knowledge of events which took place around 1688. Trinity College was, after all, the bastion of Protestant culture in Ireland, and, as such, it had felt some of the Catholic backlash.

Tyrconnell attempted to foist two Catholics upon the College, one as lecturer, one as fellow. True, they were Trinity graduates, but they had since been converted to Catholicism. From his graduation onwards, Jonathan Swift would have been acutely aware of this religious confrontation. Whether or not the 'tumult' in which he took part in November 1688 had a political motive is impossible to say, but rumours implicating Trinity College students in plots to assassinate the Deputy had been circulating ever since Tyrconnell's return to Ireland in February 1687. When the Prince of Orange invaded England, Trinity College became a centre for Protestant resistance should it come to blows in Ireland itself. And while some prepared for the worst in Dublin, others, including Swift, left for England.

Swift's subsequent concern for the security of the Church of Ireland can only be fully appreciated in the light of the events of the 1680s. In Dublin, he was in a position, as he grew to manhood, to witness the threat posed by Popery to the religion in which he had been schooled. 'I look upon myself, in the capacity of a clergyman', he wrote many years later, 'to be one appointed by providence for defending a post assigned me, and for gaining over as many enemies as I can.'[29] The revealing martial imagery is deliberate. Swift saw the maintenance of the Church of Ireland as a battle, and his advocacy of a militant Anglicanism was a legacy of his student days. But the events in Ireland were only one aspect of the threat posed by James II, and in order to interpret Swift's political ideas correctly, it is necessary to explain the causes of the Revolution of 1688, for only then do his views become intelligible.

When James, Duke of York, announced his conversion to Roman Catholicism and married the Italian, Mary of Modena, in 1673, waves of anti-Papist sentiment were felt across England. Charles II, James's elder brother, was also thought, with reason, to sympathise with the Roman Church. His wife, Catherine of Braganza, was also a Papist. Of more importance, they were childless. The heir-apparent, then, was a Roman Catholic.

As early as 21 February 1671 the House of Commons complained to the King about 'the growth of Popery'. Its fears were hardly allayed when Charles chose to suspend the penal laws against Catholics and Protestant Dissenters in March 1672. A year later he was forced to make a complete turnabout, cancelling his Declaration of Indulgence, and stepping up the enforcement of the penal laws, which exacted fines from all who failed to attend the Established Church. This change of policy was endorsed by the Test Act, which operated against both Recusants and Dissenters. In order to hold a public office, appointees had not only to supply evidence that they had recently taken communion in the Church of England, they were required to take oaths of allegiance and supremacy to the King, and to renounce the doctrine of transubstantiation. At this juncture, James, Duke of York, resigned his office of Lord High Admiral.

Swift's championing of the Test Act can be seen in numerous works, from the *Letter Concerning the Sacramental Test* of 1709, to *Some few Thoughts concerning the Repeal of the Test* in 1733. If he blamed the rise of atheism on the Great Rebellion, he claimed to be persuaded that the repeal of the Test Act would result in 'an entire Alteration of Religion among us, in a no great Compass of Years'.[30] And yet he could not have remembered the shock of the years following the imposition of the Test. With anti-Papist fervour gaining ground, only a spark was necessary to set the nation on fire, and this was supplied by the so-called 'Popish Plot'.

The mythology of Catholic subversion already had a long history, stretching back to Gunpowder Plot and beyond. The Great Fire of London of 1666 was believed by many to have been started by Papist agents. When Titus Oates revealed the existence of a plot to assassinate the King, and to restore Popery in England, he had a fund of similar plots to fall back on in appealing to English credulity.[31] The details of the plot were unconvincing at the time, and they seem even more so today. Oates's evidence was often vague and peculiarly conflicting. But he had two extraordinary pieces of luck. He made the first of his depositions before a Justice of the Peace on 6 September 1678. Six weeks later the body of the Justice, Sir Edmund Berry Godfrey, was found in a ditch. Then Edward Coleman, Secretary to the Duchess of York, was found, when arrested, to have been involved in, if not a plot, at least a conspiracy of some kind against the Protestant religion in England.

Unfortunate coincidences perhaps, but certainly there was enough circumstantial evidence to support the idea of a Popish Plot, and the popular imagination did the rest. Panic set in. The House of Commons resolved, on 31 October 1678, 'that there has been and still is a damnable and hellish plot, contrived and carried on by popish recusants for the assassinating and murdering the king, and for subverting the government and rooting out and destroying the Protestant religion'.[32] Anti-Papist feeling began to take shape in the agitation for the exclusion from the line of succession to the throne of James, Duke of York, on account of his Catholicism. Instead it was suggested that Charles should legitimise his bastard but Protestant son, the Duke of Monmouth.

The Exclusion Crisis of 1679 witnessed the rise of political parties both in the House of Commons and, to an extent, in the nation at large. Those who sought to exclude James from the succession were christened Whigs by their opponents after the fanatical Scottish Covenanters who were obsessed with Popery. Rallied by the Earl of Shaftesbury – Dryden's Achitophel – they carried the battle to the King in three Parliaments between 1679 and 1681. In each, the issue of exclusion was paramount, and bills were introduced in the Commons to this purpose. One passed the Lower House only to be thrown out by the Lords. When, in January 1681, the Commons resolved that no further supply would be granted to the King until the exclusion bill was given the royal assent, Parliament was dissolved. A new one was summoned, not to London, but to the royalist stronghold of Oxford. It lasted a week, as the Commons immediately brought in a new exclusion bill. For the rest of his reign, Charles II dispensed with Parliament.

With the threat of civil war, bringing anarchy in its train, the propertied rallied to the Crown. The King's party was by now distinguised by the name of Tories, 'a Name of Contempt given them by their Adversaries, from the Robbers in *Ireland* so call'd'.[33] Financed by French subsidies, Charles II resorted to a reign of terror against Whigs and Dissenters. Shaftesbury was tried for treason but acquitted. He fled to Holland. Then, in 1683, the Rye House Plot was discovered. This Whig conspiracy to seize the King allowed the arrest, trial and execution of several prominent Whigs. From 1681 onwards, Charles was in control. He even tried to remodel the House of Commons, introducing a policy of issuing new city and borough charters, restricting the electorate to potential sympathisers. When James II succeeded his brother peacefully in 1685, the Parliament which met in May was more susceptible to Court pressure than any since the Restoration.

The significance of the preceding account in relation to the life of Jonathan Swift is that he consistently claimed to uphold 'the old Whig principles',[34] in other words, the principles of the first Whigs who, led by Shaftesbury, pressed for the exclusion of James, Duke of York, from the line of succession. The full implications of this ideology will be considered in the following chapter, but it is important to state with clarity the tradition of politics in which Swift claimed to have been schooled. In Ireland in the 1680s he was in a good position to assess the threat caused by Popery to the establishment in Church and State. It was popularly believed that Popery led to arbitrary monarchy. Swift, on the other hand, was a firm believer in that 'Gothic' institution, limited, mixed monarchy, in which

> the King enjoys all the prerogatives necessary to the
> Support of his Dignity, and the Protection of his People,
> and is only abridg'd from the Power of injuring his own
> Subjects: In short, the Man is loose, and the Beast only
> bound ... an Empire of Laws, and not of Men.[35]

It was, then, not only the threat posed by Popery to the Anglican Church which disturbed Swift, but the danger to liberty and property as well. With the surrender of the people's rights and privileges, there was a genuine risk of slavery. The mature Swift regarded Ireland's dependency on England in this light, and he feared he might even 'outlive liberty in *England*', under a regime which, he believed, was systematically undermining the constitution.[36] But whereas in the 1720s and 1730s he subscribed to the view of a tiny minority, in 1688 the danger of absolutism was recognised by all. Catholics had been introduced into key positions in the expanded army, as the King claimed the right not only to suspend the law, but to dispense with it altogether. Parliament was prorogued, while James extended the policy of remodelling city and borough charters instituted by his brother. As J.R. Jones observes, 'by 1688 the whole kingdom was taking on the appearance of a country under military occupation.'[37]

The deciding factor in events was the birth of a son to the Queen in June 1688. James was only mortal. From the outset a 'short but stormy reign' had been envisaged under Papist auspices. But now the prospect of a Papist dynasty was unveiled. The propertied had supported the Crown in fear of civil war in 1681. Now the Crown was itself threatening liberty and property. On 30 June a 'Letter of Invitation' was sent to William of Orange asking him to intervene to protect the rights and privileges of James II's subjects. In itself the 'letter', signed by only seven men, is of little importance. But it indicates the mood of the country on the birth of James's heir. Witnesses were prepared to testify that they had seen the baby come 'black and reeking' from the body of the Queen, and that a live baby had been substituted for this still-born child, smuggled into the bedchamber in a warming-pan immediately after the birth.

This myth is significant in that it provided a legal excuse for William's intervention. He was the husband of James II's elder daughter by his first marriage. William had Mary's rights to uphold, as well as those of the kingdom. In the teeth of opposition which was becoming active rather than passive, James backed down, reversing his policy of Catholicisation. It was too late. On 5 November 1688 the Prince of Orange landed at Torbay with 11,000 Dutch infantry and 4,000 cavalry, posing as a defender of the rights and privileges of Englishmen. William waited patiently at Torbay while the King's support gradually evaporated. Finally James fled, setting foot on French soil on Christmas Day 1688.

The Revolution of 1688 was a bloodless revolution. The political nation was not prepared to watch its rights being eroded by an enroaching monarchy, nor was it going to allow the situation to slide into a state of anarchy. Stability was all-important. But, above all, the Revolution confirmed that the monarchy of England was a limited, mixed monarchy in which the King had to respect the liberty and property of the subject. Jonathan Swift's formative years encompassed virtually the whole of the developments which led to the Glorious Revolution. The influence of the events of the 1680s on his political ideas must not be underestimated. The Revolution did more than merely prevent him from taking his MA at Trinity College, Dublin. As James II crossed the English Channel into France at the end of 1688, young Jonathan Swift crossed St George's Channel to try his luck in the country of his father.

3
Moor Park

Swift arrived in England sometime during the weeks following his twenty-first birthday. 'The Troubles then breaking out', he noted in his autobiographical fragment, 'he went to his Mother, who lived in Leicester, and ... continu[ed] there some Months.' In all probability it was his first visit since his 'kidnapping' – perhaps his first ever.[1] But little is known of his activities in Leicester, other than that he succeeded in attracting the attention of at least one local young lady. 'When I went a lad to my mother, after the revolution, she brought me acquainted with a family where there was a daughter with whom I was acquainted,' he recalled many years later. 'My prudent mother was afraid I should be in love with her; but when I went to *London*, she married an inn-keeper in *Loughborow*.'[2] The young lady in question, Betty Jones, was doubtless charmed by the newcomer from Dublin, whose piercing, prominent, blue eyes appeared full of intelligence and mischief, expressing, as Pope was later to put it, a 'very uncommon archness'.[3] In the taste of his day, Swift would have been considered a well-built, handsome young man.

From Leicester, Swift moved to London, to join the household of the retired diplomat, Sir William Temple. We do not know for certain when Swift met Temple, but, considering his claim that he lived with his mother in Leicester for 'some Months' during 'the Troubles', it would seem reasonable to place his arrival at Sheen, near Richmond in Surrey, in the summer of 1689. Temple had been established for some two years in his new house, Moor Park, just outside Farnham, when William of Orange landed at Torbay.

To avoid being trapped between the forces of King and liberator, Temple withdrew to his old house at Sheen.[4]

But these were not to be happy months for Temple, for on 19 April, his mind disturbed, his only son threw himself into the Thames near London Bridge and drowned. The loss of John Temple affected Sir William deeply. It was a few weeks after this tragic death that he welcomed a penurious young Irishman into his household. The timing is perhaps significant. With good cause, the relationship between Jonathan Swift and his mentor, Sir William Temple, was to develop along filial lines. Temple was Godwin Swift's age. Swift had found another father-figure. Temple acquired a replacement for the son he had just lost.[5]

Rumour went one stage further. It was suggested that the new arrival was a product of an earlier indiscretion of Temple's. As Temple was in Holland, not Ireland, when Swift was conceived, it can be seen how flimsy the grounds were for such an accusation, however much, like a similar murmur regarding Hester Johnson, it suited the imagination of the age.[6]

But Temple's generosity needs to be explained. The answer lies in the emigration of several members of the Swift family from England to Ireland just before the Restoration. At the time, Temple's father was Master of the Rolls in Dublin. According to Swift himself, Sir John 'had been a great Friend to the Family', while Sir William, writing to Sir Robert Southwell in 1690, confirmed that the 'whole family hav[e] been long known to me'. The financial troubles of the Swifts in Ireland in the 1680s, and of Uncle Godwin in particular, prompted Jonathan Swift to make himself known to an old friend of the family. Hawkesworth notes that it was 'In the Year 1688' that Godwin Swift 'was seized with a Lethargy, and soon after totally deprived both of his Speech and his Memory: As by this Accident *Swift* was left without Support, he took a Journey to *Leicester*', and thence to Moor Park. Temple felt 'obliged ... to take care of Him', as his friends had 'for the present lost their fortunes in Ireland'.[7]

It is unlikely that Swift knew Temple personally before travelling from Leicester to London in the early summer of 1689, and it seems probable that the approach was made on the advice of his mother. Temple generously took him into his family, and gradually – perhaps very gradually – learned to value Swift's merits. 'He has latine and greek[,] some French, writes a very good and current hand, is very honest and diligent, and has good friends,' he wrote on his protégé's behalf in 1690. But by the end of 1692, during Swift's second spell at Moor Park, Temple was finding his 'secretary' a 'little necessary to him ... upon some accounts'. We shall consider the nature of these 'accounts' in due course. When Swift decided to leave the Temple household once more in 1694, the retired diplomat was reported to be 'extream[ly] angry'.[8] Two years later Swift returned to the fold a third time, and remained at Moor Park until Temple's death in 1699.

Swift's years at Moor Park, then, were his first outside the educational establishments he had been attending since the age of six. To this insecure but socially ambitious Irishman, Temple and his circle represented a level of importance, sophistication and taste which eclipsed in an instant the most that his Dublin could offer. While Temple remained at Sheen in the summer of 1689, he was 'often' visited by the new King, William III, who 'took his advice in affairs of the greatest consequence'. Temple was William's 'old Friend'.[9] He had served two terms as English ambassador at The Hague (before and after the Third Dutch War), where he became friendly with the Stadholder of the United Provinces, the future King of England. He was even involved in negotiating the marriage alliance between William and Mary. Thereafter he threw up his career and retired to his estate, refusing to be drawn into the machinations of later Caroline and Jacobean politics. But when William III offered to consult him about his affairs, Temple could hardly refuse. John Temple became William's Secretary-at-War, and it was an unfortunate betrayal of the Secretary's trust by the man he had sent to negotiate with Tyrconnell in Ireland, General Richard Hamilton, which seems to have led to his suicide. Hamilton defected. Having badly let down his royal master, John Temple killed himself in a paroxysm of remorse, for Hamilton's treachery contributed to the outbreak of civil war in Ireland.

Sir William Temple's achievements as a statesman can be

overestimated. He was one of the chief architects of the ill-fated Triple Alliance between England, the United Provinces and Sweden. But this embryonic attempt to operate a 'balance of power' policy to guard against French hegemony was directly contrary to Charles II's secret strategy which, in return for French subsidies, involved an alliance with Louis XIV to work against Dutch interests. As one contemporary opponent pointed out, Temple 'had but a small share in the secrecy of the late King *Charles*'s Designs in the greatest part of the Affairs, for which he was employed, from [16]72, till [16]79'.[10]

None the less Temple's influence on the maturing mind of Jonathan Swift should not be underestimated. The Triple Alliance may not have halted French encroachments, but the 'balance of power' theory was to figure prominently in Swift's *Discourse,* while a dispute involving Temple was not only the stimulus for *The Battle of the Books* and the digressions on modern learning and criticism in *A Tale of a Tub* itself, but for what may have been Swift's first prose work, *An Answer To A Scurrilous Pamphlet, Lately Printed, Intituled, A Letter from Monsieur de Cros, to the Lord—*. Although the question of influence is always a thorny one, Temple left his mark on Swift. Not only his opinions on politics and society, but his literary taste can be said to have affected the formulation of Swift's own. It was not simply that Swift learned to agree with Temple. Far from it. Filial relationships often involve rebellion, and this quasi-filial relationship also had its conflicts.

Temple's genius was as a prose writer and polite philosopher. He disliked wit, humour, raillery and satire. Instead, he used the vehicle of the essay, and, especially in *Upon the Gardens of Epicurus,* propounded what he understood to be Epicurean moral philosophy. He sought happiness in retirement from the world and believed this to be what Epicurus advocated. The mature Swift's forte, on the other hand, was wit, humour, raillery and satire. In *A Tale of a Tub* he attacked Epicureanism as shallow, and singled-out Epicurus' disciple, Lucretius, for particular ridicule. Clearly Swift reacted *against* Temple's ideas; he was not led to adopt them in his own writings. Nevertheless he was influenced by them, rejecting them only after he had had the opportunity to consider them at length.

When Swift arrived at Moor Park, he evidently disliked logic and science, mathematics and abstract study of any kind. Instead he devoted his time and energy to history and poetry, and he nourished literary amibitions, partly, it must be said, to compensate for his social inadequacy. If he could not aspire to status and wealth, at least he could aspire to be a man of letters or, still better, a poet. Temple was not only a man of status, friend of the new King, but he already possessed the literary reputation Swift sought. The contrast between the two was marked, and at first Swift tried to be like Temple. At Moor Park Swift received a training in the liberal arts which was, in all probability, as important to his subsequent career as his formal education. Temple advised him in his literary pursuits. This much can be documented. Finally Swift chose to turn his back on Temple's way. He rejected his mentor's ideas on philosophy and poetry and began to write satire. But he retained his respect for Temple's achievement. 'It is generally believed', he wrote in 1700, 'that this Author, has advanced our English Tongue, to as great a Perfection as it can well bear.'[11] There seems no reason to discount this statement, and Temple's influence on Swift's prose was almost certainly crucial. As Macaulay put it: 'It is impossible to doubt that the superiority of Swift is to be, in a great measure, attributed to his long and close connexion with Temple.'[12] The process was a long and complex one; it did not happen as if by osmosis. Over an extended period, Swift weighed what Temple had to offer, sifting nuggets of gold from the dross of Temple's ideas.

Swift's time at Moor Park was limited during this first visit. Temple stayed on at his late son's house at Sheen until November 1689. Perhaps Swift was introduced to William III during these months. 'I own myself indebted to Sir William Temple', he acknowledged in retrospect, 'for recommending me to the late King, although without success.'[13] With the details missing, it is impossible to fix with any certainty the date of Temple's recommendation, which could have taken place at almost any stage between 1689 and his death ten years later. For the time being, Swift lived with Temple and acted as a sort of private secretary. In describing Swift's services to Southwell, Temple noted that he had 'read to mee, writ for mee, and kept all accounts as farr as my small occasions required'.[14] This function appears to have been fulfilled not only at Sheen, but at Moor Park, where Swift 'accompanied' Temple in the autumn of 1689.[15]

But Swift's first sojourn at Moor Park was to last for little more than six months. At Sheen he had the first attack of the recurring ailment which has since been diagnosed as Ménière's disease. This condition of the inner ear leads to bouts or 'fits' of vertigo, accompanied more often than not by nausea and deafness. Swift himself put his illness down to 'eating a hundred golden pippins at a time, at Richmond', that is, Temple's estate at Sheen.[16] In the *Journal to Stella* for October 1712 he dated the onset of his illness with what was, for him, unusual precision. 'I have had my Giddiness 23 years,' he remarked, 'by fits.'[17] As the years went by, he became accustomed to the 'pair of disorders' which 'usually seize[d him] once a year',[18] but he was never able to come to terms with the debilitating effect they had on him. And the initial sickness was severe. The 'Surfeit of fruit' caused him 'to contract a giddyness and coldness of Stomach', or so he thought, 'that almost brought him to his Grave.' Seeking medical advice, he was told to return to Ireland to take his 'native air'.[19]

Thus, in the spring months of 1690, Swift was soliciting for any place which could bring him advancement in Ireland. On two separate occasions he implied that he visited the Court around this time. According to the autobiographical fragment, 'the first time' Swift ever had 'any converse' with Courts was when he was 'sent to Kensington' on account of the triennial bill, 'to convince the King and the Earl [of Portland] how ill they were informed' on the matter. Although he was then under 'three and twenty years old', Swift evidently 'gave the King a short account' of the issues it raised, 'but all in vain'.[20]

Difficulties arise over Swift's faulty memory of the incident. The triennial bill was vetoed by William III in 1693 when Swift was twenty-five, not twenty-two. Further, Swift himself was uncertain of his age at this time when writing his account of the 'Family of Swift', as he erased 'three and twenty' in the manuscript and substituted 'under twenty one years old'. This is clearly impossible, for Swift was in Dublin studying for his MA when he was in his twenty-first year, and William had not yet replaced James II on the throne of England. Perhaps Swift was confusing his visit to the Court for 'the first time', with a subsequent mission on Temple's behalf around the time of the triennial bill. On another occasion, in a letter dated 3 May 1692, Swift referred to the time he 'usd the Court above two years ago'.[21] If the business of Swift's visit related to his impending return to Ireland, then it would indeed make sense to date his introduction to the ways of Courts in the early months of 1690 when he would have been under twenty-three years old. As he remarked in retrospect, 'it was the first incident that helped to cure him of vanity.'[22]

Swift was being forced to rely on the good nature of others, and it is this dependence which characterises his life in the 1690s. He could never quite free himself from the chains of necessity, and for a spirit so fiercely proud as Swift, this was anathema. Certainly Temple was exerting himself on his protégé's behalf, as we know from his letter of recommendation of 29 May 1690 to Sir Robert Southwell, who was travelling with the King to Ireland, where he would take up an appointment as Secretary of State. Temple, therefore, ventured to make Southwell 'the offer of a servant, in case you may have occasion for such a one as this bearer'. Presumably Swift 'used the Court' in delivering Temple's letter. 'If you please to accept him into your service', Temple wrote, 'either as a gentleman to waite on you or as Clarke to write under you, and either to use Him so if you like his service, or upon any establishment of the Colledge [of Dublin] to recomend him to a fellowship there, which Hee has a just pretence to I shall acknoledge it as a great obligation to mee, as well as to him.'[23] Apparently Swift had designs on an academic career, and a fellowship at Trinity College. It was not to be.

William was crossing to Ireland to defend his newly acquired position as King of England. When James II landed in France on Christmas Day, 1688, he effectively surrendered the Crown to William of Orange. The Convention Parliament debated the legal niceties of the situation in January and February 1689 – whether the throne was vacant after James's flight so that it could now be filled by another at the behest of the 'people', or whether James had in fact abdicated by seeking voluntary exile – but one thing was abundantly clear: the political realities demanded a divergence from the strict line of succession to the Crown. If James had indeed abdicated, and if his son really had been still-born, then Mary, his elder daughter, was rightful heir to the throne. But Mary refused to accept the Convention's offer unless her husband was declared joint-sovereign. Whichever way the fiction was elaborated, one inescapable fact remained: the 'people' had decided the succession. Whether or not the offer of the Crown of England to William and Mary was suggestive of a 'contract' between sovereign and subject,[24] it could hardly be denied that the Convention Parliament had fixed the line to the throne. The logical outcome of this process was enshrined in the Act of Settlement of 1701 which determined the Succession down to our own monarch, Elizabeth II. Passing over the mass of Catholic claimants, Parliament placed the Crown on the head of the distant Protestant House of Hanover.

The reign of William III (Queen Mary died in 1694 and William ruled on alone) was characterised by a working-out of the implications of the Revolution of 1688. In the first place, not everyone recognised William as the 'rightful and lawful' monarch, but merely as King *de facto*. Only in 1702 was an oath of allegiance to William as King *de jure* made obligatory for office-holders and other men in positions of authority. Jacobitism was usually passive, but an element of active Jacobites remained a factor in politics for the rest of Swift's lifetime. These men sought to restore James II (and then his son, the Old Pretender, James III) to his throne in accordance with a strict theory of divine right of hereditary succession. At home this led to an assassination plot, uncovered in 1696, and the execution of some of those involved. In Ireland, William had to fight to defeat James II's forces and to pacify the country. On the continent, the allied war against Louis XIV was in one way a war of the English Succession. On all fronts, William and his supporters had to defend the Revolution Settlement.

Prompted by Sir William Temple, Swift was a wholehearted supporter of William III. 'As to what is called a Revolution-principle', Swift wrote in 1721:

> my opinion was this; That, whenever those evils which usually attend and follow a violent change of government, were not in probability so pernicious as the grievances we suffer under a present power, then the publick good will justify such a Revolution; and this I took to have been the Case in the Prince of Orange's expedition, although in the consequences it produced some very bad effects, which are likely to stick long enough by us.[25]

The 'consequences' of the 'expedition' were far-reaching indeed. Not only was the question of the Succession to dominate English politics until the year of Swift's death, but the very problem of interpreting the events of 1688 was a vital issue for many years to come.

Apart from replacing one sovereign with another, what was the character of the Glorious Revolution? Essentially it was a conservative attempt to preserve a limited monarchy in the face of the apparently absolutist policies then being pursued by James II. It sought to protect the liberty and property of the political nation against the encroachment of royal prerogative. When the Crown was offered to William and Mary, it was accompanied by a Declaration of Rights which stated the conditions on which they were to hold their kingship. Although in practice the powers of the monarch were not very precisely defined, the overall tone of the Declaration is unmistakable. William and Mary swore to govern 'according to the statues in Parliament agreed on'. The limited nature of their sovereignty was emphasised. It was a Parliamentary monarchy, with a constitution based on law. The Revolution of 1688 was justified in that James II had allegedly tried 'to subvert and extirpate the Protestant religion, and the laws and liberties of this kingdom'.

Swift's adherence to the 'Revolution-principle' enunciated in the Declaration of Rights should be stressed. 'I always declared my self against a Popish Successor to the Crown, whatever Title he might have by the proximity of blood', he claimed, clarifying his views on the legal nature of the monarchy. He supported the line 'as it was established by law.'[26] In later life, he was unable to stand by idle when, as he saw it, 'all things' were 'tending towards absolute Power'.[27] 'I could never discover the necessity of suspending any Law upon which the Liberty of the most innocent persons depended', he remarked, 'neither do I think this practice hath made the taste of arbitrary power so agreeable as that we should desire to see it repeated.'[28] Clearly Swift would have concurred with one contemporary explanation of the Revolution which stressed that it had been necessary for 'the recovery and security of our Rights and Liberties, which had been so unjustly invaded'. 'This is the thing we must always keep in our eye', Englishmen were reminded, 'and steer our whole course by this pole-star.'[29]

Swift appears to have travelled through life guided by such principles. In the 1690s, Parliament, too, sought to safeguard the achievements of 1688. The consensus of opinion which had allowed the Revolution to be bloodless soon gave way, in the Convention Parliament, to the re-emergence of Whig and Tory parties. The Whigs recognised the new monarchs as Kings *de jure* without any qualms. Most Tories were unable, in all conscience, to recognise William and Mary as more than sovereigns *de facto*. The 'pole-star' of liberty and property, however, depended to a large extent on the nature of the relationship between Crown and Parliament. In the years following the Revolution, the Court tried to control Parliament by buying off potential opponents with places in the government, and pensions from secret service funds.[30] The clause of the Bill of Rights relating to free proceedings in Parliament was being quietly but wilfully ignored.

'As to Parliaments', Swift noted:

I adored the wisdom of that Gothic Institution, which made them Annual: and I was confident our Liberty could never be placed upon a firm foundation until that ancient law were restored among us. For, who sees not, that while such assemblies are permitted to have a longer duration, there grows up a commerce between the Ministry and the Deputies, wherein they both find their accounts to the manifest danger of Liberty, which traffick would neither answer the design nor expence, if Parliaments met once a year.[31]

Annual parliaments were never implemented. But the reaction to the 'corruption' of the legislature by the executive from an alliance of outraged Whigs and Tories was the introduction of place bills to prevent pensioner parliaments and triennial bills to forestall standing parliaments.

This vision of a legislature working for the national good, and separate from the executive, owed much to a 'Country theory' of the respective roles of King and Parliament. 'It was for the Crown to govern, and for Parliament to exercise a jealous surveillance of government; "corruption" would follow if the Crown discovered any means at all of attaching members to it in the pursuit of business.'[32] The place bill, or self-denying ordinance, would have made it impossible for a member of the House of Commons to hold public office, while the triennial bill would have made a new Parliament mandatory every three years. Swift, as we have already observed, believed that all 'well-instituted States' made sure that the executive and legislative powers were placed 'in different Hands', and he went so far as to suggest that this confounding of the two elements of the state was 'the Foundation of all the political Mistakes in' Hobbes's *Leviathan*.[33] In this, as in other matters, he was following a well-established 'Country' tradition.

The debates in Parliament on the question of the 'corruption' of the House of Commons by the Court in the 1690s informed Swift's view of politics in a striking way. In 1693 the King vetoed both the place bill and the triennial bill after they had passed both Houses of Parliament. At this point, according to the autobiographical fragment, Swift 'was sent' to explain the purpose of the triennial bill to William III, 'who was a stranger to our Constitution'. As he was 'well versed in English History', Swift 'gave the King a short account of the Matter, but a more large one to the Earl of Portland; but all in vain: For the King was prevayled upon ... to refuse passing the Bill.'[34] Clearly Temple agreed with the principle of frequent parliaments, and if we take this further to include belief in the free proceedings of Parliament *tout court*, we have an important key to the character of Swift's own political perspective. His subsequent complaints about the 'corruption' of Parliament under the regime of Walpole can be traced back to the anxiety he felt over events that took place just after the Revolution of 1688.

Although it was vetoed by the King in 1693, the triennial bill became law in 1694. Finally the principle of the place bill was accepted by William III in 1701 as one of the clauses restricting the future prerogative of the House of Hanover. Even if this law was never put into practice, its place in the Act of Settlement indicates the seriousness with which the 'Country' party had fought to protect liberty and property *after* the Revolution. There were other related issues upon which 'Country theory' was unequivocal. One principle was stated with clarity in the Bill of Rights: 'the raising or keeping of a standing army within this kingdom in time of peace unless it be with consent of Parliament is against the law'. Once again we can document Swift's firm opinions on the question. He declared himself to have 'a mortal antipathy against Standing Armies in times of Peace', and this stance is mirrored in the King of Brobdingnag's amazement at Gulliver's talk of 'a mercenary standing Army in the Midst of Peace, and among a free People'.[35] Not only was a standing army against the law, unless it was with the consent of Parliament, but it inevitably posed a threat to the rights and privileges of the individual. 'The standing army was a bogey intended for country gentlemen,' J. G. A. Pocock observes, 'part of a hydra-headed monster called Court Influence or Ministerial Corruption, whose other heads were Placemen, Pensioners, National Debt, Excise, and High Taxation.'[36] It is crucial to an understanding of Swift's political ideas to note that he shared the country gentleman's fears about such things. We have already seen his reaction to placemen and pensioners, but he subscribed to the full complement of 'Country' phobias. 'Standing armies in times of peace; projects of excise, and bribing elections' were the abuses he railed against in the 1730s, 'not forgetting septennial Parliaments, directly against the old Whig principles, which always have been mine.'[37]

This, then, was the background to English politics during the decade that Swift was in contact with Sir William Temple, and in occasional converse with the King and his Court as Temple's messenger. It is important to keep it firmly in mind when approaching his politics. This was the political world of his twenties and early thirties. If he was often, if not habitually, anachronistic in his views, we need look no further for the explanation. His stance against what he believed to be the corruption of the Walpole ministry can be followed back to his earliest political experiences, when he was 'bred under Sir William Temple'.[38] Similarly, it is a vital clue to interpreting his actions in 1710 when he began to write in support of the ostensibly Tory ministry of Robert Harley. For it was Harley who had led the Country Opposition to William III.[39]

As the implications of the Revolution were being painfully worked out by political theorists, political propagandists, and practical politicians, William III took steps to secure his position as King of England. In May 1689 he declared war on France as part of the continental alliance against Louis XIV, and for nineteen of the next twenty-four years the two countries were at war. A vital part of William's strategy involved the subjugation of Ireland which, after Hamilton's defection, had declared for James II. In 1690 William left for Ulster. If Swift sailed with Southwell, he would have embarked at Hoylake on 11 June, arriving three days later at Carrickfergus.[40] After gathering its resources, William's expeditionary force pressed on in two main bodies towards Dublin. On 1 July an encounter occurred which has been seen by succeeding generations as the decisive battle in Ireland. Against an entrenched Jacobite force commanded (if not actually led) by James II himself, the Williamites managed to force the crossing of the Boyne, upon which the main Jacobite army fled in some confusion to the south.

Dublin was in Williamite hands by the following week, but the war dragged on for over a year. Not until the signing of the articles of the Treaty of Limerick on 3 October 1691 was the fate of Ireland finally sealed, and the prevailing conditions that have dominated Irish affairs for the past three centuries irrevocably imposed. Roman Catholics were excluded from all political power, and penal laws 'to prevent the further growth of Popery' effectively ruined the Roman Catholic gentry of Ireland. But the Protestant Ascendancy was not the only result of the Revolution of 1688 and the victory of William III in Ireland, as England took decisive steps to place Ireland under firm economic and political control. In 1699 the English Parliament prohibited the export of Irish woollen manufactures to any country whatsoever apart from England, from which they were already effectively excluded by high import duties. As well as ensuring that England would have a virtual monopoly of Irish wool (except for that which could be smuggled to France), the measure was designed to protect the English woollen industry. This set the pattern for the exploitation of Ireland by England, and throughout the eighteenth century Irish interests were systematically sacrificed to those of the mother country.

In this way, Ireland's colonial status was confirmed. Swift approved of the penal laws, but he was indignant about English oppression of Ireland, demanding to know 'whether a Law *to bind Men without their own Consent,* be obligatory *in foro conscientiae*'.[41] He was not alone in his complaints. William Molyneux's *The Case of Ireland's Being Bound by Acts of Parliament in England Stated* (1698) was the definitive argument against Ireland being dependent on England, and it provided Swift with much ammunition for his subsequent Irish tracts. The logical conclusion of English policy was an Act 'for the better securing the Dependency of ... Ireland' which passed the British Parliament in March 1720. The 'Sixth of George I' deprived the Irish House of Lords of appellate jurisdiction. It also provoked Swift to enter the lists, and led more or less directly to *The Drapier's Letters* and *A Modest Proposal*.

All this was thirty years in the future. We know nothing of Swift's movements in Ireland in 1690, and by the late summer of 1691 he was back in England.[42] Presumably Southwell did not take him on as his secretary or 'Clarke', and no new fellows were appointed at TCD until the spring of 1692. Swift returned to Moor Park via Leicester and Oxford. In Leicester he succeeded once more in attracting attention to himself on account of his conduct to the fair sex. He lightly brushed aside 'this kind of folly', and dismissed 'the inhabitants of

Leicester' as 'a parcel of very wretched fools'. 'I coud remember twenty women in my life to whom I have behavd my self just the same way', he claimed in justification of his conduct, 'and I profess without any other Design, than that of entertaining my self when I am very Idle, or when somthing goes amiss in my affairs.'[43]

Although this was scarcely a satisfactory explanation of his attitude towards the young women of Leicester, there can be no doubt that Swift had experienced disappointment. Having failed to find a position in Ireland, he turned to the Church. On his twenty-third birthday, 30 November 1690, Swift had reached the required minimum age at which a priest could be ordained. Prevented from pursuing an academic career in Dublin, Swift made alternative plans involving the taking of his Master's degree at Oxford. Thus his visit in December 1691 was part of his long-term scheme. In February 1692 he revealed a resolution of 'entring into the Church', and he proceeded to resume his studies. 'I have gott up my Lattin, pretty well, and am getting up my Greek', he wrote to his cousin, Thomas, already a postgraduate student at Oxford, 'but to enter upon causes of Philosophy is what I protest I will rather dy in a ditch than go about.'[44]

Having received a testimonial from his tutor in Dublin, St George Ashe, Swift arrived in Oxford a second time in late May or early June 1692, and on 14 June he was incorporated as a member of the University from Hart Hall (now Hertford College). Swift's Oxford career was very brief. No examination was required for the degree of Master of Arts, and his studies at TCD were deemed sufficient to warrant its conferment. After only three weeks as a student at Hart Hall, he received his degree. 'I never was more satisfied than in the behaviour of the University of Oxford to me', he wrote, 'I had all the civilities I could wish for, and so many [showed me] favours, that I am ashamed to have been more obliged in a few weeks to strangers, than ever I was in seven years to Dublin College.'[45]

And yet Swift did not proceed with his ordination straight away. 'I am not to take orders till the King gives me a Prebendary,' he explained, 'and Sir William Temple, tho' he promises me the certainty of it, yet is less forward than I could wish; because, I suppose he believes I shall leave him, and upon some accounts, he thinks me a little necessary to him.'[46] Without a living to take up, Swift could not be ordained; and without Temple's favour, Swift would have no means to secure a living. Despite his efforts to stand on his own two feet, he was still dependent on the kindness of others.

We must now consider the reasons for Temple's apparent reluctance to allow Swift to leave his household once more. In his letter of recommendation to Southwell, Temple had summarised Swift's duties at Moor Park. Swift 'writ' for him 'as farr as [his] small occasions required'.[47] One of Swift's major tasks was the supervision of Temple's writings as they were prepared for publication. He was Temple's amanuensis, working on *Miscellanea: the Second Part* (1690), *Memoirs of what past in Christendom* (1692), and *An Introduction to the History of England* (1695). In retrospect, Swift explained that everything was printed from copies he had made in his own hand during his time with Temple. 'They were all copied from the Originals by Sr Wm Temples direction, and corrected all along by his Orders.'[48] This applied not only to the three works already mentioned which were published in Temple's lifetime, but the three volumes of *Letters* (1700, 1703), *Miscellanea III* (1701) and *Memoirs III* (1709).[49]

Swift's part in these transactions was not a simple one. The circumstances surrounding the publication of *Memoirs of what past in Christendom* remain a mystery. According to Swift, Temple himself deliberately burnt the first part of his memoirs. And although he copied out the documents which eventually were printed as *Memoirs of what past in Christendom*, he did not play a part in their appearance in print. Temple scrupulously refused to publish them until after all those named in them were dead. But the manuscript of the *Memoirs* was left in the hands of Sir Robert Southwell, whence it 'fell into Booksellers Hands'.[50] It was published on 30 November 1691 *without* Temple's consent by 'a reverend Prelate of our Church.' Contemporary correspondence identifies this man as Dr Samuel Freeman, in whose Church of St Anne and St Agnes, Aldersgate, John Temple had been buried.[51]

The *Memoirs* were printed by Freeman's own printer, Richard Chiswell. But the details of how, precisely, the manuscript came to fall into the hands of a bookseller are missing. Temple had, no doubt, meant his son to prepare the papers for the press. After all, the *Memoirs* had been written at John Temple's request for his own instruction. The task had devolved on Jonathan Swift. But Temple's reluctance to publish the *Memoirs* in his own lifetime was fully justified when the book's unsolicited appearance was sufficient to spark off a reaction from Joseph August DuCros, whom Temple had allegedly treated 'comme on traitteroit le dernier des hommes'.[52] This in turn led to the publication of Swift's first prose work, *An Answer to A Scurrilous Pamphlet, Lately Printed, Intituled, A Letter from Monsieur De Cros.*

Swift's authorship of this pamphlet, which came out in the middle of February 1693, cannot be documented, but it can be asserted on the grounds of strong circumstantial, supported by internal, evidence. In *A Letter from Monsieur de Cros,* not only Temple's interpretation of events was attacked. The style was *'too luscious and affected'*, with *'Every Leaf ... charged with Gallicisms.'*[53] The *Answer*, too, was replete with Gallicisms. Moreover it deliberately gave the impression of being written at Temple's instigation and with his consent.[54] 'If Sir *W. T.* is that vain-glorious and ill-natured Animal as Monsieur *de Cros* represents him to be', the author notes at one point, 'he here solemnly promises him that he will never come to him to learn either Humility or good Manners.'[55] Clearly the author of the *Answer* is claiming Temple's own authority in dealing with the upstart DuCros. It would seem reasonable to assume that it was written by an amanuensis. And Temple's amanuensis at this time was Jonathan Swift.

That Swift admired Temple's prose style cannot be seriously doubted. 'I never read his writings', he wrote in 1692, 'but I prefer him to all others at present in England.'[56] What, then, would be more natural than for Swift to attempt to imitate his style, down to the affectation of his Gallicisms? The *Answer* reveals a number of Swiftian traits: a digressive, story-telling style; a reductive argument; a lofty assumption of superiority; classical references. But most of all it is the sarcastic aside which suggests Swift's hand, and bears comparison with the prose of *A Tale of a Tub*, which was largely written during the same decade. 'The only Hero of [the] piece shall be Truth',

DuCros had written in the *Letter*. But the author of the *Answer* complained that:

> Monsieur *de Cros* never so much as introduces his Hero in one single Paragraph of his Letter: He threatens indeed to bring him in Play one time or another, but for all that keeps him still as invisible as a Fairy Treasure, and his Hero has no more to do throughout the whole piece, than one of the *Mutae Persona* in the ancient *Drama*.[57]

In the preface to *Memoirs III*, Swift observed that the publisher of *Memoirs II* 'sent them into the World without the Author's Privity', which echoed the *Answer*, which also pointed out that they were 'published ... without the Author's Privity'.[58] If Swift wrote the *Answer*, he was working under Temple's direction, as he had been when preparing Temple's writings for the press. Temple recommended 'the Care of his Writings' to Swift on his death.[59] It was Swift's role as his amanuensis which made him a 'little necessary' to Temple in the winter of 1692-3. By the time he finally did leave Moor Park once more in 1694, Swift had also revised Temple's *Introduction to the History of England* which was published the following year. In his study of Temple's manuscripts and his management of Temple's literary affairs, Swift gained an invaluable grounding in literary matters. But Temple had found a diligent and gifted secretary.

If Swift wrote *An Answer To A Scurrilous Pamphlet*, it was not his first published work. Temple had encouraged him from the first to indulge his creativity. Poetry and history, it will be recalled, were his principal pursuits in Dublin. Swift wrote an ode to William III in Ireland, and, on his return to Moor Park at the end of 1691, he resorted to a literary regimen. He wrote to the Rev. John Kendall on 11 February 1692 that

> there is somthing in me which must be employ'd, & when I am alone, turns all for want of practice into speculation & thought; insomuch That in these seven weeks I have been here, I have writt, & burnt and writt again upon almost all manner of subjects, more perhaps than any man in England.[60]

For almost fifty years this was to be Swift's practice. In the 1730s he is still to be found writing and burning and writing again in pursuit of *la bagatelle*. But three days after his letter to Kendall, Swift addressed a covering letter to the Athenian Society, enclosing an ode submitted for consideration. It was published, early in 1692, in the supplement to the fifth volume of the *Athenian Gazette*.[61]

The *Ode to the Athenian Society* was almost certainly Swift's first publication. With affected modesty, he 'claim[ed] the Priviledge of an English-man' to offer his own 'Folly' for the inspection of the Society and of the world. During Swift's absence in Ireland, the opportunist publisher and would-be wit, John Dunton,[62] had launched on to an unsuspecting public a dubious *Gazette* which purported to carry the proceedings of the imaginary Athenian Society. Temple appears to have given his blessing to the project, and various aspiring wits sang the Society's praises, including the thirty-years-old Daniel Defoe. The worth of the undertaking was not, of course, the only consideration which spurred on these young poets. The opportunity to see one's name in print was a powerful stimulus and this worked strongly on Jonathan Swift.

He had few doubts about the merit of his *Ode*. It had been encouraged not only by 'the best of [his] Acquaintance', but by 'a Person of very great *Learning and Honour*', presumably Temple himself. He self-consciously drew attention to his Muse:

> Pardon *Ye great Unknown,* and far-exalted Men,
> The wild exursions of a youthful pen;
> Forgive a young and (almost) *Virgin-muse* ...[63]

One might be tempted, with the benefit of hindsight, to read irony into such a confession, especially the coy sexual innuendo suggested in the phrase, '(almost) *Virgin-muse*'. It is hard to see how one can be *almost* a virgin! But Swift is in deadly earnest, the highflown language of his Pindaric stanzas sharply accentuated by the tortuous syntax which, at times, renders the meaning so obscure that the poem is almost unreadable. No, Swift's muse is 'almost' virginal because,

although the *Ode to the Athenian Society* is his first published
piece, an unpublished poem preceded the present effort.
When he was in Ireland 'last year', Swift's '*Dove-muse* ... took
wing', and landing 'On the high Top of peaceful *Ararat* ...
pluckt a *Laurel Branch*,' from which it made 'an *Humble Chaplet
for the King.*' Here a marginal note refers to 'The Ode I writ to
the King in Ireland'. The awkwardness of an almost virgin-
muse, far from being ironic, is merely a puff for Swift's *Ode to
the King.* [64]

Swift's first venture into print was without question his
worst. In general, his early verse is marred by his choice of
medium. His first four surviving poems are all Pindaric odes,
like the *Ode to the Athenian Society,* and it must be concluded
that the form was far from congenial to him. Only when he
veers towards an openly satiric stance can we recognise at all
the hand of the mature writer. At the outset, in the letter
which introduces the *Ode,* we can detect the animus towards
the present which is often the prevailing spirit of the satirist.
In contrast to the virtuous past, modern times are effete and
degenerate. Although there is none of the irony of *A Tale of a
Tub* in the heartfelt assertion that folly is 'just suitable to the
Age, which God knows, I little expected ever to produce
any thing *extraordinary*', the sentiment is the same. And it is
when Swift attacks the moderns, in anticipation of the
controversy which led to the composition of *The Battle of the
Books,* that the *Ode* just manages to rise above abject
mediocrity:

> *The Wits,* I mean the Atheists of the Age,
> Who fain would rule the Pulpit, as they do the Stage,
> Wondrous *Refiners* of Philosophy,
>   Of Morals and Divinity,
> By the new *Modish System* of reducing all to sense,
> Against all Logick and concluding Laws,
>   Do own th'Effects of Providence,
>   And yet deny the Cause. [65]

If the *Ode* does not suit today's palate, there can none the
less be little doubt that Swift was thrilled to see his poem in
print. Secure in the confidence of youth, he boasted that it

was 'all ruff drawn in a week, and finishd in 2 days after, and yet it consists of 12 stanza[s] and some of them above thirty lines, all above 20'.[66] If anything, we may feel surprised that Swift had lavished so much time on his 307 lines, and be more inclined to concur with Dr Johnson's apocryphal story that it was this poem which led Dryden to remark: 'Cousin Swift, you will never be a poet.'[67] But Swift's literary stirrings had taken a firm hold. Like most aspiring poets he was, he admitted, 'overfond of [his] own writings': 'I would not have the world think so for a million, but it is so, and I find when I writt what pleases me I am Cowley to my self and can read it a hundred times over.'[68] If we are honest, we can all recognise this 'desperate weakness'. It is a common failing.

As well as the *Ode to the Athenian Society* and the *Ode to the King,* two other Pindarics survive from this period, the *Ode to Temple* and the *Ode to Dr. William Sancroft.* The influence of Abraham Cowley pervades these early offerings. Swift himself observed that, at this juncture, he could 'not write anything easy to be understood', and this is certainly the dominant feeling of the modern reader. The long, complex verse paragraphs of the odes, punctuated by parenthetical matter, and containing a redundancy of embedded clauses, display little of the rhythmical vitality we have come to expect from Swift's mature verse. And yet to the young Swift, Cowley's obscurity was a quality to be emulated if at all possible. In 'some of Mr. *Cowley's* Love Verses', he discovered 'a Strain that [he] thought extraordinary at Fifteen'. But it is interesting to note that when Cowley leads the light horse of the Moderns in *The Battle of the Books,* he was 'cleft ... in twain' by the poet, Pindar, whom he imitated in 'Address, and Pace, and Career, as well as the Vigour of his Horse, and his own Skill would allow'.[69] Within a very few years of the composition of his own Pindaric odes, Swift had rejected Cowley as a model for his own verse.

While Cowley provided the example for Pindaric obscurity, it was Temple's dislike of humour and satire which coloured the panegyric hyperbole of the odes. His own poetry reflected a conventional 'seriousness'. He also translated Virgil, Horace and Tibullus. Swift, too, was encouraged to imitate the classics, and it was not a task he found altogether congenial.

.'This Virgil sticks plaguily on my hands', he wrote to Thomas Swift, 'I did about 200 lines and gave it to my Lady G[iffard] for a Sample, and she and Sr W. T. like it as I would have them, but He wont allow that I should leave out what I mentioned to you.'[70] Temple really did supervise Swift's early attempts at poetry, and it is therefore not surprising that the *Ode to Temple,* which Swift may have begun as early as 1689,[71] is in the same highflown style as the *Ode to the Athenian Society.* The mentor deserved the bathos of Swift's eulogy.

In the later poems one of Swift's favourite rhetorical devices is to frustrate conventional expectations, raising them merely in order to dash them to the ground from a greater height. The beautiful young nymph slowly disintegrates before our eyes. The proffered description of the morning records not a rapturous dawn, but a dismal tale of urban degradation. Swift's 'rapsody' on poetry suggests that modern verse is scarcely worth the implied 'rap' of the title. When, therefore, in these early efforts, Swift attempts to scale the heights of Parnassus, we wait for a pay-off which never comes, anticipating a non-existent punch-line. We are disappointed in another, more fundamental sense, as Swift fails to satisfy the criteria of either the sublime itself, or the contrived anticlimax of his later poetry.

It has been claimed that 'perhaps the chief value of Swift's poetry is not what it tells us about its subject at all but rather what it shows us about its author.'[72] Certainly this must be true for the biographer. From the early odes we can begin to chart Swift's literary development, as first he embraces and then rejects the Pindaric form. We can observe his attachment to Archbishop Sancroft, 'the brightest pattern Earth can shew/ Of heav'n-born Truth below',[73] and use it to document his attitudes towards the Established Church at this date. We can discern the occurrence of imagery which was to find its way into *A Tale of a Tub,* and confirm the claim of the 'Apology' that the book was the work of the 1690s.[74] But the critic will return from the early odes with a sense of aesthetic unease and an awareness of missed opportunity.

Swift is a child of the seventeenth century, but at his best he does not imitate the high Renaissance style – he exploits it for a vastly different effect. As he put it in 1733 in *An Epistle to a Lady:*

> THUS, Shou'd I attempt to climb,
> Treat you in a Stile sublime,
> Such a Rocket is my Muse,
> Shou'd I lofty Numbers chuse,
> E'er I reach'd *Parnassus* Top
> I shou'd burst, and bursting drop.[75]

Swift quickly recognised his own shortcomings as a poet. 'I have had an ode in hand these 5 months inscribed to my late Ld of Canterbury Dr Sancroft, a gentleman I admire ... more than I can express,' he wrote to Thomas Swift on 3 May 1692. 'I cannot finish it for my life, and I have done nine stanzas and do not like half of them, nor am nigh finished, but there it lyes.' The *Ode to Sancroft* remained unfinished.[76] Swift had done with the Pindaric ode. When next we hear of his poetical activities, Swift was writing verses 'for Will Congreves next Play' and, significantly, they were 'almost 250 lines, not Pindarick'.[77]

The heroic couplets thus described are much closer to Swift's mature manner. The diction still veers towards the sublime, but the several occasions on which Swift draws attention to his Muse assume a much less self-conscious character, and a clear satirical design can be discerned, albeit that he half-apologises for his presumption:

> Perish the Muse's hour, thus vainly spent
> In satire, to my CONGREVE's praises meant;
> In how ill season her resentments rule,
> What's that to her if mankind be a fool?[78]

More important, perhaps, is the humorous approach through which Swift manages to suggest the familiar, conversational tone of his later octosyllabic, story-telling style. To all appearances, *To Mr. Congreve*, like the Pindaric odes, is a panegyric. But it is not quite as simple as that. Like Swift's subsequent eulogies, it operates through raillery. As Irvin Ehrenpreis observes, 'eulogy was always to be his talent, but it would be best expressed ironically, through mock-insults.'[79] In this poem, there is even a hint of self-mockery: 'Nor tax the goddess of a mean design/ To praise your parts by publishing of mine.' The caution is none the less a sound one. What is apparently an occasional poem, written in celebration of Swift's younger, but much better-known, school and college colleague, has indeed a disconcerting tendency to wander from its ostensible subject. It was simply a vehicle for Swift's poetic ideas. The verses were 'calculated for any of [Congreve's plays]', not for a particular occasion, and Swift wanted to know how the play 'succeeded, whether well, ill or indifferently', before sending them to Congreve.[80] The element of eulogy had acquired a cynical, self-interested veneer.

One final poem has survived from this period,[81] *Occasioned by Sir William Temple's Late Illness and Recovery*. Written in December 1693, and also in heroic couplets, it provides a suitable conclusion to this phase of Swift's literary development. A complicated discussion between the poet and his Muse finally results in his abandonment of poetical pretensions as if, symbolically, with Temple's physical recovery. When Swift returned to the pursuit of literary ends, he looked not to verse, but to prose. *Occasioned by Sir William Temple's Late Illness and Recovery* is the least unsatisfactory of Swift's early poems. The lexical complexity lingers on, but the structure is much less baffling: a speech by the Muse upbraiding her protégé for not launching into verse on the restoration of Temple's health is answered by the poet in accusatory terms, as he questions the validity of the grounds upon which he courts fame through his writings. Then, his own illness diagnosed as 'madness', the poet rejects his Muse in peculiarly fitting lines:

> There thy enchantment broke, and from this hour
> I here renounce thy visionary pow'r;
> And since thy essence on my breath depends,
> Thus with a puff the whole delusion ends.[82]

The first stage in Swift's relationship with Sir William Temple was similarly about to end. Within six months Swift had left Moor Park to return to Ireland. The delusion had indeed ended. Temple had used Swift as his secretary, 'often trust[ing him] with matters of great Importance', as the two men grew into a situation of 'some confidence'.[83] Swift had acted as Temple's amanuensis. He had been his companion. He had been sent to the Court at Kensington as occasion demanded, the visit in the first months of 1693, when the debate in Parliament on the triennial bill was at its height, being the most obvious and well-documented one. In this way, Swift had been on hand to supervise the publication of *An Answer To A Scurrilous Pamphlet* in the February of that year, as a contribution to the controversy over *Memoirs of what past in Christendom*. He had done all this in Temple's service, and yet reward was not forthcoming. Swift desired a living in the Church, but Temple kept fobbing him off with promises of one of the more sought-after prebendaries in Canterbury or London. It was not good enough.

Eventually Swift took steps on his own behalf to secure his ordination. His own account of the developments which led to this decision is worth quoting:

> Mr Swift lived with [Temple] some time, but resolving to settle himself in some way of living, was inclined to take orders. However, although his fortune was very small, he had a scruple of entring the Church meerly for support, and Sr Wm Temple then being Master of the Rolls in Ireland offered him an Employ of about 120 ll a year in that office, whereupon Mr Swift told him, that since he had now an opportunity of living without being driven into the Church for a maintenance, he was resolved to go to Irel[an]d and take holy Orders.[84]

An element of rebellion can be detected in Swift's refusal either to wait upon Temple's good offices, or to accept his offer of a post in connection with the Mastership of the Rolls in Ireland. Swift had rejected Temple's advice with regard to literature, and found his own genius in humour, wit and raillery. Now he was able to recognise Temple's fallibility as a human being.

4
Swift and the Church

Swift left Moor Park around the beginning of May 1694. Ill-feeling was apparent on both sides. Clearly Swift was concerned about Temple's inability or reluctance to procure anything for him but promises. 'I left Sir William Temple a month ago,' he told his cousin, Deane Swift, on 3 June. 'He was extream angry I left Him, and yet would not oblige Himself any further than upon my good Behaviour, nor would promise any thing firmly to Me at all; so that every Body judged I did best to leave Him.'[1] As ever, Swift was keen to justify his own actions. The rupture had not been his fault. He was the one who had been let down.

His immediate resolution was to go to Ireland and take orders. The biggest obstacle was his lack of a living 'in readiness'. Deane Swift and Willoughby Swift were merchants in Portugal. 'I design to be ordained September next, and make what Endeavours I can for something in the Church', Swift wrote to Deane Swift from Leicester, *en route* to Ireland, 'I wish it may ever lye in my Cosin [Willoughby]'s way or Yours to have Interest to bring me in Chaplain of the Factory [in Lisbon].' It was Swift's fate in his youth and early manhood always to be soliciting favours. Deane Swift was barely twenty. His poor relation, Jonathan Swift, was reduced to suing not for an English prebend at Westminster or Canterbury, but for the lowliest place the Church offered – if not the chaplaincy óf an English merchant company in Portugal, then 'some small Readers Place'.[2]

Swift was unable to secure his ordination during the 'embertides' of September. Having taken 'all due Methods' to achieve his advancement 'without effecting it', he was forced to make use of Temple's name. His three years' absence from Ireland required an explanation. Why had he not already embarked upon a career? Why had he delayed his ordination if the priesthood were his vocation? Narcissus Marsh, Provost of Trinity College during Swift's undergraduate days and now Archbishop of Dublin, expected 'a Certificate' from Temple relating to Swift's 'Conduct' in his family. 'Morals and Learning' were the areas in which Marsh was interested, and Swift begged Temple 'to excuse my many Weaknesses and Follyes and Oversights' in supplying 'the Reasons of quitting your Honor's Family, that is, whether the last was occasion'd by any ill Actions of mine'.[3]

Swift's path to preferment in the Church, then, was far from smooth, although it proved to be the 'type' of subsequent difficulties. He had not anticipated any problems. He was known in Dublin and his family was acquainted with several Irish bishops. And still his ordination had been delayed. Nor had he a living to go to after he had taken orders. In the case of 'those who are not ordained', Swift told Temple, 'the usuall Method is to admit them first to some small Readers Place till by Preaching upon Occasions they can value themselves for better Preferment'. Until he was ordained as a priest, Swift, as a deacon, would merely be able to hold a curacy or a readership, not a benefice with cure of souls. Even this small advance was subject to his prior ordination as deacon, and time was short. 'The Ordination is appointed by the Arch-Bishop by the Beginning of November', Swift anxiously advised Temple, 'so that if Your Honor will not grant this Favor immediatly I fear it will come too late.' With his pride in his pocket, Swift mailed his plea to England on 6 October 1694.[4]

To his credit, Temple did not allow any pettiness to intervene between himself and his erstwhile secretary. On 25 October 1694 Swift was ordained deacon by William Moreton, Bishop of Kildare.[5] Instead of missing the November date set by the Archbisop of Dublin for his ordination, Swift had been able to anticipate it. His progress into the priesthood was just as punctual. We know nothing of the brief period of Swift's diaconate, nor of his prospects after sending Temple the celebrated 'penitential' letter, but on 13 January 1695 he was ordained priest, also by Moreton. As such he was able to be preferred to a living with cure of souls. A prebend was not slow in forthcoming. According to the autobiographical fragment, Swift 'was recommended to the Lord Capel, then Ld Deputy, who gave him a Prebend in the North, worth about 100 ll a year.'[6] On 28 January 1695 – barely a fortnight after his ordination as priest – Swift was presented to the prebend of Kilroot. It is hard to resist the impression that, although the details are missing, this had all been pre-arranged.[7]

It was not a rich living, nor was it in a reputable diocese. Prior to Swift's presentation to Kilroot, the Bishop of Down and Connor had been Thomas Hackett, 'facetiously known as the Bishop of Hammersmith because of his prolonged residence there instead of in his own diocese'.[8] He was deprived of his position, along with a long list of his subordinates in Down and Connor, including Swift's predecessor as prebendary of Kilroot, William Milne. Despite this reformative step, the state of the Church of Ireland in the far-flung northern outpost was very weak. The diocese of Down and Connor did not have a cathedral, and Swift, as vicar of Kilroot, did not have a parish church. Not only were church buildings in the area run down, but the legacy of the previous incumbents was hard to overcome. 'A Memorandum concerning the Diocese of Down and Connor' relating to its examination by an ecclesiastical commission in 1693 revealed manifold corruption, and resulted in 'suspensions, excommunications, and deprivations for such varied offences as drunkenness, fornication, adultery, neglect of cures, pluralism, diversion of funds, excessive procuration and visitation fees, non-residence, illegal use of the bishop's seal, and simony'![9]

Down and Connor represented the ills from which the Church of Ireland suffered in their most exaggerated form. It had been a Church of the minority of the population ever since the Reformation. Not only did Roman Catholics vastly outnumber Protestants, but even amongst Protestants the adherents of the Established Church were merely a small proportion in comparison with the numbers of Protestant Nonconformists. This situation had obtained for over a century. In 1600 the Church of Ireland had been 'in a state of confusion, inefficiency and neglect'.[10] At the end of the seventeenth century it was in a similar decayed condition. The Revolution Settlement of 1689 had failed once again to implement a bill to comprehend the vast majority of Protestant Dissenters within the Established Church, as many Anglicans had hoped and desired. In Scotland the Established Church became Presbyterian and hundreds of Anglican clergymen were deprived of their livings. In England, Ireland and Wales the effect of the Toleration Act, which allowed freedom of worship, was severe, as Church of England congregations decreased from year to year.

The Toleration Act implied liberty of conscience, so churchwardens were increasingly reluctant to 'present any for not going to church, though they go nowhere else but to the alehouse, for the liberty they will have'.[11] Swift's experiences in the north of Ireland presented the phenomenon of empty churches in its most acute form in a parish in which the inhabitants were either Roman Catholic or Presbyterian, and so coloured his already hostile attitude to nonconformity. As G. V. Bennett puts it, 'In the generation after the Revolution the Church of England was torn apart by a great conflict of parties.'[12] It was to affect Swift's whole career, and inform many of his opinions on Church affairs. After the victory over Popery and James II which had been consolidated in the Treaty of Limerick, the Church set about putting its house in order. Swift was a beneficiary of the new policy. Preferred to a living deep in Presbyterian territory and reduced by decay, he learned at the outset that there was an unavoidable relationship between the economic basis of the Church of Ireland and the spiritual well-being of its members. He also experienced at first hand the importance of the struggle with Presbyterianism, and the necessity of employing the type of clergyman who would not succumb to the pressures such a conflict inevitably exerted. During his predecessor's time as vicar of Kilroot 'several considerable persons in the Parrish ... were forced to frequent the Presbyterian meetings for want of a fitt minister to attend that Cure.'[13] True, the efficiency of the system depended to a very large degree on the diligence of the bishops and archbishops, but the responsibility of the individual clergyman was vital. Swift looked upon himself 'in the capacity of a clergyman, to be one appointed by providence for defending a post assigned me, and for gaining over as many enemies as I can.'[14]

The prebend of Kilroot in the cathedral of Connor was a union of three parishes, Kilroot, Templecorran and Ballynure, in the county of Antrim. Only by joining the incomes of several parishes together could an adequate living be attained in many cases. Swift's income was composed almost entirely of tithes, princially deriving from the parish of Ballynure, where he was both rector and vicar. In Kilroot and Templecorran he was merely vicar and, as such, received only vicarial tithes, the rectorial tithes being impropriated by the Earl of Donegal and the See of Connor respectively.[15] In addition, the income of Swift's prebend was further reduced by an annual £20 to be paid as a pension to William Milne, the deprived previous incumbent, on account of his 'great age, poverty & long being in the Church & of the Clergy'.[16] Swift's constant concern for decayed and impropriated temporalities was not simply pecuniary; it was connected with the health of the Church of Ireland itself. Louis A. Landa refers to 'the jealous guardianship which he later came to exercise over the actual physical possessions of the Church, his keen recognition of the vital relation between worldly prosperity and spiritual health in the Church.'[17] Only by ensuring that clerical incomes were adequate for the job could the right men be recruited – men who would work for the revitalisation of Anglicanism in Ireland.

From the first, Swift was acutely conscious of his financial situation as a clergyman, and his subsequent efforts to purchase glebe land for the support of his living are a direct result of his down-to-earth attitude to his function. As he informed his successor, John Winder, 'I assure you *(for I am an understanding man in that Affair)* that the Parish of Balinure upon a fair view, at eighteen pence per acre [of] Oats, amounts to better than 100[11] a year, with Cows, Sheep, Cats and Dogs &c.'.[18] Swift never neglected the basics. In theory, every parish had some land for the priest's personal use. This glebe or smallholding was a welcome supplement to the income of the living. But there is no certainty that glebe land was to be found in any of his three parishes.[19] Presumably they had been alienated back in the mists of time. One of the main complaints aired in 1693 about the diocese of Down and Connor had been the 'want of Gleab-lands & Manse-houses',[20] and Swift appears to have had neither. There is no firm evidence of the existence of a manse in any of the three parishes. 'He may have lived either in the village of Temple-corran or in Carrickfergus.'[21] We just don't know. Viewed in perspective, Swift's efforts to purchase glebe land for Laracor and to build a log cabin there, both at his own expense, can be seen as a throwback to his experiences in Kilroot.

At the very least one would have expected Swift to have had a church in each of his parishes. But the church at Kilroot was in ruins in 1679. Significantly, Swift did not read assent at Kilroot on his institution on 5 March 1695, although he read assent at Templecorran on the 24th and at Ballynure on 21 April. Instead he finished the ritual at the parish church of Connor on 28 April. If there were church buildings at Ballynure and Templecorran, they were not in a good state of repair. Swift subsequently referred to the sermons he wrote at this time as 'calculated for a Church without a company or a roof'.[22] His clerical duties can hardly have been arduous. Almost the entire population was of Scottish extraction, and therefore of Presbyterian persuasion. In 1683 Kilroot was described as having 'not one natural Irish in the parish not papist', whereas in Templecorran the inhabitants were 'all presbyterian except the parson and clark'.[23] For one who had been bred up to have a strong dislike of 'sectaries' of any kind, it must have been a baptism of fire to serve in parishes so totally devoted to Presbyterianism.

We know very little about Swift's stay at Kilroot. That he 'tarried only briefly', Louis A. Landa remarks, is 'perhaps an eloquent comment in itself.'[24] He arrived in Ulster in March 1695 and left just over a year later. For information about his life in Antrim we must use our imagination. We do not even know whether or not he made use of a curate, or preached alternately at Templecorran and Ballynure, or followed the example of his predecessor in not serving Ballynure. Swift must have moved in a rather limited social circle, based on Carrickfergus, still the largest town in the area, not yet surpassed by Belfast. The rectorial tithes of Kilroot were impropriate to the Earl of Donegal, and Swift became acquainted with the Countess. But his other friends appear to have been fellow churchmen. His most enduring friendship seems to have been with John Winder, Vicar of Carnmoney, adjacent to Ballynure. 'I am not likely to be so pleasd with any thing again this good while, as I was with y^r Letter', Swift wrote to him on 13 January 1699, almost three years after leaving Ulster, 'I believe had I been [assurd of your] Neighberhood, I should not have been so unsatisfied with the Region I was planted in.'[25]

Swift did not relish Ulster, and when Temple encouraged him to return to Moor Park, he had little inclination to remain at his northern outpost. However, he did 'solemnly offer to forego' what he was offered – 'the same acquaintance with greatness that I formerly enjoyed, and with better prospect of interest' – for the hand in marriage of Miss Jane Waring of Belfast.[26] Winder's friendship had brought with it the emotional entanglement of incipient romance. Swift found himself involved with a young lady whom he celebrated fancifully under the name of Varina, as he would later celebrate Vanessa and Stella. 'I here solemnly protest, by all that can be witness to an oath', he wrote to her on 29 April 1696 before leaving for Moor Park, 'that if I leave this kingdom before you are mine, I will endure the utmost indignities of fortune rather than ever return again, though the king would send me back his deputy.'[27]

Interpretation of Swift's relationship with Varina is complicated by more than merely the hollow hyperbole of his parting protestations. True, he did return to Ireland in 1699 as much less significant a personage than the king's deputy. But it is his sincerity which is in question. It has been suggested that women were Swift's weakness. He may not have been a deflowerer of virgins, but he certainly seems to have been a philanderer. In Leicester, he had already caused his behaviour to be criticised. In excuse, he had offered the explanation that his 'conjur'd spirit' tended to 'do mischief if I would not give it employment'. In company, his humour turned to talk of love, but 'without any other Design than that of entertaining my self when I am very idle'. 'This I have always done as a man of the world,' he claimed, 'when I had no design of any thing grave in it, & what I thought at worst a harmless Impertinence.' There were at least 'twenty women' to whom Swift had behaved himself 'just the same way'.[28] Was Jane Waring the twenty-first? In England, Swift received a number of poison-pen letters 'censuring [his] Truth in relation to a certain Lady', and when Winder mentioned 'a dangerous Rival for an absent Lover', Swift readily resigned himself to 'Fortune', observing that 'it requires more *charms and Address in Women* to revive one *fainting Flame* than to *kindle* a dozen *new ones*'.[29]

It would be unwise to set too much store by Swift's unsuccessful suit of Jane Waring in 1696. On his return to Ireland three years later his behaviour was so very different that she wished to know 'what gave [his] temper that sudden turn, as to alter the style of [his] letters'.[30] One wonders how much he regretted being turned down. It might in fact have been more of a means to shrug off the unwanted effects of a flirtation that had gone too far. Swift's love-letters read more like ultimatums than genuine protestations of affection. Perhaps the unhappy attentions of the delectable Varina served more to inflame his desire to leave Kilroot than his ardent admiration as a lover. When Jane Waring desperately tried to fan the flames of a cold fire, his response was almost callous. While acknowledging his former professions of esteem, Swift made it abundantly clear that he no longer wished for her hand. Jane Waring died a spinster.

Swift's experiences in Ulster were ones he would wish to put behind him. Other than confirming his commitment to the well-being of the Church of Ireland, his close proximity to Calvinist doctrine may have contributed to his satire in *A Tale of a Tub*, which he appears to have begun work on once back at Moor Park.[31] Swift's first position as a clergyman was short-lived, and his time in Antrim was brief. He arrived at Kilroot in March 1695: by May 1696 he was back in England. In the bare fourteen months he might have spent in the vicinity of Carrickfergus, he made at least one trip, of unknown duration, to Dublin. Swift's own terse account of the tenure of his prebend offers no additional insight. 'Growing weary in a few months,' he wrote, 'he returned to England; resigned his Living in favor of a Friend, and continued in S^r W[illiam] Temple's house till the Death of that great Man.'[32] Swift's sister subsequently noted that Temple was 'so fond' of her brother 'that he made him give up his living in ... [*Ireland*] to stay with him at Moore-Park, and promised to get him one in *England*'.[33] This is substantially the the same as Swift's explanation to Jane Waring that his return to Moor Park was to be accompanied 'with better prospect of interest.'[34]

Swift did not resign his living at Kilroot for a further eighteen months. Then, early in January 1698, he made way for his friend, John Winder of Carnmoney, to succeed him. In the meantime he lived at Moor Park as Temple's private secretary, reading voraciously. He held a licence of absence from Kilroot which was extendable, but he had his eyes on a more profitable and prestigious living in England. It was not to be. '10 days before my resignation', he wrote, 'My Ld Sunderland fell and I with Him.'[35] Swift's relations with the Lord Chamberlain, Robert Spencer, second Earl of Sunderland, are obscure. True, he was friendly with Temple, and visited him at Moor Park,[36] but the extent of Sunderland's influence in Church matters, even at the height of his power in the 1690s, is to be suspected. If Temple's interest lay with the Lord Chamberlain, Swift's real prospects of preferment were slight. Yet this is what Swift's remarks suggest. Since Sunderland's resignation in December 1697, he explained, 'there have been other Courses, which if they succeed, I shall be proud to own the Methods, or if otherwise, very much ashamed.'[37] We know nothing of the methods employed by Swift at this juncture, for they did not meet with success. He was doomed to stay at Moor Park until the death of his great patron – a man of thirty without a home of his own, without a position, without an income.[38] He was still dependent on the kindness of friends and relations.

But, as far as we can judge, life at Moor Park was far from unhappy during this further sojourn. In the first place, Temple had *sent* for Swift, and he had returned not like the prodigal, but as Temple's cherished amanuensis. Swift had asserted his independence in leaving for Ireland despite having no firm prospects. He returned as prebendary of Kilroot. He may have had no intention of going back to

Ireland. He may have detested Ulster. Yet his relationship with Temple could not fail to be on a different footing than it had been previously. Changes had taken place at Moor Park. Lady Temple was dead. She had been buried in Westminster Abbey in February 1695, just after Swift's appointment to Kilroot. Swift's cousin Thomas, who appears to have assumed the role of Temple's secretary and chaplain on Swift's abrupt departure from his household, was now Rector of Puttenham, to the west of Moor Park.[39] And little Hetty Johnson had grown into a young woman.

An illustration of Swift's new style of living at Moor Park might be supplied by a letter to an unknown correspondent (but almost certainly Hester Johnson) written in 1698 while Temple, his sister Lady Giffard, and their retinue were in London. Swift was master of the house. 'I desire your absence heartily', he writes in comic vein, 'for now I live in great state, and the cook comes in to know what I please to have for dinner: I ask very gravely what is in the house, and accordingly give orders.'[40] Swift's position had altered out of all recognition. He continued to be Temple's messenger to William III. 'I have sent him with another compliment from Papa to the King', Lady Giffard explained on one occasion, 'where I fancy he is not displeased with finding occasions of going.'[41] No, indeed, and Temple's increasing frailty meant that 'Papa' required more and more looking after. 'Expeditions to London were not Swift's only errands for Temple,' Irvin Ehrenpreis observes. 'He kept the household accounts, acted as amanuensis, paid out moneys, and supported conversation.'[42]

In addition to Lady Giffard and her companion, Hester Johnson, Temple's household comprised six other women: Hester's mother, Temple's French daughter-in-law and her mother, and his two grand-daughters, and a waiting woman to Lady Giffard called Rebecca Dingley. Tremendous opportunities presented themselves for Swift to indulge his pride and his fancy in front of such feminine company. It is possible that Jane Waring had genuine grounds for imagining that Swift had found another mistress worthy of his attention. When Swift returned to Moor Park in 1696, Hetty Johnson was fifteen. We can merely speculate about the nature of their relations at this time. He had been her 'writing-master',[43] and certainly his fondness for little Hetty seems to have been beyond doubt. But we would gain nothing by speculation.

Swift's final stay at Moor Park must have been a pleasant one. For one thing, he was free to study. As well as making some preliminary essays towards a history of England, using Temple's *Introduction*,[44] he had time to spend on the extensive research which went into *A Tale of a Tub*. Our knowledge of Swift's reading in this period is unusually sure. 'While he was at *Moor Park*', John Lyon noted, 'he kept an Acct one year of the Books he read.' This important record dates from 7 January 1697. As Irvin Ehrenpreis observes, 'history – political and ecclesiastical – accounts for a third of the titles.'[45] But Swift read more than he would have required merely for a history. Classical literature expectedly figures largely in the list, but so do works of the early Christian fathers. If Lucretius had the distinction of being read three times, Irenaeus's attack on Gnosticism also finds a place. Both Lucretius and Irenaeus, it will be remembered, are quoted on the title-page of the *Tale*.[46] Swift's 'account' of his reading is a feast for source-hunters.

The *Tale* itself will be treated in a separate chapter, for its confused and protracted life means that only one date can be taken for granted – that of publication. Lyon asserts that it was begun at TCD, and concurs with Hawkesworth that it was 'corrected and improved' at Moor Park, the digressions being 'added' at this time.[47] But no dates are supplied for this revision, and Hawkesworth implies that it took place not on Swift's return from Ulster, but from Oxford in 1692.[48] Conflicting versions of the circumstances of composition render very little certain. Short of entering the realms of speculation, we have little recourse but to examine the *Tale* on its appearance in print. It bears the marks of long gestation and difficult birth, but we have no way of knowing how much of the published work was ready in 1697, or how much was added between then and 1704. The claim, made in the 1710 'Apology', that the work would have been the better for time spent in revision had the author 'been Master of his Papers for a Year or two before their Publication',[49] must, in the absence of corroborating evidence and in the light of the ironic structure of *A Tale of a Tub,* be taken *cum grano salis.*

Swift's time at Moor Park came to an end in 1699. From June 1698 onwards Temple's illness, supposedly gout, became increasingly debilitating. With prescience, Swift began to compile a record entitled *Journal d'Estat de Mr T— devant sa Mort*. Beginning on 1 July 1698, this was a 'Register of ye variations, wch: appeared in [Temple's] Constitution', terminating with his demise on 27 January 1699. Although we only have Lyon's word that such a document existed, it bears all the marks of Swift's usual reaction to impending or recent death. Swift's final entry noted that Temple 'dyed at one o'clock in the morning & with him all that was great & good among Men'. The apostrophe is similar to those which greeted news of the death of his mother and of Stella.[50] 'My poor brother has lost his best friend Sir William Temple,' Jane Swift remarked, 'death came in between, and has left him unprovided both of friend and living.'[51]

Swift's legacy from Temple was intellectual rather than monetary. True, he received the advantage to be derived from the publication of Temple's remaining writings, in addition to the sum of £100 bequeathed 'to Mr. Jonathan Swift, now dwelling with me.'[52] But preferment in England was not forthcoming, and the inheritance was hardly sufficient to set Swift up for life. We must look for Temple's endowment elsewhere, in the formulation of Swift's mature outlook. The question of influence is an impossible one about which to be precise, but it is hard to resist the conclusion that the environment of Moor Park produced a forced growth. The confident ironic touch of *A Tale of a Tub* is a world away from the callow Pindaric odes, and yet it seems that only a very few years separated the two performances. True, Swift's experiences in Ireland from 1694 to 1696 must be taken into account. But all in all it seems safe to lay the wonderful development of Swift's literary genius at the feet of Sir William Temple, as Swift first learned how to imitate and please his mentor, and then unlearned such skills before embarking on the pursuit of satire.

We know very little about Jonathan Swift *before* his acquaintance with Temple. Most of the comments upon his youth that he has handed down to posterity were retrospective. As a result many are distorted, and some deliberately misleading. In addition to the early poems, we have only ten letters to assist 'us in the task of sketching the character of Swift at thirty. From the letters to Jane Waring, and from his comments upon women in general, we gather that he could be selfish, inconsiderate, headstrong, overbearing and, above all, proud. This pride – the confidence he always possessed in his own ability – was to be the mainstay of his life. Despite many vicissitudes Swift was priggishly certain of his own worth, and merely waited for the world to endorse his opinion. The legacies of his childhood lay heavy on Swift's adult character. He was determined to make his way in the world, to show them, as it were, whether through a career in the Church, or as a man of letters.

In our search for evidence of Swift's character, a unique formulation of his views on various subjects should not be overlooked. Throughout his life, Swift put pen to paper to note his opinions on a multiplicity of topics. The curious manuscript headed 'When I come to be old 1699—' offers first-hand insight into his thoughts at this time:

Not to marry a young Woman.

Not to keep young Company unless they reely desire it.

Not to be peevish, or morose, or suspicious

Not to scorn present Ways, or Wits, or Fashions, or Men, or War, &c.

Not to be fond of Children, ~~or lett them come near me hardly~~ [*sic*]

Not to tell the same story over & over to th[e] same People

Not to be covetous.

Not to neglect decency, or cleenlyness, for fear of falling into Nastyness.

Not to be over severe with young People, but give Allowances for their youthfull follyes, and Weeknesses

Not to be influenced by, or give ear to knavish tatling Servants, or others.

Not to be too free of advise, nor trouble any but those that desire it.

To desire some good Friends to inform me wch of these Resolutions I break, or neglect, & wherein; and reform accordingly.

Not to talk much, nor of my self.

Not to boast of my former beauty, or strength, or favor with Ladyes, &c

Not to hearken to Flatteryes, nor conceive I can be beloved by a young woman. Et eos qui herdetetatem [*sic*] captant odisse ac vitare.

Not to be positive or opiniatre.

Not to sett up for observing all these Rules; for fear I should observe none.[53]

It is difficult to judge the extent to which these resolutions were a conscious reaction to life with Sir William Temple. If some of them sound like a young man's thoughts on the peevishness of opinionative old age, others, the last in particular, evince Swift's own capacity for self-deflation. 'If a Man would register all his Opinions upon Love, Politicks, Religion, Learning and the Like; beginning from his Youth, and so go on to old Age', he observed on another occasion, 'What a Bundle of Inconsistencies and Contradictions would appear at last?'[54] Prudent advice to anyone who wishes to characterise Swift's mature philosophy.

And yet there are certain controlling ideas that can be seen to have been fairly consistent in relation to Swift. We have noted his attitude to love and marriage in his twenties. He remained a man who entertained and liked to be entertained by the ladies. Nor did he ever overlook the 'thousand Household thoughts' which always drove matrimony out of his mind when he was only twenty-four.[55] In religion and learning Swift's views as expressed in *A Tale of a Tub* appear to have undergone only slight modification as the years went by. As far as politics are concerned, Swift's principles display a similar remarkable consistency, although it should be stressed that at this stage, as he himself conceded, he had not begun 'to trouble [him]self with the differences between the principles of Whig and Tory'. But having been 'long conversant with the Greek and Roman authors', he found himself 'a lover of liberty'. He was to remain so throughout his life. And he was a strong supporter of the Established Church – 'an High-churchman' – and he could not 'conceive how any one, who wore the habit of a clergyman, could be otherwise'.[56]

Swift, at this juncture, was blissfully unaware of the exigencies of practical politics. He gleaned his ideas from his family background, his association with Temple, and his wide reading.

But Swift's reliance on Temple was over. He had to make his own way in the world once more. No doubt he stayed on at Moor Park some few weeks, tidying up Temple's affairs. Then he moved to London, where he evidently lived for around six months in 1699.[57] Applying himself to the king on account of old promises allegedly made to Temple, Swift sought 'a Prebend of Canterbury or Westminster', expecting the Earl of Romney, who 'professed much friendship', to support his suit.[58] But he was setting his sights far too high, and no prebendal stall was vacant at either location. Bereft of friends with influence at Court (Romney 'said not a word to the King'), Swift had little alternative but to return, yet again, to his native soil. He took up an invitation to be the Earl of Berkeley's chaplain. When Berkeley sailed from Bristol in August 1699 to assume his duties as one of the Lords Justices in Ireland, Swift sailed with him. Landing near Waterford, he 'acted as [Berkeley's] Secretary the whole Journy to Dublin'.[59]

Swift hoped to retain his position as secretary, but one of his 'enemies' interposed. This brazen fellow, one Arthur Bushe:

> so far insinuated himself into the Earls favor, by telling
> him, that the Post of Secretary was not proper for a
> Clergyman, nor would be of any advantage to one who
> aimed onely at Church-preferments, that his Lordship after
> a poor Apology gave that Office to the other.[60]

The episode is worth dwelling on for a moment to illustrate the bitterness Swift still felt in his old age regarding his failure to secure the position he felt his merits deserved. Throughout his life he held grudges. His expectations were quickly aroused, and he was never satisfied with second best. Instead he invented fictions to excuse his own inadequacy. As Lord Justice, Berkeley was able to exercise considerable influence in Church appointments in Ireland. Early in

January 1700 one of the most lucrative deaneries fell vacant. Swift thought his ship had come in, but once again the coveted place was conferred elsewhere.

Swift was certain that Bushe was to blame. According to the autobiographical fragment, 'things were so ordered that the Secretary having received a Bribe, the Deanry was disposed of to another, and Mr Swift was put off with some other Church-livings not worth above a third part of that rich Deanry.'[61] But once again he was aiming at something well out of his range, and there is no reason to countenance the allegation of simony. Far from desiring the vacant deanery of Derry, John Bolton, Vicar of Ratoath and Prebendary of Dunlavin in St Patrick's Cathedral, Dublin, was reluctant to move. Why, then, should he have bribed Bushe? Nor does it appear that Swift's name was ever openly connected with Derry. William King, Bishop of Derry, mentioned five possible candidates, 'Dr. Stearn of Trim, Dr. Singe, Dr. Bolton, Mr. Span and Mr. Perkinson', adding the rider, 'I shall thank God if I get any of them.'[62] All these suggestions, it should be noted, were men with much greater experience than Swift, and when he hints that the reason he did not get the preferment 'was his being too young', we can see that it was all a figment of his own imagination; the heartfelt desire of an ambitious man. And so responsibility is placed elsewhere, on the shoulders of the Earl of Berkeley's secretary, and an elaborate story of corruption is invented to excuse Swift's failure to gain his ends.

On his appointment as Dean of Derry, Bolton resigned one of his livings – the least lucrative – Laracor. It was given to Swift. This union of three parishes, Agher, Laracor and Rathbeggan, in the diocese of Meath, provided Swift with an income, in 1700, of £230 a year. True, it was initially reduced by uncollected tithes, but at least he had secured a regular income and a permanent position.[63] Swift was instituted Vicar of Laracor on 22 March 1700. He remained domestic chaplain to Berkeley. A dispensation allowed him to postpone reading assent and consent at Laracor and Rathbeggan until June. Moreoever, his circumstances quickly improved when, in September 1700, he was given the prebend of Dunlavin in St Patrick's Cathedral, Dublin. As Louis A. Landa remarks, it was 'in the light of subsequent developments the most significant single event in his early clerical career'.[64] His introduction to men of power in England stemmed from his ability to move in the mainstream of Dublin life. He was never in regular residence at Laracor, where there was no manse. He preferred to live in Dublin Castle as Berkeley's chaplain.

Swift explained the circumstances of his life to Jane Waring in a letter of May 1700. Offering a 'dismal account' of his benefice, which he assured her was 'a true one', he did all he could to dissuade her from joining her own to his 'poor income'. Under no circumstances was she to think of journeying down from Belfast, his attendance on Lord Berkeley was 'so close, and so much required'. Besides, where would they live, with no manse at Laracor? 'There is no other way but to hire a house at *Trim*', the next village, he told her, 'or build one on the spot: the first is hardly to be done, and the other I am too poor to perform at present.'[65] But Swift was hardly being fair. The true reason for not wishing to waste away in provincial air was the fact that he was enjoying himself in Dublin, and he did not want to be encumbered by a wife. Lodging in Dublin Castle with the Earl and Countess of Berkeley, he was free to indulge himself to the full in the pleasures of a bachelor's life in Dublin. It was not a situation he was prepared to throw up just yet. He was staying put. The days of deference were over.

Part Two
Friend of the Great, 1701–1714

5
Swift and the Whigs

In April 1701 Swift accompanied Lord Berkeley to England. It was his fourth adult journey from his native Ireland to the country of his ancestors. By his thirty-fourth year, Swift's features and physique had settled into the lines which would prevail for virtually the rest of his life. In person he was of middle size, tending to stoutness, despite a firm belief which he retained to his old age in the virtues of physical exercise. His bearing seemed to indicate a more robust constitution than he actually possessed. Scrupulously careful about his diet, and temperate in his drinking habits, Swift none the less suffered excruciating attacks of nausea and giddiness. These he blamed on certain foodstuffs of which he was inordinately fond, such as fruit and malt liquor. Despite his great liking for them, he rarely indulged himself. His firm moderation in such matters may have helped to build a strong character, but did nothing to forestall or alleviate the symptoms of what is now diagnosed as a syndrome of the inner ear.

Berkeley was travelling back to England to be replaced by a new Lord-Lieutenant of Ireland, Laurence Hyde, Earl of Rochester. Swift was more concerned with literary affairs. During his time in Ireland after Temple's death, he had been working on his edition of the *Miscellanea. The Third Part,* which he proceeded to see through the press in the course of his visit. He had also been extending his projected history of England, begun at Moor Park. Two fragments have survived, bearing out his retrospective comment that his intention was 'not a voluminous work, nor properly an abridgment, but an exact relation of the most important affairs and events, without any regard to the rest'. 'I was diverted from pursuing this history', he remarked in retrospect, 'chiefly by the indignation I conceived at the proceedings of a faction, which then prevailed.'[1] The conclusion of his interest in political affairs was the publication of his first political work, *A Discourse of the Contests and Dissensions between the Nobles and Commons in Athens and Rome, with the Consequences they had upon both those States.*

As we have seen, the division into the old Whig and Tory parties which had been one of the most immediate effects of the Convention Parliament had soon been replaced by an alignment in Parliament which cut across party lines. Gradually, in the course of the 1690s, the realities of practical politics centred upon the conflict betwen Court and Country, executive and legislature. The end of the Nine Years War in 1697, as well as heralding the fall of the second Earl of Sunderland, upon whom Swift's hopes of preferment are largely supposed to have rested, precipitated a fierce battle in Parliament and in the country over the future of the large army which had fought the war. The session of 1697-8 proved to be principally concerned with the question of a standing army, as the King, his ministers, and his propagandists, fought an unavailing rearguard action to save the successful English regiments from disbandment.

It will be remembered that the standing army was a symbol of Court intentions – a potential threat to liberty and property. Whigs and Tories in office joined to ward off the attack of Whigs and Tories out of office. The Revolution Principle appeared to be at stake, for, according to the Bill of Rights, Parliamentary approval was needed for a standing army to be kept on foot in peacetime. Other issues between Court and Country came to the forefront of affairs. In addition to disbanding the army against the wishes of the King, the House of Commons took steps to resume the grants William III had made to his favourites out of the forfeited rebels' estates in Ireland. The Court had totally surrendered control of Parliament to opposition politicians like Robert Harley. After a confrontation between the Lords and the Commons in April 1700, the administration passed into the hands of the leaders of the so-called 'New Country Party'. A ministerial reshuffle resulted in the sacking of a number of Court Whigs, culminating in the dismissal of Lord Chancellor Somers.

William III had been forced to implement changes by the intractable opposition coalition. His plight was made still worse by the death in July 1700 of the Duke of Gloucester, sole surviving heir of the Protestant heir-apparent, Princess Anne. A firm settlement of the Crown in the Protestant line became imperative. Parliament was dissolved and elections took place in January 1701. The new House of Commons, dominated by elements of the Tory Party and the Country opposition, met in February 1701, and fell to immediate consideration of the question of the succession. In March a bill settling the Crown in the Protestant line, the Act of Settlement, became law.

But the rampant Tory majority in the House of Commons was not content to stop there. The previous Whig ministers were under investigation. And when it became known that secret Partition Treaties had been signed between William III and Louis XIV of France without the prior consent of Parliament, and that several Lords, Somers, Halifax, Orford and Portland, were involved, Tory tempers raged. The four Whig lords were impeached by an angry Lower House in April 1701. This caused further conflict between the two Houses of Parliament, and a propaganda campaign, organised by the Whigs, including petitions from the freeholders of Kent and a letter supposedly from the electors of England and Wales to their representatives in Parliament, designed to discredit the Commons.[2]

This, then, was the situation when Swift arrived in London in May 1701, after visiting his mother in Leicester on the way from Ireland. He witnessed the potentially destructive forces at work in the conflict between Tories and Whigs, the House of Commons and the House of Lords. Observing how 'the same manner of proceeding' as that followed by the Lower House 'had ruined the liberties of Athens and Rome', he thought that 'it might be easy to prove it from history'.[3] His reading was 'fresh in his Head' and his 'Invention at the Height'.[4] Making free use of the classics as authorities for his argument, he began to write an essay in defence of the impeached Whig lords, and against the overweening might (as he saw it) of the House of Commons.

The *Discourse* is not a satire, and for this reason there has been considerable critical disagreement over its merit. It is a vastly different piece of work from *A Tale of a Tub*, which was presumably being revised around the same time. Earlier scholars found it dry, possessing little of the universality with which Swift usually managed to invest the 'bones of a forgotten dispute'.[5] In an attempt at reassessment, it has been suggested that the *Discourse* is a satire proceeding 'by way of Allegory.'[6] But this is to misinterpret the pamphlet, and to misunderstood Swift's method. The polemical strategy adopted is that of parallel history, with events in Athens and Rome compared to the contemporary English situation. With this in view, Swift predicted dire results if the deadlock between the two Houses of Parliament over the impeachments were allowed to continue for any length of time. 'I cannot possibly see, in the common Course of Things,' he wrote, 'how the same Causes can produce different Effects and Consequences among us, than they did in *Greece* and *Rome*.'[7]

Swift's cyclical view of history and his distrust of the 'people' are ideas that can be traced back to Sir William Temple, and indeed his urbane method of argument in the *Discourse*, despite some stylistic similarities to the *Tale,* appears to be another attempt to emulate Temple's sophisticated manner, down to the vagueness of some of the postulates upon which his case is founded. In establishing a cyclical theory of history. Swift needed to prove, firstly, that it was 'an eternal Rule in Politicks, among every free People' that there was 'a Ballance of Power' within the state, and secondly, that when this balance was impaired, the ruin of the constitution would result. Applying these rules to the situation in 1701, he was then able to argue that the behaviour of the House of Commons was threatening to tip the scales in favour of the 'people', just as had been the case, in his view, in 1642. The resulting tyranny of the many would, he suggested, endanger the structure of the state.

To demonstrate his thesis, Swift provided classical analogues. Although it has been argued that these are sufficiently precise to constitute an allegory, with particular persons from the history of Athens and Rome characterising or representing contemporaries such as the four impeached lords, it is clear that the examples Swift gives are meant as parallels, nothing more:

I MIGHT easily produce many more Examples, but these are sufficient: And it may be worth the Reader's Time to reflect, a little, on the Merits of the Cause, as well as of the Men who had been thus dealt with by their Country. I shall direct him no further, than by repeating, that *Aristides* was the most renowned by the People themselves for his exact *Justice, and Knowledge in the Law.* That *Themistocles* was a most fortunate Admiral, and had got *a mighty Victory over the great King of* Persia's *Fleet.* That *Pericles* was *an able Minister of State, and excellent Orator, and a Man of Letters*: And lastly, that *Phocion,* besides the Success of his Arms, was also renowned for his *Negotiations abroad; having, in an Embassy, brought the greatest Monarch of the World, at that Time, to the Terms of an honourable Peace, by which his Country was preserved.* [8]

Allegory – literally 'speaking otherwise than one seems to speak' – would have required the reader himself to have made the connexion between Aristides, Themistocles, Pericles and Phocion and their modern counterparts, Somers, Orford, Halifax and Portland respectively, much as Dryden, in *Absalom and Achitophel*, leaves him to recognise Charles II as David, Monmouth as Absalom, and Shaftesbury as Achitophel. Instead Swift tells the reader that he is employing analogy, the process of reasoning from parallel cases.

In order to make his analogues more convincing, Swift distorts his classical sources throughout the *Discourse*.[9] The method he was subsequently to make use of in *The Conduct of the Allies* is already apparent in his first political tract. The rhetorical ploy is recourse to history to supply ostensible objectivity. In this way, despite deep partisanship, Swift can maintain the fiction of impartiality. But any hopes he might have had of actively assisting the cause of the Whig lords were lost when the impeachment charges were dismissed by the Upper House at the end of the parliamentary session in June 1701. Swift's book was not then ready for the press. Loath to waste what he had so painstakingly written, Swift appended a fifth chapter which attempted to make the *Discourse* less topical. Pointing out that 'all Forms of Government having been instituted by Men, must be mortal like their Authors', and that only a handful of men bothered to consider how 'Diseases in a State are bred, that hasten its End,' Swift hoped to shed light on the constitution of the body politic, in the cause of preventative medicine.[10] He hoped that, in the process, the *Discourse* would become less political pamphlet than political theory. Retaining a learned tone to the end of his work, he contrived to preserve his air of authority.

It was this feature of the *Discourse* which most impressed Swift's contemporaries. When it was published on 22 October 1701, Swift was already back in Ireland. Several Tory pamphlets took notice of the 'doubty Piece' in print, and it was widely assumed to have been written by that experienced Whig controversialist and historian, Gilbert Burnet, Bishop of Salisbury.[11] On Swift's next visit to England, his performance would prove to be the passport to the society of Burnet and his friends. The *Discourse* was the foundation of Swift's stock with the Whigs. It may have come too late actually to assist in the dismissal of the charges of impeachment, but it was effective in the paper war which followed on from the Parliamentary battles of the spring and early summer, and which was given new importance by the dissolution of the Tory Parliament in November 1701. Swift's pamphlet was viewed as a Whig party piece, and treated as such by the Tories. At the same time it was enlisted by the Whigs under their banner.

If the *Discourse* proved to be influential in Swift's subsequent literary career, an equally important event took place in the personal sphere in 1701. Hester Johnson, in her twenty-first year, decided to join her former writing-master in his Irish exile. Accompanied by her life-long friend, Rebecca Dingley, she crossed over to Dublin. Details of the move (and of the sum of Swift's activities in London in 1701) are almost entirely lacking. The immediate consideration was apparently financial. Hester had received a legacy on Temple's death, but it was hardly sufficient to live on in England. Ireland was much cheaper. To his 'own satisfaction', Swift 'prevailed with her and her dear friend and companion ... to draw what money they had into Ireland', where the funds were at 10 per cent, 'and all necessaries of life at half the price'.[12]

Presumably Swift visited Hester at Sheen during his months

in England, where she was still living in Lady Giffard's household. But he did not travel with the ladies to Ireland. They reached Dublin while Swift was still in London. When he joined them early in October the rumours started. Clearly it was singular for an unattached clergyman to arrange such a *modus vivendi*. Swift himself could see that 'the adventure looked so like a frolic', that it was no surprise that 'the censure held, for some time, as if there were a secret history in such a removal'. But Mrs Johnson's 'excellent conduct' soon dispelled doubts about her setting up house under the auspices of a bachelor. In addition, Swift operated a strict set of rules regarding his relations with the ladies. They did not live together at any point, nor were they ever to be found in compromising situations. There is a tradition which, as Irvin Ehrenpreis observes, 'no one has disproved',[13] that Swift and Stella were never left alone together. A third person always acted as chaperone. Morality had not merely to be maintained; it had to be seen to be maintained.

This was one of the supreme uses of Mrs Dingley. Fifteen to twenty years Hester's senior, she was a relation of Sir William Temple on his mother's side, possessed of a very scanty annuity of £14 on the death of her father on 28 September 1700 which Swift regularly supplemented out of his own pocket.[14] With few personal attractions, Rebecca Dingley was ideally suited to her role as Mrs Johnson's 'intimate friend'. Swift characterised her as 'a woman of as much piety and discretion as I have known'.[15] But Swift's feelings for Stella were of quite another sort. She proved to be 'the truest, most virtuous, and valuable friend, that I, or perhaps any other person ever was blessed with', possessed of great 'gifts of the mind', which she took care to improve 'by reading and conversation'. She filled an empty place in Swift's life, for at this time he had 'few friends or acquaintance in Ireland'. As she 'rather chose men for her companions', having 'little knowledge of, and less relish' for the 'usual topics of ladies discourse', she was an ideal companion for the Vicar of Laracor. Her judgment, advice and wit were, he professed, second to none.[16]

Whether there was more to Swift's relations with Hester Johnson than merely a close friendship is one of the puzzles of his biography. After all, in 1701 when she chose to cross over to a strange land on his advice, she was a young woman of twenty, and, according to Swift, 'looked upon as one of the most beautiful, graceful, and agreeable young women in London, only a little too fat'. 'Her hair was blacker than a raven', he continued, 'and every feature of her face in perfection.'[17] It would be curious if there was no sexual attraction between the two, particularly as they remained intimate for over a quarter of a century, until Stella's raven-black locks had turned all to grey, and age had printed 'a furrow'd Trace/On ev'ry Feature of her Face'.[18] Cynical observers were not satisfied with the steps Swift took to secure her reputation. It was said that he had taken Mrs Johnson to him 'hoping the World would esteem her his wife, though not own'd by him as such', and that, 'his humour being confessedly odd, they would pass over this part of his conduct what ever they imagined'.[19] And yet there is no firm evidence to hint at a physical side to their relationship. Lyon stresses that Swift's housekeeper, Mrs Brent, thought it 'all Platonick Love'.[20] This is certainly what Swift himself would give us to believe, in his *Journal to Stella*, in the birthday poems, and in his account, 'On the Death of Mrs. Johnson'.[21]

Swift spent comparatively little time with his newly disembarked friends before the call of England forced him to cross the Irish Sea yet once more. On 16 February 1702 he was granted the degree of Doctor of Divinity from Trinity College. Three weeks later William III died as a result of a riding accident. The new prospect which was opening on the accession of Queen Anne, a Church-of-England Prince whose heart was 'entirely English', was enough to tempt the Vicar of Laracor. Leaving towards the end of April, he was soon in London after his customary visit to Leicester. He found the Whigs out of favour. The man who 'was born to a million of disappointments',[22] had backed the wrong horse during the excitements of 1701. Queen Anne's first ministry was a coalition of Tory and Country party elements, led by the Duke of Marlborough as Captain-General and Sidney, Lord Godolphin as Lord Treasurer. Whigs were largely excluded from the Cabinet and from high office. Swift's hopes of preferment were severely jolted.

This did not prevent him making the most of the response to his *Discourse*. Its reception was gratifying, and there were two editions.[23] Swift let it be known that he was the author. Soon he was acquainted with not only Burnet, but with Somers and Halifax, two of the lords whom he had defended as best he could in the tract. In addition he renewed his acquaintance with the son of the second Earl of Sunderland, who had inherited the title on his father's death. In the course of his visit in 1702, then, Swift became friendly with three of the five Whig lords known as the Junto. To Somers he would dedicate *A Tale of a Tub*. With Halifax he 'soon grew domestic'.[24] With the perversity of which he was to give ample illustration in the years to come, Swift chose to cultivate men who were, at that moment, powerless to help him. Men, moreover, whose ideas on several key issues were diametrically opposed to his own, especially concerning the role of the Church of England in state affairs. As he claimed to have told Somers, he was 'what they called a Whig in politics', but a High Churchman 'as to religion'.[25] To Somers, such distinctions must have seemed strange.

John, Baron Somers, came from small origins and a lawyer's calling to be worth a considerable fortune and to hold the office of Lord Chancellor of England. Renowned for his abilities and his learning, he always retained an aloofness, a 'formality of his nature', as Swift called it, which often alienated potential friends. The last of the Whigs to fall before the Country onslaught at the end of the 1690s, Somers's mutual hostility to Robert Harley was well-known, even though they had been sometime friends.[26] It is interesting that soon after Swift became acquainted with Harley in 1710, he discovered that Somers was 'a false deceitful rascal.'[27]

Charles Montague, Earl of Halifax, was another man of exceptional abilities. His financial genius had made him a natural choice as First Lord of the Treasury during the mid-1690s, and the emergence of the Bank of England owed much to his careful management. Small but gifted, Halifax was both artistic and a powerful public speaker. His ways were less reserved than Somers's and he affected to be a patron of men of letters. As a result Swift remained on rather better terms with him throughout the reign of Queen Anne, without ever receiving the preferment he thought his due.

In contrast, the younger Charles Spencer, Earl of Sunderland and son-in-law to the Duke of Marlborough, was a pushy, irreligious young man of extreme Whig views. He would be the first of the Modern Whigs of the Junto to regain office in the new reign. Sunderland, too, took an interest in books and literature, and subsidised the distribution of Whig propaganda.[28] Yet despite their early acquaintance (Sunderland, as Lord Spencer, visited Moor Park in the 1690s),[29] Swift and Sunderland were never on particularly friendly terms.

It was to these men, together with the Bishop of Salisbury, that Swift looked to satisfy his clerical ambitions. He sought to impress them with his brilliance, not only in conversation, but in literature. This, most probably, was the reason that *A Tale of a Tub* was brought out of wraps, and revised for ultimate publication in 1704. The satire on abuses in religion and learning, Swift fondly imagined, would help to establish his reputation as a young man of genius, reinforcing the good impression made by the *Discourse*. Not only could he put his considerable erudition to practical use in political debate, he could employ it in a witty attack on vulgar errors. It is ironic that the *Tale*, on its own, was the single most potent argument used against Swift's preferment in the Church.

It is worth emphasising, at this juncture, how far Swift's views were removed from those of the Whig Lords of the Junto. On only one point were they agreed – the paramount importance of 'Revolution Principles' – and even in interpreting the Revolution of 1688 they differed to a greater or lesser extent. Swift viewed the Revolution Settlement as a return to a situation which had obtained in the past: the Modern Whigs increasingly regarded the events of 1688 as the foundation of a new political system. Thus although both Swift and the Modern Whigs subscribed wholeheartedly to the Act of Settlement which entailed the succession in the Protestant line, they concurred in little else.

From this single common belief, Swift allowed himself to become entangled with a party of men whose other articles of faith were anathema to him. The Whigs, for instance, did not subscribe to the High Churchman's view of the close relationship between Church and State. Christ's kingdom was not of this earth, and precise distinctions were drawn between secular and spiritual authority. We have seen Swift's hatred of Papist and Dissenter alike. The Whigs, on the other hand, championed the cause of Protestant Dissenters. The question of occasional conformity was to become a principal bone of contention between Whig and Tory in the reign of Queen Anne. It well illustrates the divergence of opinion between Swift and the Whigs. Under the terms of the Test and Corporation Acts, anyone who wanted either to qualify for public office or to be eligible for office in a borough had to have taken communion in the Church of England the previous year. This automatically ruled out Roman Catholics. Presbyterians and other Nonconformists were not so scrupulous. Instead they adhered not to the spirit but to the letter of the law. They received communion annually in the Established Church – literally once a year to qualify for office. The rest of the time they attended their Dissenting meeting-houses.

To Swift, as to most High Churchmen, this practice was utterly reprehensible. However, the Whigs were in favour of occasional conformity for political, if for no other, reasons. Dissenters tended to support the Whig party with votes and money. When bills were introduced into the House of Commons to prevent occasional conformity, then, they were vigorously opposed by the Whigs. Swift was sufficiently confused by this behaviour. He could not approve of the practice of encouraging the Dissenters which the Whigs endorsed 'to make their bottom as wide as they could, by taking all denominations of Protestants to be members of their body.'[30] Over issues such as these Swift discovered that, in all conscience, he was not a *Modern* Whig.

What, then, did Swift mean when he said that, in 1702, he found himself 'much inclined to be what they called a Whig in politics'?[31] He was writing retrospectively, and this hedging was far from unconscious. Aware of his mistaken notions about the Whig party of Queen Anne's reign, he was right to use words such as 'inclined' and phrases like 'what they called.' The Modern Whigs of the Junto were not the Old Whigs who had supported Shaftesbury and the Exclusion Bill. The theory of the relationship between King and 'people', executive and legislature, that was known as 'Country', and to which, as we have seen, Swift adhered, was not consistently held by men like Somers, Halifax, and Sunderland. Swift was insufficiently versed in the practical politics of post-Revolution England to know of the arising distinction between 'Old Whigs' such as Robert Harley and the 'Modern Whigs' of the Junto. For Swift's 'Whig' views we must recall his political axioms: advocacy of the Revolution and support for the Protestant Succession; annual Parliaments in order to ensure the free proceedings of Parliament; the upholding of the law to protect the rights and privileges of the propertied against the abuse of royal prerogative, down to opposition to standing armies in peacetime without the consent of Parliament.

Swift, on his own admission, had not troubled himself 'with the difference between the principles of Whig and Tory' until 1702. He knew that he was 'a lover of liberty'. In *Verses on the Death of Dr. Swift* he was to claim that 'Fair LIBERTY was all his Cry'.[32] Liberty, in his eyes, consisted in the separation of executive and legislature, and this, allied to his firm belief in the Established Church, provides a reasonably clear picture of Swift's political creed. But in 1702 he was a political naif. He recognised only that the Whigs held Revolution Principles, and this was enough, for the Revolution Principle was the foundation of his own beliefs. Only gradually did he realise that his other views were not in accord with those of the Whigs of the reign of Queen Anne.

However, the years from 1701 to 1715 were dominated by the dichotomy between Whig and Tory, and Old Whig or Country principles were virtually forgotten. The conflict between the two parties permeated English society, as party organisation not only at the centre of power but in the constituencies approached, in a number of ways, the sophistication of modern politics. Religion – the issue which most obviously divided Swift and his new Whig friends – was at the heart of the matter. The cry, 'the Church in Danger', was raised long and loud by High Churchmen who saw, or claimed to see, a rising threat from the forces of Dissent. Occasional conformity was used as a symbol for the rallying of the 'true sons of the Church'. Alongside this fundamental difference between Whig and Tory ranged a number of secondary issues. From 1702 to 1713 England was at war as part of the continental alliance against France. The War of the Spanish Succession also concerned the English succession, for a defeat by Louis XIV would almost inevitably have led to an attempt to restore James III, son of the deposed James II, to the Crowns of the three kingdoms. Whigs wholeheartedly supported the war, in all its aspects, and tainted those who were less enthusiastic as supporters of the Pretender. In this way, attitudes towards the war and the Pretender often served to categorise men as either Whig or Tory. Five general elections in the twelve years of Anne's reign kept the political temperature at a constant high level.

When Swift next returned to London, in November 1703, he found 'the highest and warmest reign of party and faction that [he] ever knew or read of, upon the bill against Occasional Conformity.'[33] The first occasional conformity bill had been lost in February 1703 in a dispute between the two Houses of Parliament. A more determined effort to enact this piece of legislation was made at the start of the new Parliamentary session in November 1703. On its own, it was enough to raise the spirit of party. Even 'the dogs in the streets' were 'much more contumelious and quarrelsome than usual; and the very night before the bill went up, a committee of Whig and Tory cats, had a very warm and loud debate upon the roof of our house.'[34]

Swift admitted to being 'much at a loss' about how to regard the occasional conformity bill. Despite his misgivings he was encouraged to write against it, being reassured by Somers, Burnet and Charles Mordaunt, Earl of Peterborough, that it would not harm the Church. 'I know not what to think', he wrote, 'and therefore shall think no more.' This signal illustration of Swift's lack of political nous at this stage reveals his dependence on his new friends. The Whigs were against the occasional conformity bill to a man, and Swift believed himself to be a Whig. He did indeed write against the bill. In the light of his later printed attacks on those who sought to repeal the Test Act this seems scarcely credible. But the pamphlet was 'too late by a day', and, remaining unpublished, has sunk without trace. The bill was headed off in the House of Commons, the government secretly manoeuvring against it. Swift's awareness of the importance of timing in the production of political propaganda was not yet fully developed.

At this time he was putting the finishing touches to *A Tale of a Tub*, at least in the state in which it finally appeared. It was dedicated to Somers as the 'worthiest', and was an attempt to cement his relationship with 'the best friends in nature, [who] only want that little circumstance of favour and power' in order to help his career. 'The Queen and Court, and House óf Lords, and half the Commons almost, are Whigs', Swift confidently claimed, 'and the number daily increases.'[35] Swift's assessment of the political situation was hardly sound. True, a general swing away from the High Church zealots who had begun the reign with such confidence could be discerned, but the Tory party was still far stronger than the Whig, both at Court and in the constituencies. It was against this backcloth that Swift at last released the dangerously brilliant *Tale*. It was meant to make his fortune. It did nothing of the kind.

6

A Tale of a Tub

The web of mystification which Swift spins around *A Tale of a Tub* extends to the circumstances surrounding its publication. The copy was supposedly given to the publisher by a 'Gentleman' who was a 'Friend of the Author,'[1] and yet it is claimed that the appearance of the work in print was without the author's knowledge, 'for he concludes the Copy is lost, having lent it to a Person, since dead, and being never in Possession of it after' (p. 17). Already the curious distancing effect of the *Tale* is at work, confounding fact and fiction, leaving the reader unsure of his ground until, at the end, reality itself is called into question. In this sense, if in no other, the quotation from Irenaeus which appears on the title-page seems apt: 'Basima eacabasa eanaa irraurista, diarba da caeotaba fobor camelanthi.' Couched under these allegedly sublime mysteries, is a meaningless succession of words derived from Hebrew, a jargon repeated by Marcosian heretics in initiation ceremonies, 'in order the more thoroughly to bewilder those who are being initiated.'[2] The reader, like the convert to Gnosticism, is being initiated into the mysterious world of *A Tale of a Tub*, through the rites of mystification.

Of course Swift desired the *Tale's* publication, but the pains he takes to heighten the sense of esotericism and uncertainty are an important clue to interpretation of this most difficult of his works. It is written 'for the Universal Improvement of Mankind', and it proffers help both practical and spiritual to navigate the hidden shoals of life. Above all, it is new. Lucretius, like Irenaeus, cited on the title-page as if to suggest a place as one of the presiding deities of the *Tale*, promises to pursue things unattempted yet in verse as he pretends to reveal the secret of the universe.[3] The putative author of the *Tale* is avowedly following the example of Lucretius. Ostensibly, *A Tale of a Tub* is a work of the occult. It rightfully belongs among cabbalistic, hermetic, Gnostic and Rosicrucian books dealing with magic in one form or another. No wonder that the 'authorities' most cited in the *Tale* are ancient atheists like Epicurus and Lucretius, or alchemists such as Paracelsus Bumbastus or Thomas Vaughan, or creators of 'systems' of the vastness of those propounded by Hobbes and Descartes.

Similar mystery surrounds the composition of *A Tale of a Tub,* and once again this is deliberate on Swift's part. No direct statement relating to the process exists. Swift's silence is profound. In 1708 he wrote 'An Apology for the, &c.' Even in his extant letter to the publisher, Benjamin Tooke, Swift refers consistently to the *Tale* as 'the *&c.*', and this significant contraction was not expanded when the 'Apology' was prefixed to the fifth edition in 1710.[4] In this addition, Swift supplies information. The 'greatest Part' of the *Tale* was 'finished above thirteen Years since, *1696,* which is eight Years before it was published' (p. 1). For once Swift's arithmetic, at least, is correct. The 'Apology' was dated 3 June 1709. And there is consistency within the 'Apology' about the date of composition of the 'greatest Part' of the *Tale.* At another point Swift says that the 'Author' read one of Buckingham's works (which appeared in 1704) 'about ten Years after his Book was writ, and a Year or two after it was published' (p. 7). The relevant dates are 1696 and 1704.

But the 'Apology' states that the 'greatest Part' of the *Tale* was *'finished'* in 1696. The ambiguity is unfortunate. Does this mean that the *Tale* was *begun* that year, and that most of it was finally published in the state in which it was left at the end of 1696? Or does 'finished' in 1696 imply that its conception was much earlier? The point is of real importance to Swift's biography. There is a tradition that the religious allegory of the three brothers and their coats was being written while Swift was at Trinity College in the 1680s. Deane Swift noted that the *'Chamber Fellow'* of young Swift at TCD told a second party 'that he saw *The Tale of a Tub* in the

88

Handwriting of Dr. Swift, when the Doctor was but nineteen Years old.'[5] Again the distancing effect that seems to be one of the *Tale's* main attributes is clearly seen at work. Deane Swift's account is already second-hand before he adds his own pennyworth. Somebody told somebody else who told the author of these memoirs, etc. True, Deane Swift's account is corroborated by John Lyon in his notes to Hawkesworth's *Life* of Swift. Lyon agreed that the *Tale* was begun at TCD, and that several people had seen it in manuscript at the time.[6]

But this indirect evidence would seem to be contradicted by the *Tale* itself, the wit of which, we are told, was 'calculated for this present Month of *August*, 1697' (p. 26). Mystification is very much to the forefront. In the 'Apology', much is made of the fact that the author was not in control of his papers at the time they were published. Had he been 'Master of his Papers for a Year or two before' (p. 2), it is claimed, the finished product would have been rather different. For one thing, the *Mechanical Operation of the Spirit*, a 'fragment' appended, along with *The Battle of the Books*, to the *Tale* proper, would have been omitted. It was 'a most imperfect Sketch with the Addition of a few loose Hints, which he once lent a Gentleman.' No part of the original idea, it was 'wholly out of the Method and Scheme he had intended' (p. 9).

This leads us to consideration of the very question of authorship, for it, too, has continued to be befogged, even to the present day. With his love of mystery, Swift did not acknowledge authorship of the *Tale*. On its publication, several names, including Sir William Temple's, were put forward as possible authors. The book was soon enveloped in an air of scandal, as it was said that it had attacked religion itself, and so those accused of responsibility were quick to repudiate it. An exception was Swift's cousin, Thomas. When a *Complete Key to the Tale of a Tub* appeared in 1710, some account was given of the 'authors'. Thomas Swift was held to be responsible for the tale of the three brothers, plus the 'fragment'. Swift himself was stated to be the author of only the prefatory matter and the digressions, in addition to the *Battle of the Books*.[7]

One of the main reasons for the 'Apology' was the question

of authorship, for Swift, although he cultivated his anonymity, knew 'nothing more contemptible in a Writer than the Character of a Plagiary' (p. 7). As he wrote to Tooke, he suspected that his 'little Parson-cousin' was 'at the bottom' of this additional unwanted mystification over authorship. The circumstance had at least one favourable side-effect. Swift explained that he lent Thomas 'a copy of some part of, &c.', and that after he had left for Ireland in 1704, Thomas had 'affected to talk suspiciously, as if he had some share in it.'[8] Jealous of the monstrous offspring of his fertile imagination, Swift, without acknowledging his own authorship, none the less repudiated his cousin Thomas's in the 'Apology'. He challenged anyone to 'prove his Claim to three Lines in the whole Book' (including, one supposes, the *Mechanical Operation*), upon which the 'Claimant' would 'be acknowledged the undisputed Author' (p. 12).

But of course the 'Apology' itself cannot be used as unimpeachable evidence of either Swift's intention, or the circumstances of the *Tale*'s composition and publication. We merely have to note the curious manner in which the narrative changes from the first person to the third person, and back again. In the undoubted guise of the author of the book himself, Swift observes that because of the great obscurity of the *Tale*, 'I am content to convey some Apology along with it,' by way of explanation (p. 1). Immediately inverting this apparently open manner, he then proceeeds to give a detached, objective account of the work: 'The Author was then young, his Invention at the Height, and his Reading fresh in his Head' (p. 1). The different expository styles continue to interchange and overlap throughout the 'Apology'. The result, once again, is mystification. Is the author of the *Tale* writing the 'Apology', or is someone else? Can we believe what is said in the 'Apology'? The effect is one of distancing Swift from his text, for, of course, he did write the 'Apology', as he wrote the *Tale*, and 'Men of Tast' will realise that 'there generally runs an Irony through the Thread of the whole Book' (p. 4).

All that we can safely conclude is that *A Tale of a Tub* was largely composed from 1696 onwards. There may have been a sketch of the tale of the three brothers dating from an earlier period, but evidence for this is unconvincing and second-hand at best. Swift's reading in 1697 indicates that much of the *Tale,* particularly the Digressions, could not have been written prior to this time. Topical references also indicate that it was in a fluid state until very near the year of its actual publication. The Dedication to Somers, for instance, could hardly have been written before Swift became acquainted with him in the early years of the reign of Queen Anne.[9] It would seem reasonable to assume that Swift was revising the *Tale* during the months he was in England prior to its publication.

Despite the recent arguments of R. M. Adams in favour of *A Tale of a Tub* being a work of collaboration,[10] it must also be concluded that the sole author was Jonathan Swift. True, he may have discussed the content of his book, with his cousin, say, and he himself notes that he left a portion of the copy in Thomas's hands in 1704, but this does not constitute joint-authorship. Swift's monster had only one parent. And we must also reject any notion that Swift was not 'Master of his Papers' prior to their publication. *A Tale of a Tub* is a work belonging to the year 1704, however much it owes to the legacy of the seventeenth century. This leaves the question of censorship by the publisher to consider. Swift notes in the 'Apology' that the 'Gentleman' who conveyed the copy to the press 'expung[ed] certain Passages where now the Chasms appear under the Name of *Desiderata*' (p. 12), and he claims that in the original version there were four, not three, wooden machines. This, too, if Swift is to be believed, is an example of censorship; a most unfortunate one, indeed, for by changing four to three 'some have endeavour'd to squeeze out a dangerous Meaning that was never thought on' (p. 4).

Now it is true that four is a 'much more Cabalistick' number than three – the Gnostic heretics observed the virtues of the monad, the tetrad and the ogdoad, whilst the trinity is a peculiarly Christian symbol – but the question of the censorship of the *Tale* appears to be yet one more example of mystification. It also, of course, allowed Swift to lay the blame for the 'excesses' of the religious allegory on nameless accomplices. After all, part of the reason for the 'Apology' was to vindicate the real author from charges of atheism, which was why he stressed his youth at the time of the *Tale*'s composition. A much more important consideration when approaching the 'Chasms' is that the force of some of Swift's best jokes would be lost if the gaps were removed, as it were. 'THERE is in Mankind a certain * * *', the author remarks in 'A Digression on Madness' when he is about to reveal the mysteries of human nature. No wonder the marginal comment on the hiatus reads '*Hic multa desiderantur*' – 'here many things are wanted' (p. 107)!

The strategy of mystification is experienced by every reader on opening *A Tale of a Tub* for the first time. Nowadays it is customary to follow the text of the fifth edition which includes the 'Apology'. This means in practice that the reader is distanced from the text itself by wad after wad of prefatory matter. We are familiar with the mock owlishness of *The Dunciad Variorum*, in which the *apparatus criticus* far outweighs the pages devoted to the poem itself. Pope's model was the *Tale*, in which, sandwiched between the title-page and section I of the *Tale* proper, we find the 'Apology', the Dedication to Somers, 'The Bookseller to the Reader', 'The Epistle Dedicatory to His Royal Highness Prince Posterity', and finally the Preface. Even having waded through these multifarious excuses for postponing the actual beginning of the book, we discover that section I of the *Tale* is also an introduction. Only at the start of section II do we encounter those magical words, 'ONCE upon a Time' (p. 44). Students, understandably, are sufficiently bewildered by this practice, and it often seems that the *Tale* is in danger of disappearing altogether, pushed back by the pressure of prefaces and introductions so that ultimately there will be no room left to begin the proper subject of the book. Then, as soon as the reader is launched on the surface of the tale of the three brothers and their coats, he is infuriatingly interrupted not once, but five times, by so-called digressions.[11] These seem strange lengths to go to create and preserve an aura of mystification.

Of course on a mature contemplation of the satire of the *Tale*, the place of each preface and each intrusion into the body of the narrative can be recognised. But a first impression is hard to overcome when the book is actually being read. At the outset, the reader of the *Tale,* like any other reader of fiction, is prepared to suspend his disbelief if this is called for. The most disorientating feature of Swift's satire, however, is that we are never really sure whether it *is* calling for such a conventional approach. The shift from first person to third person which characterises the 'Apology' is not a problem in the work to which it is prefixed, to be sure. Two sections have the bookseller as their putative author, but thereafter we are in the undoubted presence of an insistent 'I'. The 'Epistle Dedicatory' to Prince Posterity begins with this statement of personality ('I HERE present *Your Highness* with the Fruits of a very few leisure Hours, stollen from the short Intervals of a World of Business' (p. 18)), and the rest of the *Tale* is narrated in the first person.

But one of the most disconcerting effects of Swift's method is related to the very question of whether or not it is a work of fiction. Like *The Dunciad* it retains an essential quality of 'thinginess'.[12] The bookseller is not marketing a work of art, a creation of the imagination, so much as a manuscript, or a collection of words which, we are assured, has some wonderful mystical attributes connected to it. The *Tale,* above all, is matter. The bookseller supposedly forbore publishing these papers for some time 'because I thought I had better Work upon my Hands' (p. 17). And so we are once more distanced from the narrator of the *Tale.* What we know about him is only to be gleaned from those details he lets drop in the course of his writing. Therefore we are unsure whether or not he is a fictional character in the mould, presumably, of Tristram Shandy. He, too, is writing a book about a book. As Ronald Paulson remarks, 'one of the facts about the *Tale* that contribute[s] to its curiously unique air is that a reader is never wholly convinced of the fiction, nor unconvinced.'[13]

The emergence of the insistent I of the *Tale* from the bookseller's announcements to the reader onwards is accompanied by quite a number of pieces of information about the 'author' of the work. We learn that the *Tale* is written 'during a long Prorogation of Parliament, a great Dearth of Forein News, and a tedious Fit of rainy Weather' (p. 18). Thus the temporal dimension appears to be established. But we cannot be sure whether or not this statement relates to the 'real' world, or to an 'imagined' world such as we find in *Tristram Shandy*. More data is supplied. The 'author' has been asked to provide a tale of a tub to divert the 'Wits of the present Age', who are 'so very numerous and penetrating,' from picking holes 'in the weak sides of Religion and Government' during this period of dullness (p. 24). Like seamen, who throw out an empty tub to occupy a whale so that it will not attack the ship, so the 'author' of the *Tale* is letting go a metaphorical tub of his own. He seems oblivious of the fact that the metaphor he has set working requires his *Tale* to be as empty as its literal counterpart.

This is not the first clue we have been given into the character of the putative author of the *Tale*. His works, for instance, do not survive for very long once they have been published. The governor of Prince Posterity has professed 'a peculiar Malice' (p. 19) for our author's writings. In accordance with his favourable impression of modern wit, the author of the *Tale*, whom Ronald Paulson christens 'the Hack', is 'a most devoted Servant of all *Modern* Forms' (p. 27). He is attempting to emulate his 'more successful Brethren the *Moderns*' (p. 25); indeed, he has just been initiated (like a modern Gnostic) into the 'Illustrious Fraternity' of Grub Street. The Hack proceeds fully to adopt the attitudes of the '*Grub-street* Brotherhood', defending its place in the world of letters against 'two *Junior* start-up Societies,' the Royal Society, and the *literati* who meet at Will's Coffee-house (p. 38).

That the putative author of *A Tale of a Tub* is a hack, there can be no doubt. Further details of his life and character can be discerned. He is zealous and splenetic (p. 19), but despite his 'slender Abilities' (p. 21), he has written 'Four-score and eleven Pamphlets ... under three Reigns, and for the Service of six and thirty Factions' (p. 42). We are told that he is living in a garret, and that the *Tale* is being written in this very location (p. 106). In this way, an apparent spatial dimension is supplied. The Hack, in fact, is in very poor health. He has led 'an unfortunate Life', his head 'broken in a hundred places' for his pains, while his body is racked with the pains of 'Poxes ill cured'. 'Bawds and surgeons' are his 'profess'd Enemies' (p. 42). Paranoia is only one of his symptoms, for as well as being poor and hungry, it transpires that he is out of his wits, perhaps as a result of venereal disease. All in all, as he admits, he is 'a Person, whose Imaginations are hard-mouth'd, and exceedingly disposed to run away with his *Reason*'; it is because of this that his friends will never trust him to be left alone, 'without a solemn Promise, to vent my Speculations in this, or the like manner, for the universal Benefit of Human kind' (p. 114).

Clearly we have enough biographical detail about the putative author of *A Tale of a Tub* to treat him as a fictional character. But the *Tale* isn't a novel, and the so-called Hack is not consistent. He observes that ''Tis a great Ease to my Conscience that I have writ so elaborate and useful a Discourse without one grain of Satyr intermixt' (p. 29), and then proceeds to display that very 'Satyrical Itch' for several pages. 'It becomes hard to resist the conclusion that the narrator is, of set design, an eclectic: too much of a chameleon to focus very narrowly a unidirectional current of satire', writes Pat Rogers. 'It does not do to strive officiously to keep The Hack alive at such moments.'[14]

The Hack, then, is not a fully developed fictional character, but a rhetorical device. Clearly Swift is not addressing the reader 'directly' in the *Tale*. But because of the odd mixture of fiction and reality, it is difficult to decide when, if ever, to take statements at face value. When the narrator argues that without madness, 'all Mankind would unhappily be reduced to the same Belief in Things Invisible',[15] we can be certain that this is not Swift's view. A simple ironic inversion, however, would reveal his true opinion. Unfortunately it is rarely easy as that in *A Tale of a Tub*. If the Hack is not a full-blown *persona*, then he is a mouthpiece for Swift – he *may* at times speak Swift's mind, but we can never be sure. Once again mystification is the principal effect, and the proliferation in the last thirty years of studies of Swift's *personae* or masks, particularly in the *Tale*, has been truly staggering.[16] Recently critics such as John Traugott have attempted to sidestep the question. 'We *know* perfectly well that we are in the presence of Swift,' he writes, 'not of some novelistic fiction.'[17] We know perfectly well that Swift is the real author of the *Tale*, but we do not know with any certainty how to

95

interpret the conclusion the narrator has manipulated us into accepting as unavoidable: 'This is the sublime and refined Point of Felicity, called, *the Possession of being well deceived*; The Serene Peaceful State of being a Fool among Knaves' (p. 110). Some critics believe that here Swift emerges from the mask that he tends to hide behind in this work. If so, he is a very strange Christian indeed, and deserves to be taken at face value even when discussing 'the Qualities of *Acamoth*' (p. 119).

The *Tale* is a disturbing and fascinating book for the very reason that the reader is unsure of his ground. Swift parades outrageous theories upon the virtues of numbers or the use and improvement of madness in a commonwealth and invites us to decide whether, in this topsy-turvy world, they don't deserve to be treated seriously. Of course it is a satire, as the 'Apology' emphasises, in which much use is made of parody, of styles and ideas. Swift *impersonates* various characters, moulding aspects of each into the composite narrator, which is what gives the Hack his eclecticism. It may be true, as John Traugott observes, that Swift 'conjures up his repertoire of voices' with 'demonic joy', and that he 'speaks his deepest thoughts in their tongues,'[18] but these are not his heart-felt opinions. They are his nightmares. Like a Boschian landscape, the bedlam of *A Tale of a Tub* is a Swiftian terror. In that Swift formulated these visions of hell, they must perforce express his 'deepest' and darkest thoughts. The *Tale* plumbs the depths of the heart of darkness. But above all it invites, cajoles, nay, forces readers to think. And Swift's polemical strategy manipulates the reader through his diabolical devices to tread the paths of orthodoxy.

In the 'Apology', Swift defended the *Tale* against the charge of irreligion. It was not a satire upon religion itself, he observed with justice, but upon its abuses and corruptions. Surely he could ridicule those. The *Tale*, moreover, 'Celebrates the Church of *England* as the most perfect of all others' (p. 2). Of course it was subject to the same imperfections as all human institutions, but the satire was levelled at Papists and Dissenters. Swift was adamant: the author 'will forfeit his Life, if any one Opinion can be *fairly* deduced from that Book, which is contrary to Religion or Morality' (p. 2). But *A Tale of*

a Tub is not merely a satire on abuses in religion. It also
attacks corruptions in learning. In Swift's original scheme, if
the 'Apology' is to be believed, the religious theme was to be
handled in the allegory of the brothers and their coats, 'which
was to make up the Body of the Discourse', whilst the abuses
in learning were to be treated 'by way of Digressions' (p. 1).
Of course the structure of the *Tale* is far from symmetrical,
with additional matter both prefaced and appended to the
book proper, and at the climax, in the 'Digression concerning
Madness', the abuses in religion and learning merge as they
are shown to be two sides of the same coin.

The allegory of the brothers and their coats can only be
rehearsed very briefly here.[19] Their father dies, leaving them
with coats which they have to keep in pristine condition. For
this purpose he supplies 'full Instructions' in his will, 'upon
which your future Fortunes will entirely depend.' These coats
are the fabric of Christianity which Christ, the father of the
religion, left to the primitive Christians. Their treatment of
their coats is what will determine whether they are saved or
damned, so for the sake of their 'future Fortunes' they are
admonished to 'wear them clean, and brush them often' (p.
44). Each century is represented by a year in the lives of the
brothers, and so for the 'first seven years' the brothers fight
the enemies of Christianity and heretics ('Gyants' and
'Dragons'), before succumbing to the secular pressures exerted
upon religion ('they came up to Town'). As a result of these
pressures, the outward appearance of religion becomes more
important than inward purity. Men worship tailor-gods,
parodying the mass and the sacraments (pp. 44-7), until
ultimately the mere observance of custom replaces spirituality (*That Fellow ... has no Soul; where is his Shoulder-Knot.?"* (p.
49)).

Thus worldly circumstances bring about an alteration in
the fabric of Christianity. To follow the fashion, the brothers
need to wear shoulder-knots on their coats, that is, they need
to embellish the authority of the gospels in deciding their
religious practices. They search their father's will in vain for
guidance about shoulder-knots. Peter interprets the will,
subjecting it to a variety of distortions in meaning to justify
the brothers' following the changing fashions, until it is

finally decided that the literal sense of the text is to be ignored in favour of 'a *Mythological*, and *Allegorical* Sense' (p. 53). The *Tale* proceeds to chronicle the decline of primitive Christianity in the Dark Ages, as Peter leads the way in the acceptance of tradition as an authority alongside the gospels themselves.

The doctrine of transubstantiation is ridiculed at some length in section IV of the *Tale*. One of the best comic scenes, which, as Frederik N. Smith points out, is also dealing with 'the source of linguistic authority,'[20] is when Peter, who has assumed authority over his brothers, offers them a crust of brown bread for their victuals, assuring them at the same time that it is really *'excellent good Mutton'*, and, moreover, *'true natural Juice from the Grape'* (pp. 72-4). Swift mercilessly plays on the Roman Catholic insistence that the actual flesh and blood of Christ are contained in the consecrated bread alone when used in holy communion – the brothers question Peter's authority:

> *By G—, My Lord*, said [one], *I can only say, that to my Eyes, and Fingers, and Teeth, and Nose, it seems to be nothing but a Crust of Bread.* Upon which, the second put in his Word: *I never saw a Piece of Mutton in my Life, so nearly resembling a Slice from a Twelve-peny Loaf. Look ye, Gentlemen,* cries *Peter* in a Rage, *to convince you, what a couple of blind, positive, ignorant, wilful Puppies you are, I will use but this plain Argument; By G—, it is true, good, natural Mutton as any in* Leaden-Hall *Market; and G— confound you both eternally, if you offer to believe otherwise.* Such a thundring Proof as this, left no farther Room for Objection ... (p. 73)

Swift's comic literalisation of a metaphorically based statement ('*G— confound you both eternally*') anticipates the joking Jove of *The Day of Judgement* who, setting his wit to the sectaries, 'damn[s] such Fools.'[21] It is a typical Swiftian rhetorical ploy. The 'authority' assumed by the Pope, based not on biblical justification, but simple decree, is exposed to ridicule, and this gives a flavour of Swift's satire on the abuses perpetrated by the Roman Catholic Church between 700 and 1400.

Corruptions such as these bring on the Reformation. Transubstantiation is called 'a principal Occasion' of 'that great and famous *Rupture*' which happened between the brothers, 'and was never afterward made up' (p. 74). Peter 'grew so scandalous', that his brothers finally resorted to their father's will – the gospels – determined to submit to his authority no longer. He refused them a copy, but they 'made a shift' to consult the original will. This showed them how seriously they had been misled by Peter. Of course this represented allegorically the translation of the scriptures out of the classical and into the vulgar languages, which demonstrated that there was no biblical authority for many of the Church's practices, such as not administering the cup to the laity in communion, or the celibacy of priests, or auricular confession, or the absolution of sins.

When Peter discovered the brothers in the throes of their reformation (they had broken open the cellar-door and taken wine, and had sent for their wives after discarding their concubines), he kicked them 'out of Doors' (p. 76). At this time the two other brothers also 'began to be distinguished ... by certain Names' – Martin and Jack (p. 84). Turning to their coats – the fabric of Christianity – which were disfigured by the various trimmings stitched on to the original cloth as fashion dictated, the brothers consulted their father's will. Martin (Luther) was first to pull off 'a large Handful of *Points*' (p. 85). Proceeding carefully, and diligently picking at the threads, Martin decided to leave alone embroidery which could not be removed without damaging the cloth. In this way Swift 'celebrates' the Church of England as the 'most perfect of all others' – in other words, the least corrupt. For Jack's method of dealing with his coat was altogether different. In a frenzy, he tore at the trimmings, 'honoring it with the Title of *Zeal*' (p. 86), and was not satisfied until he had pulled off a 'whole Piece, Cloth and all, and flung it into the Kennel' (pp. 86-7). Ignoring Martin's warnings '*not to damage his Coat by any Means*', Jack (Calvin) ends up with his 'either wholly rent to his Shirt; or those Places which had scaped his cruel Clutches ... still in *Peter's* Livery' (p. 88).[22]

This is the beginning of Swift's satire on the Dissenters, for Jack is the central character of the rest of the *Tale*, and after the famous, climactic sections surrounding the 'Digression concerning Madness', the Hack returns to the narration of Jack's escapades. The allegory, like the rest of the fable, is not hard to interpret. According to Swift, the Dissenters, in their zeal to dissociate themselves from the corruption of the Church of Rome, have actually torn the fabric of Christianity, failing to observe practices for which scriptural authority exists. Martin's coat ends up 'so well reduced into the State of Innocence', whilst Jack's own is in rags, that Jack runs 'mad with Spleen, and Spight,.and Contradiction' (p. 88). Further, in that both Peter and Jack refused to behave in strict accordance with their father's will, they were continually being taken for each other. 'Their Humours and Dispositions were not only the same, but there was a close Analogy in their Shape, their Size and their Mien', so that Jack bore 'a huge Personal Resemblance with his Brother *Peter*.' And this despite 'that Aversion, or Antipathy, which *Jack* and his Brother *Peter* seemed, even to an Affectation, to bear toward each other', 'the singular Effects' of which the Hack relates in Section XI of the *Tale* (p. 127).

In this way Swift contrives to show the zeal and enthusiasm of the sectaries in an unfavourable light, and he does not bother to distinguish between the various groups of Protestant nonconformists. Jack has many sobriquets. 'Sometimes they would call Him, *Jack the Bald*; sometimes, *Jack with a Lanthorn*; sometimes, *Dutch Jack*; sometimes, *French Hugh*; sometimes, *Tom the Beggar*; and sometimes, *Knocking Jack of the North*' (pp. 88-9). Thus, he is not only Calvin, but the personification of numerous sects. Their hatred of the Established Church stems from their rage at the Reformation. Jack is unhinged – 'in a few Days it was for certain reported, that he had run out of his Wits' – and it is in this state that he gives rise to 'the most Illustrious and Epidemick Sect of *AEolists*, who … do still acknowledge the Renowned *JACK* for their Author and Founder' (p. 89). In a cutting note, Swift describes the Aeolists as '*All Pretenders to Inspiration whatsoever*'.

Swift was suspicious of inspiration. 'It may be thought perhaps a strange thing, that God should require us to believe Mysteries, while the Reason or Manner of what we are to believe is above our Comprehension, and wholly concealed from us', he wrote. 'But this is a great and dangerous Mistake.'[23] A 'mighty Weight' was laid upon faith, and the mere revelation of spiritual mysteries through the scriptures was sufficient for their acceptance. 'This faith', he observed about belief in the Trinity, 'we may acquire without giving up our Senses, or contradicting our Reason.'[24] But this was not the view of the Aeolists, who believed that they were individually in touch with God, and that they were of the elect. Through inspiration, they could comprehend the incomprehensible. And so, adopting a reductive approach in Section VIII of the *Tale*, Swift attacked inspiration as nothing but wind. Wind was the basis of life, the Hack claimed ingenuously; further, among the Aeolists 'all Learning was esteemed ... to be compounded from the same Principle' (pp. 95-7).

Through synecdoche, the Aeolists link errors in religion and learning; they link Irenaeus and Lucretius, cited on the title-page; they link those who spin fictions in religion, elaborating systems out of their own minds to mystify their votaries, and those who spin fictions in learning to explain the universe to their own satisfaction. Phillip Harth has suggested a second syllogism to complement Swift's Hack's syllogism about words and wind. This too links the Aeolists – those who profit by mystification in religion – and the occultists who peddle mystification in learning.

> All occultists are Aeolists.
> The Puritans are Aeolists.
> Therefore, the Puritans are occultists.[25]

It is crucial to an understanding of *A Tale of a Tub* to recognise the reasons that the section on the Aeolists immediately precedes the famous 'Digression concerning Madness'. Life is herein reduced to wind; to matter. Hence madness is also a material condition, reduced to the vapours, which is simply another name for wind. The Aeolists worship mad Jack, the founder of Aeolism. Madness equals happiness – 'a perpetual *Possession* of being well deceived'. This madness possesses the Gnostic heretics against whom Irenaeus wrote; it possesses Lucretius and the Epicureans; it possesses Paracelsus and the

ists; it possesses Hobbes and Descartes, the creators of
s.

instead of trying to establish universal Christianity, so that
mankind would indeed be 'happily reduced to the *same* Belief
in Things Invisible', they perpetrate error. This leads to
mystification in the minds of men, and to uncertainty about
what to believe. 'I believe', Swift wrote, 'that thousands of
men would be orthodox enough in certain points, if divines
had not been too curious, or too narrow, in reducing
orthodoxy within the compass of subtleties, niceties, and
distinctions, with little warrant from Scripture, and less from
reason or good policy'.[26] But this is precisely what the
Aeolists were working against. Instead of orthodoxy, they
promoted error. It is wrong, and dangerous, in Swift's view, to
propound systems. This is the abuse of learning and religion;
the abuse of reason. 'I am not answerable to God for the
doubts that arise in my own breast, since they are the
consequences of that reason which he hath planted in me,' he
pointed out, adding the important rider, 'if I take care to
conceal those doubts from others, if I use my best endeavours
to subdue them, and if they have no influence on the conduct
of my life.'[27] Patently the Aeolists acted otherwise. In *A Tale of
a Tub*, Swift satirised all those who, in Rochester's terms,
wished to 'pierce/The limits of the boundless universe'.[28] And
he censured those who claimed to have succeeded. It is an
attack on error.

Ultimately Swift's satire on Gnosticism, alchemy and
Epicureanism is linked. Just as Book IV of *Gulliver's Travels*
attacks the two broad errors which might be classified as
Epicurean and Stoic – the one indulging the flesh to the
exclusion of all spirituality; the other repressing totally all
carnal impulses and emotions – through the Yahoos and
Houyhnhnms respectively, so the *Tale* concentrates on those
who seek to mislead. Both the Gnostics and the alchemists
employed the terms of the New Testament to formulate their
allegories and enigmas. Both used the symbolic number
four – the Gnostic tetrad, the hermetic four elements. Further,
there is a direct connection with Lucretius. As Miriam
Starkman observes, 'all occultism may be traced to an
ultimate quest for the original of all things; a quest of which

the ultimate aim was the achievement of universal systems'.[29] But this applies not only to Swift's attack on abuses in learning; it is the essence of his attack on abuses in religion. Irenaeus, cited on the title-page, is used to categorise the *Tale*. Irenaeus, a primitive father, was trying, in his work *Against Heresies,* to counter movements away from the primitive spirit of Christianity – movements which eventually resulted in the abuses of religion perpetrated by both Peter and Jack. This is why they are often mistaken for each other. They both propagate error, the error that the Hack champions, and the supposed reason for writing *A Tale of a Tub*:

> For, *Night* being the universal Mother of Things, wise Philosophers hold all Writings to be *fruitful* in the Proportion they are *dark*; And therefore, the *true illuminated* (that is to say, the *Darkest* of all) have met with such numberless Commentators, whose *Scholiastick* Midwifry hath deliver'd them of Meanings, that the Authors themselves, perhaps, never conceived, and yet may very justly be allowed the Lawful Parents of them: The Words of such Writers being like Seed, which, however scattered at random, when they light upon a fruitful Ground, will multiply far beyond either the Hopes or Imagination of the Sower.
>
> AND therefore in order to promote so useful a Work, I will here take Leave to glance a few *Innuendo's* that may be of great Assistance to those sublime Spirits, who shall be appointed to labor in a universal Comment upon this wonderful Discourse. And First, I have couched a very profound Mystery in the Number of O's multiply'd by *Seven*, and divided by *Nine* ... (pp. 118-19)

Several things should be said about this passage, for it is the true climax of the satire of *A Tale of a Tub*. Note the linguistic complexity, as Swift changes the accepted meaning of words through double meanings, metaphor and oxymoron.[30] Here it is darkness and not light which brings forth fruit, so that the '*true illuminated*' are the '*Darkest* of all'. This is mystification in action. Scholastic midwives confuse the issue further by delivering monsters of their own begetting and fathering them on authors who are not responsible for them. This is the

103

abuse of scholarship, and, in glancing at 'those sublime Spirits' whom he expects to be 'appointed to labor in a universal Comment upon this wonderful Discourse', Swift draws an implicit comparison with the true scholars who worked on the Authorized Version. His note on this passage refers instead to 'what the *Cabbalists* among the *Jews* have done with the *Bible*', and the 'wonderful Mysteries' the cabbalistic method is alleged to have uncovered. Finally the seed metaphor indicates Swift's fears about the abuses of religion and learning: words 'being like Seed ... when they light upon a fruitful Ground, will multiply far beyond either the Hopes or Imagination of the Sower.' In this perverse parable of the sower, the *Tale,* and all works of the occult, are shown to operate on mankind to the detriment of true religion and genuine learning, because the ground is so abundantly fruitful. Conversely, Swift's desire is that mankind will be 'happily reduced to the *same* Belief in Things Invisible.' But even language itself is against him, as linguistic authority is as liable to be subverted as the three brothers' father's will.

A Tale of a Tub is an allegorical account of the degeneration of Christianity from the pristine condition of the primitive Church. At the same time it comments on the decline of learning from the classical standards of the 'ancients' to the ephemerality of 'modern' authors. Criticism is no longer an art form following 'Those RULES of old *discover'd*, not *devis'd*',[31] 'by observing which, a careful Reader might be able to pronounce upon the productions of the *Learned,* form his Taste to a true Relish of the *Sublime* and the *Admirable,* and divide every Beauty of Matter or of Style from the Corruption that Apes it.' Instead the 'modern' or *'True Critick'* is *'a Discoverer and Collector of Writers Faults'* (pp. 56-8). Similarly, 'modern' scholars like the Hack, who professes to be 'so entirely satisfied with the whole present Procedure of human Things, that I have been for some Years preparing Materials towards *A Panegyrick upon the World'* (p. 32), are concerned with providing 'a just Defence of the *Moderns* Learning and Wit, against the Presumption, the Pride, and the Ignorance of the *Antients'* (p. 42).

In alluding to the controversy between the 'ancients' and the 'moderns', Swift is referring not merely to questions of literature, but to a wide-ranging debate which had been going on in Europe throughout the seventeenth century concerning the relative achievements in learning of the Greeks and Romans and of present-day civilisation. It was an issue which greatly interested Sir William Temple, whose *Essay upon the Ancient and Modern Learning,* written in 1690, embroiled him in a public conflict with, first, the brilliant young academic, William Wotton, and, subsequently, with the distinguished scholar and critic, Richard Bentley. 'Have the Studies, the Writings, the Productions of *Gresham* College, or the late Academies of *Paris*', he asked, 'outshined or eclipsed the Lycaeum of *Plato*, the Academy of *Aristotle,* the Stoa of *Zeno,* the Garden of *Epicurus?*'[32] No, he answered, most emphatically.

Temple's involvement in controversy with Wotton and Bentley partly informed the satire of *A Tale of a Tub.* But it also caused Swift to write, in 1697, the greatest prose mock-heroic in English, *A Full and True Account of the Battel Fought last Friday, Between the Antient and the Modern Books in St. James's Library,* commonly called *The Battle of the Books,* which was appended to *A Tale of a Tub* on its publication in 1704. A brief outline of the events leading to its composition is necessary. In 1694 Wotton published *Reflections upon Ancient and Modern Learning,* which 'proclaim[ed] open war against Sir *William Temple* for having written an *Essay* in Honour of the Ancients'.[33] Then, in January 1695, an edition of the *Epistles of Phalaris* appeared from the pen of Charles Boyle. Now Temple had praised these letters extravagantly, with Aesop and Phalaris heading a long list of ancient prose writers whose efforts far surpassed the best the moderns could offer. In the course of working on his edition, Boyle had differed with the librarian of the Royal Library at St James's Palace (where the battle of the books was located by Swift) over a manuscript he had wished to consult. In the Preface to his edition he ironically thanked the librarian, Richard Bentley, for his 'humanity'. When the second edition of Wotton's *Reflections* came out in 1697, Bentley added an appendix in which he proved the *Epistles* to be spurious, and Boyle's edition to be riddled with errors. The following year a work of collaboration, but published under Boyle's name, and purporting to be an *Examination* of the import of Wotton's and Bentley's scholarship, was issued as a rejoinder. It was 'as witty as it was faulty, and as malicious as it was untruthful.'[34]

It was in response to the second edition of Wotton's *Reflections*, it appears, that Swift penned the *Battle of the Books*.[35] Although they had been subjected to a modicum of criticism in the *Tale* itself, Wotton and Bentley were attacked more pointedly in the *Battle,* especially for their views on Aesop and Phalaris. The finale describes, with superb mock-epic similes, a skirmish between these particular ancients and moderns:

> As when two *Mungrel-Curs*, whom *native Greediness,* and *domestick Want*, provoke, and join in Partnership, though fearful, nightly to invade the Folds of some rich Grazier; They, with Tails depress'd, and lolling Tongues, creep soft and slow; mean while, the conscious *Moon*, now in her *Zenith*, on their guilty Heads, darts perpendicular Rays; Nor dare they bark, though much provok'd at her refulgent Visage, whether seen in Puddle by Reflexion, or in Sphear direct; but one surveys the Region round, while t'other scouts the Plain, if haply, to discover at distance from the Flock, some *Carcass* half devoured, the Refuse of gorged Wolves, or ominous Ravens. So march'd this lovely, loving Pair of Friends, nor with less Fear and Circumspection; when, at distance, they might perceive two shining Suits of Armor, hanging upon an Oak, and the Owners not far off in a profound Sleep. The two Friends drew lots, and the pursuing of this Adventure, fell to *Bentley* ... (pp. 161-2)

The armour, obviously enough, belongs to Aesop and Phalaris. Aesop has already figured in the fable, having been 'of late most barbarously treated by a strange Effect of the *Regent's Humanity*' – a clear echo of Boyle's ironic phrase in the Preface to his edition of Phalaris – 'who had tore off his Title-page, sorely defaced one half of his leaves, and chained him fast among a Shelf of *Moderns*' (p. 150). Now, Bentley is pictured seizing on the armour of both writers, as they sleep.

Finally Wotton and Bentley come upon Temple and Boyle at the 'Fountain Head' of the 'limpid Stream' Helicon, the home of the Muses. Wotton's lance, flung at Temple as he is drinking 'large Draughts in his Helmet, from the Fountain', 'reach'd even to the Belt of the averted *Antient,* upon which, lightly grazing, it fell to the Ground'. '*Temple* neither felt the Weapon touch him', the narrator stresses, 'nor heard it fall.' But Boyle is shown what has happened by Apollo.

> As a young Lion, in the *Libyan Plains*, or *Araby Desart,* sent by his aged Sire to hunt for Prey, or Health, or Exercise; He scours along, wishing to meet some Tiger from the Mountains, or a furious Boar; If Chance, a *Wild Ass*, with Brayings importune, affronts his Ear, the generous Beast, though loathing to distain his Claws with **Blood** so vile, yet much provok'd at the offensive Noise; which *Echo*, foolish Nymph, like her *ill-judging Sex,* repeats much louder, and with more Delight than *Philomela*'s Song: He vindicates the Honor of the Forest, and hunts the noisy, long-ear'd Animal. So *Wotton* fled, so *Boyle* pursued. (pp. 163-4)

When he discovers, further, that Bentley has stolen 'the Helmet and Shield of *Phalaris*, his Friend, both which he had lately with his own Hands, new polish'd and gilded', Boyle diverts his attention from Wotton. The friends make a stand, and Bentley throws a spear at Boyle 'with all his Force'. Taking it on his shield, Boyle transfixes both Bentley and Wotton with 'a Launce of wondrous Length and sharpness', as 'a skilful Cook' trusses 'a Brace of *Woodcocks*' (p. 164).

This, then, is Swift's representation, in mock-heroic terms, of the scholarly dispute between Temple and Boyle, Wotton and Bentley, from which *The Battle of the Books* takes its occasion. But to regard Swift's work as merely another document in the history of the *querelle* between the ancients and the moderns is to do scant justice to one of his most satisfying productions. True, there is none of the obscurity or complexity of the *Tale* itself, or of the fourth book of *Gulliver's Travels,* but the *Battle* is a piece of comic bravura displaying Swift's talents at their peak. Wisely, he leaves the actual battle undecided, moderating between those who refuse to recognise the achievements of the modern scientists, and those who fail to acknowledge their debt to their classical predecessors. This issue is brilliantly imaged in the dialogue between the spider and the bee. The spider is 'furnisht with a Native Stock within [it]self', the materials of his web 'extracted altogether out of [his] own Person' (p. 149), just like those who spin webs of mystification out of their own minds, blind to the fact that they, too, need the 'light' of revelation to discern the mysteries of religion and nature. As a result the spider, 'by a lazy Contemplation of four Inches round; by an overweening Pride, which feeding and engendering on it self, turns all into Excrement and Venom; producing nothing at last, but Fly-bane and a Cobweb' (p. 150). The bee, on the other hand, is like the ancient poets, who 'pretend to Nothing of our own, beyond our *Wings* and our *Voice*: that is to say, our *Flights* and our *Language*; For the rest, whatever we have got, has been by infinite Labor, and search, and ranging thro' every Corner of Nature'. The result is '*Sweetness* and *Light*', as, once again, the abuses in religion ad learning are linked (p. 151).

The confusion between matter and spirit, outer and inner, is also the subject of *The Mechanical Operation of the Spirit*, but this is an unsatisfactory exercise, well fulfilling Swift's own description of it (in the 'Apology') as 'a most imperfect Sketch' (p. 9). In fact even the suggestion that it is the work of a different hand (p. 169) appears plausible, and the 'Fragment' need not detain us long. At times it seems almost to be a loose plan or sketch of the *Tale*'s satire on the Aeolists. The same analogy between spiritual ecstasy and sexual orgasm is made, but the rather crude wordplay of the 'Fragments' retains little of the subtlety of Section VIII of the *Tale*, with its accompanying latinate puns. The mechanical, as opposed to the natural, operation of the spirit, 'is wholly an Effect of Art', proceeding, like the Aeolist's inspiration or the spider's web, 'entirely from within' (pp. 175, 177). In 'working up the *Spirit*', canting preachers, possessed with 'a Competent Share of *Inward Light*' (like the '*true Illuminated*') get carried away to the point at which a tussle between the spirit and the flesh takes place:

> However it came about, the *Saint* felt his *Vessel* full *extended* in every Part (a very natural Effect of strong *Inspiration*;) and the Place and Time falling out so unluckily, that he could not have the Convenience of Evacuating upwards, by Repetition, Prayer, or Lecture; he was forced to open an inferior Vent. In short, he wrestled with the Flesh so long, that he at length subdued it, coming off with honourable Wounds, all *before*. (p. 184)

The puns are obvious ones, the sexual innuendo unmistakable, and, of course, the preacher succumbs to venereal disease – hardly an unanticipated punch-line. Swift attacks hypocrisy many times in his writings, but rarely so predictably. Instead of using sexuality as a means to strip man of his pretensions, reminding him of his mortality, the 'Fragment' is content simply to draw heavy-handed parallels between the workings of the flesh and the alleged operation of the spirit in the various fanatical sects, the history of which forms the conclusion of the piece.

It was not the first time that Swift had made this point. In his satire on the Aeolists he comments on the application of wind 'in *certain Mysteries* not to be named, giving Occasion for those happy Epithets of *Turgidus*, and *Inflatus*, apply'd either to the *Emittent,* or *Recipient* Organs' (p. 95). Or again, he compares inspiration 'to certain subterraneous *Effluviums* of *Wind*' delivered by the Aeolist priest, noting that

> these were frequently managed and directed by *Female* Officers, whose Organs were understood to be better disposed for the Admission of those Oracular *Gusts,* as entring and passing up thro' a Receptacle of greater Capacity, and causing also a Pruriency by the Way, such as with due Management, hath been refined from a Carnal, into a Spiritual Extasie. (p. 99)

But what the *Mechanical Operation of the Spirit* fails to exploit is the potential *humour* of the situation. For we must never forget that, above all, *A Tale of a Tub* is very funny. It may, in essence, be an anatomy of the seventeenth century and its concerns – its hopes, its fears, its strengths and its weaknesses –

as Swift saw them. Like all great satire, it is a very serious work. But great satire also works through humour, otherwise it becomes simply denunciation. And denunciation is not satire.

A Tale of a Tub is a difficult work, and much of its humour is of a peculiarly cerebral kind, calling for at least a competent knowledge of the classics, albeit in translation. And if one has read Irenaeus and the odd hermetic tome, so much the better. It often works through wordplay of an extraordinarily inventive kind, as if to point up the quixotic nature of language itself, and its capacity to confuse rather than clarify. Swift's intention was to satirise the abuses of religion and learning, and many of his themes are timeless and universal. But elements of the *Tale* are of a topical nature, and too often this is allowed to obscure the reason that it is one of the greatest – if not the greatest – satire in English. *A Tale of a Tub* shows Swift's hilarious comic genius at a pitch he would never again attain, 'his Invention at the Height, and his Reading fresh in his Head' (p. 1), displaying perfectly the effectiveness of satire when it is handled correctly, by a man who knew what a dangerous weapon laughter is, and how to employ it 'to laugh the Follies of Mankind out of Countenance.'[36]

Satire's superiority to the dry denunciation of error might best be illustrated by a final example from the *Tale*. One passage is glossed thus in footnote: 'The Villanies and Cruelties committed by Enthusiasts and Phanaticks among us, were all performed under the Disguise of Religion and long Prayers.' It is a perfectly reasonable representation of the excesses of the Protestant Dissenters. But it bears little similarity to the fun of the passage to which it refers, in which Swift manages to inject such life into the bare bones of the subject of religious bigotry in his portrayal of the Aeolists and their founder, mad Jack.

> WHEN he had some Roguish Trick to play, he would down with his Knees, up with his Eyes, and fall to Prayers, tho' in the midst of the Kennel. Then it was that those who understood his Pranks, would be sure to get far enough out of his Way; And whenever Curiosity attracted Strangers to

Laugh, or to Listen; he would of a sudden, with one Hand out with his *Gear*, and piss full in their Eyes, and with the other, all to-bespatter them with Mud. (pp. 124-5)

At bottom, the *Tale* may be a savage exposure of nonconformist cant. But it is also refreshingly unsanctimonius. We've all been pissed on by Aeolists; it takes Swift to point it out and remind us of the fact. At times such as these we realise, as if for the first time, the glorious potential of satire.

7

Vicar of Laracor

Swift remained in Ireland from 1704 until the end of 1707. It was the longest period he had stayed in his native land as an adult. There were several reasons for his restless feet to restrict their movements for a time to one side of the Irish Sea. His finances were far from healthy, and for three years we can see his best energies being spent on Church affairs. But a further consideration may have been much more personal. It is perhaps significant that when Swift next set sail for England, he was followed by Hester Johnson and Rebecca Dingley. Early in that year, 1707, Thomas Swift, the 'little Parson-cousin', was enquiring 'whether JONATHAN be married? or whether he has been able to resist the charms of both those gentlewomen that marched quite from *Moore-Park* to *Dublin* (as they would have marched to the *north* or any where else) with full resolution to engage him?'[1]

Marriage had been in the forefront of relations between Swift and Mrs Johnson on Swift's return to Ireland in 1704. While he had been in London, the Rev. William Tisdall, a Fellow of Trinity College, had virtually assumed Swift's role as the ladies' intellectual mentor. He visited them in a new house in William Street on the outskirts of Dublin, and was soon 'mighty proud' of his place in Hester's 'good graces'. One thing led to another. He made a proposal of marriage and asked Swift to 'make overtures' on his behalf to Hester's mother at Moor Park. Swift questioned the propriety of such a manner of proceeding 'without the daughter's giving me leave, under her own or her friend's hand.' Yet he acquainted the mother with the proposal and, as he told Tisdall rather ambiguously, 'spoke with all the advantages you deserve.'[2]

However, Swift's behaviour does not quite rise above suspicion. Tisdall's small fortune was cited as sufficient reason for Swift to question the prudence of the match. Once again he had his own parents' unfortunate marriage as a model, but when he resorted to justifying his own conduct in relation to Mrs Johnson, we may feel that he protests too much:

> I will upon my conscience and honour tell you the naked truth [he wrote]. First, I think I have said to you before, that if my fortunes and humour served me to think of that state [matrimony], I should certainly, among all persons on earth, make your choice; because I never saw that person whose conversation I entirely valued but hers; this was the utmost I ever gave way to. And, secondly, I must assure you sincerely, that this regard of mine never once entered into my head to be an impediment to you; but I judged it would, perhaps, be a clog to your rising in the world; and I did not conceive you were ... rich enough to make yourself and her happy and easy.[3]

Swift's urgent desire to appear disinterested and totally free from any selfish motive is intriguing. True, it was a lofty pose he loved to adopt, however much it was his incapacity to remain aloof which provided the stimulus for his satire. Despite his protests, his ingenuousness in this affair is open to doubt.

Swift's reaction to Tisdall's courtship of Hester Johnson offers evidence of his own feelings towards his dear friend. He admitted that he valued her conversation above all others, and that 'this was the utmost [he] ever *gave way to*.' Surely this is a clear indication that, however much he resisted, he was attracted by more than Stella's mind. Details are entirely lacking, but Hester Johnson did not marry Tisdall. On 20 April 1704 Swift wished the happy couple 'joy of [their] good fortunes', and bemoaned his own rambling nature. He felt that things had gone too far for the engagement to 'be decently broken.'[4] Yet after he landed at Dublin on 1 June there is no further mention of the matter. We must suppose that Tisdall was refused, and that Hester was content to await developments with her friend Mrs Dingley and her closest counsellor, Swift himself. It is impossible to say whether she

113

had designs on marriage with Swift. For his part, Swift succeeded in not giving way to any marital inclinations he might have had. Neither his 'fortune' nor his 'humour' encouraged him to succumb to such desires.

On disembarking, Swift went straight to Laracor, almost certainly on account of the state of affairs in William Street. He was still in residence at Trim at the end of the year. He spent his time recouping his resources, both mental and physical. As Louis A. Landa remarks of Laracor, 'Primarily it was a place of retirement where he could find relief from the vexed problems he faced elsewhere.'[5] He did not serve the cure himself, but paid his curate, a Mr Smith, a generous salary to do so.[6] Swift preached the occasional sermon at Laracor, and that was all. With no manse there, he was forced to take lodgings in nearby Trim. 'The undeveloped state of Laracor gave Swift his opportunity,' writes Landa. 'It was an outlet for his passion for improvement; indeed his attitude towards his little acre of ground was more that of the gentleman bent on improving his estate than that of a priest concerned with the cure of souls.'[7]

Already, by 1704, Swift had spent over £200 on his glebeland. He had put down a walk, and had supervised the digging of trenches and a ditch on his property. With his eyes on more long-term developments, he had also arranged to have willows planted. Subsequently he was to purchase additional glebe for the living, and his improving zeal culminated in the building of, if not a manse, then at least a 'neat cabin' on the site (as a visitation report of 1723 called it)[8] – all that at his own expense. Here at Laracor Swift licked his wounds. He had suffered sadly in the course of the previous six months. His visit to England had brought no tangible reward, merely 'the good words and wishes of a decayed ministry, whose lives and mine will probably wear out before they can serve either my little hopes, or their own ambition'.[9] In fact his hanging on in England in the prospect that something might turn up had severely depleted his resources. 'If I love Ireland better than I did, it is because we are nearer related, for I am deeply allyed to its Poverty,' he wrote in 1706. 'My little Revenue is sunk two Parts in three, and the third in Arrear.'[10]

At this juncture, Swift's 'little Revenue' amounted to around £200 per annum – Laracor and Rathbeggan brought in just over £180, and the Prebend of Dunlavin an additional £15 or £20. But his outgoings were more than this. He paid his curate £57 plus supplementary fees. His servant, John Kemp, received £4 a year but, in addition, Swift had to provide him with clothes and board. Travelling cost money, and hiring or buying horses (he bought two in 1703) involved the considerable expense of stables and fodder. On top of other incidental expenses such as Crown rents at Laracor, he was responsible for multifarious acts of charity that ultimately rivalled the Primate's in munificence. In one sense, his annual 'payment' to Mrs Johnson of £50, like his later pensions to his sister and to Mrs Dingley, were also forms of charity. Swift had been living beyond his means. He had gambled on preferment as a result of his acquaintance with the Whigs, and he had lost. There was only one answer. He had to retrench.

In time Swift returned to Dublin and was soon caught up in the politics of St Patrick's Cathedral, defending the right of the Chapter to elect its nominee, Swift's friend John Stearne, Rector of Trim, as Dean on the death of the incumbent, Jerome Ryves, who died on 1 February 1705. In conjunction with the Archdeacon, Enoch Reader, Swift wrote to Archbishop King in England 'to present to you our new elected Dean in order to receive the usuall confirmation'.[11] Swift was well aware of the rights of his Chapter, a knowledge he would put to good use when in time he became Dean of St Patrick's himself, and the episode reveals him taking an active part as Prebendary in Cathedral affairs. Further evidence of his growing importance was his election in July 1707 to succeed Daniel Jackson as Proctor in Convocation, the governing body of the Church of Ireland. Serving until the prorogation of Convocation on 30 October of that year, Swift distinguished himself as a champion of the rights of churchmen, and a supporter of the Lower House in the perennial conflict with the bishops who formed the Upper House. He was not afraid to voice his own opinion and to stand out against the body of the Lower House if occasion demanded.[12] His experiences informed not only his attitudes towards Chapter affairs, but his views on the administration of the Church of Ireland itself, and his involvement brought an early indication of his increased consequence when he was chosen to sue for the gift of Queen Anne's Bounty. In the long run this was to prove the stepping stone, if not to a bishopric, then at least to intimacy with the highest ministers in the state, and a hint of political power in his own right.

But the years in Ireland were not fruitful in a literary sense. In verse he wrote drafts of two poems subsequently published in rather different form, *The History of Vanbrug's House* and *Baucis and Philemon,* a vitriolic attack on Lord Cutts, *The Description of a Salamander,* and a satire on the Union of England and Scotland. Prose fared little better. A poor allegorical representation of the plight of Ireland, *The Story of the Injured Lady,* can be supplemented by only *Various Thoughts, Moral and Diverting* and *A Tritical Essay upon the Faculties of the Mind.* The *Thoughts,* dated 1 October 1706 and published in the *Miscellanies* of 1711, show how comfortable Swift could find the aphorism *qua* aphorism as a vehicle. But it is the *Tritical Essay,* an exercise in the parody of utter banality, which is of most interest, 'proposed as a Pattern for young Writers to imitate'.[13] Cliché follows cliché, much as in *Polite Conversation* which, Swift suggests, was first being collected around this time.[14] It is in pieces such as these and in the Anglo-Latin word-games that his obsession with words, with wordplay and with the character of speech and writing in general can be seen most clearly. As Irvin Ehrenpreis notes, 'The inevitable parallel in our own day is Joyce,'[15] and it seems probable that Joyce owes more to Swift than merely the allusions in *Ulysses* and *Finnegans Wake* would suggest. Swift could almost be said to anticipate the technique of *Finnegans Wake,* as he takes words apart, experimenting with the very sounds themselves, as if trying to comprehend the way in which these noises can somehow convey meaning.

The *Tritical Essay* was dated 6 August 1707 and addressed, in the form of a letter, to 'a Lover of Antiquities'. Swift had found new friends. A new Lord-Lieutenant had arrived in Dublin in June 1707. Thomas Herbert, Earl of Pembroke, brought with him a young scholar as Black Rod to the Irish Parliament. Sir Andrew Fountaine was the lover of antiquities, author of a monograph, *Numismata Anglo-Saxonica et*

Anglo-Danica, on the old coins which he collected along with paintings and drawings. Swift discovered mutual interests in punning and wordplay with both Pembroke and Fountaine, and soon a coterie was meeting at Dublin Castle, including Swift's old tutor, St George Ashe, now Bishop of Clogher, and his brothers Dillon and Thomas Ashe. Two examples of Swift's ingenuity have survived from this period, 'A Dialogue in the Castilian Language' and 'The Dying Speech of Tom Ashe', addressed to Pembroke himself. While the quality of the puns is often in some doubt ('Little did I think you would so soon see poor *Tom stown* under a *tomb stone*'),[16] these pieces show Swift in his element, in congenial company, playing games with the signs and sounds of language.

Swift's new friendship with Pembroke and Fountaine had other, more important, results. When they returned to England at the end of 1707 Swift decided to go with them. He had a legitimate reason to absent himslf from his benefices. As a recognition of his growing prominence in Church of Ireland business, and of his personal intimacy with the Lord-Lieutenant, he was asked by Archbishop King to act as solicitor for the gift of the First Fruits and twentieth parts – Queen Anne's Bounty – to the Irish clergy.[17] Aware of Swift's official backing, Pembroke was expected to add his own support to the request. When, on 28 November, the Lord-Lieutenant's entourage sailed from Dublin, the Vicar of Laracor sailed with it. He arrived at Parkgate on the eve of his fortieth birthday.

Swift was glad to be back in England. He found that the very 'Buildings, the Improvement, the Dress and countenance of the People putt a new spirit into one.'[18] Leaving Pembroke's party and travelling to Leicester by way of Derby, he was ensconced in Fountaine's house in London by the end of the year. Soon after his arrival he was joined in England by the ladies. But although Swift's visit was to last for eighteen months, it was not, in purely practical terms, a fruitful one. The negotiations over the First Fruits dragged on to an unsuccessful conclusion, and he remained no nearer to the preferment in the Church he hoped to secure from his relations with the Whig leaders. Opportunities came and went without his capitalising on them.

Soon after his arrival, he hoped to be given the vacant bishopric of Waterford. But Thomas Milles was appointed even though, according to Swift himself, 'The Court and Archbishop of *Canterbury* were strongly engaged for another Person, not much suspected in *Ireland*.' Somers's friendship gave him 'a Glimpse that Things would have gone otherwise', but it was not to be. Although he was 'stomach sick' at this most recent setback, he felt he had now to 'retire to my Moralls[,] pretend to be wholly without Ambition, and to resign with Patience.'[19] Not even little things would go right for him. He had had his eyes on the curacy of the parish of St Nicholas Without in Dublin, and believed it had been promised to him. Over twenty-five years later he was still complaining that Dean Stearne had gone back on his word, and had 'thought fit, by concert with the Archbishop, to hold' the curacy of St Nicholas Without himself.[20] This, too, came to a head when Swift was in London trying to inveigle the Court into consenting to the gift of Queen Anne's Bounty for the Church of Ireland.

It took several months for Archbishop King to forward a representation on that score to be given to Pembroke, through whom, at this juncture, the application was to be made. But Pembroke did nothing. Finally, observing 'the Nicety of Proceeding in a matter where the Ld. Lt was engaged', Swift followed Somers's advice and applied directly to Lord Treasurer Godophin 'in Behalf of the Clergy of *Ireland*.'[21] An interview between Swift and Godolphin took place in June 1708, but the latter refused to commit himself. For a further five months little headway was made. Then, almost out of the blue, Swift announced that 'the Thing is done'.[22] To his chagrin, Pembroke failed to take care of the matter before being replaced as Lord-Lieutenant by the Earl of Wharton. It was back to square one.

In March 1709, over a year after receiving the representation of the archbishops and bishops of Ireland from King, Swift was instructed to approach the new Lord-Lieutenant. Wharton 'thought fit to receive the Motion as wholly new, and what He could not consider (as He said) till he were fixed in the Governmt, and till the same Application were made to Him, as has been to His Predecessors.'[23] The coldness of the reception afforded him by first Godolphin and then Wharton goes a long way to explaining Swift's animosity towards the outgoing Whig ministers in 1710. Louis A. Landa remarks that the interview with the Lord Treasurer 'was a turning point in Swift's relation with the Whigs.'[24] His subsequent treatment of Wharton in print is well-known. None of this alters the fact that when Swift landed in Ireland on 30 June 1709, the First Fruits had still not been granted to the Irish Church, and that had been the ostensible purpose of his visit to England.

It was not that Swift was ignored by the Whigs. He renewed his friendships with Somers and Halifax during this visit. But the swing to the Whigs failed to make any appreciable difference to his personal situation. Godolphin largely controlled preferment in England and Ireland, and those posts not in his gift were in the Lord-Lieutenant's. The path of clerical advancement remained blocked. Swift's grasp of political realities even at this stage is of a piece with his other early interpretations of political events. 'I never in my life saw or heard such divisions and complications of parties as there have been for some time,' he observed on 12 February 1708 in the wake of Robert Harley's resignation from the position of Secretary of State. 'You sometimes see the extremes of Whig and Tory driving on the same thing.'[25] By the beginning of 1709 he was sufficiently aware of the difference in principles between himself and the Whigs of the Junto that he was learning to call himself a 'moderate' Whig, and amusing himself 'with Projects of uniting of Partyes, which I perfect over night, and burn in the morning'.[26]

It was this dissatisfaction with the extreme views of his Whig acquaintances which ultimately forced Swift into Harley's camp. Their disregard for the security of the Church of England in particular troubled him deeply, and prompted him to write several pamphlets in its defence and against the projected repeal of the Test Act in Ireland during these months. As he assured Archbishop King, 'no Prospect of making my Fortune, shall ever prevail on me to go against what becometh a Man of Conscience and Truth, and an entire Friend to the established Church.'[27] In 1710 he was represented to Harley as 'a discontented person, that was used ill for not being Whig enough', and he recalled that Harley had 'formerly made some Advances towards [him]'.[28] It was the logical conclusion of his disillusionment with Modern Whiggery. Gradually he learned to distinguish between the professions of men like Somers, Sunderland and Wharton and those who were more interested in keeping alive the authentic spirit of the Old Whigs.

Swift's time in England in 1708 and 1709 was spent in the company of Whigs, as he widened his circle of acquaintance. Once his responsibility for *A Tale of a Tub* was known, his character as a man of genius and learning was quickly told abroad. 'The author of the *Tale of a Tub* goes Queen's Secretary to Vienna,' Erasmus Lewis wrote to Robert Harley on 21 August 1708, 'Lord Berkeley will follow in the spring with the character of Envoy Extraordinary.'[29] In the end, like the rumours which circulated over the grant of the First Fruits, this information proved to be mistaken after genuine prospects of such a visit had been offered to Swift.[30] However, Lewis's report indicates not only Swift's reputation as author of the *Tale,* but that Harley was aware of his abilities, even though we have no knowledge of the 'Advances' he 'formerly made' towards the Vicar of Laracor.

The Whig men of letters took Swift to their bosom during this latest visit to England. The most important friendship he made was with Sunderland's Under-Secretary, Joseph Addison. By the end of February 1708 Addison was inviting Swift to 'the George in Pal-Mal', and soon the 'Triumvirate' of Addison, Swift and Richard Steele was meeting, if somewhat irregularly.[31] It was Addison's company that Swift found most congenial, and the feeling was mutual. 'I love your Company and value your Conversation more than any Man's,' Addison assured him in 1710, and as late as 1718, long after the 'curse of party' had blighted their friendship, he still lived 'in hopes of seeing' Swift, and wistfully wondered whether they would ever again 'talk together in Laconick?'[32]

Addison was already an established wit when he was introduced to Swift in the winter of 1707-8. He had published poems, *Rosamond: An Opera,* and *Remarks on Several Parts of Italy,* which 'gradually became the one work any Englishman interested in Italy felt obliged to consult'.[33] He, too, had tried to use his literary reputation to secure advancement. Step by step he progressed until, for a few months in the reign of George I, he actually held the office of Secretary of State. Addison provided Swift with a useful link between powerful acquaintances like Somers and Halifax and the Whig *literati*. As Under-Secretary, he was in constant contact with the ministers, and thus Swift's hopes of preferment in the English Church were prolonged. Swift took every opportunity of reminding the Whigs of his existence. Halifax was to promise 'duly once every Year' to wish Swift 'removed to England', and to 'sometimes putt, My Lord President [Somers] in mind of me'. In the same grovelling letter, Swift asked Halifax to 'desire Dr South to dy about the Fall of the Leaf', so that he could succeed to his Prebend at Westminster and the Rectory of Islip. Such episodes reveal Swift at his most grasping as well as his most tasteless. He subsequently burned all his letters from Halifax and Somers except one, which he retained 'as a true Original of Courtiers & Court promises.'[34] His claim never to have heard Halifax 'say one good thing or seem to tast what was said by another' must be set against his desperate attempts to use him to his own advantage.[35]

Swift's relations with Addison were tainted by these transactions, as Swift tried 'to procure so[me] Additions to [his] Fortunes',[36] but the genuine warmth of their friendship was of lasting significance in the field of letters. It is not simply that Addison wished to correct the drafts of some of Swift's poems, reducing his comic rhymes and polishing his natural conversational tone, but, thank goodness, without any permanent effect.[37] Addison introduced Swift to Richard Steele who, in 1709, launched *The Tatler*. Out of *The Tatler* grew *The Spectator,* a journal which, on its own, introduced a new species of polite essay writing, establishing a vast new audience, and contributing markedly to the enormous growth in the reading public which occurred in the course of the reign of Queen Anne.[38] As Herbert Davis remarked over forty years ago, Swift's role in the birth of *The Tatler* was more 'than is implied by his lending Steele the pseudonym Bickerstaff'.[39]

Isaac Bickerstaff, Esquire, made his first appearance in *Predictions for the Year 1708,* which Swift published early in the same year. Thus Swift introduced an unsuspecting public to one of his repertoire of characters. Bickerstaff is not as fully rounded as Lemuel Gulliver, or even the Modest Proposer. He is more of an impersonation than a fully developed persona. And yet the assumption of the name of Isaac Bickerstaff had consequences not only for *The Tatler,* as Steele borrowed the pseudonym made famous by Swift, but for Swift's subsequent prose writings. Polemical strategy is practised by the most artless writer, as he seeks to manipulate the reader; to impose upon him either consciously or unconsciously the fictional world in which he wishes him to believe.[40] From his first publications in prose and verse onwards, Jonathan Swift had been exploiting, either consciously or unconsciously, the art of fictional projection. The *Ode to the Athenian Society* presents a fictional Jonathan Swift as author as much as the *Discourse* or the more openly polemical *Answer to a Scurrilous Pamphlet,* even though the first is signed, and the two others published anonymously. *A Tale of a Tub,* free from a specific political purpose, had signalled a considerable advance in Swift's awareness of the techniques of reader manipulation. His adoption of the pseudonym of Isaac Bickerstaff denotes a further advance in the purely practical sphere where oblique irony can be counter-productive, if not actually dangerous, as Defoe's *The Shortest Way with the Dissenters* well illustrates.

Swift's methods in the Bickerstaff pamphlets bear comparison with those used in his more explicitly polemical pieces. The attempt to perpetrate and maintain a hoax on the general public at the expense of the astrologer, John Partridge, served to sharpen Swift's perception of the requirements of political writing. In attacking Partridge, he was extending the attack he had made in *A Tale of a Tub* on abuses in religion and learning. Belief in astrology was simply another form of Aeolism. Partridge was singled-out because of his outspokenness in his almanacs about the Church of England.[41] Claiming to vindicate the art of casting nativities from the frauds and cheats of charlatans such as Partridge, Swift, as Isaac Bickerstaff, first parodies the practices of almanac-makers, and then offers predictions of his own, beginning with a 'Trifle' relating to Partridge himself. 'I have consulted the Star of his Nativity by my own Rules', he alleges, 'and find he will infallibly die upon the 29th of *March* next, about eleven at Night, of a raging Fever.'[42] True enough, *The Accomplishment Of the First of Mr. Bickerstaff's Predictions* duly supplied an account of Partridge's death within four hours of Bickerstaff's calculation!

This further pamphlet from the pen of Swift indicates where his real interest in Partridge lay. Certainly the *Predictions* had offered an opportunity for the author 'and his friends in the secret, [to] laugh often and plentifully in a corner, to reflect how many hundred thousand fools they have already made.'[43] But the hoax had a serious purpose. Partridge is alleged to have declared himself a Nonconformist on his death-bed, and to have had 'a fanatick Preacher to be his spiritual Guide'. He was said to have been so obsessed with Bickerstaff's prediction that 'it had the perpetual Possession of his Mind and Thoughts.'[44] Swift is still exposing vulgar errors. And when Partridge had the audacity to claim in his *Merlinus Liberatus* for 1709 that he was 'still alive, and (excepting [his] Age) as well as ever [he] was in his Life; as [he] was also at that 29th of *March* [1708]',[45] Swift pressed home his attack on Aeolism. Surely Partridge was dead. As proof, *A Vindication of Isaac Bickerstaff, Esq;* offered the testimony of 'Above a Thousand Gentlemen' who, having bought Partridge's almanac for 1709, 'at every Line they read, they would lift up their Eyes, and cry out, betwixt Rage and Laughter, *They were sure no Man* alive *ever writ such damned Stuff as this*'![46]

If Partridge had been roasted alive, the name of Bickerstaff acquired a currency all of its own, and was tacked on to many publications merely to make them sell. From 1710 onwards almanacs *qua* almanacs began to appear carrying what they alleged to be Bickerstaff's new predictions. But the most vital use of Bickerstaff's name was made by Richard Steele. On 12 April 1709, in its first number, *The Tatler* drew attention to Bickerstaff's *Vindication*, and explained the founding of the periodical as an extension of the original purpose of the attack on Partridge:

I have in another Place, and in a Paper by it self,
sufficiently convinc'd this Man that he is dead, and if he
has any Shame, I don't doubt but that by this Time he
owns it to all his Acquaintance: For tho' the Legs and

123

Arms, and the whole Body of that Man may still appear and perform their animal Functions; yet since, as I have elsewhere observ'd, his Art is gone, the Man is gone. I am, as I said, concern'd, that this little Matter should make so much Noise; but since I am engag'd, I take myself oblig'd in Honour to go on in my Lucubrations, and by the Help of these Arts of which I am Master, as well as my Skill in Astrological Speculations, I shall, as I see Occasion, proceed to confute other dead Men, who pretend to be in Being, that they are actually deceased.[47]

Steele was taking over Swift's pseudonym, as 'the Name of *Bickerstaff*' had 'created an Inclination in the Town towards any Thing that could appear in the same Disguise.'[48] He did Swift the justice of acknowledging the extent to which *The Tatler* was indebted to the Vicar of Laracor's encouragement. It became 'well known' that Swift wrote 'several *Tatlers,* and some *Spectators*', although 'he would never tell his best Friends the particular Papers.'[49] Clearly it would be fruitless to speculate, at this late stage, upon which may have come from Swift's pen. Certainly he supplied 'hints' to Steele, who benefited, as he was to put it, from 'a certain uncommon Way of Thinking, and a Turn in Conversation peculiar to [Swift]'.[50]

This extraordinary inventiveness can be seen in one contribution to *The Tatler* which was undoubtedly Swift's, *A Description of the Morning:*

> NOW hardly here and there an Hackney-Coach
> Appearing, show'd the Ruddy Morns Approach.
> Now *Betty* from her Masters Bed had flown,
> And softly stole to discompose her own.
> The Slipshod Prentice from his Masters Door
> Had par'd the Dirt, and Sprinkled round the Floor.
> Now *Moll* had whirl'd her Mop with dext'rous Airs,
> Prepar'd to Scrub the Entry and the Stairs.
> The Youth with Broomy Stumps began to trace
> The Kennel-Edge, where Wheels had worn the Place.
> The Smallcoal-Man was heard with Cadence deep,
> 'Till drown'd in Shriller Notes of Chimney-Sweep,
> Duns at his Lordships Gate began to meet,

And Brickdust *Moll* had Scream'd through half the Street.
The Turnkey now his Flock returning sees,
Duly let out a Nights to Steal for Fees.
The watchful Bailiffs take their silent Stands,
And School-Boys lag with Satchels in their Hands.[51]

In these eighteen lines, Swift displays his most accomplished poetry hitherto, and considerable critical attention has, quite rightly, been paid to them recently.[52] It is, of course, a town-eclogue, and the mock-pastoral mode allows the ironic inversion of values between town and country to be exploited to the full. Instead of a genuine dawn chorus, we are presented with a sham medley of notes from smallcoalman, chimney-sweep and 'Brickdust *Moll*'. This comparison between country wildlife and civilised town-life is taken further. An unnatural hackney-coach is the harbinger of the dawn. Betty flutters from one, illicit, nest to her own. The turnkey's flock returns home, but unlike country sheep, this flock is nocturnal and predatory. Such implicit comparisons reveal what is wrong with contemporary society.

This is one aspect of Swift's ability to treat 'obvious and common Subjects ... in a new and unbeaten Method'.[53] But the most remarkable feature of a poem such as this is the manner in which it relates to a coherent satiric vision. The *Description* is gentle satire, to be sure, employing none of the harshness of which Swift is capable. 'Last Week I saw a Woman *flay'd*,' he wrote with grim irony in *A Tale of a Tub,* 'and you will hardly believe, how much it altered her Person for the worse.'[54] Instead of involving the reader on a personal level (*'you* will hardly believe'), the *Description* is a detached, passive observation of the movements and sounds that herald the dawn in London. Swift contrives to arouse the curiosity of the reader without fully satisfying it, just as he deliberately does in much of his satire. Why does Brickdust Moll scream? Is she calling attention to her services, or is she being abused in some way? Like the derelict in *A Beautiful Young Nymph Going to Bed* who 'feels the Lash, and faintly screams' – are her screams faint because she is inured to pain, or because she is too debilitated to scream other than faintly? – the reasons for Brickdust Moll's screaming remain tantalisingly imprecise.

One thing *is* clear: she should not be screaming. In an ideal world or an idyllic pastoral landscape screaming has no place. There is no need for Betty to fly from her master's bed. Apprentices are not slipshod. Debt-collectors do not gather at gates, nor do bailiffs stand in watch. In an ideal world, or a pastoral golden age, schoolboys do not lag with satchels in their hands. True satire condemns society by reference to an ideal. Such is Swift's satire. More often than not his ideal may be implicit rather than explicit, but it is one of his great strengths as a satirist that he is constantly asking us to compare two orders – what is, and would should be – in such a way that once one comparison is forced upon us, the full range of discrepancies between actual and ideal are brought into play, even in a poem so superficially innocuous as *A Description of the Morning*.[55]

Swift's satire draws on his own deeply rooted principles for the ideal which is used as a yardstick against which the shortcomings of contemporary society can be measured. In this sense, if in no other, his corpus is political. He still believed himself to be a Whig, and yet he recognised discrepancies between his own strong views on various issues and those professed by the supporters of the Whigs of the Junto. In no area did this marked divergence of opinion make itself felt so strongly as in attitudes towards the Established Church. During his visit to England from 1707 to 1709, Swift was forced to reconsider his position, and to formulate the tenets on which his beliefs were based. *The Sentiments of a Church-of-England Man, With Respect to Religion and Government*, published in 1711 but written in 1708, put forward his own views on the relationship between Church and State, while his own keen concern for the decline in moral standards was made evident in 1709 in *A Project for the Advancement of Religion and the Reformation of Manners*. These are straightforward apologies for Anglicanism in which the reader is addressed 'directly', not through a mask or persona. In *An Argument against Abolishing Christianity in England*, he unleashed the incredible force of his wit, employing irony with all the power of the man who had been born to introduce it, refine it, and show its use.

Swift's ironic works have certain things in common. One is parody. *A Tale of a Tub* parodies or 'personates', as the

'Apology' puts it, 'the Style and Manner of other Writers, whom [the author] has a mind to expose.'[56] *A Meditation upon a Broom-Stick* is written 'According to The Style and Manner of the Honourable Robert Boyle's *Meditations*'. While *Gulliver's Travels* proceeds as if it were a *bona fide* travel-book, *A Modest Proposal* adopts the form and tone of the 'humble petitions' and other projecting pamphlets which abounded, especially in the 1720s. Similarly, *An Argument against Abolishing Christianity* was written to expose 'the Trumpery lately written by *Asgill, Tindall, Toland, Coward,* and Forty more' Deists and Freethinkers who, in Swift's view, were threatening the foundations of the Church of England.[57]

A second characteristic of his ironic manner is a tactical shifting of ground in the middle of a work. Just as the reader is beginning to be sure of his footing, confident in the reliability of the narrative voice, he is forced to come to terms with a disconcerting dislocation, as he becomes aware either that the narrator is not to be trusted, or that his postulates are unsound, or his conclusions unacceptable. Gulliver's clarity of vision is gradually but irreversibly impaired as we are made to recognise the narrowness of his insight. The Hack manoeuvres us into a position in which it seems we must choose between being fools or knaves. The Modest Proposer's solution to the ills of Ireland is to eat the babies of beggars. In the *Argument*, after four paragraphs setting out his reasons for holding such a tendentious theory as wishing to retain Christianity, the narrator changes tack. 'BUT here I would not be mistaken', he announces:

> I hope, no Reader imagines me so weak to stand up in the Defence of *real* Christianity; such as used in primitive Times (if we may believe the Authors of those Ages) to have an Influence upon Mens Belief and Actions: To offer at the Restoration of that, would indeed be a wild Project; it would be to dig up Foundations; to destroy at one Blow *all* the Wit, and *half* the Learning of the Kingdom; to break the entire Frame and Constitution of Things; to ruin Trade, extinguish Arts and Sciences with the Professors of them; in short, to turn our Courts, Exchanges and Shops into Desarts ...[58]

Swift's irony suggests that it is ludicrous, in this topsy-turvy world, to expect anything more than the pursuit of nominal Christianity. The narrator of the *Argument* is not advocating *real* Christianity at all, and the false assumption the reader may have been led into rebounds upon him with redoubled force. All the narrator is defending is a mere paying of lip-service to an ethical code which will permit a civilised lifestyle to continue unhindered by any real adherence to a doctrine of love thy neighbour. Notice the way in which Swift's persona inverts, or rather perverts, the orthodox viewpoint. In his version of things, it is not the foundations of the Church of England that are under threat, but the status quo. Should anyone offer to restore the conditions in which religion influenced belief and action, it would, it is suggested, result in the destruction of English society. In an incredible parody of the famous passage in Hobbes's *Leviathan,* in which the breakdown of order resulted in a return to a state of nature so that there would be no industry, no navigation, no trade, no 'commodious Building', no arts, no letters and no society, and 'the life of man, solitary poore, nasty, brutish, and short', Swift insinuates that the reversion to primitive faith would lead to the sort of anarchy feared by his contemporaries.[59] Christianity is thus reduced to the level of other 'systems', such as Hobbes's. We may recall *A Tale of a Tub* when we read the view that the 'System of the Gospel, after the Fate of other Systems is generally antiquated and exploded.'[60]

It is this feature of Swift's irony which at once makes it so compelling and so complex. Irony says one thing and means another. As it never says what it means, how can we be sure that we are interpreting it properly? Is Swift arguing for the retention of *nominal* Christianity? Does he really see a threat to his own society in the restoration of *real* Christianity? Or, despite the categorical denial of his persona ('I would not be mistaken'), is this what he is actually advocating? If the rules of simple irony operate, then this is surely what he is proposing. 'I hope, no Reader imagines me so weak to stand up in the Defence of *real* Christianity' would simply be inverted to read: 'I hope the reader will understand that I am actually suggesting that we try to behave as true Christians, and not the nominal Christians we are at the moment.' But how can we know for sure whether this is what Swift is saying?

The same problem recurs time and time again in his ironic works. Do we have to choose, with the Hack, between being fools or knaves? Are the Houyhnhnms supposed to present an ideal that man should aspire to emulate, or are they meant to show what an excess of reason can result in? It is at times like these that we must be careful not to let our own prejudices influence our reading of Swift. *A Modest Proposal* is far from being a simple, warm-hearted, egalitarian response to the plight of the beggars in Ireland. How do we know? By reading Swift's sermons on the condition of Ireland, and his serious proposals for curing her economic ills.[61] In the case of *An Argument against Abolishing Christianity*, it is interesting to look at Swift's other statements on behaviour and belief. *A Project for the Advancement of Religion*, written around the same time, but 'without Exaggeration or Satyr', advocates 'Hypocrisy' rather than 'open Infidelity and Vice', as it wears 'the Livery of Religion, it acknowledgeth her Authority, and is cautious of giving Scandal.'[62] 'I am not answerable to God for the doubts that arise in my own breast', Swift wrote twenty years later, 'since they are the consequence of that reason which he hath planted in me, if I take care to conceal those doubts from others, if I use my best endeavours to subdue them, and if they have no influence on the conduct of my life.'[63] In both cases Swift is defending the simple paying of lip-service to Christianity, *even if genuine faith is sadly lacking.*

This is not to say that Swift wished only for the existence of a nominal Christianity. On a number of occasions he writes of 'the great and constant Love' the early Christians 'bore to each other' in ways that suggest he himself yearned for such a Golden Age.[64] But he was a realist in so much as he recognised the degeneration in human nature which had taken place since those halcyon days. He wrote to 'mend the world', although fully aware of the unlikelihood of success. It was his 'rage and resentment' which urged him on.[65] The relationship between the *Argument* and *A Project for the Advancement of Religion* is similar to that between *A Modest Proposal* and his sermon, *Causes of the Wretched Condition of Ireland,* which also dealt with the question of the beggars: a savage ironic satire is balanced by a serious argument on the same subject which addresses the reader 'directly'. Such combinations of tracts mirror Swift's own oscillation between the belief that a sane discussion can have some practical effect and the concession that only the lash of satire could leave any mark at all on the minds of men. The two sides of the Vicar of Laracor – idealist and realist – are clearly to be seen.

While Swift was in England it began to be rumoured that the government was working towards the repeal of the Test Act in Ireland, perhaps in return for the gift of the First Fruits.[66] He viewed the projected move as a precedent for the future removal of the Test in England, and he expressed his indignation both in private and in *A Letter from a Member of the House of Commons in Ireland to a Member of the House of Commons in England concerning the Sacramental Test* ('If your little Finger be sore, and you think a Poultice made of our *Vitals* will give it any Ease, speak the Word, and it shall be done').[67] When Wharton made his way to Ireland in 1709 to take up residence as Lord-Lieutenant, he was expected to 'drive directly at repealing the Test.'[68] But Addison, who travelled to Dublin as Wharton's Secretary, thought it could wait to 'a new parlament where parties are not settled and confirmed', in which 'He will be able to Lead them into anything that will be for their Real Interest and Advantage.'[69]

This, then, was the situation in Ireland when Swift returned from England at the end of June 1709, after arranging for the publication of the third part of Temple's *Memoirs*.[70] He had come back empty-handed, having secured neither the First Fruits nor his own advancement. In Ireland he had an extended opportunity to cultivate Wharton's acquaintance and appears to have been on friendlier terms with the Lord-Lieutenant than one would have expected, or would have liked to expect, from the tone of *A Short Character of His Excellency the Earl of Wharton*. He was also able to maintain his friendship with Addison, though unable to approve of any scheme to repeal the Test Act. He, too, realised the importance of the new Parliament. Early in 1710 he wrote *A Letter to a Member of Parliament in Ireland, Upon the chusing a new Speaker there*.

The pamphlet was never published in Swift's lifetime. It is, none the less, of great interest on several counts. Firstly, it is perhaps the earliest example of Swift's involvement in Irish as opposed to English politics, and, as such, it reveals his distrust of Wharton. 'There is nothing a chief Governor can be commanded to attempt here [in Ireland]', he observed, 'wherein he may not succeed, with a very competent share of Address, and with such Assistance as he will allways find ready at his Devotion.'[71] This is a remarkably perceptive appreciation of the current situation in Ireland, which almost echoed Addison's private thoughts on the potentialities of Wharton's careful management of the Irish House of Commons. Secondly, the pamphlet illustrates perfectly the stock Swift placed in the Test Act as an Anglican bulwark against the encroachments of Nonconformity, and serves to document his growing awareness of political realities. Although 'the High-flying Whigs' might desire a repeal of the Act, 'the Moderate Men, both of High and Low Church, profess to be wholly averse from this Design, as thinking it beneath the Policy of common Gardners to cutt down the onely Hedge that shelters from the North.'[72]

In this tract, Swift chooses to distinguish between Whigs and moderate men of both High Church and Low Church leanings. He has learnt that his views do not conveniently fall into any simple dichotomy between Whig and Tory, and so he is groping for further party qualifications. The Modern Whigs of the Junto are characterised as 'High-flying Whigs', and are explicitly linked with the fanatical Scottish Covenanters who gave the first Whigs their name. Significantly, Swift does not associate himself with these men. His very attitude towards the Speakership contest is a signal indication of his much more mature political outlook. He is beginning to accept the way in which practical politics work, when principle is so apt to be sacrificed to expediency. He notes that 'the bare acting upon a Principle from the Dictates of a good Conscience, or prospect of Serving the Publick, will not go very far under the present Dispositions of Mankind.' No, indeed. In this way, the choice of a Speaker is crucial. In a typical anecdote, Swift refers to a former Speaker of the House of Commons in England, Sir Thomas Littleton, who thought 'that a House of Commons, with a stinking Breath (supposing the Speaker to be the Mouth) would go near to infect every thing within the Walls, and a great deal without'.[73]

Swift's new-found political awareness is crucial, in that less than a year later he would be writing pamphlets that, in style, manner and ideology, are very similar to *A Letter to a Member of Parliament in Ireland,* but he would be writing them against the interest of his Whig friends, and in support of the ostensibly Tory administration of Robert Harley. Clearly this new alliance needs to be explained. Too often it is claimed that Swift 'joined the Tory party', as if in 1710 he resigned from the Labour Party and became a card-carrying member of the SDP. The party political machinery was vastly different from that of modern political parties. To those who wish to define eighteenth-century English politics in strict terms of Whig and Tory, the idea that Swift 'changed party' and became a Tory might suggest a compromise of political principle and expediency, much as he outlines in the *Letter.* This would be very far from the truth.

Without whitewashing Swift's conduct in joining the Harley camp, it is possible to recognise his change of political allegiance as not an alteration but a confirmation of his principles. True, from 1710 onwards he consorted with men who were politically opposed to the Whigs amongst whom he had moved since coming to England on the accession of Queen Anne. It would be easy to accuse him of disingenuousness, cowardice or time-serving, but it would be unfair. We have seen Swift's growing disillusionment with the policies of the Modern Whigs. His dissatisfaction became profound. He had hoped for preferment from his Whig friends and although promises had been made, nothing was forthcoming. Certainly personal elements cannot be ruled out. The prospects could only be better under a new regime. And yet it was a conjunction of principle which led to the close friendship between Jonathan Swift and Robert Harley.

When Swift left England in the summer of 1709, the Whigs were rampant. Harley's fall in February 1708 had signalled the full-scale infiltration of the ministry by the Junto. By the end of 1709 four of the five great Whig lords – Sunderland, Wharton, Somers and Orford – had assumed office, and the

General Election of 1708 had returned the most Whiggish Parliament since the Revolution. The turnaround since the early days of the reign, when not a single Whig held a senior ministerial position, was complete. Yet this was viewed as merely the prelude to a thoroughgoing Whig government. Ultimately this would entail the removal of Lord Treasurer Godolphin. In November 1709 an opportunity to isolate Godolphin utterly from the Tory party occurred. On 5 November a fiery High Church orator called Henry Sacheverell preached a sermon in St Paul's on the text: 'In perils among false brethren'. The sermon was printed and bought in tens of thousands. Soon it began to be said that Sacheverell had attacked the Revolution Settlement. Pressed by the Junto, Godolphin reluctantly agreed to an impeachment.[74]

Swift's views on the Sacheverell affair are not explicitly recorded, and certainly he would have had mixed feelings about the sermon. True, Sacheverell had warned against the dangers of permitting too much latitude to the forces of Dissent, but he had also implicitly condemned the Revolution, and Swift would have had no part of this. The stage was set for a full-scale dress trial in Westminster Hall. Although the verdict went against Sacheverell and in favour of the government, it was a pyrrhic victory. The trial was the occasion for a tremendous display of popular feeling in favour of the Church and against the government, as High Church mobs roamed London threatening all who refused to salute Sacheverell.[75] This powerful demonstration of dissatisfaction with the Whig-dominated Godolphin ministry had far-reaching consequences.

On 13 April 1710 the Duke of Shrewsbury replaced the Earl of Kent as Lord Chamberlain. Two months later Queen Anne's intentions became clearer when she dismissed Sunderland and appointed the Tory, Lord Dartmouth, Secretary of State. Swift watched these developments in Ireland with growing interest. Planning a return to England, he told his publisher, Benjamin Tooke, that he hoped to see him soon, 'since it is like to be a new world, and since I have the merit of suffering by not complying with the old.'[76] Tooke confirmed that 'All here depend on an entire alteration.'[77] Finally, on 8 August, Godolphin was told to break his white staff of office.

Four days later Harley re-entered the ministry as Chancellor of the Exchequer and Second Lord of the Treasury (which had been put into commission). He had not yet replaced Godolphin as Lord Treasurer, but he was universally regarded as the new Prime Minister.

When Swift left Ireland on 31 August 1710 in the company of the Lord-Lieutenant, he was indeed entering a new political world. He had every intention of making his way in it. Since returning from his previous, unprofitable, visit to England, he had entertained Addison in his friend's two sojourns in Dublin as Wharton's Secretary. He had corresponded with leading Whigs in London who had promised to help him find preferment on their side of St George's Channel. But nothing had come of it. 'I am ashamed for my selfe and my Friends to see you left in a Place, so incapable of tasting you, and to see so much Merit, and so great Qualitys unrewarded by those who are sensible of them', Halifax had written, 'Mr Addison and I are enter'd into a New Confederacy, never to give over the pursuit, nor to cease reminding those, who can serve you, till your worth is placed in that light where it ought to shine.'[78]

Now the Whigs were once again powerless to help the Vicar of Laracor, even had they intended to turn their fine words into deeds. In view of the change of ministry, the Irish bishops once more decided to seek the remission of the First Fruits and Twentieth Parts, this time from Harley. Swift was again commissioned to act on their behalf. This meant that he had an official reason to leave Ireland, and an official reason to approach the new Prime Minister, the man who had 'formerly made some Advances towards [him]'. This time he would be dealing with someone who was fully conscious of the power of the press as a means of manipulating public opinion.[79] Soon the old ministry would be smarting under the lash of the Vicar of Laracor, and lamenting their failure to accommodate him while they still had time.

8
Swift and the Tories

Swift arrived in London on 7 September 1710 after a tedious journey. 'I am perfectly resolvd to return as soon as I hav done my Commission whethr it succeeds or no', he told the ladies on disembarking, 'I neer went to Engd with so little desire in my Life.'[1] In the event Swift was to tarry for month after month, long after his application for the gift of Queen Anne's Bounty to the Irish clergy had met with success, as he was welcomed by the new ministers with open arms. But the first few weeks were strange enough. 'The Whigs were ravished to see me, and would lay hold on me as a twig while they are drowning,' he explained with morbid satisfaction, 'the great men making me their clumsy apologies, &c.' All except Godolphin, who greeted the Vicar of Laracor with as much coldness as ever he had done when he was Lord Treasurer, which 'enraged [Swift] so' that he came away 'almost vowing revenge'.[2]

Still, Swift's friends were Whigs, and he moved within Whig circles for the time being at least. Letters were to be addressed to him 'inclose[d] to Richd Steele Esqr. at his Office at the Cockpitt, near Whitehall', except for the ladies, who were privileged enough to be able to send them to him at St James's Coffee-house, 'that I may have them the sooner.' He found all his acquaintances 'just as I left them', and on every side he was asked why he had been so long in Ireland, 'as naturally as if here were my *Being*; but no soul offers to make it so.' 'I protest I shall return to Dublin, and the Canal at Laracor', he continued, 'with more satisfaction than ever I did in my life.'[3]

Gradually he became sated with the good words of the

135

Whigs. Anticipating 'such a winter as hath not been seen in England', with the world turned 'upside down' and 'every Whig in great office ... to a man ... infallibly put out', Swift was soon 'talk[ing] treason' against their 'baseness and ingratitude'. It was in this frame of mind, 'heartily weary of this town', and equally 'weary of the caresses of great men out of place', that he was introduced to Harley. 'We are amazed to find our mistakes', Swift wrote sardonically to Dean Stearne on 26 September, 'and how it was possible to see so much merit where there was none, and to overlook it where there was so much.'[4] His disillusionment with the Modern Whigs was almost complete.

Robert Harley was a Shaftesburian Whig of the Old School. He had supported the banner of William of Orange with a troop of horse raised at his own expense, and had distinguished himself in the Convention Parliament as a hot Whig, as he urged on extreme measures against those who had assisted and advised James II. As a Commissioner of Public Accounts in the 1690s, he actively pursued a working separation of executive and legislature, keeping a check, on Parliament's behalf, on Court expenditure.[5] Becoming a leading figure in the alliance of Opposition Whigs and Tories known as the Country party, he dominated the proceedings of the House of Commons in the late 1690s, and was chosen Speaker in three successive Parliaments from 1701 to 1705. In the process, he was appointed Secretary of State in 1704 in the room of the Earl of Nottingham.

Harley's position as a member of the Tory-dominated Godolphin ministry gave rise to comments that he had turned his coat. Just as Swift could be said to have 'changed party' in 1710, so Harley was accused of 'changing party'. He saw it somewhat differently. It was not he that had turned his coat, but Whigs like Somers and Halifax who had been bought off by places in the ministry in the mid-1690s. As *Faults on Both Sides,* that important Harleyite pamphlets put it in 1710: 'it was their deserting the true interest of their country, and running into and supporting all the mismanagements of the late reign, that made him join with those that were called Tories.' And he had a cast-iron reason for doing so: 'to rescue the nation from the rapine of that corrupt ministry'.[6] 'I have the same principles I came into the House of Commons with,' he wrote on one occasion. 'I never have willingly, nor never will change them.'[7] It was his refusal to be satisfied with the ministry's growing dependence on the Whigs of the Junto which led to the tension between Harley and Godolphin which resulted in the trial of strength in 1708 that ended in his fall.

Harley's plan, even at this late stage, was to cut across party lines in the formation of a single-party House of Commons working 'for the good of England'.[8] He sought to 'Graft the Whiggs on the bulk of the Church Party'.[9] As *Faults on Both Sides* put it in 1710, Whigs who concurred 'in the promotion of the public good' would be 'as freely admitted to employments and as well regarded as ever, nothing more being desired than a coalition of the honestest men of both sides.' As for Harley, it was suggested, 'If his conduct shall be impartially considered, it will be found that his actions have shown him much more a patriot and a true Whig than his adversaries.'[10] It is in the light of Harley's political career, and comments such as these, that we should review Swift's own professions. He claimed to be 'of the old Whig principles, without the modern articles and refinements'.[11] Harley embodied the Old Whig principles that Swift admired so much. In this context, Swift's alliance with Harley seems understandable, perhaps unavoidable.

Harley was having problems with the implementation of his 'coalition' scheme. The Whigs were proving as intractable as ever, and by 23 September Somers, Orford, Wharton, Cowper and the Secretary of State, Henry Boyle, had resigned. With the credit crisis encouraged by the outgoing ministers severely handicapping the government's chances of continuing the war, Harley was forced to appoint Tories to a number of key ministerial positions. Instead of a non-party administration comprising the 'honestest men of both sides', he was faced with a Tory *fait accompli*, and their triumph was confirmed at the polls in October by a landslide electoral victory. It was at this juncture that Swift made his approach over the First Fruits. 'I have been told, that Mr. Harley himself would not let the Tories be too numerous', he wrote, 'for fear they should be insolent, and kick against him.'[12]

Harley had little choice in the matter. 'They *were* too numerous, and finally they *did* kick against him, aided and abetted by Henry St John, the new Secretary of State.

St John was a staunch Tory, but he had been schooled in politics under Harley. When Harley was appointed Secretary of State in 1704, St John had accompanied him into office as Secretary-at-War. When Harley resigned in 1708, St John resigned with him. St John's extreme Tory outlook made him a dangerous choice for a coalition-scheme, and he would not have been appointed to a Cabinet post if Harley had succeeded in persuading Somers, Cowper and Boyle not to resign in September 1710. Boyle would have retained the post of Secretary of State, and St John would have had to satisfy himself with his former position as Secretary-at-War. Over the course of the next four years, St John was to advance from his subordinate position to challenge Harley for the leadership of the ministry, but without success. This, however, is the background to Swift's extensive dealings with the two men, from whose 'quarrel', as he was later to put it, 'all our misfortunes proceeded'.[13]

Through the offices of Erasmus Lewis, Lord Dartmouth's Under-Secretary, Swift was introduced to Harley, 'who received [him] with the greatest respect and kindness imaginable', on 4 October 1710. The contrast with the cold meetings he had had to endure with Godolphin was marked. At the end of his second audience with Harley on the 7th, Swift had been completely won over, and was 'inclined half to believe what some friends ha[d] told [him], That he would do every thing to bring [him] over'. Harley touched Swift on his tenderest spot, his thirst for greatness, and applied the balm of kindness and flattery. When Swift asked leave to attend his levee, Harley replied shrewdly that 'That was not a place for friends to come to.' 'The Tories dryly tell me, I may make my fortune, if I please,' Swift observed, 'but I do not understand them, or rather, I do understand them.'[14] He understood them only too well.

Harley did not merely fob off Swift with promises like the Whigs had done. The affair of the First Fruits proceeded smoothly, and soon Swift was able to tell Archbishop King that his solicitation had been successful.[15] True, it took some months for the official seal to be set to the arrangement, but this time there were no misunderstandings. The Vicar of Laracor had managed to win for the Irish Church the gift of Queen Anne's Bounty. Harley's interest in an obscure Irish clergyman was not without an ulterior motive. He had a job for Swift; one for which he was supremely well-equipped. Harley was, of all his contemporaries, the most aware of the power of public opinion, and how it could be manipulated by the press. He had need of a propagandist; one who was not an everyday Grub Street scribbler, but a stylist who might control ministerial propaganda. He found such a writer in Swift.

Swift had published nothing during his months in Ireland between the end of June 1709 and the end of August 1710. True, he had been planning the volume of *Miscellanies* which finally appeared in February 1711, and a fifth edition of *A Tale of a Tub* to carry the 'Apology'.[16] He had also written without publishing *A Letter to a Member of Parliament in Ireland*. But his first publications since *Memoirs III* were a number of pieces in verse and prose that he began to compose on his arrival in London. These included two contributions to *The Tatler* – one on the abuse of language, the other *A Description of a City Shower* – a lost ballad made up of puns on the Westminster election, and his promised revenge on Godolphin, *The Virtues of Sid Hamet the Magician's Rod*.

If Harley needed any reminding of the power of Swift's pen, this poem was sufficient to do it. He recognised the Vicar of Laracor's hand, and pulled the broadside out of his pocket in company, 'and gave them to a gentleman at the table to read, though they had all read them often'. Peterborough insisted on reading the lines himself, and, as Swift relates, 'Mr. Harley bobbed me at every line to take notice of the beauties. Prior rallied lord Peterborow for author of them; and lord Peterborow said, he knew them to be his; and Prior then turned it upon me, and I on him.' The flattery was obvious, but welcome to a man like Swift. Here he was, sitting in the company of the Prime Minister, listening to his own verses being read out to the general applause of the assembled company. He lapped it up as if it were manna from heaven.[17]

The Virtues of Sid Hamet the Magician's Rod is not one of Swift's best poems. It is very much a topical piece, which relies heavily not only on fairly obvious sexual innuendo, but on current political reference for its effect. Godolphin is portrayed as a covetous old man, who uses the wealth he has accrued through office to maintain his position. His white staff of office is represented as the archetype of various rods throughout the ages (even Hermes' rod 'was just a Type of *Sid's*'), and its peculiar virtues are celebrated ironically, as Sid's enchanted wand searches out not water, like a normal divining rod, but hard cash. It is also employed to catch those who are prepared to be bought off with places in the government:

> *SID*'s Rod was slender, white and tall,
> Which oft he us'd to *fish* withal:
> A *PLACE* was fastned to the Hook,
> And many Score of *Gudgeons* took ...[18]

Note that this is a perpetual Country complaint. Swift and Pope were later to censure Walpole for buying off potential opposition. In 1710 Swift was already condemning Godolphin for doing the same thing. The magic he was master of is human cupidity: '*Sid*'s Scepter, full of Juice, did shoot/ In Golden Boughs, and Golden Fruit', and his Christian name of Sidney permits Swift to draw the parallel with Sid Hamet in *Don Quixote,* as he lampoons Godolphin mercilessly for his misconduct in office, concluding with a suitably belittling comparison of the *quondam* Lord High Treasurer of Great Britain and a child in a tantrum:

> DEAR *Sid*, then why wer't though so mad
> To break thy *Rod* like naughty Lad?[19]

It is worth pointing out that the criticisms Swift makes of Godolphin in *The Virtues of Sid Hamet the Magician's Rod* were to re-appear in rather different form in Swift's *Examiner* essays in the months to come, as he exposed the greed of the old ministry, and in particular the circle surrounding Marlborough and Godolphin, with the avaricious Duke of Marlborough himself as his principal target. No wonder Harley 'bobbed' Swift at the poem's 'beauties', as he looked forward to as yet unwritten attacks on the disgraced ministers. Despite its deficiencies as a serious poem, *The Virtues of Sid Hamet the Magician's Rod* is a minor masterpeice of political literature, combining humour and scathing wit and abuse in the ridiculing of a public figure of major importance. Not only were the half-sheets highly commended, they were selling 'prodigiously'.[20]

If he was pleased with the reception of *Sid Hamet,* Swift was even more happy with the praise *A Description of a City Shower* received. 'They say 'tis the best thing I ever writ, and I think so too,' he told the ladies. Matthew Prior and Nicholas Rowe 'both fell commending [it] beyond any thing that has been written of the kind.'[21] Like *A Description of the Morning,* it works through the inversion of conventional expectation. Instead of a sweet, refreshing rain, we are offered a 'Sable Cloud' which, having 'swill'd more Liquor than it could contain ... like a Drunkard gives it up again'; a 'drizzling Show'r' that could be best compared to 'that Sprinkling which some careless Quean/Flirts on you from her Mop, but not so clean'.[22]

Originally Swift called his verses 'my poetical *Description of a Shower in London*'.[23] The change of title is significant, for the phonetic difficulty of 'City Shower' is quite deliberate. The poem is concerned with the excrement of the city, and, through metonymy, with the products of civilisation itself. By implication, the shower is a type of Noah's flood, 'Threat'ning with Deluge this *Devoted* Town'. The after-effects can be seen as the cleansing waters wash away the corruption of the city both literally and metaphorically:

> NOW from all Parts the swelling Kennels flow,
> And bear their Trophies with them as they go:
> Filth of all Hues and Odours seem to tell
> What Street they sail'd from, by their Sight and
>   Smell.
> They, as each Torrent drives, with rapid Force
> From *Smithfield,* or St. *Pulchre*'s shape their Course,
> And in huge Confluent join'd at *Snow-Hill* Ridge,
> Fall from the *Conduit* prone to *Holborn-Bridge.*
> Sweepings from Butchers Stalls, Dung, Guts,
>   and Blood,

Drown'd Puppies, stinking Sprats, all drench'd
   in Mud,
Dead Cats and Turnip-Tops come tumbling down
   the Flood.[24]

These, it is suggested, are the genuine works of urban civilisation, as Swift displays the wonderful rhythmical sense of which he was master in the concluding triplet – a 'modern' poetical refinement he detested – moving with effortless ease from an iambic to a dactylic beat for two-and-a-half lines, before resuming the original pulse. *A Description of a City Shower* may not be 'the best thing [he] ever writ', but it is an accomplished piece nevertheless.

Swift was to give up trifles such as these for more important work. During the shower, 'underneath a Shed', 'Triumphant Tories, and desponding Whigs,/Forget their Fewds'. During his previous visit to London, Swift had toyed with the idea of uniting parties.[25] Under Harley's auspices, he was to be given the chance to air such conciliatory views in print. *Faults on Both Sides* had attempted to moderate between the extremes of Whig and Tory during the October elections. On 2 November *The Examiner,* a hitherto staunch Tory periodical launched around the time of Godolphin's dismissal, announced in its thirteenth number that it intended 'to converse in equal Freedom with the deserving Men of both Parties'. Two issues later, on 16 November, following a disquisition on the art of political lying, *The Examiner* revealed its resolution 'to let the remote and uninstructed Part of the Nation see, that they have been misled on both Sides, by mad, ridiculous Extreams, at a wide Distance on each Side from the Truth; while the right Path is so broad and plain, as to be easily kept, if they were once put into it.'[26] The author of all three papers was Jonathan Swift.

The details of Swift's recruitment are missing, but clearly Harley had asked him about the possibility of his taking over the authorship of *The Examiner* during their meetings over the First Fruits in October 1710. Swift himself offered this retrospective account of his 'conversion' to the ministerial view:

142

Mr. Harley told me, he and his friends knew very well
what useful things I had written against the principles of
the late discarded faction; and, that my personal esteem for
several among them, would not make me a favourer of
their cause: That there was now an entirely new scene:
That the Queen was resolved to employ none but those
who were friends to the constitution of church and state:
That their great difficulty lay in the want of some good
pen, to keep up the spirit raised in the people, to assert the
principles, and justify the proceedings of the new ministers.[27]

While it would be imprudent to accept Swift's version uncri-
tically, the key element is an emphasis on principles –
the word is used twice – and the insinuation is that to write for
Harley did not involve a sacrifice of integrity on Swift's part.
The call was for 'those who were friends to the constitution of church *and* state'. It was over the Church that Swift had
differed with his Whig friends and had 'written against the
principles of the late discarded faction'. Further, he was being
asked to 'assert the principles' of the new ministers.

And yet the *Examiner* is often assumed without question to
be a Tory organ, preaching views far removed from those
associated with Whiggery. Certainly when the authors of the
first twelve papers put pen to paper, a distinct Tory air was
exuded. Henry St John, John Freind, Francis Atterbury,
Matthew Prior and the supposed general editor, William
King, were all Tories with unimpeachable credentials.[28] But
in his 'faults on both sides' *Examiner* – his third – Swift
questioned the validity of party terminology:

I would be glad to ask a Question about *two Great Men* of
the late Ministry [Marlborough and Godolphin], how they
came to be *Whigs?* And by what figure of Speech, half a
Dozen others, lately put into great Employments, can be
called *Tories?* I doubt, whoever would suit the Definition to
the Persons, must make it directly contrary to what we
understood it at the Time of the Revolution.[29]

This is the clue we need to interpret Swift's own political
attitudes in 1710. Harley and his closest followers can, indeed,

only be called Tories by a 'figure of Speech', because they are claiming to pursue principles and policies that, before 1688, would have been called Whig.

Swift went on to give the reasons for his disillusionment with the Modern Whigs, expending on his examination of the grave deleterious effects of the modern art of political lying:

> Here, has this Island of ours, for the greatest Part of twenty Years lain under the Influence of such Counsels and Persons, whose Principle and Interest it was to corrupt our Manners, blind our Understandings, drain our Wealth, and in Time destroy our Constitution both in Church and State; and we at last were brought to the very Brink of Ruin; yet by the Means of perpetual Misrepresentations, have never been able to distinguish between our Enemies and Friends. We have seen a great Part of the Nation's Money got into the Hands of those, who by their Birth, Education and Merit, could pretend no higher than to wear our Liveries. While others, who by their Credit, Quality and Fortune, were only able to give Reputation and Success to the Revolution, were not only laid aside, as dangerous and useless; but loaden with the Scandal of *Jacobites,* Men of *Arbitrary Principles,* and *Pensioners* to *France;* while Truth, who is said to *lie in a Well,* seemed now to be buried there under a heap of Stones.[30]

This was no mere cant – it was a *cri de coeur.* In this passage from the *Examiner,* we can recognise Swift's own firmly held beliefs jumping out at us from the page. Through the corruption of the nation's manners, the enemies of the constitution in Church and State could debauch the people's principles and blind their understandings. The figure of blindness predominates in Swift's series of *Examiner* essays, 'that Blindness, which Prejudice and Passion cast over the Understanding'.[31] We might recall that *A Tale of a Tub* was, according to the 'Apology', written by a man who, 'By the Assistance of some Thinking, and much Conversation ... had endeavour'd to Strip himself of as many real Prejudices as he could.'[32] Swift was still exposing vulgar errors, this time of a political nature. Above all, he was provoking his readers, and challenging them to think for themselves.

At last, at the age of almost forty-three, Swift was beginning to grasp the realities of the post-Revolution political
world, and to shuffle off the misconceptions and half-truths
he had worn since entering the home of Sir William Temple.
Harley had learned long ago that the present-day Whigs had
very little in common with the first Whigs other than their
name. Under Harley's tutelage, Swift shed the last prejudices
he possessed about politics. As he sought to pierce the
blindness of his audience, to give them his version of the
truth, he was himself dispelling the rosy haze through which
he had previously viewed the conduct of his Whig friends.
'Get the *Examiners,* and read them', he advised the ladies on
the first day of 1711, 'the last nine or ten are full of the
reasons for the late change, and of the abuses of the last
ministry; and the great men assure me they are all true.'
'They are written by their encouragement and direction,' he
added, to endorse the fact that he had become the full-time
author of the ministerial paper of opinion.[33]

Was Swift simply exchanging one set of political prejudices
for another? Perhaps he was, but he continued to believe in
Harley's version of things for the rest of his life, and, in
essence, it was fully in accord with the principles he claimed
to have always held. Since the Revolution, he explained, the
corruption of manners had allowed the constitution to be
undermined by men of mean birth, while the natural leaders
of the nation, the aristocracy, degenerated from year to year.
Liberty itself was threatened, and those who sought to uphold
the rights and privileges of the propertied were condemned as
Jacobites, just as Swift himself was to be in the reigns of
George I and George II. If he was deceived about the reality of
politics after 1710, however, the deception was of his own
making. He was a willing contributor to Harley's cause. 'I am
at present a little involved with the present ministry in some
certain things', he explained on his birthday, 'But, to say the
truth, [they] have a difficult task, and want me, &c.' Swift
liked to be wanted. 'Perhaps they may be just as grateful as
others', he continued, 'but, *according to the best judgment I have*,
they are pursuing the true interest of the public; and
therefore I am glad to contribute what is in my power.'[34] It

was this which allowed Swift to talk of principle with genuine sincerity as he wrote on the ministry's behalf.

Understandably, critics are more interested in the famous *Examiner* essays, the attacks on Marlborough in 'A Bill of British Ingratitude' and the 'Letter to Crassus', say, or the indictment of Wharton as Verres.[35] But to the biographer, the series of essays offers signal insight into the development of Swift's political ideas. 'WHOEVER is a true Lover of our Constitution', he wrote in the *Examiner* for 28 December 1710, 'must needs be pleased to see what successful Endeavours are daily made to restore it in every Branch to its antient Form, from the languishing Condition it hath long lain in, and with such deadly symptoms.'[36] Through the *Examiner*, and other writings in support of the Harley ministry, Swift sought to restore a measure of purity to the degenerate British constitution by exposing and rooting out the corruptions that tainted it. To the defence of the new ministry, he brought the wit of which he was capable, and the various polemical strategies he adopted are a testimony to the fertility of his abundant imagination, as he endeavoured, as Examiner, 'to undeceive or discover those deluded or deluding Persons' who had the temerity to mislead well-meaning people.[37]

As author of *The Examiner*, Swift came into prolonged contact with the new ministers. As a result, he is sometimes credited with wielding real power in the government. Some writers refer to 'inner cabinet meetings', beginning in the spring of 1711, to which he was invited, and in which he played a decisive role.[38] Swift himself tends to supply the evidence of his influence, largely in the *Journal to Stella*, that unique record of Swift the man and his life in London from 1710. There are a number of ways of interpreting this correspondence. Perhaps Swift chose to exaggerate his own importance within the ministerial circle to impress his lady friends in Dublin. On the other hand, perhaps he consciously played down his immense interest with the ministers, concealing secrets of his involvement. Who can tell? The playful tone of his correspondence in general, and his letters to Hester Johnson and Rebecca Dingley in particular, makes it supremely difficult to decide when Swift is being serious.

Take, for instance, his account of a thanksgiving day at

Court, 'where the queen past by us with all Tories about her'. 'The queen made me a curtsy, and said, in a sort of familiar way ... How does MD?', Swift jokes, 'I considered she was a queen, and so excused her.'[39] Despite talk of him giving a sermon at Court,[40] Swift was never introduced to Queen Anne. The difficulty does not lie in interpreting such obviously ironic passages, but in deciding whether or not less obvious accounts should be taken at face-value. It is much less easy to analyse the following description of a dinner at Harley's, given after he became Earl of Oxford and Lord Treasurer in May 1711:

> Ld Bol— told me I must walk away to day when dinner was done, because Ld Tr and he and anothr were to enter on Business: but I sd it was as fit I should know their Business as any body; for I was to justify; so the rest went, and I stayd and it was so important I was like to sleep over it.[41]

Certainly Swift himself undercuts his great achievement in being allowed to attend an 'inner cabinet' meeting, but does this invalidate the fact that he was permitted to hear what was said? True, he no doubt felt that it was his role to justify the proceedings of the ministry in print, but more than that, it flattered him to think that he was a valued member of a charmed inner circle. What about Bolingbroke's initial reluctance to suffer Swift to remain in the room when government business was being discussed? Was this genuine or feigned? Was Swift a valued companion at such times, or did he thrust his nose into matters which did not concern him? Were the ministers careful not to offend their chief propagandist, or merely indifferent to his presence? They had been made well-aware of his fiercely independent spirit. He refused to 'be treated like a school-boy' – even at the hands of ministers of state – having 'felt too much of that in [his] life already'.[42]

Orrery denied Swift's importance in the Oxford ministry, alleging that although he 'enjoyed the shadow' of power, the 'substance' was lacking. He was 'employed, not trusted'.[43] Contemporary Whigs like White Kennett similarly deflated Swift's pretensions as Courtier, describing him as affecting the role of 'the principal man of business', and acting 'as a Master of Requests', all the time trying desperately to draw attention to his own significance to the ministers and hovering around the great like a moth around a flame.[44] This is far removed from Swift's own account of his behaviour at Court, and of the cavalier way in which he treated the Prime Minister himself. He fancied himself to be 'better known' at Court 'than any man that goes there' by the end of 1711. When he saw Harley at Court he 'affect[ed] never to take notice of him'. 'People seeing me speak to him causes me a great deal of teazing,' he explained, offering a very different version of his conduct from that supplied by Kennett. On one occasion Swift 'avoyded' Harley so assiduously that the Lord Treasurer was forced to 'hunt' him 'thrice about the Room'![45]

The temptation, then, is to regard Swift's statements with a degree of scepticism when they relate to his own importance within government circles. Certainly he was never in Harley's confidence to the extent he supposed; no man was. And yet evidence of his influence in state affairs does exist. Increasingly, from the spring of 1711 onwards, Swift assumed a large share of the responsibility for government propaganda under the Oxford ministry.[46] This was especially evident after the 'peace crisis' of December 1711, when *The Conduct of the Allies* effectively outlined the 'official' position on the actions of the allies and of the Godolphin ministry during the War of the Spanish Succession. Swift also claimed to have been instrumental in the unsuccessful attempt to mediate in the developing power struggle between Harley and St John. 'Do you know', he told the ladies in August 1711, 'that I have ventured all my credit with these great ministers to clear some misunderstandings betwixt them; and if there be no breach, I ought to have the merit of it? 'Tis a plaguy ticklish piece of work, and a man hazards losing both sides. 'Tis a pity the world does not know my virtue.'[47]

There can be little doubt, despite the *Journal's* ironic tone, that Swift firmly believed he had been the man who had done most to reconcile Harley and St John.[48] While this might smack of self-importance, and seem to support Orrery's suggestion that 'at the same time that he imagined himself a subtil diver, who dextrously shot down into the profoundest region of politics, he was suffered only to sound the shallows nearest the shore, and was scarce admitted to descend below the froth at the top',[49] there can be no hesitation about interpreting Swift's assistance in the composition of Queen's speeches. The Queen's speech, delivered at the opening of each Parliamentary session, is an important statement of the government's programme in Parliament for the ensuing weeks. As Prime Minister, Harley had overall responsibility for deciding the content of such speeches, and he invited comments from a select band of ministerial assistants – Dartmouth and Buckingham in 1711; Bromley in 1714.[50] Swift was also involved, not only in 1713, when he 'corrected' the draft of the speech 'in sevrall Places and penned the vote of Address of thanks for the Speech',[51] but in 1714, as he commented on successive drafts of the speech which opened the new Parliament on 2 March. The content may have been Oxford's preserve; the formulation owed much to the hand of Swift. His involvement in such important matters strongly suggests that his role was not limited to menial tasks. Not even Bolingbroke was consulted about the Queen's speech at this stage. Clearly Swift's influence at the centre of power was real enough.

However, he was unaware of many ministerial matters. It was only gradually, for instance, that he realised that all was not as it should be between Harley and St John. In February 1711 the weekly dinners, which have erroneously been referred to as 'inner cabinet' meetings, began at Harley's house. They were sufficiently prestigious to impress the Vicar of Laracor, who was glad to be one of the number. At the same time, Harley was experiencing the first of many difficulties with Secretary St John. It was at the 'beginning of February 1710[11] [that] there began to be a separation in the House of Commons, and Mr Secretary St John began listing a party, and set up for governing the House'.[52] The emergence of the October Club, whose motto was 'we will not be harled',[53] was used by St John to embarrass Harley. As Swift observed, the October Club wanted to 'drive things on to extreams against the Whigs, to call the old ministry to account, and get off five or six heads'.[54] These were also St John's wishes.

Harley prescribed 'gentler measures', but *The Examiner* began to reflect the views of St John, as Swift fell under the spell of the charismatic Secretary of State. In four successive papers from 25 January 1711, Swift subjected the Whigs and the old ministry to a withering assault. First he discussed the sort of measures they might be expected to take on their hypothetical return to power. Then he eulogised the new ministry in an explicit comparison of the virtues of the two administrations. The following issue was the brilliant 'Letter to Crassus' – a bitter *exposé* of the avarice of the Duke of Marlborough which, he assured the ladies, 'has ruined us'.[55] And finally, in 'An Answer to the *Letter* to the EXAMINER', he drew attention to the 'Conduct of the late Ministry, the shameful Mismanagements in *Spain*, [and] the wrong Steps in the Treaty of Peace.'[56] His tactics were not vastly dissimilar to those of the October Club, which wanted to 'drive things on to extreams against the Whigs'.

Throughout January 1711 he had been closeted in business conference with Secretary St John, 'forwarding an impeachment against a certain great person'.[57] St John, in the *Letter to the Examiner,* published soon after the journal's appearance in August 1710, had stated baldly that Britain had been imposed upon by the allies, encouraged to act as principals in a war that was not strictly in her own interests, and had been forced to pay for the privilege. 'I must talk politicks', Swift wrote on 7 January. 'In my opinion we have nothing to save us but a Peace, and I am sure we cannot have such a one as we hoped.'[58] As his subsequent *Examiner* papers confirm, he had been converted to St John's way of thinking. At this juncture he was evidently oblivious of the fact that it was not Harley's. He appears to have been unaware of the ill feeling between the two men which dated from this time.

He was disabused after Harley was dangerously wounded by the Marquis de Guiscard on 8 March 1711. He published an account of the incident in *The Examiner*:

The Murderer confessed in *Newgate*, that his chief Design was against Mr. Secretary *St John,* who happened to change Seats with Mr. *Harley*, for more Convenience of examining the Criminal: And being asked what provoked him to stab

the Chancellor? He said, that not being able to come at the
Secretary, as he intended, it was some Satisfaction to
murder the Person whom he thought Mr. *St John* loved
best.[59]

Although, as Swift remarked in retrospect, this representation
of the assassination attempt gave 'Mr. St John all the merit,
while Mr. Harley remained with nothing but the danger and
the pain', he had derived it from the Secretary himself, who
had even 'perused' the passage 'before it was printed' without
offering to make any changes.[60] Understandably, Harley was
hurt by St John's affectation, and Swift decided not to provide
a full narrative of the affair, leaving it to his 'under-strapper',
the author of *chroniques scandaleuses*, Delarivière Manley, who
now lived with the printer, John Barber. 'I was afraid of
disobliging Mr. Harley or Mr. St John in one critical point
about it', he explained, 'and so would not do it myself.'[61]

Swift was conscious of the strained relations between
Harley and St John for the first time. 'I am heartily sorry to
find my friend the secretary stand a little ticklish with the rest
of the ministry', he noted on 27 April.[62] Harley later referred
to the 'perverseness of some of the Tory's during the time that
[he] lay sick of his wounds'.[63] St John was behind this as, with
Harley incapacitated, he sought to remodel the House of
Commons to his own advantage. But many MPs stayed loyal
to the Prime Minister, as did most of the Cabinet. There was
such an upsurge of popular feeling on behalf of the wounded
man in fact, that St John was in danger of losing his place as a
result of his machinations. On 23 May Harley was raised to
the peerage as Earl of Oxford and Earl Mortimer. Six days
later he was given the Lord Treasurer's white staff. St John
had been routed.

Oxford asked Swift to be his chaplain, but he refused. 'I
will be no man's chaplain alive,' he emphasised; he had had
enough of that, too, during the Lord-Lieutenancy of the Earl
of Berkeley. As far as the ministry was concerned, it was this
proudly independent attitude which made him unreliable.
During these weeks the decision was made for his regular
series of contributions to *The Examiner* to cease. The details
are as scanty as those of his recruitment. 'If they go on', he

wrote, 'they may probably be by some other hand, which 'in my opinion is a thousand pities; but who can help it?'[64] Why, then, did Swift stop writing *The Examiner*? Was it a voluntary decision? 'One cannot avoid thinking', W.A. Speck pertinently observes, 'that he was glad to relinquish a post which had brought him directly into the firing line between the chief ministers.'[65] Yet he spoke of his failure to continue as Examiner as 'a thousand pities'. Clearly he had mixed feelings. True, he had been caught between Harley and St John, Oxford and Bolingbroke, the 'colonel' and the 'captain', but perhaps it was this which led to his removal from the *Examiner.*

Swift may have objected to being used like a 'school-boy', and yet that is precisely the way he reacted to adversity. In the months following his giving up the authorship of the *Examiner*, he became increasingly anxious lest these ministers would treat him the same way as all the others had done. 'Remember if I am used ill and ungratefully', he wrote to the ladies on 29 June, three weeks after his last complete *Examiner* appeared (no. 44):

as I have formerly been, 'tis what I am prepared for, and shall not wonder at it. Yet, I am now envied, and thought in high favour, and have every day numbers of considerable men teazing me to solicit for them. And the ministry all use me perfectly well, and all that know them, say they love me. Yet I can count upon nothing, nor will, but upon MD's love and kindness.—They think me useful; they pretended they were afraid of none but me; and that they resolved to have me; they have often confessed this: yet all makes little impression on me.—Pox of these speculations! They give me the spleen; and that is a disease I was not born to.[66]

Certainly Oxford had need of the pen of the Vicar of Laracor. St John, too, recognised its power, and sought to make use of it. For his part, Swift hoped for a bishopric, or an English deanery at the very least, as a reward for his public services on behalf of the government. He refused payment.[67] But these worldly concerns should not obscure the genuineness of

Swift's feelings for Oxford and St John. A bond of friendship existed between them which held them together long after the events of these years were merely a faint memory.

Oxford had infuriating habits as a politician. Obsessed with secrecy, he seems to have had real difficulty in making himself understood, and he turned procrastination into a fine art. This was not wasted on Swift. 'I always loved you just so much the worse for your station,' he wrote to him in 1714, when Oxford was trying desperately to maintain his position. 'For in your publick Capacity you have often angred me to the Heart, but as a private man never once.'[68] Swift loved Oxford as a private man, and it was as a private man that his best characteristics could be seen. He was friendly, trustworthy, and scrupulously honest. He liked to practise politics on the personal level, buttonholing individuals and convincing them of his sincerity. It was this ability to get along with people which explains his subtle manipulation of Swift. He wanted Swift on his side, and he went out of his way to make him his.

Swift remained loyal to Oxford to the last, justifying the conduct of the disgraced minister even when he was in the Tower of London, awaiting trial for treason. He was prone to two sorts of hero-worship. Often he would cultivate the friendship of an older man whom he admired and respected. Invariably he would discover, in the end, that even these paragons had failings just like everyone else. It is tempting to suggest that in such relationships Swift was looking for a father-figure. Perhaps he was. In the case of Oxford, he never surrendered the belief he had in his abilities as a statesman, nor in his integrity as a public servant. 'I shall take the Liberty of thinking and calling You', he wrote on Oxford's committal to the Tower in July 1715, 'the ablest and faithfullest Minister, and truest Lover of Your Country that this Age hath produced.'[69]

Swift's relationship with St John was of another kind. If he admired the virtue of a Sir Thomas More, he could also appreciate the brilliance of a Charles XII of Sweden.[70] It was St John's intellect that first attracted Swift, and a love-affair of the mind, rather than of the heart, soon developed. 'I am thinking what a veneration we used to have for sir William

Temple, because he might have been secretary of state at fifty', he wrote on meeting St John, 'and here is a young fellow, hardly thirty, in that employment.'[71] When Swift was with St John in the first few months of 1711, almost to the exclusion of Harley, he forgot the Secretary's less admirable qualities – his debauchery and his freethinking – and surrendered himself in admiration of his genius. 'I think Mr. St. John the greatest young man I ever knew,' he told the ladies in no uncertain terms, 'wit, capacity, beauty, quickness of apprehension, good learning, and an excellent taste; the best orator in the house of commons, admirable conversation, good nature, and good manners; generous, and a despiser of money.'[72] Praise indeed, which goes a long way to explaining Swift's long patience with the man of mercury. When he became conscious of a division of loyalties, his heart remained with Oxford, but his appreciation of the Secretary's gifts was unfeigned.

Gradually the depression Swift felt after giving up responsibility for *The Examiner* lifted, as it became clear that the ministers were not prepared to let him go just yet. 'There is now but one business the ministry wants me for', he explained, 'and when that is done, I will take my leave of them.' 'I never got a penny from them', he stressed, 'nor expect it.'[73] The care which was lavished on *The Conduct of the Allies, and of the Late Ministry, In Beginning and Carrying on the Present War,* both on the part of Swift and of the ministers themselves, meant that he was to tarry in London for many months more, prolonging and extending his contact with the great men, until his destiny was so bound up with that of the government that he could not make a decisive break with England until its fall.

The Conduct of the Allies was a carefully prepared piece of propaganda intended to fulfil a crucial public relations job for the Oxford ministry. The Tories had been borne into office on a wave of war-weariness. Despite being offered extremely advantageous terms by Louis XIV in 1709, the Whigs had failed to make peace. Understandably enough, the country gentlemen who financed the war through their taxes suspected that someone was making money out of the prolongation of hostilities. St John gave substance to this vague feeling in *A Letter to the Examiner*: 'if the War continue much longer on the present Foot', he asserted, not only would the objectives of the war – 'To restore the *Spanish* Monarchy to the House of *Austria*, who by their own Supiness, and by the Perfidy of the *French*, had lost it; and to regain a Barrier for *Holland* which lay naked and open to the Insults of *France*' – be thwarted, but

> *Britain* may expect to remain exhausted of Men and
> Money, to see her Trade divided amongst her Neighbours,
> her Revenues anticipated even to future Generations, and
> to have this only Glory left Her, that She has proved a
> Farm to the *Bank,* a Province to *Holland,* and a Jest to the
> whole World.[74]

These were the themes upon which Swift would play variations in his peace pamphlets, *The Conduct of the Allies* and *Some Remarks on the Barrier Treaty.*

It is worth pointing out that we know next to nothing about Swift's opinions on the question of war and peace prior to 1710. But his views, as expressed in the *Journal to Stella,* were remarkably consistent. 'In my opinion we have nothing to save us but a Peace,' he wrote on 7 January 1711, and seven months later his attitude had not changed. The Earl of Peterborough was 'violent against a Peace.' 'He reasons well,' Swift noted, 'yet I am for a Peace.'[75] The *Examiner* had promised 'a Discourse' on 'the Conduct of the late Ministry, the shameful Mismanagements in *Spain*, [and] the wrong Steps in the Treaty of Peace'.[76] On 30 October Swift revealed that he had been

> to-day in the city concerting some things with a printer,
> and am to be to-morrow all day busy with Mr. secretary
> about the same. I won't tell you now; but the ministers
> reckon it will do abundance of good, and open the eyes of
> the nation, who are half bewitched against a Peace. Few of
> this generation can remember any thing but war and taxes,
> and they think it is as it should be: whereas 'tis certain we
> are the most undone people in Europe, as I am afraid I
> shall make appear beyond all contradiction.[77]

Swift's anger – the belief that 'we are the most undone people in Europe' – needs to be explained. Although the

Revolution of 1688 had, in his terms, re-established the 'antient Form' of the English constitution, it had had to be defended by force of arms. The long wars waged to remove the threat of French hegemony had necessitated a new system of public credit, inaugurated with the Bank of England in 1694. Those who lent money to the government to allow it to anticipate the revenue of taxation were paid an annuity. While some men welcomed the new development, conservative-minded thinkers like Swift and St John viewed it with horror, seeing it leading to the undermining of the constitution itself.

Swift, we recall, believed that 'power' should 'always follow property', and in the first of his contributions to the *Examiner* he explained that *'Power*, which, according to the old Maxim, was used to follow *Land*, is now gone over to *Money'*.[78] The previous year, in a private letter, St John had remarked bitterly on the growth of 'a sort of property' – stocks and shares – 'not known twenty years ago, [which] is now increased to be almost equal to the terra firma of our island'.[79] This unhealthy situation had come about because of the war. It was, therefore, in England's interests to bring it to a close as soon as possible. Instead, the Whigs seemed to be prolonging it. Indeed, in 1710 they had engineered a credit crisis to try to forestall the change of ministry. If the new government had been unable to find the money to continue the war, then Harley, the Chancellor of the Exchequer, would have been forced to resign. In Swift's eyes, the increase in the monied interest not only threatened the constitution, it was self-perpetuating. When he wrote that in his opinion 'we have nothing to save us but a Peace', he was scarcely exaggerating. It was of a piece with his other ideas on politics.

On his return to office, Harley had taken positive steps to initiate peace negotiations. Particularly through the offices of the Earl of Jersey, he had secretly set about formulating preliminaries upon which official negotiations could begin. In May 1711 the Cabinet learned of the existence of these moves, and in the summer Matthew Prior was sent to France to build upon them. He returned with the French diplomat, Mesnager, and by the autumn the two sides had reached agreement upon these preliminaries. But as yet no one outside the government circle knew of the Mesnager Convention, although the Whigs had their suspicions. Swift was to be instrumental in manipulating opinion to create a favourable response to the news that peace talks had begun, and that official negotiations were ready to commence.[80]

The problem was that, under the terms of the Grand Alliance between England, Holland and Austria, it was not permissible to negotiate a separate peace with France. While Oxford sought to make a nice distinction between separate treating and a separate treaty, St John advocated more extreme measures. He preferred 'shock tactics', the deliverance of a *fait accompli* to Holland, which would result either in a separate peace or a constrained Dutch concurrence. The Emperor could shift for himself.[81] Peace was the priority, even if it meant that Spain remained in the hands of the Bourbons. Ostensibly it had been a war for the Spanish succession; in English eyes it had, in many ways, been a war for the *English* succession. In Swift's eyes, it was now a war which threatened not merely the Protestant Succession, but the very constitution. His brief was to put forward arguments for a peace but, even more than that, to provide government supporters in Parliament with a line to follow in debate with the Whigs who would inevitably come out strongly against a peace without Spain.

Swift's thesis in *The Conduct of the Allies* was straightforward. He claimed that

> no Nation was ever so long or so scandalously abused by
> the Folly, the Temerity, the Corruption, the Ambition of its
> domestick Enemies; or treated with so much Insolence,
> Injustice and Ingratitude by its foreign Friends.

This he sought to prove 'by plain Matters of Fact', centring his argument on three points:

> *First*, That against all manner of Prudence or common
> Reason, we engaged in this War as Principals, when we
> ought to have acted only as Auxiliaries.
> *Secondly*, That we spent all our Vigour in pursuing that
> Part of the War which could least answer the End we

proposed by beginning of it; and made no Efforts at all
where we could have most weakned the Common Enemy,
and at the same time enriched our Selves.

Lastly, That we suffered each of our Allies to break every
Article in those Treaties and Agreements by which they
were bound, and to lay the Burthen upon us.[82]

This final point was designed to draw the anticipated fire of
the Whigs over the question of the government's infringement
of the articles of the Grand Alliance. How could they object to
British transgressions if it could be demonstrated that the
allies had already broken the treaty? How could they justly
blame the British for opening separate peace negotiations
with France, or for sacrificing the Austrian claim to Spain? It
is for this reason that Swift points out the 'Insolence, Injustice
and Ingratitude' of the allies, and prints the eighth article of
the Grand Alliance to prove that 'No Peace without Spain'
was never a condition – it contained 'not a Syllable of
engaging to dispossess the Duke of *Anjou*' of his Spanish
inheritance.[83]

Swift's pamphlet does more than simply state with clarity a
case for the ministry's conduct over the peace negotiations. It
indicts the Godolphin ministry of conspiring to defraud the
kingdom. What Swift succeeds in doing is to create a fictional
world in which he wishes his audience to believe. In this
fictional world, a land called Britain has been the victim of a
plot. 'They' are all in on it: the Whigs, the allies, the
stockjobbers who have created a new sort of property out of
stocks and shares, and, above all, the Marlboroughs – 'the
Family'. Now this much is fiction. No doubt Marlborough
made a fortune from the war. No doubt the allies did their
best to use the resources of Britain to fight their own battles.
No doubt the stockjobbers made money out of the prolongation of hostilities. No doubt the Whigs wished to retain office.
But this is no proof of a conspiracy. The conspiracy is in the
minds of Swift's readers. They desperately wanted to *believe*
that such a conspiracy existed, and Swift's careful parading of
selected facts within the rhetorical framework of *The Conduct
of the Allies* supplies ostensible evidence.

The target reader of Swift's pamphlet was not a truculent

Whig but a sympathetic Tory. Swift did not try to win over the adherents of the 'No Peace without Spain' lobby. As Herbert Davis observes, the *Conduct of the Allies* was 'intended to provide a statement of policy for the Ministry and their friends in the House'.[84] Dr Johnson noted that the 'efficacy' of 'this wonder-working pamphlet' was supplied 'by the passions of its readers'. He goes on to say that 'it operates by the mere weight of facts, with very little assistance from the hand that produced them.'[85] But he misunderstands Swift's polemical strategy. He is taken in by the apparent 'plain speaking' of the narrator, for even in this seemingly straightforward work the manipulation of the reader is uppermost in Swift's mind. He uses his knowledge of the fears of the target reader to outline a fictional political situation against which his audience will react violently, and he supplies unimpeachable facts to convince the country squire that this fictional situation is not fictional at all, but fact. In its use of prejudice, *The Conduct of the Allies* has much in common with other pieces of propaganda that set up a scapegoat to explain away the uncongenial situation which exists, and seek to stimulate hatred for specific political purposes. It looks forward to the victimisation of William Wood in *The Drapier's Letters*.

It served its turn well. The manuscript had been circulated among the senior ministers for their comment and suggestions. Both Oxford and St John offered advice, and the Prime Minister made a number of amendments to the pamphlet after the first edition was published on 27 November 1711.[86] Parliament was due to meet on 7 December. The piece was designed to prepare the way for the Queen's speech, carefully concocted between Oxford and his closest associates,[87] which would reveal the existence of the Mesnager Convention. It sold in staggering proportions, assisted by the 'great men' who 'subscribe[d] for hundreds' to distribute throughout the nation. The fifth edition was printed 'in small' for that very purpose.[88] Its usefulness was apparent when the House of Commons debated the Whig motion of 'No Peace without Spain', and decided decisively in favour of peace. 'The house of commons have this day made many severe votes about our being abused by our allies,' Swift gleefully noted on 4 February 1712. 'Those who spoke, drew all their arguments from my book, and their votes confirm all I writ; the Court had a majority of a hundred and fifty: all agree, that it was my book that spirited them to these resolutions; I long to see them in print'. When they finally appeared, he was fully confirmed in his suspicions: the 'Resolutions' were 'almost quotations from it; and would never have passed, if that book had not been written'.[89]

The Conduct of the Allies, then, was an unqualified success. It was an exemplary political pamphlet which had a job to do, and which did it well. By the end of January 1712 it had passed through six editions and had sold over 11,000 copies. Swift's reputation with the ministry was secure. However the 'peace crisis' of December 1711 had not passed without giving him a severe shock. The Tory majority in the Commons had guaranteed the passage of any vote on the question of peace. Swift's rhetoric merely gave polish to the inevitable outcome. In the Lords the government's strength was much less convincing, and in December 1711 Oxford was guilty of one of his worst errors in Parliamentary management. It was common knowledge that the Earl of Nottingham had made a bargain with the Whigs: in return for the safe passage of a watered-down occasional conformity bill, he was to open the debate on the Queen's speech with a resounding cry of 'No Peace without Spain'.

Nottingham was called Dismal on account of his lugubrious appearance. His family name was Finch. 'Lord treasurer was hinting as if he wished a ballad was made on him', Swift wrote on 5 December, 'and I will get up one against to-morrow.' He composed the ballad, 'Two degrees above Grubstreet', the following morning.[90] *An Excellent New Song, Being The Intended Speech of a Famous Orator against Peace* was published the same day. In it Swift travestied Nottingham's expected speech, and made free use of his names to contrive the most awful puns:

> An Orator dismal of *Nottinghamshire,*
> Who has forty Years let out his Conscience to hire,
> Out of Zeal for his Country, and want of a *Place,*
> Is come up, *vi & armis,* to *break the Queen's Peace.*

160

> He has vamp't an old Speech, and the Court to their
> sorrow,
> Shall hear Him harangue against PRIOR to Morrow.
> When once he begins, he never will flinch,
> But repeats the same Note a whole Day, like a *Finch.*
> I have heard all the Speech repeated by *Hoppy.*
> And, *mistakes to prevent,* I *have obtain'd a Copy.*[91]

Swift was hoping to prevent the mistakes that might result
from Nottingham's speech, and to secure a speedy peace. He
makes it quite clear that the real reason that Nottingham
refuses to concur in the peace negotiations is personal rather
than public: ''tis a great Shame/ There should be a Peace,
while I'm *Not in game'*. The punning chorus, *'Not in game'*, is
repeated at the end of every verse of the ballad, and it is true
that Nottingham had been disappointed by his failure to be
accommodated in the Oxford ministry. It may well have been
that he chose to make a deal with the Whigs on a matter of
principle – the occasional conformity bill – but his actions
could readily be construed otherwise. Nottingham never
forgave Swift for daring to interpret them in this way, and
was instrumental in forwarding the prosecution of *The Publick
Spirit of the Whigs* in 1714.[92]

Despite these preparations against the possible ill consequences of Nottingham's speech, Oxford allowed Parliament
to assemble on 7 December 1711 without ensuring that the
government was at full strength in the House of Lords.
Nottingham duly made his speech in response to the Queen's
call for a peace, and the motion of 'No Peace without Spain'
was carried as an additional clause to the address of thanks
for the speech.[93] Swift was thunderstruck. 'I am horribly
down', he told the ladies, and he began to suspect all sorts of
secret intrigues involving betrayal by the Queen, Mrs
Masham, Oxford or all three in conjunction. He was unim-
pressed by the Lord Treasurer's advice not to fear, 'for all
would be well yet'. 'I told [him], I should have the advantage
of him', he explained, 'for he would lose his head and I should
only be hanged, and so carry my body entire to the grave.'[94]

Swift's reaction to the 'peace crisis' reveals the depth of his
political understanding. Even at this late stage, he failed to

appreciate the way in which practical politics work, and seems genuinely to have believed that the Queen's female favourites had more influence than her ministers, and that she was being misled by the Whig Duchess of Somerset. Timorously daring, he added fuel to the flames by penning a mock prophecy foretelling the embarrassment of the Whigs in 1711, and advising Queen Anne to dismiss Somerset, and to put her trust in Mrs Masham. *The Windsor Prophecy,* published in a mixture of roman type and Gothic black letter, purported to be genuine. But Swift miscalculated its effect, much as he had done that of *A Tale of a Tub.* Mrs Masham warned him 'not to let the *Prophecy* be published, for fear of angering the queen', but it was too late. It almost certainly confirmed Anne's distrust of the Vicar of Laracor, and became yet one more obstacle on the road to preferment.[95]

In Swift's defence, it must be said that he thought he was witnessing 'the ruin of an excellent ministry'. He even began to speculate on the ministerial changes he expected to take place. He had no confidence in Oxford's statesmanship, and could not accept the sanguine view of St John that in time 'my lord treasurer's wisdom would appear greater than ever; that he suffered all that had happened on purpose, and had taken measures to turn it to advantage'.[96] It is doubtful whether Oxford deliberately sought to let the vote in the Lords go against him, but in the event he *did* turn it to his advantage, amply endorsing Swift's subsequent explanation of his success as a politician. His 'Rule in Politicks', according to Swift, was 'to watch Incidents as they come, and then turn them to the Advantage of what he pursues, [rather] than pretend to foresee them at a great Distance.'[97]

This, at any rate, appears to have been what happened in December 1711. The Whigs had a majority in the House of Lords. Oxford wanted to remedy that situation. The vote of the upper House over the peace had meant that additional ministerial strength was needed there in order to reverse the decision. At a stroke, on 31 December, Queen Anne created twelve new peers, ensuring a government majority in the Lords. 'I have broke open my letter, and tore it into the bargain', Swift wrote, 'to let you know, that we are all safe.'[98] He might not have liked the expedient – not many did – but now the ministry was safe, the peace was safe, and the Vicar of Laracor was safe. 'We are all extremely happy', he concluded, 'Give me joy, sirrahs.' At the same time, the Duke of Marlborough was dismissed from all his employments so that, as Swift observed, 'The last ministry people are utterly desperate.'[99] The Oxford ministry was firmly ensconced in power, and official steps towards a peace were being made. The Whigs had been defeated.

At the beginning of 1712, then, there was no pressing reason for Swift to stay on in London. The First Fruits had been granted, and his role as peace propagandist was virtually over. 'I am sick of politicks,' he assured the ladies. 'I will set out in March, if there be a fit of fine weather':

> unless the ministry desire me to stay till the end of the session, which may be a month longer; but I believe they will not: for I suppose the Peace will be made, and they will have no further service for me. I must make my canal fine this Summer, as fine as I can. I am afraid I shall see great neglects among my quick-sets. I hope the cherry-trees on the river-walk are fine things now. But no more of this.[100]

Swift did not leave for Ireland in March 1712. Spring and summer both passed away without him at Laracor. Winter found him still in London, the confidant of the greatest ministers in the land. He might miss his glebeland in Ireland and regret not having the company of the ladies, but he was unable to leave. Like a tired child at a noisy party, he gazed around him at all that was happening with eyes wide open in wonderment, afraid to go away lest something else occurred and he should miss it. He remained where he was.

163

9

Dean of St Patrick's

Swift enjoyed being in London. He found city life exciting, a mixture of congenial society and stimulating atmosphere. In addition to the 'Saturday Club' dinners at Oxford's (which declined in attraction from May 1711 onwards, as far as Swift was concerned),[1] there were the fairly regular meetings of the Brothers' Club held on Thursdays, 'to advance conversation and friendship, and to reward deserving persons with our interest and recommendation'.[2] Although the Lord Treasurer was rather pointedly excluded from their gatherings, 'The Society' took in 'none but men of wit or men of interest.' In such company Swift took great delight, and was allowed to shine. Less formal dinners punctuated his calendar, as he dined with friends and acquaintances at taverns and coffeehouses. In London, Swift was never idle. At times he might yearn for the peace of the Irish countryside, but these moods did not affect him for long. Only when he was depressed or anxious over some setback or disappointment did he regret his long stay on the wrong side of St George's Channel. Then he felt himself becoming splenetic – a condition which, as he often explained, he was not 'born to'. Normally, as Charles Ford told him, Swift's 'spirits' were 'greater than any man's I ever met'.[3]

Swift's attitude to the metropolis is well reflected in the ambivalence of poems like *A Description of the Morning* and *A Description of a City Shower*. He was not blind to the dirt and congestion of the capital, but he accepted that nowhere else could he move in a society that comprised men of such genius, learning or quality. A grudging affection for London can be discerned, glinting through the unattractiveness and

164

squalor of his portraits of city life. And so he hung on and on, until he could hang on no longer. And then he forced himself to turn his back on the attractions of polite society.

In London, Swift had to marshal his resources with care. After all, he was not a rich man. His income from Laracor and the Prebend of Dunlavin was soon eaten up. At times, particularly in the pages of the *Journal to Stella*, it seems as if he were possessed by his own impecuniosity. A successful day, we are given to understand, was one during which he did not have to pay his way, and his letters to the ladies are permeated with references to his social scrounging. On the other hand, his comic distress when obliged to dig deep into his own pocket makes amusing reading. 'To-day I was all about St. Paul's, and up at the top like a fool, with sir Andrew Fountain and two more', he noted on one occasion, 'and spent seven shillings for my dinner like a puppy: this is the second time he has served me so; but I'll never do it again, though all mankind should persuade me, unconsidering puppies!' He pretended to be positively distraught when his turn to treat the Brothers' Club came round, or when he was forced to hand out Christmas boxes to the porters of coffee-houses or of important men. 'The rogues of the Coffee-house have raised their tax,' he explained on Boxing Day 1710, 'every one giving a crown, and I gave mine for shame, besides a great many half crowns to great mens porters, &c.'[4]

Such comments seem humorous enough, and are recounted in the playful tone we associate with the *Journal to Stella,* and yet poverty was a real threat to Swift. He 'left off going to Coffee-Houses' six months or so after arriving in London. Similarly he began to refuse to dine with Whigs like Halifax at his country house, because it would cost him 'a guinea to his servants, and twelve shillings coach hire; and he shall be hanged first'. He complained bitterly about the 'humour' of 'all rich fellows' who tended to use 'all people without any consideration of their fortunes; but I'll see them rot before they shall serve me so.' Lines of *A Description of a City Shower* owed something to his personal experience: 'If you be wise, then go not far to Dine,/You'll spend in Coach-hire more than save in Wine.' Such financial logistics were always in the forefront of Swift's mind.[5]

was not only the 'quality' who had no concern for his pocket. Patrick, his manservant, was constantly infuriating him by his lack of thought. 'I have gotten half a bushel of coals', Swift announced in October 1710 – an unavoidable expense with winter coming on – but Patrick, 'the extravagant whelp, had a fire ready for' him even though he was coming home late, and so he 'pickt off the coals' before going to bed. Stories like this have a poignancy which often takes the edge off the comedy of the situation. Swift's frequent rubs with careless servants make up a recurring theme in the *Journal*, and contribute to his collection, *Directions to Servants*. Impecunious gentlemen were at their mercy. Yet Patrick's grasp of the realities of London life was sound. On bespeaking a lodging, Swift refused to pay key-money. 'Patrick would have had me give [the landlord] earnest to bind him', he explained, 'but I would not.' For once Swift's niggardliness let him down, as 'the dog let it ... to another'.[6]

He changed lodgings on several occasions during his stay in London. Initially he had lived in the heart of things, occupying three successive sets of rooms in the area of Pall Mall and St James's from his arrival in London until he moved to Chelsea, then a pleasant little village, on 26 April 1711, 'for the air, and [to] put myself under a necessity of walking to and from London every day.' During the summer of that year he returned to Suffolk Street in the west end, and thence, in October, to St Martin's Street, Leicester Fields, where he paid 'ten shillings a week; that won't hold out long, faith', he told the ladies. True enough, he left at the end of November for 'little Panton Street', where he also paid '10s a week', and stayed there until moving to Kensington in June 1712. Visits to Windsor, which Swift loved, in the summers of 1711 and 1712, punctuated his sojourn in London.[7]

There was more to Swift's moves than mere financial considerations, however. A family with which he was growing ever more familiar, the Vanhomrighs, lived 'but five doors off' from his lodgings in St Albans Street to the north of Pall Mall. Evidently it was no coincidence that, on his arrival in London in 1710, Swift chose to live in that area. Bartholomew Vanhomrigh, of Dutch extraction, had been a Dublin merchant of considerable social standing. When he died in

1703, he left a widow, two sons and two daughters. The family settled in London on a permanent basis in December 1707, just as Swift arrived from Ireland to solicit the gift of the First Fruits. Whether or not he knew them in Dublin, he certainly visited them in England, and initiated a correspondence with the elder daughter, Esther.

Esther Vanhomrigh is, of course, the Vanessa known to posterity, and from the first her relationship with Swift appears to have been a special one. It was sufficiently obvious to provoke a revealing enquiry from Stella about Swift's activities in London in 1710, and an equally defensive response. 'What do you mean *That boards near me, that I dine with now and then?*', he complained, 'I know no such person: I don't dine with boarders.' Nor were the Vanhomrighs boarders at this juncture. They rented rooms, and could entertain at will. 'What the pox! You know whom I have dined with every day since I left you, better than I do,' he continued, referring to the *Journal*, 'What do you mean, sirrah?'[8]

The problem of interpreting such comments, as is often the case with Swift's letters, is particularly acute. But two things combine to suggest that he was especially furtive as far as the Vanhomrighs were concerned. Firstly, he habitually adopted a defensive tone when admitting that he had, indeed, visited them. He dined with them only when it was wet and miserable, or when he had no other company, or when he was invited along with Sir Andrew Fountaine. Stock phrases used to explain away his presence at their table almost become nervous tics. 'I dined to-day at Mrs. Vanhomrigh's, being a rainy day', is a theme upon which many variations are played. There was a good reason for playing down his involvement with the family. Stella appears to have been jealous. 'Sir Andrew Fountain and I dined, by invitation, with Mrs. Vanhomrigh', Swift wrote on 26 February 1711, 'You say they are of no consequence: why, they keep as good female company as I do male.'[9]

And yet, despite his brief acknowledgments in the *Journal*, Swift was more intimate with the Vanhomrighs than the bare entries might suggest. When he first mentions dining with them, on 20 October 1710, he had been in London for seven weeks. As Harold Williams remarks, 'it can hardly have been his first visit since he arrived.' He would have seen his 'neighbour' Vanhomrigh before then, in which case the ladies would *not* have known 'whom [he had] dined with every day since [he] left [them]', as he claimed. A similar disingenuousness characterises his very infrequent references to Esther Vanhomrigh. She is mentioned on only three occasions in the entire *Journal*, and never by name.[10] But Swift's unguarded representations of his visits, supplied in his letters to Vanessa herself, were very different. 'I will come as early on Monday as I can find Opportunity', he wrote from Windsor in the summer of 1712, 'and will take a little Grubstreet Lodging; pretty near where I did before; and dine with You thrice a week; and will tell You a thousand Secrets provided You will have no Quarrells to me.'[11] This, surely, is Swift's authentic voice, not the taciturn mumblings we find in the *Journal*.

Throughout his months in Chelsea, Swift visited the Vanhomrighs every day. He kept his 'best gown and periwig' at their house, changing into them on his walk *into* town, and out of them again in the evening as he retraced his steps. Swift committed sins of omission in his letters to the ladies in Dublin. Why? 'Adieu till we meet over a Pott of Coffee, or an Orange and Sugar in the Sluttery,' he wrote to Esther Vanhomrigh – 'Misshessy' – in the earliest extant letter between the two, 'which I have so often found to be the most agreeable Chamber in the World.' 'I can say no more being called away', he wrote in 1721, 'mais soyez assurè que jamais personne du monde a etè aimee honoreè estimeè adoreè par votre amie [*sic*] que vous, I drank no Coffee since I left you nor intend till I see you again, there is none worth drinking but yours, if my *self* may be the judge.'[12] Such superlatives suggest the depth of feeling involved in Swift's friendship with Vanessa. It was for this reason, no doubt, that he chose to deal disingenuously with Stella.

Vanessa was twenty-two when Swift returned to London in 1710. She was not an extraordinary beauty, as far as we can tell. An old woman 'who was intimate' with her at Celbridge, described her as 'neither tall nor handsome, (probably *dutch-built*) but lively, & fond of promoting mirth'.[13] It was probably her vivacity which most excited Swift. 'People in

[Ireland] do very ill understand Raillery,' Swift wrote to Archbishop King from London. 'I can railly much safer here.'[14] Vanessa could 'railly very well',[15] and Swift was inordinately fond of that sort of humour. He could, then, indulge his passion for raillery (and for the company of women who admired him) in safety, over 'a dish of Coffee in the Sluttery' with Vanessa. What else went on there is shrouded in mystery.

It is difficult to judge at what stage Vanessa began to nourish a passion for Swift, but there can be no doubt that such a feeling developed in her breast. The affair is fancifully chronicled in Swift's poem, *Cadenus and Vanessa*. Vanessa, 'A Nymph so hard to be subdu'd,/ Who neither was Coquette nor Prude', is given Cadenus, 'A Gownman of a diff'rent Make', for her 'Coadjutor'. For a frolic, to make 'Her Sex, with universal Voice ... laugh at her capricious Choice', Cupid fires 'A Dart of such prodigious Length' that it pierces 'the feeble Volume' of Cadenus' 'Poetick Works' quite through, 'And deep transfix'd her Bosom too':

> Some Lines, more moving than the rest,
> Stuck to the Point that pierc'd her Breast;
> And, born directly to the Heart,
> With Pains unknown increas'd her Smart.[16]

The lines are ironically phrased. It has been objected that, at this stage, Swift had not published a volume of poems. True enough, but evidently Cadenus had, even though his importance as a poet is undercut in the reference to 'the feeble Volume'. The tone is light, the tale fanciful.

But *Cadenus and Vanessa* has been increasingly weighed down with the lumber of academic scholarship. Leslie Stephen thought it 'less remarkable' as a poem 'than as an autobiographical document'.[17] However, it will not do to use it as a source for the reality of Swift's relations with Esther Vanhomrigh. It is a poem, not an autobiographical statement and, as such, Cadenus is a fictional character. Peter J. Schakel, on the other hand, claims that the poem's 'allusive matrix' raises it from 'mere biography to a serious statement on love, self-understanding, and human nature'.[18] True, Cadenus 'understood not what was Love'. True, we again have a hint that, at bottom, Swift was a Hobbesian:

> Self-Love, in Nature rooted fast,
> Attends us first, and leaves us last ...

True, love is characterised as an impure passion in a passage peculiarly reminiscent of Rochester:

> *Love,* why do we one Passion call?
> When 'tis a Compound of them all;
> Where hot and cold, where sharp and sweet,
> In all their Equipages meet;
> Where Pleasures mix'd with Pains appear,
> Sorrow with Joy, and Hope with Fear.
> Wherein his Dignity and Age
> Forbid *Cadenus* to engage.[19]

But, in view of the poem's ironic structure, I am uncertain about the seriousness of Swift's statement on love. Similarly, when John Irwin Fischer calls it 'a failure' because Swift 'refused to acknowledge a part of his own experience', resulting in the 'inconsistency' of its 'thesis', I begin to wonder whether *Cadenus and Vanessa* is a poem at all, and not some doctoral dissertation *manqué* on love.[20]

The critic will wish to ask other questions of the poem than the biographer. After all, it is by far Swift's longest. And it is inevitable that the path to its door will continue to be trodden by those seeking clarification about the nature of the relations between Swift and Esther Vanhomrigh. Swift was fully aware of Vanessa's feeling for him. That much is clear. Moreover, he anticipated the judgment of those who would say he was 'no good':

> ... grant her Passion be sincere,
> How shall his Innocence be clear?
> Appearances were all so strong,
> The World must think him in the Wrong;
> Wou'd say, He made a treach'rous Use
> Of Wit, to flatter and seduce:

The Town wou'd swear he had betray'd,
By Magick Spells, the harmless Maid;
And ev'ry Beau wou'd have his Jokes,
That Scholars were like other Folks:
That when Platonick Flights were over,
The Tutor turn'd a mortal Lover.
So tender of the Young and Fair?
It shew'd a true Paternal Care—
Five thousand Guineas in her Purse?
The Doctor might have fancy'd worse.—[21]

As far as the 'world' was concerned, whatever the character of
Swift's relationship with Vanessa, he would be seen to be in
the wrong.

But we will look in vain in *Cadenus and Vanessa* for an
unequivocal statement about the outcome of the affair:

But what Success *Vanessa* met,
Is to the World a Secret yet:
Whether the Nymph, to please her Swain,
Talks in a high Romantick Strain;
Or whether he at last descends
To like with less Seraphick Ends;
Or, to compound the Business, whether
They temper Love and Books together;
Must never to Mankind be told,
Nor shall the conscious Muse unfold.[22]

Swift was as good as his word. Mankind has not been
vouchsafed the secret of any of his amours, just as the
outcome of the liaison between Cadenus and Vanessa was
never revealed by his Muse. And yet there have not been
wanting those who wish to find evidence of sexual relations
between Swift and Esther Vanhomrigh. Some have claimed
that the tone of *Journal to Stella* changes 'from March 1712 to
the end', attributing this to their growing intimacy.[23]
Frequent references to coffee in letters between the two have
been taken, not as a private joke, but as covert allusions to the
sex act. Certainly they have some hidden meaning. 'Without
Health you will lose all desire of drinking your Coffee', Swift

arned, 'and *so low* as to have no Spirits.'[24] Did he take advantage of his young admirer? Was he 'no good'? Is it possible that such cryptic allusions refer to sexual intercourse? Did Swift actually consummate his relationship with Esther Vanhomrigh?

The evidence is inconclusive, but there is sufficient to suggest that he did not. As we have observed, Swift was obsessed with female cleanliness. This *idée fixe* even finds a place in *Cadenus and Vanessa*. Venus 'sprinkles thrice the new-born Maid':

> From whence the tender Skin assumes
> A Sweetness above all Perfumes;
> From whence a Cleanliness remains,
> Incapable of outward Stains ... [25]

This is a compliment from Swift of the highest order. He constantly sought to remind man of his own mortality, using scatological imagery as a satiric device. And yet this must not obscure the fact that he was trying desperately to come to terms with his own physical nature at the same time. Sex was perhaps the greatest single manifestation of his own sullied flesh.

Instead Swift extolled the virtues of friendship in his poetry, which, 'in its greatest Height', was

> A constant, rational Delight,
> On Virtue's Basis fix'd to last,
> When Love's Allurements long are past;
> Which gently warms, but cannot burn;
> He gladly offers in return:
> His Want of Passion will redeem,
> With Gratitude, Respect, Esteem:
> With that Devotion we bestow,
> When Goddesses appear below.[26]

Swift's 'love' poetry is the poetry of friendship. He reserves his satirical verse for the exploration of physical union, and celebrates the feelings he has for Stella and Vanessa under a different name.

The World shall in its Atoms end,
E'er *Stella* can deceive a Friend.[27]

This, from Swift, was the highest of all compliments. As he put it in the *Journal to Stella:* 'I can count upon nothing, nor will, but upon MD's love and kindness.'[28] If the tone of the *Journal* changes, it never quite erases the pervading quality of affection which permeates it.

I have dwelt on *Cadenus and Vanessa* for the insight it offers into Swift's relations with Esther Vanhomrigh. But we must not lose sight of the fact that it is, above all, a playful poem. It is not rehearsing a reasoned argument on the nature of love so much as celebrating a genuine love affair in verse. Whether or not there was a sexual element in this liaison hardly matters as far as criticism of the poem is concerned. Nor does Swift's stance have to be seen as consistent. Perhaps in *Cadenus and Vanessa* he wanted to excuse his own reluctance to consummate the relationship. Perhaps he wished simply to put off any ideas Vanessa might have had about marriage. Who can tell? It is just as likely – perhaps more likely – that he was merely teasing, using raillery at the expense of both. One can imagine him showing his verses to Vanessa as they flowed from his pen, as Sidney perhaps showed *Astrophil and Stella* to Penelope Devereux, the one feeling flattered that such lines had been written about her, the other basking in the compliments that were sure to ensue.

Despite the efforts of latter-day critics of Swift's poetry to recruit *Cadenus and Vanessa* into their lists of universal concerns and controlling metaphors, it is, as Harold Williams rightly pointed out, a personal poem, 'written for Vanessa, and not intended for publication'.[29] This is an important consideration, and should be the basis for any analysis, whether critical or biographical. As a high-spirited flight of fancy, *Cadenus and Vanessa* is unique in Swift's canon. It must not be overburdened with the weight of serious statements it was not designed to carry, lest it sink without trace. Nor can we set too much store by the opportunities it appears to present for deriving biographical information. When Swift ridicules the character of Cadenus it must be remembered that he is indulging in raillery; it is not necessarily an accurate representation of how he saw himself, nor is it necessarily meant to be. He is playing games. Let us enjoy *Cadenus and Vanessa* for its own sake, not sacrifice it to the sacred cow of scholarship.

The date of composition of *Cadenus and Vanessa* is problematic. Swift's retrospective dating, 1712,[30] might indicate that the poem was begun during his stay at Windsor during the summer of that year. But clearly it cannot have been completed, at least in its published form, at that time. The name, Vanessa, is quite obviously a poetical version of Vanhomrigh. Cadenus is an anagram of Decanus – the latin for dean – and Swift was not appointed Dean of St Patrick's, Dublin, until April 1713, and installed two months later. It may be that *Cadenus and Vanessa* is the work of the summer of 1713, when Swift also visited Windsor. His notoriously unreliable memory for dates could account for his being a year out in this case. It remains to chronicle and explain his preferment, not to an English bishopric, not even to an English deanery, but to the deanery of St Patrick's.

Even though Swift had suggested that his work for the Oxford ministry was almost over with the resolution of the peace question and the dismissal of Marlborough, he nevertheless continued to meet with the ministers. From the spring of 1712 onwards he began to assume the role of unofficial *chef de propagande*. Previously, although he had been in contact with a number of Tory scribblers, he had largely confined his activities to the production of his own writings on behalf of the government. His sphere of influence widened markedly after the publication of *The Conduct of the Allies*. 'I have got an under spur-leather to write an *Examiner* again', he wrote on 5 December 1711, 'and the secretary and I will now and then send hints.' However, St John's involvement in the undertaking appears to have been minimal. The emphatic '*I* have got' indicates where the initiative lay – with Swift. Soon he was acting as supervisor of not only William Oldisworth's *Examiner*; a number of government publications fell under his scrutiny. Abel Roper, editor of the principal Tory newspaper, *The Post Boy,* worked in St John's office, but he was Swift's 'humble slave'. Papers were sent to Swift 'before they were printed', so that he could amend them as he saw fit. 'I have

often scratched out passages from papers and pamphlets',
he told the ladies, 'because I thought them too severe.'[31]

As time passed, the amount of such work increased, and so
did the number of pieces of propaganda that he arranged to
be printed. His own printer, John Barber, was a vital assistant
in this respect. Swift's business often took him to Barber's
shop in the City. In return, Swift secured for him the printing
of the official *Gazette*.[32] William King and Charles Ford were
Gazetteers in succession, and both were Swift's nominees.
Ford was his strong personal friend, deeply involved from
time to time in the production of Swift's own writings, and a
favourite of both Vanessa and Stella. He was 'an easy
companion, always ready for what I please, when I am weary
of business'.[33] For the next quarter of a century, Ford would remain one his most affectionate admirers, even if, as Gazet-
teer, his indolent, pleasure-seeking manner was hardly ideal.

Swift's role as organiser of propaganda was of real importance to the Oxford ministry, and he was an ideal man for the
job. 'Grubstreet is dead and gone last Week,' he observed on
the implementation of the stamp duty on newspapers and
pamphlets on 1 August 1712. 'I plyed it pretty close the last
Fortnight, and publisht at least 7 penny Papers of my own,
besides some of other Peoples.'[34] He was always ready to put
pen to paper in the common cause of ministerial propaganda,
and the 'Genius, which could raise such pleasing Ideas upon
Occasions so barren to an ordinary Invention'[35] could also be
relied upon to provide 'hints' to be applied, improved upon
and finished off by 'understrappers'. He acted as editor of the
government press agency, checking the copy of his underlings
for aberrations in style and content, as well as contributing
the occasional leading article himself. It was no coincidence
that he was called upon to 'correct' drafts of the Queen's
speeches in 1713 and 1714, and to compose important
Parliamentary addresses and votes

Additionally, Swift liked to think of himself as the official
historian of the peace negotiations. The Utrecht Congress met
from January 1712 until April 1713. As G. M. Trevelyan put
it, 'the battle for the Peace had been decided at home, but it
had still to be won abroad.'[36] It was at this point that St John
began to exert himself in the negotiations. True, there has

tended, until recent years, to be 'a wild exaggeration of the Secretary's initiative and a distortion of the whole nature of the negotiations'. Oxford's hand remained firmly on the controls. 'The traditional picture of Henry St John as the new arbiter of Europe, battling with de Torcy, fighting for the ministry at the conference table', writes A. D. MacLachlan, 'accords ill with the repeated comments of foreign ministers on his insubordination.'[37] Oxford retained until the last the hope that a collective peace was possible, adhering to the letter of the Grand Alliance. He had the satisfaction of being able to inform Parliament in April 1713, in the Queen's speech which, appropriately enough, Swift 'corrected in sevrall Places',[38] that the Dutch had also agreed to put an end to hostilities. But St John expended a considerable amount of energy in the course of the Congress at Utrecht in his attempt to make the allies 'swallow' the peace 'with a pox'.[39]

St John, for instance, was notoriously responsible for the 'Restraining Orders' issued to the Duke of Ormond, Marlborough's replacement as Commander-in-Chief of the British forces, which instructed him to 'avoid engaging in any siege, or hazarding a battle, till you have farther orders from her Majesty'.[40] They may have led to the signing of the Armistice of June 1712, but provided the Whigs with ammunition for the charge of high crimes and misdemeanours levelled at Oxford, Bolingbroke and Ormond in 1715. Oxford persistently denied all complicity in the affair. When St John claimed his reward, the revival in him of the title of Earl of Bolingbroke, he was fobbed off with the lower title of viscount. The blow was made even worse by the fact that both Oxford and Dartmouth, the other Secretary of State, had received earldoms since 1710. 'I was dragged into the house of lords in such a manner, as to make my promotion a punishment, not a reward', was Bolingbroke's own retrospective comment.[41] Nor would Swift write the preamble for his patent. 'I excused my self from a Work that might lose me a great deal of Reputation, and get me very little', he explained, 'we would fain have the Court make him an Earl, but it will not be.'[42]

Despite his misgivings, Bolingbroke accepted his peerage, prepared to have a title, whatever the cost. The following month, August 1712, he made a disastrous visit to France. True, during his stay he managed to extend the Armistice – an important achievement – but he also took further steps towards a separate peace with France. In addition, he lapped up the attention which was lavished upon him at Versailles, and committed the indiscretion of appearing at the opera at the same time as the Pretender. All these things widened the division between Oxford and Bolingbroke, and provided fuel for the Whigs to use after 1714. The cavalier manner in which Bolingbroke treated the allies laid him open to charges of treason. It was only through Oxford's persistence, in October 1712 and March 1713, that peace was not concluded without the Dutch. Bolingbroke had replaced the 'subtle, if tortuous, diplomacy of Oxford ... by insensitive bullying'.[43] In a bitter Cabinet meeting held on 28 September 1712, the feud between the two men was brought out into the open, and Bolingbroke's conduct was condemned. The Treaty of Utrecht of April 1713 was a triumph for the Lord Treasurer.

It was this devious peace-making that Swift felt himself obliged to defend in print. He saw his task as one of justifying the proceedings of the ministers. He denied all knowledge of activities that might be construed as treasonous, and made great efforts to research into the history of the peace. But there was a lot of which he was unaware. No wonder, then, that his industry went unappreciated by the ministers themselves. 'My large Treatise stands stock still; some think it too dangerous to publish, and would have me print onely what relates to the Peace,' Swift wrote on 18 January 1713. 'I can't tell what I shall do.'[44] Twenty-four years later the cry remained the same, when Erasmus Lewis offered his opinion of the finished *History of the Four Last Years of the Queen*:

I know very well it is your intention to do honour to the then lord treasurer. Lord Oxford knows it: all his family and friends know it; but it is to be done with great circumspection. It is now too late to publish a pamphlet, and too early to publish a history.

It was always my opinion, that the best way of doing honour to the treasurer, was to write a history of the peace

of Utrecht, beginning with a short preamble concerning
the calamitous state of our debt, and ending with the
breaking our army and restoring the civil power; that these
things were completed under the administration of the
Earl of Oxford, and this should be his epitaph.[45]

In 1713 Swift saw the matter somewhat differently. His 'large
Treatise' was his offering to Oxford – his opus magnum on
the Lord Treasurer's behalf – it was to pave the way to his
preferment in the Church.

In a curious way, then, *The History of the Four Last Years of
the Queen* had always been linked in his mind with a reward
for his services. In the same letter, dated 11 October 1712, in
which he revealed that he was writing an account of the
peace-making, he also affirmed that 'Something or nothing
will be done in my own Affairs ... if the Latter, I have done
with Courts for ever.' By April 1713, with the conclusion of
peace at Utrecht, and with Swift putting the finishing touches
to his book, the two matters were again connected in his
mind. 'I shall pass next winter here [in London]', he
explained, 'and then I will dun them to give me a Summ of
money.'[46] Defoe had been receiving a quarterly payment of
£100 from secret service funds for his writings on behalf of the
government throughout the years of the Oxford ministry.[47]
That was not Swift's way. He did not consider himself a
hireling, but a private man who had done his country what
service he could out of a disinterested public spirit. Paradoxi-
cally, with peace concluded, he felt entitled to claim his dues.
'I sh[a]ll be ruined or at least sadly crampt unless the Qu—
will give me 100011,' he noted. 'I am sure she owes me a great
deal more.'[48]

Swift's pretence to disinterestedness was stretching a point.
He may have believed in the cause for which he was writing,
but ever since the publication of *The Conduct of the Allies* he had
been waiting for suitable English deaneries to become vacant.
He was not slow in hinting to Oxford when opportunities
arose. On 5 February 1712 he wrote to point out that the
deanery of Wells was now available, with the death of the
incumbent the previous day. 'I entirely submit my good
Fortune to your Lordship,' he claimed rather disingenuously.

A few weeks later he was forced to deny all knowledge of the matter. 'No – if you will have it, I am not Dean of Wells, nor know any thing of being so', he told the ladies, 'nor is there any thing in the Story: & that's enough.'[49]

It was his eagerness for preferment, as much as anything else, that stopped Swift from returning to Ireland in the spring of 1712. True, he suffered a very painful attack of shingles which incapacitated him for a couple of months. The symptoms first appeared on 26 March, and, when the discomfort was at its worst, he did not leave his chamber for a fortnight.[50] But he was determined not to leave England without tangible acknowledgment of his services on behalf of the ministry. The deanery of Wells remained vacant for over a year. Others became available at Ely and Lichfield. Swift would have been happy with any of them, but he was to be disappointed yet again. 'This Morning My Friend Mr Lewis came to me, and shewed me an Order for a Warrant for the 3 vacant Deanryes, but none of them to me', he wrote, 'this was what I always foresaw, and receive the notice of it better I believe than he expected.' Although he professed not to be bitter about the affair, and not to blame Oxford for anything other than 'his not giving me timely notice, as he promised to do, if he found the Qu— would do nothing for me', this time Swift resolved to bring matters to a head. He told Oxford that he 'had nothing to do but to go to Irel[an]d immediatly, for [he] could not with any Reputation stay longer here, unless [he] had somethink honorabl immediatly given to [him].'[51]

Thus Swift came to accept the deanery of St Patrick's, Dublin. He had been working on this safety net for several months, just in case his hopes of preferment in England came to nothing. He exerted all his energy to procure the vacant bishopric of Dromore for the incumbent dean, John Stearne, so that he could take his place at St Patrick's. For once he succeeded. 'I am less out of humor than you would imagine,' he consoled the ladies, '& if it were not that impertinent People will condole with me, as they used to give me Joy, I would value it less.'[52] Swift had got his deanery, but at the price of exile in Ireland. Thus, inauspiciously, began his tenure of the deanery of St Patrick's, which was to last for over thirty years until Dean Swift would become such a well-n name that he could be recognised merely by his initials – J.S.D.D.D.S.P.D. – Jonathan Swift, Doctor of Divinity, Dean of St Patrick's, Dublin.

Why did Swift fail to secure preferment in England? Was it simply that Oxford was unwilling to reward his chief propagandist? Or was there some other reason? Firstly, all English and Irish bishoprics, and English deaneries, were in the gift of the Crown. Queen Anne could be advised whom to appoint, but the responsibility for granting preferment was hers, and hers alone. However much Oxford might wish to press the claims of the Vicar of Laracor, there was no guarantee that he would succeed. And there were a number of reasons for Queen Anne's dislike of Dr Swift. *A Tale of a Tub*, despite the argument of the tardily-issued 'Apology', was firmly believed to have satirised not the abuses of religion, but religion itself, and the last Stuart was a staunch upholder of the Church of England. It is ironic that she thought that one of its most vociferous defenders was a dangerous opponent. Had Swift turned his talents to respectable religious controversy instead of satire, there is every possibility that he would have achieved more in his career in the Church.

The second factor which militated against his rise in the Church appears to have been the ill-advised publication of *The Windsor Prophecy*. Sir David Hamilton, the Queen's Whig physician, offered to show the poem to her, but 'she declin'd to see' it. Subsequently, discussing the vacant deanery of Wells, 'she discours'd of Dr. Swift's Character': 'He was good for some things she said But had not dispos'd of that Benefice to him, nor woud not.' Hamilton knew that 'she was teaz'd to preffer Dr. Swift', but she would not give in. Finally, when Swift was given St Patrick's, 'She discours'd of Dr. Swifts being a Dean in Ireland, saying that all the Deanerys in Ireland were of the Lord Lieutenants gift, but the Bishopricks of Hers.' 'I told Her most knew that she was pressd to prefer him', Hamilton continues, 'and it was Honourable to Her as a Pious Queen, to refuse it!'[53]

The ministers, then, cannot be justly accused of neglecting to push Swift's claims to preferment. He himself exculpates Oxford, who exerted himself to make sure that Swift could be preferred to St Patrick's without any difficulty.[54] He had to settle for the deanery of his own cathedral because the gift was the Lord-Lieutenant's, and the Duke of Ormond was his friend. As Queen Anne steadfastly refused to have anything to do with the author of *A Tale of a Tub* and *The Windsor Prophecy*, there was simply no other way of rewarding his services to the ministry. And so Swift was in no mood to be overscrupulous about money-matters at this juncture. Two and a half years in England had sorely depleted his meagre resources. When he said he intended to 'dun' the ministry for money he was not joking. He wanted an assurance that he would get the sum of £1000 to offset the expenses of installation as dean, and he was certain that the figure was a reasonable one. He looked on the prospect with grim resignation. 'The prints will tell you that I am condemned to live again in Ireland', he wrote to the poet, William Diaper, 'and all that the Court and Ministry did for me, was to let me chuse my station in the country where I am banished.'[55]

Swift set out for Ireland on 1 June 1713, hoping that the journey would restore his health, for he had been suffering from a prolonged attack of his condition of the inner ear. He trusted that 'Riding, and a Sea Voyage' would put him right. Reaching Holyhead on the 10th, he crossed over to Dublin the same day. But far from alleviating his ailment, travel had aggravated it. He hurried to Laracor, having been installed Dean of St Patrick's on the 13th. 'My health has been so ill that I was forced to steal away', he wrote, 'and here I am riding for life.'[56] At Trim, Swift recruited his spirits, just as he had done in 1704 and 1709 on returning from previous visits to England. Although much had happened to him since 1710, he still had had his share of disappointments to vex him and grievances to nurse. Instead of a glorious homecoming, he had had to cross over with an aching head, to take up a post that was hardly his first choice. He 'endeavour[ed] to forget every thing' relating to his life in London. 'At my first coming I thought I should have dyed with Discontent', he wrote, 'and was horribly melancholy while they were installing me, but it begins to wear off, and change to Dullness.'[57]

He had plenty to forget about affairs in England. Oxford and Bolingbroke were once more at each other's throats, and a power struggle was fought out 'in the corridors of

Kensington and Whitehall' in Swift's absence in July and August 1713.[58] 'We are all running headlong into the greatest confusion imaginable', Erasmus Lewis informed him on 9 July. 'I heartily wish you were here, for you might certainly be of great Use to Us by yr endeavours to reconcile, and by representing to 'em the infallible consequences of these Divisons'.[59] Swift had resolved not to leave Ireland 'till I am sent for, and if they have no further service for me, I will never see England again.' Instead he intended 'to look after Willows, and to cutt Hedges than meddle with Affairs of State', as he swallowed the 'bitter Draughts' given him by the 'public'.[60] But he could not fail to respond to a second prompting from Lewis, dated 30 July 1713 from Whitehall, in which Swift was told that 'my Lord Treasurer desires you will make all possible hast over, for we want you extreamly'.[61] On being assured that he would be needed before October, Swift sailed from Dublin on 29 August, and by 9 September he was back in London.[62]

While Erasmus Lewis was encouraging Swift to resume his residence in England, Lord Treasurer Oxford was putting paid to Bolingbroke's hopes – for the time being at least – of replacing him at the head of the ministry. It was in the session of Parliament beginning on 9 April 1713 that Oxford discerned the first indications of a real split in the ranks of the government, 'during which time', he later noted, 'a confederation was made against the Treasurer'.[63] At the end of the session Bolingbroke remarked unequivocally to Auditor Harley that 'if your brother will not set himself at the head of the Church party, somebody must.'[64] Although he was ill for the last fortnight in July, Oxford still managed to defeat the cabal of Bolingbroke, Harcourt, the Bishop of Rochester and Lady Masham. His opponents were 'forced to submit not just to his continued premiership, but to a remodelling of ministerial offices which directly curtailed their own departmental authority and placed "Treasurer's men" at almost every strategic point available'.[65] The appointment of that staunch Harleyite, William Bromley, as Secretary of State in place of Dartmouth, who was 'promoted' to the office of Lord Privy Seal, out of Bolingbroke's firing line, strengthened Oxford's position as Prime Minister. Bolingbroke had not merely been headed off, he had been routed.

When Swift returned from Ireland, then, he found that the 'Quarrells and Coldness' between Oxford and Bolingbroke had got worse. He 'laboured to reconcile them' and 'expostulated with them both, but could not find any good Consequences'. 'Things went on at the same Rate,' he recalled many years later. 'They grew more estranged every day.'[66] This was the background to his final dealings with the Oxford ministry. But he was required to defend the ministry from Whig allegations regarding the safety of the Protestant Succession. Now, if ever, the government needed him to justify the proceedings of the ministers. His first contribution to the common fund of ministerial propaganda was published soon after the October elections, which returned an even larger number of Tories to Parliament than three years before. In *The Importance of the Guardian Considered* and the subsequent *The Publick Spirit of the Whigs: Set Forth in their Generous Encouragement of the Author of the Crisis,* he subjected Richard Steele to a withering attack which reflected not only on his integrity, but upon his 'Candor, Erudition, and Style'. They were Swift's final writings on Oxford's behalf, and were motivated by a mixture of public duty and personal resentment.

Since becoming involved with the ostensibly Tory ministry, Swift's relations with the Whigs had been strained to say the least. For a while he kept on seeing Halifax, but 'very seldom'. Somers, who had proved 'a false decitful rascal', he met for the last time in December 1710. His friendship with Addison declined. As early as October 1710, Swift explained, *'Party* had so possessed him, that he talked as if he suspected me, and would not fall in with any thing I said.' They parted coldly, and by the end of the year were 'hardly meet[ing] once a fortnight'. Soon they were merely 'common acquaintance[s]'.[67] Yet Swift claimed, with some justice, to have stuck to his old friends. He was 'a constant advocate with the Earl of Oxford' for 'many of' them: 'He knows how often I press'd him in favour of Mr. Addison, Mr. Congreve, Mr. Row, and Mr. Steel,' he remarked.[68]

This did not prevent Swift being subjected to more and more abuse in print as the leading ministerial propagandist. His authorship of *The Examiner* and the *Conduct of the Allies* was widely suspected. As far as the Whigs were concerned,

Swift was the 'master genius' called upon by the government to 'take the work' of propaganda 'in hand', and they did not care for what they regarded without compunction as his apostasy.[69] When, on 4 November 1712, he saved Oxford's life by opening a bandbox in which two pistols were placed to go off as a booby-trap, he was accused of attempting to gain preferment for himself by inventing the whole thing. The Whig press ridiculed him mercilessly with suggestions that 'surely now the Bandbox whim/Will help him down to Wells'.[70] 'I believe you have heard the Story of my Escape in opening the Banbox sent to Ld Treasr', he wrote to the ladies, 'the Prints have told a thousand Lyes of it.'[71]

The final indignity, as far as Swift was concerned, occurred in May 1713 as he was about to set out for Ireland. Five weeks earlier he had been present at the rehearsal of Addison's *Cato*, and relations between the Whig wits and himself seemed to be less strained than usual.[72] Then, as Swift wrote to Addison, Steele, in the pages of his journal, *The Guardian*, 'insinuated with the utmost malice, that I was the author of the Examiner; and abused me in the grossest manner he could possibly invent, and set his name to what he had written.'[73] He called Swift a 'miscreant' – an unbeliever. Swift was genuinely shocked. Not only had he been instrumental (or so he believed) in persuading Oxford to allow Steele to retain his position as Commissioner of the Stamp Office in 1710, but, as he explained to Steele himself, when printers brought him their papers in manuscript, he 'absolutely forbid them to give any hints against Mr. Addison and you, and some others; and ... frequently struck out reflexions upon you in particular.' And this was how he was repaid! He wanted to know how Steele would 'be able to defend himself from the imputation of the highest degree of baseness, ingratitude, and injustice'.[74]

Steele was unmoved by Swift's cries of shame. 'They laugh at you', he told him, 'if they make you believe your interposition has kept me thus long in office.' With reason, he believed that Swift was 'an accomplice of the Examiner's', and of course he was. Not only did Swift arrange for William Oldisworth to revive the *Examiner* in December 1711, but he knew how to contact him through Barber the printer, and contributed to his paper from time to time even at this late state.[75] He may never have 'exchanged one syllable' with Oldisworth in his life, as he claimed, nor have seen him 'above twice, and that in mixt company', but he was the *Examiner*'s accomplice nevertheless.[76] 'There are solecisms in morals as well as in languages,' he reminded Steele, but the latter was content to let the matter rest in print with an offhand: 'It is nothing to me whether the Examiner writes against me in the character of an estranged friend, or an exasperated mistress.' In this way he explicitly added insult to injury in dealing with the new Dean of St Patrick's in the same manner in which he would deal with scribblers of the kidney of Delarivière Manley, the author of *The New Atalantis*.[77]

This, then, was the background to Swift's attacks on Steele in the winter of 1713-14. Clearly they had a personal element, and *The Importance of the Guardian Considered* resorts to tactics designed to belittle Steele's character. On 4 June 1713 Steele had resigned as Commissioner of the Stamp Office to take up a Parliamentary career as member for the borough of Stockbridge. Then, in *The Guardian,* he had taken the ministry to task for failing to ensure the demolition of Dunkirk in accordance with the terms of the Treaty of Utrecht. The letter, signed with his own name, in which he repeated three times the statement that 'the *British* Nation expect the immediate Demolition of *Dunkirk*', was subsequently reprinted in its entirety in *The Importance of Dunkirk Consider'd: In Defence of the Guardian Of August the 7th. In A Letter to the Bailiff of Stockbridge.*[78] It was this which gave Swift his cue.

In representing his views (and the views of his Whig friends) as the views of the British nation, Steele was employing synecdoche. Swift pointed out that this was *'figurative Speech, naming the tenth Part for the whole'*. Considering Steele's pamphlet *'partly as a* Critick, *and partly as a* Commentator', he rapped his character, his style and his pretensions. 'To take the height of his Learning', he advised John Snow, the bailiff of Steele's borough of Stockbridge:

you are to suppose a Lad just fit for the University, and sent early from thence into the wide World, where he followed every way of Life that might least improve or preserve the Rudiments he had got. He hath no Invention, nor is Master of a tolerable Style; his chief Talent is Humour, which he sometimes discovers both in Writing and Discourse; for after the first Bottle he is no disagreeable Companion.

Not only was Steele 'the most imprudent Man alive', he had 'committed more Absurdities in Oeconomy, Friendship, Love, Duty, good Manners, Politicks, Religion and Writing, than ever fell to one Man's share'.[79] In *The Importance of the Guardian Considered*, Swift vented the anger and bitterness over the way he had been treated by Steele five months earlier.

It is, then, a different piece of work than his previous political pamphlets, owing more to his *ad hominem* attacks on Godolphin, Wharton and Marlborough, than to works like *The Conduct of the Allies*. Swift's main task was to defend the conduct of the ministry from Whig allegations that the Protestant Succession was in danger under its control. 'One of their present Topicks for Clamour is *Dunkirk*', he explained:

> *First,* It is meant to lay an Odium on the Ministry; *Secondly,* If the Town be soon demolished, Mr. *Steele* and his Faction have the Merit, their Arguments and Threatnings have frighted my Lord Treasurer' *Thirdly,* If the Demolishing should be further deferred, the Nation will be fully convinced of his Lordship's Intention to bring over the *Pretender.*[80]

In such a situation, serious argument could do little good. By denying Whig fears, Swift would be lending them further credence. Instead he sought to expose the propaganda campaign mounted by Richard Steele for what it was by highlighting its motives and objectives. By using his wit to puncture Steele's pretensions through ridicule of the man and his writing, Swift was also hoping to denounce his backers. He employed this strategy not only in *The Importance of the Guardian Considered*, but in *The Publick Spirit of the Whigs: Set Forth in their Generous Encouragement of the Author of the Crisis*.

Pressing on with his efforts to discredit the Oxford ministry,

Steele abandoned the *Guardian* in favour of the more political *Englishman*. On 22 October 1713, subscriptions were called for to promote the publication of a pamphlet called *The Crisis ... With Some Seasonable Remarks On the Danger of a Popish Successor*. Published on 19 January 1714, in the aftermath of Queen Anne's near-fatal illness at the end of December, *The Crisis* was an attempt to influence the meeting of the new Parliament on 16 February. In a rehearsal of the question of the succession since 1688, Steele, 'in a tedious but impressive recital', printed verbatim the laws that had been passed relating to the security of the Protestant Succession. Then he indulged in alarmist comments on the realities of the situation which obtained in 1714 – the recent war with France, the dishonourable peace treaty which had ended the conflict, the continuing threat of French hegemony with the consequences for the English succession, and the existence of numerous Papist claimants to the throne. All this was designed to justify the claim that there was indeed a crisis in British affairs.[81]

The Crisis was heralded by a series of press announcements. Swift was well aware of Steele's plans. *The First Ode of the Second Book of Horace Paraphras'd: And Address'd to Richard St—le Esq*, published on 6 or 7 January 1714, opened thus:

> *DICK*, thour't resolv'd, as I am told,
> Some strange *Arcana* to unfold,
> And with the help of *Buckley*'s Pen
> To vamp the *good Old Cause* again.
> Which thou (such *Bur[ne]t*'s shrewd Advice is)
> Must furbish up and Nickname *CRISIS*.[82]

But, with Parliament about to assemble, Oxford needed more than this poem to offset Steele's challenge. The definitive Swiftian response was published on 23 February and, as Irvin Ehrenpreis quite rightly remarks, 'deserves on several grounds to be described as one of his finest works'.[83]

The chief interest of the *Publick Spirit of the Whigs* lies in the 'Observations' Swift offers 'on the Seasonableness, Candor, Erudition, and Style' of *The Crisis*. Firstly he comments upon the quality of Whig propaganda, and the generosity of the

Whig patrons who require neither wit, style nor argument from their writers. Regardless of the lack of such subtleties, 'The Work shall be reported admirable, sublime, unanswerable; shall serve to raise the sinking Clamours, and confirm the Scandal of introducing Popery and the Pretender, upon the QUEEN and her Ministers'. Once again Swift offers to expose the intentions of Steele and the Whigs:

> IN Popish Countries, when some Imposter cries out, *A Miracle! A Miracle!* it is not done with a Hope or Intention of converting Hereticks, but confirming the deluded Vulgar in their Errors; and so the Cry goes round without examining into the Cheat. Thus the Whigs among us give about the Cry, A *Pamphlet!* A *Pamphlet!* The *Crisis! The Crisis!* Not with a View of convincing their Adversaries, but to raise the Spirits of their Friends, recal their Stragglers, and unite their Numbers by Sound and Impudence; as Bees assemble and cling together by the Noise of Brass.[84]

Swift knew all about this sort of polemical strategy, for *The Conduct of the Allies* had been written to rally the ministry's supporters around the banner of the 'conspiracy thesis', just as Steele was now trying to rally the opposition to the cry of 'the Succession in Danger'.

Having exposed Whig reasons for supporting the author of *The Crisis,* Swift proceeded to 'the most disgustful Task that ever I undertook' – remarking 'upon the Falsehoods and Absurdities' of the pamphlet itself. *The Publick Spirit of the Whigs* really is a critique of Steele's grammar, rhetoric and learning. Three examples will have to suffice. The preface of *The Crisis* is shown to be a plagiarism of Virgil.[85] The second sentence of the pamphlet proper is taken to task for tautology. 'By Liberty', Steele had written, 'I desire to be understood to mean.' 'He *desires to be understood to mean*', Swift mocked, 'that is, he desires to be meant to mean, or to be understood to understand.'[86] The whole of the opening of *The Crisis* is subjected by Swift to a painstaking detection of Steele's plentiful solecisms.

My final example shows Swift trying to teach Steele the art of reader-manipulation. '*We have the Laws, I say, the Laws on our Side,*' Steele had written. 'This elegant Repetition is, I think, a little out of Place', Swift observed. 'For, the Stress might better have been laid upon so great a Majority of the Nation; without which, I doubt the Laws would be of little weight.'[87] Instead of merely resorting to abuse in lieu of argument, Swift criticised the *Crisis* not so much for its content, but for its style. It is a remarkable exercise in literary deflation. Swift appealed 'to all who know the Flatness of [Steele's] Style, and the Barrenness of his Invention' – 'Was he ever able to walk without Leading-strings, or swim without Bladders, without being discovered by his hobbling and his sinking?'[88] The insinuation is clear: Steele's contributions to *The Tatler* and *The Spectator* were dull and insipid – he relied on the wit of others like Addison and Swift. In the paper war between Swift and Steele which had its origins in the May of 1713, the author of *The Crisis* was soundly beaten.

Politics do not necessarily bend to the judgments of art. It was Steele's expulsion from the House of Commons which signalled the ministry's victory over the Whigs' chief propagandist. On 2 March the Queen's speech (in which, appropriately, Swift had had a hand) spoke out against 'some who have arrived to that Height of Malice as to insinuate, that the Protestant Succession in the House of *Hanover* is in Danger under my Government'. This was clearly levelled at *The Crisis,* and the Commons resolved to 'shew their just Abhorrence of the licentious Practices, in publishing scandalous Papers, and spreading seditious Rumours' about the safety of the succession.[89] On 12 March a complaint was made about Steele's writing, and on the 18th he was expelled the House.

However, in the Lords the Queen's speech was turned against the man who had been its stylistic consultant when Wharton, holding up a copy of *The Publick Spirit of the Whigs,* said he knew a libel of the sort condemned by the Queen. Oxford denied all knowledge of the matter, and a resolution was passed that Swift's pamphlet was a 'false, malicious and factious libel'. Swift subsequently bitterly lamented the inadequacy of the protection afforded 'those who scribble for the Government'.[90] John Barber, the printer, and John Morphew, the publisher, were taken into custody, and a search was mounted for the author of the offending pamphlet.

Then a screen was lowered on the findings of the Secretaries of State. Despite the issue of a proclamation offering £300 reward for information leading to the arrest of the author of the *Publick Spirit of the Whigs*, it was common knowledge that Swift 'escaped *Discovery* and *Punishment*' because he was 'under the Wings of some great Men'.[91] Oxford even sent him a bill for £100 to relieve any exigencies he might have in relation to the pamphlet's prosecution.[92] It was a timely intervention, for Swift was 'above 150^{11} in Debt in London' by 1714.[93] But Swift had been forced to admit that he, too, 'scribbled' for the government. *The Publick Spirit of the Whigs* was his final publication on Oxford's behalf. He left London on 31 May 1714 for Letcombe Bassett in Berkshire, happy, no doubt, to be out of harm's way, as the struggle between Oxford and Bolingbroke threatened to split the Tory party asunder.

Although Swift published other writings during his years in London from 1710 to 1714 which were not overtly political in purpose, his literary activities always had an underlying political meaning. Irvin Ehrenpreis observes that:

> Swift had no ear for music, no eye for painting or sculpture, little understanding of architecture, not the faintest interest in dancing. That he was never an amateur of the arts is one of the essential differences between his genius and the modern ideal of the creative imagination. It is not simply an apparent difference in the vocabulary of awareness, but an essential difference in taste and values. Literature for Swift amounted to the intersection of two principles: craftsmanship and morality.[94]

Swift's writings reflect a world view. They recognise a degeneration from a Golden Age. As such, the decline in political institutions from a pristine state was merely one manifestation of a general trend, illustrated in *Gulliver's Travels* through the 'least corrupted' Brobdingnagians, 'whose wise Maxims in Morality and Government, it would be our Happiness to observe'.[95] In writing on behalf of the Oxford ministry, then, Swift believed he was helping to right some of the wrongs that were corrupting British society, not only in the sphere of practical politics, but in other spheres too. There were many vulgar errors to expose and correct. In fact the decay had already reached the English language itself. Swift's *Tatler* essay of 28 September 1710 had drawn attention to 'the continual corruption of our English tongue'.[96] In June 1711 Swift took the idea further in proposing the formation of 'a society or academy for correcting and settling our language, that we may not be perpetually changing as we do'. Oxford 'enter[ed] mightily' into the design, and Swift was encouraged to publish his proposals in the form of a letter to the Lord Treasurer.[97]

A Proposal for Correcting, Improving and Ascertaining the English Tongue finally appeared on 17 May 1712. Swift 'suffer[ed his] name to be put at the End of it', which, he confided to the ladies, 'I nevr did before in my Life.'[98] But by addressing his *Proposal* to Oxford, Swift suggested a political motive, and his eulogistic opening was hardly calculated to allay Whig doubts. There were some, he insinuated, who 'would not have us by any Means think of preserving our Civil or Religious Constitution, because we are engaged in a War abroad'.[99] This indictment of Whig policy was unmistakable. Oxford's achievement, according to Swift and his circle, was that he restored the 'civil power' by putting an end to the war and by 'breaking our army', thus removing the threat the Marlboroughs posed to the constitution itself. And yet Swift evinced surprise that, within two weeks of its publication, the *Proposal* had stimulated '2 Answers ... thô tis no Politicks'.[100]

True, in calling for 'some Method ... for *Ascertaining* and *Fixing* our Language for ever, after such Alterations are made in it as shall be thought requisite', the *Proposal* suggested that 'a free judicious Choice should be made of such Persons, as are generally allowed to be the best qualified for such a Work, without any regard to Quality, Party, or Profession'. The Whigs were to be included in the membership of Swift's 'society or academy', which was to be formed from 'twenty Members of both parties'.[101] But the idea behind the scheme fits in well with Swift's overriding Old Whig or Country attitude to the past. It retains the same nostalgic yearning for a bygone age and the same resistance to change. The language was to be ordered and regulated just as ideally, in Swift's view, the state should be ordered and regulated. He was not totally against neologisms, however. 'Provided, that no Word, which a Society shall give Sanction to, be afterwards antiquated and exploded', he explained, 'they may have Liberty to receive whatever new ones they shall find Occasion for.'[102]

This provides an important clue to Swift's way of thinking. He may not have consciously anticipated the consequences of Orwellian Newspeak, but his concerns were similar. According to the 'Apology', *A Tale of a Tub* 'seems calculated to live at least as long as our Language, and our Tast admit no great Alterations.'[103] Swift was anxious not primarily because of his own claim on posterity. He genuinely appears to have believed that, as a result of the corruption of the language, people 'would hardly be able to understand any thing that was written among us an Hundred Years ago'.[104] And the consequences of this were, or could be, far reaching. *A Tale of a Tub* investigates the 'consequences of linguistic distortion'.[105] So does Orwell's *1984* in which, through Newspeak, works of literature of the past will not merely be incomprehensible, they will actually be altered so that they mean something different from their original meaning. Thus the corruption of language, and the linguistic distortion which could follow on from it, could also be politically subversive.

Concern with linguistic authority is linked to Swift's interest in history. History, too, can distort. In Glubbdubdrib, Gulliver discovers 'how the World had been misled by prostitute Writers'.[106] Swift's own writings explore the relationship between historical truth and contemporary reality. His *Discourse*, as well as his *Examiner* papers on Marlborough and Wharton, exploit 'parallel' history to reveal a modern lesson, while *The Conduct of the Allies* is largely an exercise in contemporary history. But all of them distort and falsify. Whether or not Swift was conscious of this fact in his own writings, he was well aware of such ploys when they were used by his adversaries, as *Mr. C[olli]n's Discourse of Free-Thinking, Put into plain English, by way of Abstract, for the Use of the Poor* illustrates perfectly. Adopting the persona of a Whig Deist, Swift contrives to subvert the import of Anthony Collins's *Discourse of Free-Thinking*. Through distorting Collins's arguments by the addition or omission of a word here and there, Swift takes them to their logical conclusion, demonstrating how the Scriptures can be falsified to support a misleading interpretation. Thus Solomon, Isaiah, Ezekiel, Amos and Jeremiah, as well as Socrates, Plato, Epicurus, Plutarch, Varro, Cato, Cicero and Seneca, are all called Free-thinkers. Abuses in learning are once again employed to promote vulgar errors in religion.

Ultimately this is a political point. Literature is, or can be, used to project a false view of the world. History, in Swift's view, was being written by charlatans, 'prostitute Writers' who were far from objective. When Gilbert Burnet, Bishop of Salisbury, rushed out an *Introduction to the Third Volume* of his *History of the Reformation,* Swift responded with *A Preface to the B[isho]p of S[a]r[u]m's Introduction*, published on 7 December 1713. Although ostensibly a work of historical scholarship, Burnet's *History* bore the burden of Whig propaganda. Begun at the time of the Exclusion Crisis, it had been laid aside. But now *'the Reasons of his engaging in it at first, seemed to return upon him'* – *'the Danger of a Popish Successor in View, and the dreadful Apprehensions of the Power of* France' – so that *'He could delay it no longer'*. He rushed out the *Introduction* as a contribution, not to an objective history, but to the Whig propaganda campaign.[107]

Swift treated Burnet as he treated Steele, censuring both writers for 'that peculiar Manner of expressing himself, which the Poverty of our Language forceth me to call their Stile', and exposing the polemical strategy of each. Burnet's attempt to employ parallel history was taken apart by Swift:

WHEN the Bishop published his History, there was a *Popish* Plot on Foot: The Duke of *York*, a known *Papist*, was presumptive Heir to the Crown; the House of Commons would not hear of any Expedients for securing their Religion under a *Popish* Prince, nor would the King or Lords consent to a Bill of Exclusion: The *French* King was in the Height of his Grandeur, and the Vigour of his Age. At this Day the Presumptive Heir, with that whole illustrious Family, are *Protestants*; the *Popish Pretender* excluded for ever by several Acts of Parliament; and every Person in the smallest Employment, as well as Member in both Houses, obliged to *abjure* him. The *French* King is at the lowest Ebb of Life; his Armies have been conquered, and his Towns won from him for ten Years together; and his Kingdom is in Danger of being torn by Divisions during a long Minority. Are these Cases Parallel? Or are we now in more Danger of *France* and *Popery* than we were thirty Years ago? What can be the Motive for advancing such false, such detestable Assertions?[108]

The same could be said of Swift's own *Discourse*, which also puts forward false parallels for events taking place in England in 1701. He was well aware of the way in which history could be written to produce a totally untrue account of what actually happened.

It was for reasons such as these that he was anxious for his own *History of the Four Last Years of the Queen* to be published. It, too, was an exercise in propaganda – this time on behalf of the government. Swift was confident that it would supply the 'true' history of the peace-making, unlike the 'false' accounts of the Whigs. The *'Great Work'* would lay 'the whole History of' Whiggish 'Iniquity ... in so clear a Light', that there would be no further need of ministerial propaganda.[109] But *The History of the Four Last Years of the Queen* was not published in Swift's lifetime. Nor was he more successful in pressing his claim to the position of Historiographer-Royal in the summer of 1714 – a post he had coveted as early as 1710. It was not that he wanted the revenue, he explained. 'I would not give two Pence to have it for the Value of it', he wrote on 13 July, 'but I had been told ... that the Qu— had a Concern for her History &c: and I was ready to undertake it.'[110] The vacancy had been filled the previous day. Swift was denied even this official recognition of his writings on the government's behalf.

Swift, then, was thwarted in all his practical schemes for the correction of abuses in learning. His academy did not materialise, his *History* languished in manuscript, and his aspirations to the post of Historiographer remained unfulfilled. But the early months of 1714 saw the meetings of the Scriblerus Club take place, and together Swift, Alexander Pope, John Gay, John Arbuthnot, Thomas Parnell and Robert Harley, Earl of Oxford, made an unforgettable contribution to the detection and exposure of false scholarship and bad taste in literature. The Scriblerians not only projected the fictional *Memoirs of Martinus Scriblerus,* that archetypal pedant, but their activities can be seen to have influenced such diverse works as Gay's *Three Hours after Marriage* and *The Beggar's Opera,* Pope's *Peri Bathous: Or, The Art of Sinking in Poetry* and *The Dunciad,* and Swift's own *Gulliver's Travels.* Taking their cue from *A Tale of a Tub,* the Scriblerians played off works of contemporary literature, using parody and burlesque to highlight their dullness.

Pope, Gay and Arbuthnot became Swift's close friends, and their association persisted throughout the long years of exile in Ireland, cut short only by death. Arbuthnot, the Queen's physician, is first mentioned in the *Journal to Stella* in the entry for 19 March 1711.[111] Swift's affection for the author of the 'John Bull' pamphlets was unfeigned. He assured Ford that 'there does not live a better Man.' 'If the World had but a dozen Arbuthnetts in it I would burn my Travells,' he wrote when working on his account of Gulliver's experiences in Lilliput and Brobdingnag, Laputa and Houyhnhnmland.[112] Swift's acquaintance with Pope was more recent, and their friendship developed from the end of 1713 onwards. Through Pope, Swift got to know John Gay who came up to town for the winter. He already knew Parnell, an Irish clergyman whom he introduced to Bolingbroke in the hope that 'a little friendly forwarding' might make his fortune.[113]

The Scriblerus Club helped to take Swift's mind off the disturbing developments that were taking place in the spring and early summer of 1714. He was at his happiest in pursuit of *la bagatelle.* Oxford, too, was invited to 'come and take part in/The Memoirs of Martin', when the Scriblerians met at Arbuthnot's chambers in St James's Palace. It is often hard to remember that their gatherings took place for such a short space of time. Swift's involvement ended at the end of May 1714 when he left for Berkshire. Arbuthnot asked him to 'Remember Martin, who is an innocent fellow, & will not disturb your solitude', but Swift thought that 'To talk of Martin in any hands but [Arbuthnot's], is a Folly.'[114] He abandoned the project at an early stage, even though the *Memoirs of Martinus Scriblerus* were appended to editions of his works in the eighteenth century.

Not even *la bagatelle* could take Swift's mind off the quarrel between Oxford and Bolingbroke at this juncture. After a final meeting with them, during which Swift 'spoke very freely to them both', he told them he would 'retire', for 'all was gone'.[115] Despite the successes of the summer of 1713, Oxford had been unable to consolidate his position. The Whigs continued to harass him over the safety of the Protestant Succession, and they were joined by 'Whimsical' Tories like Hanmer and Anglesey in the face of Bolingbroke's manoeuvrings, who hoped that, by persuading the Pretender to turn Protestant, he might yet replace Oxford at the head of the government. The first months of 1714, therefore, saw Oxford not only defending his position against the Whigs, but fighting a rearguard action against Bolingbroke and his supporters.

He made mistakes. After finalising his son's marriage to the wealthy heiress of the late Duke of Newcastle, Oxford invoked the Queen's displeasure for the first time by asking that the dukedom be conferred on the young man. He later bitterly regretted his 'never enough to be lamented folly in mentioning to her Majesty the titles'.[116] This *faux pas* was quickly followed by the death of his favourite daughter in November 1713. Swift wrote him a compassionate letter on the occasion, and there can be no doubt that the loss affected Oxford deeply.[117] He began to appear before the Queen drunk and unfit for business. By this time he was experiencing genuine difficulty in making himself understood.[118] Bolingbroke took his chance. On two occasions in the spring of 1714 Oxford's resolution wavered, and he toyed with the idea of resignation.[119] Finally he roused himself, and made a determined effort to wreck Bolingbroke's schemes, and to stand by the Protestant Succession he had done so much to bring about.

'The Dragon dy's hard,' Arbuthnot told Swift on 26 June. 'He is now kicking & cuffing about him like the divill.'[120] He was seeing the Queen on business once more, and concerting policy with his ministerial allies. But it was too late. On 27 July a desperately weak Queen Anne relieved him of office. Four days later, she appointed to the Lord Treasurership, not the eager Bolingbroke, but the trusty Duke of Shrewsbury. The following day she died. 'The Earl of Oxford was removed on Tuesday; the Queen died on Sunday', Bolingbroke lamented,

'What a world is this and how does Fortune banter us'.[121] The event he had been working for had happened before he had had time to lay his plans, and the Hanoverians succeeded peacefully to the throne of Great Britain.

Swift was still in Berkshire at his friend, John Geree's, awaiting 'the Issue' of the 'Conflict' between Oxford and Bolingbroke. He had foreseen 'the Earl of Oxford's disgrace'.[122] He had not anticipated the premature accession of George I. Whatever plans he had made to return to London on Bolingbroke's triumph were rendered redundant. He knew that he could have no place in the new scheme of things, he was too much involved with the old ministers. Indeed he feared for his life. His days of influence were over, and all he had secured for his pains was the deanery of St Patrick's. For most of his life he had been endeavouring to 'cross the *Irish* Seas,/ To live in Plenty, Power and Ease', but without success. Now he was to be banished yet again to his native Ireland. He loved hobnobbing with the great and powerful. He had enjoyed his friendships with men of quality in England, his visits with the ministers to Windsor, his familiarity with the Court of St James's. Now all that was over. No wonder the reward of the deanery of St Patrick's turned to ashes in his mouth, for in the end his association with the Oxford ministry had brought nothing but disappointments and depression. In October 1713 he had addressed *Part of the Seventh Epistle of the First Book of Horace Imitated* to Oxford. Now some of the couplets began to ring true:

> I have Experience dearly bought,
> You know I am not worth a Groat:
> But you resolved to have your Jest,
> And 'twas a Folly to Contest:
> Then since you now have done your worst,
> Pray leave me where you found me first.[123]

But that was impossible. Swift had tasted greatness. For the rest of his life he would constantly be turning over the events of the reign of Queen Anne in his mind, refining them and polishing them until they shone with the brightness of gold in his memory, and the death of Queen Anne became emblematic of the fall of man.

Part Three
Hibernian Patriot, 1714–1745

10
Exile

On Monday, 16 August 1714, Swift mounted his horse at Letcombe Regis, and rode north to Holyhead, and thence to Ireland. Arriving on the 24th, he began a sojourn which was to last uninterrupted for more than a decade – the longest period he had stayed in his native land as an adult. Neither the country nor the inhabitants were congenial to him. 'Being in England onely renders this Place more hatefull to me', he complained, 'which Habitude would make tolerable.'[1] He was afforded the opportunity to make an extended experiment. Although he hoped to keep his resolution 'of never medling with Irish Politicks', it was to be as a patriot that he would capture the hearts of his countrymen, and engrave the name of the 'great Dean' on the national consciousness.[2]

That was in the future. The situation was far different in 1714. Ostensibly Swift had been forced to return because he needed to take the oaths of allegiance as Dean of St Patrick's to the new king within three months of George I's accession to the throne.[3] But, once in Ireland, he was removed from immediate danger at the hands of vengeful Whigs. This did not prevent him feeling the effects of the backlash in Dublin, and the erstwhile favourite of Oxford and Bolingbroke was subjected to gleeful attacks in print, and the worst that rumour could do to make him uncomfortable. Encouraged by his friends to go back to England, he offered several reasons for staying put, including his poor financial circumstances and the *Publick Spirit*. He knew that he was better off where he was. Besides, he doubted, with reason, whether 'the Present Government' would give him a licence of absence. For the time being, the Dean of St Patrick's was in residence in Dublin.[4]

Reliable news from England gradually filtered through, providing little encouragement for him to change his mind. Both Bolingbroke and Oxford had hoped for favour from the new King. They were quickly disabused. Bolingbroke was dismissed on 31 August on George I's direct order. He withdrew into the country. On hearing of his retirement, Swift wrote him a friendly letter. 'I would give all I am worth, for the sake of my country, that you had left your mantle with some body in the House of Commons', he lamented, 'or that a dozen honest men among them had ... so many shreds of it.'[5] Oxford had trimmed his sails, and might have expected some indulgence at the hand of the new King in view of his struggle with the extreme elements in the Tory party. 'I had the honour in the two preceding reigns to express my love to my country by promoting what is now come to pass,' he wrote to Hanover on 6 August, 'your majesty's succession to the crowns of these kingdoms.'[6] But he was treated shabbily when he kissed the King's hand on his landing at Greenwich on 18 September. George I stared at him in silent contempt as Dorset introduced him as 'the Earl of Oxford, of whom your majesty must have heard'.[7]

Swift's friends, then, were completely excluded from Court. Marlborough had returned from his self-imposed continental exile on news of Queen Anne's death, and was reappointed Captain-General. The Lords of the Junto were given posts to a man. Even the Earl of Nottingham – Swift's old adversary, Dismal – was found a Cabinet position in view of his apostasy in 1711. The Whigs were rampant. By December 1714, as one contemporary claimed, 'hardly one Tory [was] left in any place, though never so mean a one'.[8] The Hanoverian Succession fatally wounded the old Tory party, although Bolingbroke's despairing observation of September, 'the Tory party is gone', was premature, if in character.[9] It lingered on, without support of any kind at the centre of power, until dealt the *coup de grâce* at the polls in January 1715 when the Tory majority in the House of Commons was decimated.[10]

In this new world, who could blame the Dean of St Patrick's for remaining on the far side of the Irish Sea? He had never wielded political influence in his own right; he had merely enjoyed 'a good degree of confidence' with the Oxford ministry.[11] His small stock of personal courage dwindled perceptibly. It may simply have been bantering exaggeration which made him describe himself as 'a greater Coward than ever' soon after his arrival in Ireland,[12] and yet, his confidence shattered, Swift seems to have surrendered himself to depression. Depression gave way to illness. He found himself listless, and he complained constantly of 'the generall Languor this Country gives one'.[13] Troubled 'with perpetual colds and twenty ailments',[14] almost certainly psychosomatic in character, he felt that he could not 'think nor write in this Country'. 'My time passes in doing nothing, which makes me so busy that I have not leisure for anything else.' Write? 'I can as easily fly!'*Some Considerations upon the Consequences hoped and feared from the Death of the Queen,* which he began in England on 9 August, lay unfinished, with not 'one Syllable' added.[15]

Engulfed by waves of self-pity, Swift managed to pen some twenty-eight lines, *In Sickness,* more remarkable for their reflection of his state of mind at this juncture than for any poetical merit:

> 'Tis true, – then why should I repine,
> To see my Life so fast decline?
> But, why obscurely here alone?
> Where I am neither lov'd nor known.
> My State of Health none care to learn;
> My Life is here no Soul's Concern.
> And, those with whom I now converse,
> Without a Tear will tend my Herse.[16]

Swift felt a stranger in the country of his birth – an exile in a hostile environment. Moreover, he lived 'obscurely'. His cushion of fame and influence had been removed, and his inveterate insecurity was once again in possession of his soul. 'The Person who brought me your Letter delivered it in such a Manner, that I thought I was at Court again, and that the Bearer wanted a Place,' he wrote on receiving a letter from a new acquaintance, Knightley Chetwode, 'and ... I had my Answer ready to give him after Perusall, that I would do him what Service I could.' For a moment, he had forgotten where he was, and was, in his imagination, back where he wanted to be, rubbing shoulders with Prime Ministers and Secretaries of State, Dukes, Earls and Viscounts. And then he remembered. 'I recollected I was in Ireland, that the Queen was dead, the Ministry changed, and I was onely the poor Dean of St. Patrick's.'[17]

Swift's isolation was almost total. With the exception of the ladies, all the friends he really cared about were in England, mostly in difficulties. In this frame of mind, Swift turned, quite naturally, to justifying his own conduct, and the actions of his friends. *Memoirs, Relating To That Change which happened in the Queen's Ministry in the Year 1710*, although never published in Swift's lifetime, was written in October 1714. In its much more personal approach, it is of a piece with *In Sickness*. The timidly courageous Swift of the polemical pamphlets – the author of *The Conduct of the Allies* or *An Excellent New Song* – is nowhere to be seen. The *Memoirs* were not designed as a public utterance, simply as 'an entertainment to those who will have any personal regard for me or my memory'.[18] A work of therapy, it is the preserve of the biographer, rather than of the critic or the historian. Polemic would serve no purpose now. *Some free Thoughts upon the present State of Affairs,* which Swift had been anxious to publish prior to the Queen's death, remained unprinted; *Some Considerations* was left unfinished. 'The — take this country', Swift remarked bitterly to Bolingbroke on 14 September, 'it has, in three weeks, spoiled two as good sixpenny pamphlets, as ever a proclamation was issued out against.'[19]

Gradually, Swift regained his mental composure and his physical vigour, but it was a drawn-out process. Enforced activity was an ally in the battle against depression. His brief visit to Dublin on his installation as Dean of St Patrick's in 1713 had been insufficient to settle his affairs, and so there was work to do. 'A man who is new in a house, or an office, has so many important nothings to take up his time', he observed, 'that he cannot do what he would.'[20] And Swift had both to deal with. Even the deanery required work. He had to dismiss old servants and recruit new ones, have shelves built for his library and a chimney-piece made. All this took up time and needed supervision. Idleness was giving way to business, as Swift sought to occupy his mind not with art, nor with great affairs of state, but with the humdrum routine of being Dean of St Patrick's, Dublin.

Swift often wished to leave the tedium of Dublin life behind him. After all, he had little enough company there in the beginning, where he 'live[d] a country-life in town, see[ing] no body, and go[ing] every day once to prayers'.[21] Hester Johnson and Rebecca Dingley no longer lived in Dublin, but they were regular visitors of Archdeacon Walls and his wife in Queen Street. Otherwise, at this juncture, Swift appeares to have enjoyed the society of very few people. It is apparent that, as was his custom, he had travelled immediately to Trim on his arrival in Ireland,[22] but his 'acre of ground' at Laracor had 'gone to ruin'. 'The wall of my apartment' – the little wooden cabin he had built himself – 'is fallen down, and I want mud to rebuild it, and straw to thatch it,' he told Bolingbroke. 'Besides, a spiteful neighbour has seized on six feet of ground, carried off my trees, and spoiled my grove [of willows].'[23] He had been invited to visit Woodbrooke, near Portarlington, the country seat of Knightley Chetwode, but he was forced to postpone his journey until the end of October 1714. When he finally set out, he was met near Trim by a messenger. Vanessa had followed him to Ireland!

The arrival of Esther Vanhomrigh enlarged his small social world, but not without anguish. Clearly Stella and Vanessa were kept apart. 'I ever told you, you wanted Discretion,' Swift responded to the news that Vanessa had landed. 'Nor shall you know where I am till I come, & then I will see you.'[24] They cannot have met until his return to Dublin late in November 1714, but within a very short space of time his new association was being openly discussed. 'This morning a Woman who does business for me told me she heard I was in — with one — naming you, and twenty particulars,' he wrote towards the end of the year. 'I ever feared the Tattle of this nasty Toun; and told you so.'[25] He advised less frequent visits. 'Tattle by the help of Discretion will wear off.' Vanessa was far from pleased. 'If you continue to treat me as you do, you will not be made uneasy by me long,' she rejoined. ''Tis impossible to describe what I have suffer'd since I saw you last, I am sure I could have bore the Rack much better than

those killing, killing, words of yours.'[26] The relations of Swift
and Esther Vanhomrigh in Ireland were more complicated
than when they met in London 'over a Pott of Coffee, or an
Orange and Sugar in the Sluttery'.[27]

Swift often sought to escape from the various pressures of
Dublin life to the quiet of the countryside. At Woodbrooke,
he found himself in 'tolerable Health', though still affected by
'Lazyness'.[28] Chetwode invited him to Martry for Christmas,
but Swift went instead to Belcamp, five miles north of Dublin,
one the first of many visits to the ancestral home of the
Grattan family. By the end of March his feet were itchy once
more. 'I have been these ten weeks resolving every week to go
down to Trim,' he wrote on the 31st, revealing for the first
time his plan to go 'half round Ireland'.[29] During May 1715
he journeyed not only to Trim, where he met up with
Chetwode again, but to Martry, and thence to Gaulstown
House, the seat of the Rochfort family, where he was
entertained by Robert Rochfort, the Chief Baron of the
Exchequer. Increasingly Swift found himself being invited to
stay with friends of some consequence in a circle around
Dublin, and this gave him the opportunity to break away
from his chores as Dean of St Patrick's. From Gaulstown he
accompanied Chetwode to Woodbrooke, and spent some time
in Athy, inspecting deanery lands which he had been trying
to visit ever since his return to Ireland. He did not arrive back
in Dublin until the middle of June.[30] This first circuit was the
archetype of the many such tours he would make in the long
years to come.

All sorts of things had been going on in his absence. On 27
March 1715, Bolingbroke had fled to France to forestall Whig
attempts to exact personal retribution for his acts as Secretary
of State. It proved to be 'an enormous blunder',[31] at once
proclaiming his guilt, and preventing for many years his
return to the English political scene. Of course his correspondence with the Court of the Pretender at St Germains was
widely suspected, the General Election of 1715 had seen the
routing of the Tory party, and Bolingbroke feared for his
head. It placed his friends in jeopardy. Not only was Swift
thought to sympathise with Jacobitism, but some of his closest
associates, such as Charles Ford and Knightley Chetwode,

were tainted with support for the cause. Ford had already left for France. As for Chetwode, that distasteful gentleman, he once observed to Swift that he was 'more attached' to Bolingbroke than Swift was aware.[32] Swift moved within Jacobite circles: he could hardly avoid being smeared with the charge of Jacobitism himself.

In May, while Swift was on his travels, letters addressed to him were intercepted. They were discovered when one Mr Jeffreys was searched on landing in Ireland. Although there was little or nothing in the correspondence to incriminate Swift, the new Secretary of State, James Stanhope, was informed. His Under-Secretary expected the papers to be 'treasonable', and advocated 'confinement' for Swift, or 'very good and sufficient bail' at the very least, but Archbishop King explained that 'they seemed to acquit the Dean by complaining of his not writing, which they interpreted as a forbidding him to write'.[33] No wonder that, in *Gulliver's Travels,* Swift indignantly attacks the whole machinery of the government in relation to letters, ciphers, and the subterfuge of alleged traitors. Jeffreys was represented to be 'an ingenious man' who knew *'arcana imperii'* which was not to be passed by correspondence. One particular passage in a letter from John Barber to Swift was thought to be 'of no small importance to his Majesty's service', as it related specifically to Bolingbroke's flight:

> Two days before the *Captain* went abroad he sent for me, and amongst other things, asked me with great earnestness, If there was no possibility of sending a Letter safe to your hands. I answer'd, I knew but of one way and that was to direct to you under cover to Mrs Van[homrigh]. He reply'd no way by Post wou'd do. I then said tho I was lame and ill, I would go over with it myself if he pleased. He thanked me, and said I should hear from him in a Day or two, but I never saw him more.[34]

Clearly, as Archbishop King observed, 'could the last instructions' mentioned in this letter 'be intercepted', then Swift might be fully implicated in a plot to bring in the Pretender.[35] Swift kept in touch with developments as he journeyed around Ireland. Indeed he half expected a messenger to arrive at Woodbrooke to place him under confinement,[36] but he was allowed to return to Dublin unmolested. Meanwhile, on 10 June 1715, the House of Commons had impeached both Oxford and Bolingbroke for high treason, and for high crimes and misdemeanours against the state. 'God be thanked I have yet no parliamentary business', Swift wrote on the 28th, 'and if they have none with me, I shall never seek their acquaintance.'[37] Then on 9 July Oxford was committed to the Tower of London to await his trial. To his immense credit, Swift's loyalty to his disgraced friend never wavered. In fact there is a hint that he resolved to risk all in joining Oxford at his time of trouble. 'I was upon the balance two hours whether I should not take out a license of absence immediately upon a letter I received,' he told Chetwode, 'but at last I thought I was too late by a week for the design; and so I am dropped again into my old insipidness.'[38] None the less Swift wrote to Oxford, offering his 'poor Service and Attendance' in his distress. By then Oxford was in the Tower. 'I shall take the liberty of thinking and calling You, the ablest and faithfullest Minister, and truest Lover of Your Country that this Age hath produced,' Swift assured him, in terms that even eclipse his high praise of Sir William Temple, 'And I have already taken Care that you shall be so represented to Posterity, in spight of all the Rage and Malice of Your Enemyes.'[39]

Again we see the importance Swift placed on the accurate recording of history. No one could accuse him of ingratitude, the blackest of sins in his own eyes. On hearing news of the impeachments, and regardless of his own recent trouble over the intercepted letters, Swift sat down to write *An Enquiry into the Behaviour of the Queen's Last Ministry.* 'You know how well I lov'd both Lord Oxford and Bolingbroke, and how dear the Duke of Ormond is to me', he wrote to Pope, 'do you imagine I can be easy while their enemies are endeavouring to take off their heads?'[40] Ormond's impeachment, voted on 21 June, seems to have been the last straw, as Swift's concern for his own safety was submerged beneath his compassion for the plight of his friends, and his indignation at the treatment being meted out to them by the avenging Whigs. The first chapter of Swift's *Enquiry*, written in June 1715, drew particular attention to Ormond's attainder, 'which indeed neither ... I, nor I believe any one Person in the three Kingdoms did ever pretend to foresee; and now it is done, it looks like a Dream.'[41] As Lord-Lieutenant, Ormond had been responsible for preferring Swift to the deanery of St Patrick's.

The *Enquiry* was Swift's defence of Oxford, Bolingbroke and Ormond against the charges brought against them by the House of Commons. He proposed to examine two points:

> First how far these Ministers are answerable to their
> Friends for their Neglect, Mismanagement and mutuall
> Dissensions; and Secondly with what Justice they are
> accused by their Enemies for endeavouring to alter the
> Succession of the Crown, in favor of the Pretender.[42]

'As my own Heart was free from all treasonable Thoughts', Swift insisted, in an attempt to pre-empt the question of his friends' being in the interest of the Pretender, 'so I did little Imagine my self to be perpetually in the Company of Traytors.'[43] But Bolingbroke was already in France, to be joined by Ormond around the beginning of August 1715. True, Bolingbroke had steered well clear of the Court of the Pretender at first, protesting his loyalty to the Hanoverian Succession. In July, however, when Swift was at work on his written justification of his conduct, Bolingbroke accepted an earldom from the Pretender, and was appointed Secretary of State.

As Bolingbroke's biographer points out, 'Events were soon to prove that this was an even greater blunder than his original decision to flee from England.'[44] In September 1715 the Earl of Mar raised the Pretender's standard in Scotland. After the abortive rebellion, it would have been foolish to claim that Bolingbroke and Ormond had not wished to alter the succession. Both were among the Pretender's closest advisers. Indeed Bolingbroke was dismissed from his post as Secretary of State in March 1716 because of his part in the fiasco. No wonder, then, that Swift limited his discussion of the behaviour of the Queen's last ministry to answering the charges of neglect and mismanagement, laying as much of the blame for shortcomings as he could on the Queen herself. He left alone the accusation of treason, returning to it only in the summer of 1717 when the charges against Oxford were dismissed. Swift remained silent throughout the trials and tribulations of his friends. He was either unable or reluctant to publish anything in their defence at the time. And so the question of his own sympathy for Jacobitism is left unanswered, there existing no contemporary evidence which can be brought to bear on the case.[45]

On 28 June 1715, in a letter to Pope, Swift supplied a graphic description of his life in exile during these months:

> You are to understand that I live in the corner of a vast unfurnished house; my family consists of a steward, a groom, a helper in the stable, a foot-man, and an old maid, who are all at board-wages, and when I do not dine abroad, or make an entertainment, (which last is very rare) I eat a mutton-pye, and drink half a pint of wine: My amusements are defending my small dominions against the Arch-Bishop, and endeavouring to reduce my rebellious Choir.[46]

Chapter affairs took up an increasing amount of his time. As we have seen, he was a staunch defender of the Church of Ireland in both spiritual and temporal matters. Now he put his mind to the task of defending the rights and privileges of the Liberty of St Patrick's within the city of Dublin, and, incidentally, his own powers as Dean. Although he had enjoyed the confidence of Archbishop King to some degree when a confidant of the greatest men in England, Swift was often to find him an uncomfortable neighbour and superior in the new scheme of things, for King was an ardent Whig. As Louis A. Landa points out, the Liberty of St Patrick's was an *imperium in imperio*: 'it was geographically within the archbishop's Liberty of St. Sepulchre, yet it was essentially free of the archbishop's jurisdiction.'[47] Any attempted encroachment in the Liberty of St Patrick's was met with determined resistance by Dean Swift. In temporal matters, King was prudent enough to leave the Dean well alone. But he occasionally tried to exert his influence in the spiritual sphere, principally by supporting men within the Chapter who would counterbalance Swift's power.

In fact, in his first years in Dublin, it was relations with his Chapter which most troubled Swift. He held many of his powers as Dean only in conjunction with this Chapter, and therefore room for disagreement was large. This makes it appear as if his career as Dean existed in 'an atmosphere of bickering and litigiousness',[48] as he fought for full control of what he imagined to be his inalienable and unassailable rights. One controversy had its origins in the months following his installation. The College of the Vicars Choral possessed land endowments, and, as a corporation, sought to exercise, in its own right, the power to make leases. Swift would have none of it. He challenged this assumed right to proceed 'without the consent of the Dean and Chapter'. He threatened to 'immediately deprive every Man of them who consents to any Lease without the Approbation aforesaid, and shall think the Church well ridd of such men who to gratify their unreasonable Avarice would starve their Successors'.[49]

Here we see Dean Swift in characteristic pose, defending the rights of his Chapter, and, through theirs, his own, acting firmly and decisively to remedy an abuse of privilege. It is also worth noting his concern for the state of the Church of Ireland as an institution. This important feature of his role as clergyman can be seen quite clearly in his insistence on the temporal, as well as the spiritual, well-being of his successors. Swift, it should be emphasised, was not, on his appointment, a popular choice. 'They have made Swift Dean of St. Patrick's,' wrote Robert Molesworth. 'This vexes the godly party beyond expression.'[50] The clergy of Ireland were thought to 'Detest Dr Swift because they think him an Enemy to the Order'.[51] He was no such thing, but he had to prove his point. He was not to be taken on trust. 'I hear you will meet with great difficulty with your Chapter', Knightley Chetwode warned him in December 1714, but Swift was not so sure. 'I design great things at my visitation, and I believe my Chapter will join with me,' Swift replied. 'I hear they think me a smart Dean; and that I am for doing good.'[52]

Louis A. Landa has supplied an invaluable corrective of the

earlier view of Swift's relations with his Chapter. Orrery claimed that 'like the rest of the kingdom, [they] received him with great reluctance', but that 'in a short time after his arrival, not one member of that body offered to contradict him, even in trifles', they were so well reduced to 'reason and obedience'.[53] Swift's reception was not as uniformly and severely hostile as Orrery would make it appear. Nor, on the other hand, was his assertion of authority so speedily and universally accepted. For the first few years of his exile, the affairs of St Patrick's occupied his time more than he liked. On numerous occasions he had to turn down invitations to go into the country. It would also be reasonable to assume that one of the reaons he failed to write anything of note for several years after his return from England was his preoccupation with Church matters. His handling of problems such as the case of the 'singing men' (as he scathingly referred to the Vicars Choral) cemented his relationship with his Chapter. 'My Chapter joins with me,' he wrote on 27 September 1714, 'we have consulted a lawyer, who (as it is usuall) makes ours a very good case; my desires in that point are very moderate, only to break the lease, and turn out nine singing men.'[54] The affair was a long, drawn-out one, but in the end the singing men gave in.[55]

And yet the desired unity had not come about by 1717, when Swift wrote to Atterbury that 'To oppose me in everything relating to my station, is made a merit in my Chapter'.[56] The previous year, his Chapter had challenged his right of veto, which, he was confident, 'is what the deans of this Cathedral have possessed for time immemorial, and what has never been once disputed'.[57] Atterbury could offer no evidence to support the idea of the Dean's negative voice. Swift was not one to give in easily. He was beginning, in his own stubborn way, to enjoy these ecclesiastical power-struggles. By the 1720s he was starting to have his way in most things relating to the running of St Patrick's Cathedral, and the lines along which the Chapter would run until the time of his death had been laid. 'It is an infallible maxim', he wrote in 1721, 'that not one thing here is done without the Dean's Consent.'[58] Similarly despite disagreements with his Archbishop over preferment in particular, Swift's relations with

King subsided into an easygoing friendship, after the friction of the first years of the Hanoverian Succession. On occasion King still attempted to interfere in Chapter affairs, but he no longer even hinted at Swift's Jacobitism. Soon they were to join forces in the defence of their country against the threat posed by the copper coinage of William Wood.

In addition, Swift's prospects slowly began to improve in the wider sphere. Oxford was finally discharged from custody in the Tower of London on 1 July 1717. Bolingbroke was waiting for a pardon from George I. Swift's friends and associates were in a much better position than in 1714. Accompanying this change in personal fortunes, was the gradual return of his relish for letters. When Oxford was given his liberty, Swift not only wrote to ask if he might share his hours of retirement in Herefordshire, he returned to work on *An Enquiry into the Behaviour of the Queen's Last Ministry* – apparently the first writing he had attempted for a full two years apart from a poem also addressed *To The Earl of Oxford, Late Lord Treasurer. Sent to him when he was in the Tower, before his Tryal. Out of Horace.* With his friends out of danger, and things 'tolerably quiet' at last, Swift's urge to write returned.[59] 'If You are once got into *la bagatelle*,' Matthew Prior told him, 'You may despise the World.'[60] And increasingly Swift did begin to enjoy once again the light-hearted literary games he had played not only in London, but throughout his life.

He was greatly assisted in such pursuits by Charles Ford, Thomas Sheridan and Patrick Delany. Ford, in many ways Swift's most valuable and trusted friend, returned to Dublin in the late summer of 1718 from his voluntary continental exile, and stayed until the autumn. He found Swift employed in trifles with Sheridan, writing verse-letters with his left hand, and plagued with the latter's 'base verses'.[61] Swift also composed a verse-letter in a less flippant vein, *To Mr. Delany*, to accompany some lines in prose dated 10 November 1718:

> To You, whose Virtues I must own
> With shame, I have too lately known;
> To you, by Art and Nature taught
> To be the Man I long have sought,
> Had not ill Fate, perverse and blind,

> Plac'd you in Life too far behind;
> Or what I should repine at more,
> Plac'd me in Life too far before;
> To you the Muse this Verse bestows,
> Which might as well have been in Prose;
> No Thought, no Fancy, no Sublime,
> But simple Topicks told in Rime.[62]

Delany was 'as easy a man in conversation as I have known', Swift told Pope.[63] But although the author of *Observations upon Lord Orrery's Remarks* was singled out as 'the Man I long have sought', Sheridan was Swift's 'Viceroy Trifler', as he turned to *la bagatelle* as a form of therapy, 'to divert the vexation of former thoughts, and present objects'.[64]

Thomas Sheridan, the father of Swift's biographer, and grandfather of the playwright, Richard Brinsley Sheridan, was a schoolmaster and clergyman. He was twenty years younger than Swift. Their acquaintance 'probably began in 1717', and soon Sheridan was 'Swift's closest Irish friend'.[65] As learned as he was witty, Sheridan was not only 'the best scholar in both kingdoms', according to Swift, but 'the best School-master here in the Memory of Man'.[66] Although it was a decade after the friendship began that Sheridan implored Swift to 'Let me be your Gay, and Stella be Pope,/We'll wean you from sighing for England I hope', it is clear that he fulfilled such a function from the outset. Sheridan was the nearest Ireland had to offer to the humour, wit and raillery of the Scriblerus Club. He was of an age with Gay and Pope. When Swift, Stella and Sheridan were together, 'there's nothing that is dull.'[67] Swift agreed, assuring the absent Ford that, were he to forsake London for Dublin, 'The Dean and Sheridan, I hope,/Will half supply a Gay and Pope'.[68]

To Mr. Delany gives an idea of what Swift saw in his new Irish friends. We have seen how he loved raillery, but lamented that it was not an Irish forte. In this poem he describes the 'Three Gifts for Conversation fit' – 'Humor, Raillery and Witt'. Although hard to define, 'Wit and Humor differ quite,/That gives Surprise, and this Delight'. Raillery grew out of both. 'That Irony which turns to Praise' was 'an obliging Ridicule' – flattery 'with [a] peculiar Air'. In Swift's view, Sheridan, at this early stage in their relationship, did not understand raillery, 'Because the Diff'rence lyes abstruse/ 'Twixt Raillery and gross Abuse', and he had written a number of papers 'out of all the Rules of Raillery'.[69] The fault was quickly rectified, and Swift grew to cherish Sheridan's friendship:

> Altho a great Dunce I be
> Happy if once I be
> with my Friend Punsiby.[70]

In this recently published fragment, Swift's affection for the author of *Ars Pun-ica, sive Flos Linguarum: The Art of Punning; or the Flower of Languages* – the book which gave Sheridan the pseudonym, Tom Punsibi – is clearly to be seen.

Sheridan's contribution to Swift's rehabilitation, then, was vital. At this juncture he was still unable to concentrate on writing prose, the medium in which he expressed his serious thoughts. 'I can now express in a hundred words', he complained to Bolingbroke in 1719, 'what would formerly have cost me ten.' 'Towards six years older' than he had been in England, he was 'twenty years duller'.[71] 'I write nothing but Verses of late', he explained, 'and they are all Panegyricks.'[72] Trying desperately to fight off the effects of Ménière's disease, he thought first of a visit to England, and then as far afield as Aix-la-Chappelle, but had to content himself with a three-month 'ramble about this Scurvy Country' in the summer of 1719.[73] There was no marked improvement in his state of health. The opening months of 1720 found him 'Lazy and listless', troubled by a 'giddy head', and 'perpetuall ill Health'. He was 'deaf for three or four days together' every 'five or six weeks'. 'I cannot think of a Journy to England', he told Ford, 'till I get more Health and Spirits.'[74]

Whether or not it was a reflection of his own ill health, Swift's poems of these years display an increasing scatological element, as if his assessment of human capabilities was declining in proportion to his person vigour. He penned strange 'Panegyricks'. In 1719 the first of his 'Progress' poems were written, *Phillis, Or, the Progress of Love* and *The Progress of Beauty,* to be followed in 1722 by *The Progress of Marriage.* In a

number of ways they are the prototypes of the later 'excremental' poems, *The Lady's Dressing Room, Strephon and Chloe,
Cassinus and Peter* and *A Beautiful Young Nymph Going to Bed.*
Certain features are common to all – a desire to strip man
of his pretensions to remind him of his own mortality and
the vanity of human wishes – and rhetorical ploys recur, as
Swift, concentrating on specific instances of human folly,
works through metonymy to draw attention to the range
of mankind's weaknesses and shortcomings. It is in this
ironic sense, presumably, that he refers to them as 'Panegyricks'.

   Swift did write one genuine panegyric in 1719, *On Stella's
Birth-day*:

> Stella this Day is thirty four,
> (We won't dispute a Year or more)
> However Stella, be not troubled,
> Although thy Size and Years are doubled,
> Since first I saw Thee at Sixteen
> The brightest Virgin of the Green,
> So little is thy Form declin'd
> Made up so largly in thy Mind.
> Oh, would it please the Gods to split
> Thy Beauty, Size, and Years, and Wit,
> No Age could furnish out a Pair
> Of Nymphs so gracefull, Wise and fair
> With half the Lustre of Your Eyes,
> With half thy Wit, thy Years and Size:
> And then before it grew too late,
> How should I beg of gentle Fate,
> (That either Nymph might have her Swain,)
> To split my Worship too in twain.[75]

It was the first of his birthday poems in celebration of his
closest friend. He wrote six other poems relating to her
birthday on 13 March, as well as such miscellaneous verses as
*To Stella, Visting me in my Sickness, To Stella, Who Collected and
Transcribed his Poems, Stella at Wood-Park,*[76] and *A Receipt to
Restore Stella's Youth.* The practice ceased only on Hester

Johnson's death on 28 January 1728. Although Swift also wrote verses to Vanessa during this period, and even to Rebecca Dingley, the poems to Stella are unique. It has been rightly observed that they are written 'as if in reply' to the 'Progress' poems, stressing 'the lasting, rational values of deeper relationships', not the transient, false pleasures of sexual liaisons.[77]

At the same time, the 'Stella' poems are 'truly fanciful'.[78] To take the verses I have just quoted, Hester Johnson was thirty-eight and not thirty-four in 1719, and Swift had known her since she was eight, not sixteen. Two years later, in *Stella's Birth-day*, he implied that her age was thirty-six, when in fact it was forty.[79] Why? Is Swift merely being playful? Twice sixteen is not thirty-four, anyway. Perhaps the poems met a deeper need. As John Irwin Fischer pertinently points out, they 'celebrate her last birthdays because it was then, not earlier, she needed to be told that neither were her youth and beauty wasted nor were her age and ailments pointless'. Swift's poems were written when her health was deteriorating: 'she was fat ... in 1719, emaciated by 1723, grey by 1725, under heavy medication by 1727.'[80] It seems likely that he turned to poetry to re-assure Stella about the passing of the years.

What consolation did he offer? He foresaw the day

> When Stella's Locks must all be grey
> When Age must print a furrow'd Trace
> On ev'ry Feature of her Face ...

And yet 'All Men of Sense' would be heedless of the ravages of time, and would 'crowd to Stella's at fourscore'. Swift sought to remind her that virtue far outweighs transitory considerations of beauty:

> Now, this is Stella's Case in Fact;
> An Angel's Face, a little crack't;
> (Could Poets or Painters fix
> How Angels look at thirty six) ...[81]

The tone *is* fanciful: but the reverberations are solemn.

Various remedies were tried in a vain attempt to restóre Stella's failing health. By 1723 she was hardly eating anything, and Swift's repeated complaints about her appetite began. 'Mrs. Johnson eats an ounce a week', he explained, 'which frights me from dining with her.' By the end of 1724 she was growing still 'leaner, she eats about 2 ounces a week, and even drinks less than she did'. A few months later she was taking 'but a mouthfull a day'.[82] Summers at Ford's residence, Woodpark, in 1723, and at Sheridan's cabin at Quilca, where she repaired with Swift and Rebecca Dingley in 1725, had no permanent effect. Swift's verses on the two occasions were playful, but wishful thinking. *A Receipt to Restore Stella's Youth* explained that

> ... you have fasted
> So long till all your Flesh is wasted,
> And must against the warmer Days
> Be sent to *Quilca* down to graze;
> Where Mirth, and Exercise, and Air,
> Will soon your Appetite repair.[83]

Country air and exercise proved as ineffectual as steel. 'I wish she would go to London', Swift lamented, convinced by his own experiences that the fatigue of eighteenth-century travel was a panacea for all ills. But whatever was amiss with Stella's stomach, it refused to mend.[84]

When Swift was in England in 1726, Stella survived narrowly a further severe bout of illness. He fully expected to hear news of her death. 'What you tell me of Mrs J— I have long expected with great Oppression and Heavyness of Heart', he wrote to John Worrall on 15 July. I would not for the Universe be present at Such a Tryal of seeing her depart.' 'Pray write to me every Week, that I may know what Steps to take, For I am determind not to go to Ireld to find her just dead or dying,' he continued. 'Nothing but Extremity could make me so familiar with those terrible Words applyed to such a dear Friend.'[85] It is in the light of this knowledge of Stella's failing health, and the fact that they had 'been perfect Friends these 35 Years', that Swift's poems to Stella should be read. The final birthday poem, written in 1727, dropped the mask of playfulness, and asked her to 'Accept for once some serious Lines' from 'not the gravest of Divines':

> Although we now can form no more
> Long Schemes of Life, as heretofore;
> Yet you, while Time is running fast,
> Can look with Joy on what is past.

'Say, *Stella*', he asked, 'feel you no Content,/Reflecting on a Life well spent?' Surely 'Virtue, stil'd its own Reward' should 'shine through Life's declining Part'?[86]

Swift experienced the utmost difficulty in reconciling himself to the loss of Stella. Since hearing of her condition in 1726, he had 'not been the same Man, nor ever shall be again, but drag on a wretched Life till it shall please God to call me away'.[87] Such a display of morbid sensitivity speaks volumes about Swift's character, his tendency to brood on disappointments and tribulations. 'I was 47 Years old when I began to think of death', he told Bolingbroke in 1729, 'and the reflections upon it now begin when I wake in the Morning, and end when I am going to Sleep.'[88] By then he had seen both Stella and Vanessa buried. 'I am of Opinion that there is not a greater Folly than to contract too great and intimate a Friendship', he observed, 'which must always leave the Survivor miserable.'[89] He would 'gladly' have shared Stella's sufferings, 'Or give my Scrap of Life to you,/And think it far beneath your Due'.[90] Swift came to learn that love was painful, and even to question the value of platonic friendship.

Swift's feelings for Esther Vanhomrigh are much less easy to describe. Apart from a series of letters dating, in the most part, from around 1720, very little evidence of their relations in Ireland exists. Middleton Murry believed that 'Vanessa had broken through his plans and defences, and set a chord in him vibrating that never stopped, and that in his heart of hearts he did not want to stop.'[91] Support for such an interpretation is tenuous at best. 'I think it inconvenient for a hundred Reasons that I should make your House a sort of constant dwelling place,' Swift wrote soon after she took up permanent residence in Ireland on the death of her mother in 1714. 'I will certainly come as often as I conveniently

can.'[92] This is scarcely the language of love, and it did not
satisfy Vanessa. 'I believe you thought I only rallyed when I
told you the other night that I wou'd pester you with letters,'
she warned, 'if you have any regard for your quiate ... allter
your behaviour quickly for I do assure you I have too much
spirrite to sitt down contented with this treatment.'[93]

There is, then, more than a hint that the affection was
one-sided. It was one thing for Swift to find his curiosity
aroused by Vanessa's flattering attentions in London, far
away from his Irish friends: quite another for the Dean of St
Patrick's to be pestered on his own doorstep by an unattached
young lady. How often he visited her at her house at
Celbridge, just to the west of Dublin, is impossible to say.
Presumably they met in Dublin itself on occasion. When
Vanessa was forced to stay in the country in 1720 on account
of her sister's health, Swift finally made the effort to see her
there. He had been entreated to do so for weeks on end. Mary
Vanhomrigh died towards the end of February 1721. Swift
seems to have been genuinely upset. Vanessa's own health
was little better. When she, too, died on 2 June 1723, she left
George Berkeley, the philosopher, £3000, although he had
'never in the whole course of [his] life, to [his] knowledge,
exchanged a single word with her'.[94] She had made her will a
month earlier, on 1 May, and had not left Swift a penny, not
even 'twenty-five pounds to buy a ring' of mourning, and yet
several such bequests were authorised.[95]

Such is the bare outline of Swift's relations with Vanessa in
Ireland. Clearly interpretation is called for. Why, for instance,
should Vanessa leave money to 'a perfect stranger'? Suspicion
attaches itself to the date of her will. Did it signify a change of
heart on Vanessa's part? Needless to say, various legends have
sprung up relating to the affair. Bishop Evans of Meath, who,
it should be said at once, was a witness extraordinarily hostile
to Swift, claimed that, in April 1723, Vanessa discovered 'the
D[ean] was married to Mrs. Johnson'. Thus two traditions of
Swift's biography become intertwined. Swift's early biographers all have things to say about his marriage to Stella in
1716.[96] Similarly they offer a romantic account of a final
confrontation between Swift and Vanessa, which goes like
this. On hearing that he was married to Stella, Vanessa wrote

asking if it were true. (There is some confusion whether she wrote to the Dean or to Mrs Johnson.) Thereupon Swift rode to Celbridge, flung the letter on to a table in front of her, and left immediately without uttering a single word.[97]

Two things must be said about this story. Referring to the alleged letter, Lyon writes: 'This is all only Tattle & suspicion – For no Letter either of her or him appears in ye whole correspondence; wch she did preserve.'[98] Seeing that Vanessa kept not only Swift's letters, but copies of her own, it is indeed strange that she retained neither the original of this last letter, particularly after Swift had apparently returned it to her in such a dramatic manner, nor a copy. Secondly, the event of any 'last' meeting between Swift and Vanessa in April 1723 would hardly have been relayed first-hand to Bishop Evans, who was vindictively prejudiced against them both. The tradition of the marriage to Stella is similarly second-hand at best. ''Tis generally believed that she lived without God in ye world,' Evans wrote about Vanessa. 'When Dean Price (the Minister of her Parish) offered her his services in her last minutes: she sent him word no Price no Prayers, with a scrap out of the Tale in the Tub ... and so she dyed.'[99]

It would be fabulous to imagine Vanessa, who knew the rules of raillery so well, going out of the world with a pun on her lips. True, we have corroborating evidence of her lack of religion. 'I firmly believe could I know your thoughts (which no humane creature is capable of geussing at because never any one liveing thought like you)', she wrote to Swift on one occasion, 'I should find you have often in a rage wished me religious hopeing then I should have paid my devotions to heaven.' The way in which she continued is revealing: 'but that would not spair you for was I an Enthusiast still you'd be the Deity I should worship.'[100] One can assume that Swift would have found such professions of adoration not only distasteful, but profoundly disturbing. However, there is no real reason to countenance Bishop Evans's version of the death of Vanessa. It is gratuitously malicious.

The simple fact is that Vanessa would not leave Swift alone. Take, for example, the following undated letter:

Believe me 'tis with the utmost regret that I now complain

221

to you because I know your good nature such that you can not see any humaine creature miserable without being sensibly touched yett what can I do I must either unload my heart and tell you all its griefs or sink under the unexpressable distress I now suffer by your prodigious neglect of me T'is now ten long weeks since I saw you and in all that time I have never recieved but one letter from you and a little note with an excuse Oh— — — how have you forgott me you indeavour by severities to force me from you nor can I blame you for with the utmost distress and confusion I behold my self the cause of uneasie reflections to you yet I can not comfort you but here declair that t'is not in the power of arte time or accedent to lessen the unexpressable passion which I have for — — — put my passion under the utmost restraint send me as distant from you as the earth will alow yet you can not banish those charming Idaea's which will ever stick by me whilst I have the use of memory nor is the love I beare you only seated in my soul for there is not a single atome of my frame that is not blended with it therefor don't flatter your self that separation will ever change my sentiments for I find m yself unquiat in the midst of silence and my heart is at once pierced with sorrow and love for heavens sake tell me what has caused this prodigious change in you which I have found of late ...[101]

Here we find evidence not only of a 'prodigious change' in Swift's attitude towards Vanessa, but of her persistently chasing him. On her own admission, Vanessa 'was born with violent passions' which 'terminate[d] all in ... that unexpressible passion' she felt for Swift.[102] The last extant letter from Vanessa to Swift is of a piece with her previous recriminations. Complaining that he had 'quite forgot' her, she declared that 'I have so little Joy in life that I don't care how soon mine endes.'[103] Less than a year later she was dead.

The problem is how to reconcile Swift's apparent reluctance to see Vanessa too often, with his extravagant statements of admiration – 'mon bon goût de trouver en vous tout ce qu la Nature a donnee à un mortel, je veux dire l'honneur, la vertue, le bon sens, l'esprit, la douceur, l'agrement, et la firmitè d'ame.'[104] It seems that Swift sought to humour a woman he found he could not handle in any other way. Given his habitual playfulness in letter-writing, his cryptic epistles to Vanessa should be interpreted cautiously. He encouraged her to take an interest in life, to find something to occupy her mind other than the dangerous feelings she nourished for him. It was to no avail. That he realised how indiscreet and imprudent his behaviour towards her had been there can be little doubt. He had anticipated the noise of the 'world' in *Cadenus and Vanessa,* and was worried about the consequences of their meeting in Ireland. Ford often appears to have acted as a sort of chaperone. One can't help feeling that his relations with Vanessa added to the obstacles preventing him from living a quiet life in exile.

Swift's extant writings do not mention Vanessa's death, and yet it was his custom to respond to such events by offering a spontaneous epitaph for a lost loved one. Not only his mother and Stella were commemorated thus – Temple, Anne Long, even Sheridan – all were accorded Swift's last respects in this way. But not Vanessa. Even *Cadenus and Vanessa* was published without his approval in 1726, when he was in England and powerless to prevent it. Swift noted 'how indiscreet it is to leave any one Master of what cannot without the least Consequence be shewn to the World.'[105] Vanessa was not even to be allowed this acknowledgment of her intimacy with the Dean of St Patrick's. According to Delany, someone said that it 'must be an extraordinary woman that could inspire the Dean to write so finely upon her'. Stella only 'smiled, and answered, that she thought that point not quite so clear; for it was well known, the Dean could write finely upon a broomstick.'[106]

It is probably true that Vanessa's 'passion for the Dean ... impaired both her health & spirits'. Whether the Dean was 'no good' is another matter.[107] Throughout her time in Ireland, Swift seems to have done what he could to make Vanessa comfortable, without ever giving her the hope that he would be hers and hers alone. There is no indication that he felt any of the passion that she declared for him. Instead he tried to let her down gently. It seems highly unlikely that he fell out with her, much less that he stormed into her room at Celbridge, threw down a letter, and flounced out again. That is 'only Tattle'. Her final illness, on the other hand, reveals Swift in character. The day before she died, he expressed his intention to set out precipitately on 'a long Southern journey'.[108] Bearing in mind his urgent desire to be out of the way when Stella was thought to be dying, what could be more natural than for Swift to rush away in expectation of the death of a woman who loved him deeply? He felt love for Esther Vanhomrigh in his own way, but that had not been enough. His entanglement with Vanessa was one of the most tragic involvements of his life.

Swift's first years in exile, then, were painful ones. As well as his worries over the safety of his friends in England and over the health of Stella and Vanessa, he was plagued by his own recurring deafness and giddiness. Not all obstacles to his contentment in Ireland were personal. From 1720 onwards he became increasingly concerned about the state of the nation itself. At the same time, he was working on *Gulliver's Travels,* his massive indictment of human folly. Despite the memories of the great years of the Oxford ministry which never ceased to trouble him, despite his reluctance to live in Ireland, despite his own ill-health, despite the decline of Stella, despite the death of Vanessa, despite the fact that he was losing touch with his old friends without being able fully to replace them, the decade of the 1720s was to prove Swift's greatest creative period. True, his invention was no longer 'at the Height' it had been when he wrote *A Tale of a Tub*. He was no longer a young man. But his powers had not yet faded. This was the period of his artistic maturity, to culminate in *Gulliver's Travels,* the Irish tracts, and his most accomplished verse. The desperate situation of the kingdom of Ireland roused him to anger, and gave him a cause.

11
Swift and Ireland

It would be misleading to suggest that Swift did not concern himself with Irish affairs until the publication of *A Proposal For the universal Use Of Irish Manufacture* in 1720. Despite his 'Resolution of never medling with Irish Politicks',[1] his own fate had always been bound up with that of his native land. Irish failure to pursue its own interests was a constant source of amazement and irritation to him. England had undone Ireland by 'the common Arts practised upon all easy credulous Virgins, half by Force, and half by Consent, after solemn Vows and Protestations of Marriage'.[2] He lamented the fact that 'the Interest of our whole Kingdom is, at any Time, ready to strike to that of [the] poorest *Fishing Town*' in England and that 'we value your Interest much more than our own'.[3] 'I do profess without affectation, that your kind opinion of me as a Patriot (since you call it so) is what I do not deserve,' he wrote to Pope in 1728, 'because what I do is owing to perfect rage and resentment, and the mortifying sight of slavery, folly, and baseness about me, among which I am forced to live.'[4]

The Irish were not literally in bondage, but liberty is the opposite of slavery, and liberty was precisely what Ireland was being denied by England. Swift believed that the Irish were scarcely being allowed 'the common Rights and Privileges of Brethren, Fellow-Subjects, and even of Mankind'. As he put it in his sermon, *Causes of the Wretched Condition of Ireland,* through 'the intolerable Hardships we lie under in every Branch of our Trade ... we are become as *Hewers of Wood, and Drawers of Water,* to our rigorous Neighbours.'[5] The development of the Irish economy was restricted by the laws of England which, in regulating the export of Irish livestock and woollen manufactures, effectively ensured the continuance of poverty. Far from enjoying 'the just Rights and Privileges of Mankind', 'the whole Nation itself is almost reduced to Beggary by the Disadvantages we lye under, and the Hardships we are forced to bear.' It was the element of constraint which led Swift to represent Ireland's plight as one of slavery, and he pondered the justice of laws which could '*bind Men without their own Consent*'.[6]

But there were two other elements in the stimulation of his 'perfect rage and resentment' – 'folly, and baseness'. And here Swift did think something might be done by the Irish themselves to alleviate their economic problems. He described as the 'second Cause of our miserable State'

> the Folly, the Vanity, and Ingratitude of those vast
> Numbers, who think themselves too good to live in the
> Country which gave them Birth, and still gives them Bread;
> and rather chuse to pass their Days, and consume their
> Wealth, and draw out the very Vitals of their Mother
> Kingdom, among those who heartily despise them.[7]

The irresponsible behaviour of Irish landlords was a great contribution to the poverty of Ireland. Not only did they tend to be absentees, living in England off the proceeds of their Irish land, which did nothing to help the native economy, but the agricultural policies they adopted produced a similarly deleterious effect. Although there were prohibitions on the export of Irish woollen manufactures and livestock to England, the vast majority of Irish acres were given over to grazing, 'an Absurdity', Swift remarked, 'that a *wild Indian* would be ashamed of'.[8]

The consequences were severe. Tenants were turned off their land. Agricultural improvements were ignored, as *rentier* landlords, caring more for quick profits than gradual increases in revenue through greater efficiency, let their land on long leases. 'Middlemen' moved in, subletting to the actual tenant on short-term leases, through perhaps as many as three or four sublessees. On the expiry of these leases, the land would often be auctioned and let to the highest bidder. Thus a system of rack-renting grew up, with additional grave effects on the economic situation. With no guarantee of a stay of any duration on a given plot of land, the incentive for conscientious farmers to improve their techniques was virtually non-existent. As a result the yield was pitifully small from Irish arable land, and the import of grain from England added to the country's economic difficulties, with no prospect of the ultimate alleviation of poverty in the country at large.

Finally, in Swift's view, Ireland's wretched condition was exacerbated by 'that monstrous Pride and Vanity in both Sexes' which, resulting in 'all Kind of Expence and Extravagance', led to the import of luxury goods 'from Abroad, disdaining the Growth or Manufacture of their own Country'. This drained still more of Ireland's small wealth, and acted as a damper on her own manufacturing industries. 'THUS our Tradesmen and Shopkeepers, who deal in Home-Goods, are left in a starving Condition, and only those encouraged who ruin the Kingdom by importing among us foreign Vanities.'[9] This spirit of indolence and ostentatiousness extended downwards throughout Irish society, Swift felt, and largely accounted for 'that great Number of Poor, who, under the Name of common Beggars, infest our Streets, and fill our Ears with their continual Cries, and craving Importunity'. True, it was 'an unnecessary Evil, brought upon us for the gross Neglect, and want of proper Management, in those whose Duty it is to prevent it.' None the less, he alleged:

> it would infallibly be found, upon strict Enquiry, that
> there is hardly one in twenty of those miserable Objects
> who do not owe their present Poverty to their own Faults;
> to their present Sloth and Negligence; to their indiscreet
> Marriage without the least Prospect of supporting a
> Family, to their foolish Expensiveness, to their Drunken-
> ness, and other Vices, by which they have squandered their
> Gettings, and contracted Diseases in their old Age.[10]

This, then, was what fired Swift's 'rage and resentment' at the 'baseness' which surrounded him, amongst which he was 'forced to live'. *Causes of the Wretched Condition of Ireland,* characterised by none of the irony of *A Modest Proposal,* supplies the true picture of his attitude towards the beggars. They were symptomatic of Ireland's plight, the consequences of 'slavery, folly, and baseness'. Remedy the causes and the effects would disappear. To treat the symptoms without offering to diagnose the disease would be merely cosmetic. Swift's real concern was with the reasons for Ireland's pitiable situation, not with the incidental human suffering alone. No reformist humanitarian he, but a strict paternalist. The beggars were 'an unnecessary Evil, brought upon us for the gross Neglect, and want of proper Management, in those whose Duty it is to prevent it'. The key word is 'Duty'.

Swift's own response to such 'gross Neglect, and want of proper Managment' was *A Proposal For the universal Use Of Irish Manufacture*. Despite his own ill-health which, as he explained to Ford on 4 April 1720, meant that he had 'not been able to write', he was fully aware of the issues involved in the passing of a Declaratory Act by the English Parliament relating to Ireland which deprived the Irish House of Lords of appellate jurisdiction. The Act, 'for the better securing the Dependency of ... Ireland' – widely-known as the 'Sixth of George I' – affirmed the right of the English Parliament to legislate for Ireland. Swift went to the heart of the matter in his comments on the new law. 'I believe my self not guilty of too much veneration for the Irish H. of Lds', he wrote, 'the Question is whether People ought to be Slaves or no.'[11] Less than two months later he had sufficiently shrugged off his disabilities to publish his first piece since *The Publick Spirit of the Whigs*.

The title of *A Proposal For the universal Use Of Irish Manufacture* is somewhat misleading. It was at once an attack on English oppression, Irish folly, and universal inhumanity. 'Whoever travels this Country, and observes the *Face* of Nature, or the *Faces*, and Habits, and Dwellings of the *Natives*', he complained, 'will hardly think himself in a Land where either *Law, Religion,* or *common Humanity* is professed.'[12] But the opening of the pamphlet dealt, albeit ironically, with economic matters. 'IT is the peculiar Felicity and Prudence of the People in this Kingdom', Swift remarked, 'that whatever Commodities, or Productions, lie under the greatest Discouragements from *England,* those are what they are sure to be most industrious in cultivating and spreading'. He proceeded to offer a positive proposal to assist the Irish economy – the ostensible subject of the piece – 'What if the House of Commons had thought fit to make a Resolution, *Nemine Contradicente,* against wearing any Cloath or Stuff in their Families, which were not of the Growth and Manufacture of this Kingdom?'[13]

But the subtitle indicates the vehemence of Swift's attack on English oppression – not only is it a proposal for the 'universal Use Of *Irish* Manufacture', but also for 'Utterly *Rejecting* and *Renouncing* Every Thing wearable that comes from ENGLAND' – and he makes a free use of irony to highlight the severity of English policies towards Ireland. 'I WAS much delighted with a Person, who hath a great Estate in this Kingdom', he notes, 'upon his Complaints to me, *how grievously POOR* England *suffers by Impositions from* Ireland.' These included the fact that '*the People of* Ireland *presume to dig for Coals* in their own Grounds; *and the Farmers in the County of* Wicklow *send their Turf to the very Market of* Dublin, *to the great Discouragement of the Coal Trade at* Mostyn *and* White-haven'! Such were 'a *few* among the many Hardships we put upon that *POOR* Kingdom of *England*; for which, I am confident, every *honest* Man wisheth a *Remedy.*'[14]

Swift portrayed England as Pallas in Ovid's *Metamorphoses,* who turned Arachne into a spider and condemned her 'to spin and *weave* for ever, *out of her own Bowels*', for having the audacity almost to equal her in spinning and weaving. He suggested that a similar '*cruel and unjust Sentence* ... is fully executed upon *Us* by *England*, with further Additions of *Rigor* and *Severity*. For the greatest Part of *our Bowels and Vitals* is extracted, without allowing us the Liberty of *spinning* and *weaving* them'. Thus he allegorically presented Ireland's grievance over the prohibition on the export of Irish woollen manufactures and the English monopoly of Irish wool, the extract of '*our Bowels and Vitals*'. He had used the metaphor previously in *A Letter Concerning the Sacramental Test.*[15] In the *Proposal,* he drew attention to the tendency of English ministers, 'from their *high* Elevation, to look *down* upon this Kingdom, as if it had been one of their *Colonies* of *Out-casts in America.*' The main thrust of the pamphlet was aimed at the Declaratory Act which had confirmed Ireland's dependency on England. But George I was not allowed to hide totally behind the backs of his ministers. 'I HOPE, and believe', Swift concluded, 'nothing could please his Majesty better than to hear that his loyal Subjects, of both Sexes, in this Kingdom, celebrated his *Birth-Day* (now approaching) *universally* clad in their own Manufacture.'[16]

In this way, Swift pointed out how the Irish could assist themselves. 'Is there Vertue enough left in this deluded People', he asked, 'to save them from the Brink of Ruin?' The *Proposal* touches on each of the points made in his sermon, *Causes of the Wretched Condition of Ireland.* We find the same tirade against the vanity and extravagance in dress of both sexes, the same censure of 'the unthinking Shopkeepers' of Dublin, who were '*utterly* destitute of common Sense'. Instead of encouraging agriculture, 'which hath been the principal Care of all wise Nations', Irish landlords were 'absolutely prohibiting their Tenants from Plowing', and turning their land to grazing. This was the cause of 'the prodigious Dearness of Corn, and the Importation of it from *London*', and the depopulation of 'vast Tracts of the best Land, for the feeding of Sheep', even though wool is 'a Drug to us, and a Monopoly to [England]'. The effects of rack-renting would be seen 'in a very few Years', Swift predicted, when 'the whole *Species* of what we call *Substantial Farmers,* will ... be utterly at an End'.[17]

The *Proposal* was a severe indictment of those responsible for the poverty of Ireland. It has been suggested that, whether judged 'artistically or pragmatically', it is 'a failure',[18] but this does scant justice to its polemical strategy. It has much in common with his previous prose work, *The Publick Spirit of the Whigs,* in the way Swift moves from serious comment on the state of the nation to ironic exposure of English motives in securing the dependency of Ireland. Certainly it did little to alter the condition of Ireland, and caused England, and England's representatives in Dublin, nothing more than annoyance. But then Swift would have been realistic enough not to expect such a work to 'mend the world'. That was not its purpose. It sought, rather, to give shape to the feelings of discontent he shared with other concerned Irishmen. The *Proposal* offered a diagnosis of the country's ills, and suggested a course of action that could alleviate some of its difficulties without being blocked by the English Privy Council.

In preaching the doctrine of self-help, the *Proposal* indicated how Irish folly and avarice greatly contributed to a situation already made desperate by English oppression, and pointed forward to the method adopted to defeat the threat posed by Wood's copper coinage. There was nothing to prevent the voluntary use of Irish manufacture by the Irish people, just as no one could be forced to accept Wood's halfpence as payment. Swift's supple movement from direct address to ironic comment in the *Proposal* attempts to manipulate the reader into a position in which the *fact* of English oppression of Ireland will appear irrefutable. To this end is directed hyperbole, litotes, the very typography, in such a way that the actual disjointed nature of the 'argument' contributes to the overall effect. 'THESE are a *few* among the many Hardships we put upon the *POOR* Kingdom of *England*; for which, I am confident, every *honest* Man wisheth a *Remedy*.' This absurd inversion of the true situation, emphasised by the italicised key words, is the stuff of Swift's mature ironic style.

A Proposal For the universal Use Of Irish Manufacture may not have remedied the affairs of Ireland, but it provoked a prosecution. It was presented as 'false, scandalous, and seditious' by the Grand Juries of the City and County of Dublin on 30 May 1720, and the printer, Edward Waters, was tried at the King's Bench before Lord Chief Justice Whitshed, who refused to accept a verdict of not guilty. Nine times the jury returned this verdict, and nine times they were sent back to reconsider. Eleven hours later they offered a special verdict, leaving the decision to the Lord Chief Justice himself. Whitshed deferred the proceedings 'from one Term to another', until the Duke of Grafton granted a *noli prosequi* on his arrival from England in August 1721 to take up the office of Lord-Lieutenant.[19]

Swift satirised Whitshed's conduct in *An Excellent New Song on a seditious Pamphlet*, 'Written in the Year 1720', but not published until 1735:

Tho' a Printer and Dean
Seditiously mean

Our true *Irish* Hearts from old *England* to wean;
We'll buy *English* Silks for our Wives and our Daughters,
In Spight of his Deanship and Journeyman Waters.[20]

But there can be little doubt that the *Proposal* was seditious in intent. Although in his private correspondence, Swift claimed that the pamphlet tried merely to persuade 'People here to wear their own Manufactures exclusive of any from Engl[an]d, with some Complaints of the Hardships they lye under,'[21] he was perfectly aware of the thrust of his own rhetoric. It was, as Whitshed allegedly claimed, 'published with a design of setting the two kingdoms at variance', not necessarily with a hope 'to bring in the Pretender', but certainly with a desire to make the Irish aware of their own interests and of English exploitation.[22]

He continued to champion the cause of liberty in a series of pamphlets on Irish affairs. The concluding paragraph of the *Proposal* had referred to 'a *Thing* they call a *Bank*', to be half-funded by real money, 'and the other Half altogether imaginary'. Swift deliberately underestimated the capital of the proposed bank, and called for 'a sufficient Provision of *Hemp*, and *Caps*, and *Bells*, to distribute according to the several Degrees of *Honesty* and *Prudence* in *some Persons*'.[23] Almost certainly he miscalculated the potential benefits of a bank to Ireland, but he genuinely doubted the prudence of pursuing schemes of a speculative nature, particularly at this juncture, and he poked fun at the proposals in a series of pieces in prose and verse, such as *The Wonderful Wonder of Wonders, The Wonder of All the Wonders* and *The Run upon the Bankers*. Evaluation of his contributions to the contemporary literature on the bank is complicated by uncertainty about their extent. They are among the most ephemeral of Swift's writings, and problems of authorship arise. However, on 9 December 1721 the Irish House of Commons resolved that 'they could not find any safe foundation for establishing a public Bank', and the threat was removed. Swift perhaps had his final say on the subject in *The Last Speech and dying Words of the Bank of Ireland Which was Executed at College-Green, on Saturday the 9th Inst.*[24]

The plight of the Irish weavers was linked with the prohibition of the export of Irish manufactured woollens.

Despite a clandestine and profitable trade with France in such goods, the South Sea Bubble was sufficient to reduce the Dublin weavers to penury. As St Patrick's was in the heart of their district, Swift was personally affected by sights of distress. As these honest, industrious men were being undone though no fault of their own, he felt obliged to assist them, not only by his pen, but through actual financial aid. At this time he was lending tradesmen capital to establish themselves in business, but things were so desperate that a fund was set up to relieve their importunities. A performance of *Hamlet* raised £73 on 1 April 1721. Sheridan wrote a prologue for it; Swift an epilogue. *An Epilogue To be spoke at the Theatre-Royal This present Saturday being April the 1st. In the Behalf of the Distressed Weavers* was printed in at least three Irish editions, as well as in four London newspapers. It reiterated Swift's views on the wearing of woollens of native manufacture. 'O! Cou'd I see this Audience Clad in *Stuff*,/ Tho' Moneys scarce we shou'd have Trade enough'.[25]

Swift was perfectly sincere in his championing of the weavers. Theirs was a symbolic struggle for survival. Soon an opportunity presented itself for Swift to rally the nation around a more potent symbol of English oppression. On 12 July 1722 the Crown granted a patent to an Englishman called William Wood to mint £100,800-worth of copper coinage for use in Ireland. This was done without consultation, and without the approval of the Irish Parliament. It was yet one more instance of English interference in the internal affairs of the kingdom, and it caused an outcry in Ireland, enflaming an already heated situation. A campaign of passive resistance and non-cooperation with the scheme gathered momentum. Despite early official protests at the granting of the patent, and addresses presented to the King by both Houses of Parliament accusing Wood of fraud, nothing was done to meet Irish demands or to call an official enquiry. Wood continued his preparations to ship his coin across the Irish Sea. It was left for Swift, after consultation with Archbishop King and Lord Chancellor Midleton, to advocate a boycott of the new currency in *A Letter to the Shop-Keepers,* published in February 1724.

There was nothing illegal in such a method of proceeding.

'We have only one remedy, and that is not to receive these [coins] in payments,' King had written as early as 3 September 1722, 'the Patent oblidges none but such as are willing of themselves' to accept them. Should landlords 'refuse to take their rents in brass', he continued, 'it will break the neck of the Project'.[26] This was precisely Swift's point in the first of the *Drapier's Letters*:

> THEREFORE, my friends, stand to it One and All:
> Refuse this *Filthy Trash*. It is no Treason to rebel against
> Mr. *Wood*. His *Majesty* in his Patent obliges nobody to take
> these *Half-pence*: Our *Gracious Prince* hath no such ill
> Advisers about him; or if he had, yet you see the Laws have
> not left it in the *King*'s Power, to force us to take any Coin
> but what is Lawful, of right Standard, *Gold* and *Silver*.
> Therefore you have nothing to fear.[27]

But although the opposition to Wood's halfpence was partly political in character, the question being, as Swift put it in relation to the Declaratory Act, 'whether People ought to be Slaves or no', there were sound economic reasons for refusing to accept the new coinage, and these the English government failed to appreciate until it was too late.

Despite the claims of some contemporaries like Archbishop King, there can be no doubt that there was a severe shortage of small change in Ireland in the early eighteenth century.[28] But not only did the Irish, quite understandably, desire their own national mint, the conditions of Wood's patent were seriously troubling. £100,800 amounted to a quarter of the money already in circulation in Ireland. Swift thought it was out of all proportion to the country's needs, which he estimated at approximately £25,000.[29] This failure on the part of the English government to appreciate the real needs of Ireland was compounded by the low intrinsic value that Wood, under the terms of his patent, was obliged to meet in minting his coins. Thus the already depleted specie of Ireland was placed under further threat. Gold and silver were being drained away in payments for English and French goods as it was, and coins of low intrinsic value could only exacerbate the problem.

Not only would Wood's halfpence be exchangeable for gold and silver at a greater rate than their face-value, but increased opportunities for counterfeiting would inevitably ensue. Even without the new patent, 'many *Counterfeits*' were being 'passed about under the Name of RAPS'.[30] The conditions of Wood's patent resulted in the 'almost complete absence of safeguards [and] virtually insured a currency even more debased than the patent allowed'.[31] The consequences for Ireland would be dire indeed. Wood was not required to pay the bearer legal tender on demand, nor placed under any practicable restrictions to check that he did not exceed the generous terms of his patent. With nothing to prevent him coining more than his original £100,800-worth of copper, and with the certainty that his halfpence would be worth more than their intrinsic value but that there would be no way of forcing him to redeem them in gold and silver, Swift's fears for the already weak Irish economy are easy to understand.

The economic effects of permitting Wood's halfpence to pass into circulation in Ireland were vividly outlined in the *Letter to the Shop-Keepers:*

THESE *Half-pence*, if they once pass, will soon be *Counterfeit*, because it may be cheaply done, the *Stuff* is so *Base*. The *Dutch* likewise will probably do the same thing, and send them over to us to pay for our *Goods*; and Mr. WOOD will never be at rest, but coin on: So that in some Years we shall have at least five Times 108000 *l.* [*sic*] of this *Lumber*. Now the current Money of this Kingdom is not reckoned to be above Four Hundred Thousand Pounds in all; and while there is a *Silver* Six-Pence left, these *Blood-suckers* will never be quiet.

WHEN once the *Kingdom* is reduced to such a Condition, I will tell you what must be the End: The *Gentlemen of Estates* will all turn off their *Tenants* for want of Payment; because ... the *Tenants* are obliged by their Leases to pay *Sterling*, which is Lawful Current Money of *England*; then they will turn their own *Farmers, as too many of them do already,* run *all* into *Sheep* where they can, keeping only such other *Cattle* as are necessary; then they will be their own *Merchants,* and send their *Wool,* and *Butter,* and *Hides,* and

235

Linnen beyond Sea for ready *Money*, and *Wine*, and *Spices*,
and *Silks*. They will keep only a few miserable *Cottagers*.
The *Farmers* must *Rob* and *Beg*, or leave their *Country*. The
Shop-Keepers in this and every other Town, must *Break* and
Starve: For it is the *Landed-man* that maintains the *Merchant*,
and *Shop-keeper*, and *Handicrafts-Man*.[32]

In this way, with pardonable exaggeration, and in keeping
with his own strong views on the importance of land in the
social system, Swift successfully ties in the debate over Wood's
halfpence and the more general debate over the state of
Ireland, predicting the ruin of the kingdom should the copper
coinage be allowed to pass.

It took the English government quite a while to realise that
the opposition to Wood's patent was not solely political. 'It is
not new to see small matters aggravated and carried to a very
great height', Walpole assured Lord-Lieutenant Grafton in
1723, 'but these things seldom happen by chance, and when
there is in reality little or no reason to complain, nothing but
secret management and industry can kindle a general flame
in a kingdom.'[33] Even the shrewd Walpole failed to appreciate
the ins and outs of the affair. The Irish leaders themselves
initiated the policy of non-cooperation with England. In
August 1724 the Commissioners of the Revenue were directed
to receive Wood's coin. Swift had predicted this order in the
first *Drapier's Letter*.[34] Once into circulation, it would have
been difficult for the coins not to have been accepted in
payment. But the Irish Privy Council refused to act on the
order from England. It was really only after such marked
instances of Irish concern that Walpole began to reconsider
his attitude to Wood's patent, as the policies unofficially
enunciated in Swift's pamphlet and backed by the united
Irish leadership were put into practice.

On 9 April 1724 Grafton received notice of his dismissal.
He was replaced as Lord-Lieutenant by Swift's old friend,
Lord Carteret. Swift wrote to him on the 28th, representing
'the apprehensions' of the 'principle persons in this kingdom'
concerning Wood's patent, 'the most ruinous project that ever
was contrived against any nation'. Carteret reminded him
that the affair was 'under examination', and reserved 'judge-

ment of the matter' until the deliberations of the English Privy Council on the addresses from the Irish Parliament were completed. On 24 July Wood made a number of concessions to Irish 'Apprehensions', the most pertinent of which was an offer to limit his coinage to £40,000 unless 'the exigencies of Trade' suggested otherwise. These were reported in Harding's *Dublin Impartial News Letter* on 1 August. Four days later the same journal advertised a second letter from M.B., Drapier. *A Letter to Mr. Harding the Printer, Upon Occasion of a Paragraph in His News-Paper of Aug. 1st. Relating to Mr. Woods's Half-Pence* was Swift's response to the fresh exigency.[35]

The ground of the debate had shifted. One of the most relevant of the economic reasons for opposing Wood's patent had been the absurdly high figure of £100,800. But £40,000, although still too high, was more suited to Irish needs. Swift needed to rally Irish opposition to the patent, to harden the resolve of any waverers, and to urge a collective boycott of Wood's coinage, lest this marvellous chance for a united stance against English oppression should pass by unexploited. 'It is plain', the second *Drapier's Letter* opened, 'what I foretold in my *Letter to the Shop-Keepers, &c.* that this vile Fellow would never be at Rest; and the Danger of our Ruin approaches nearer; And therefore the Kingdom requires *New* and *Fresh Warning.*'[36] Through some inspired sophistry backed up by sound common sense, Swift falsified Wood's case, and fudged the real issues raised by his new proposals. The proposed issue of £40,000-worth of copper was 'almost double' the requirements of the kingdom, and who was to judge 'when the Exigencies of Trade' required an additional minting? Wood offered to take Irish goods in exchange for his coinage, and proposed that no-one would be 'obliged' to take more than 5½d. at one payment. 'Good God!', M.B. thundered, 'Who are this Wretch's *Advisers*? Who are his *Supporters, Abettors, Encouragers,* or *Sharers*? Mr. *Wood* will Oblige me to take Five-pence Half-penny of his Brass in every Payment. And I will shoot Mr. *Wood* and his Deputies through the Head, like *High-way Men* or *House-breakers*, if they dare to force one Farthing of their Coin on me in the Payment of an Hundred Pounds.'[37]

Thus Swift added a further dimension to the political

concepts behind the granting of the patent. In asking rhetorically who were Wood's backers, Swift insinuated that here was yet another instance of English exploitation of Ireland, connived at by Walpole and the government. His polemical strategy had perceptibly altered, Just as 'the Family' had been used as a mark against which all darts could be levelled in *The Conduct of the Allies,* so Wood was at once magnified into a monster who could bear the brunt of the anger of the Irish people, and belittled to emphasise his real insignificance. He was only a *'Hard-ware-man'* – a front-man for the real enemies of Ireland. Who was really responsible for the strenuous efforts being made to impose this patent on its unwilling victim, Swift wanted to know, and what were their motives? True, Wood was commonly supposed to have acquired his patent through bribing the King's mistress, the Duchess of Kendal.[38] But was this sufficient to account for the tenacity with which his cause was being promoted against the combined interests of an entire kingdom? These were the doubts and fears that Swift worked on in *The Drapier's Letters.*

Too much has been made of his adoption of the persona of M.B., Drapier. Swift told Ford that he had 'sent out a small Pamphlet under the Name of a Draper', and when he sent the first *Letter* to Carteret he explained that though it was 'entitled to a Weaver, and suited to the vulgar', it was 'thought to be the work of a better hand'.[39] In making use of a pseudonym, he was doing little more than thinly veiling his own authorship of the piece. It was not an elaborate attempt at subterfuge. There were rhetorical advantages, no doubt, in the figure of a draper, particularly in the first two pamphlets. 'FOR my own Part', Swift wrote in the guise of M.B.:

I am already resolved what to do; I have a pretty good Shop of *Irish Stuffs* and *Silks*, and instead of taking Mr. WOOD's bad Copper, I intend to Truck with my Neighbours the *Butchers,* and *Bakers,* and *Brewers,* and the rest, *Goods for Goods,* and the little *Gold* and *Silver* I have, I will keep by me like my *Heart's Blood* till better Times, or until I am just ready to starve ...[40]

238

Simple anonymity would have been unable to exploit the opportunity to offer such practical advice to tradesmen, and the second *Letter* also suggests what M.B. would do should Wood come to his shop. *The Drapier's Letters* were, in the main, 'suited to the vulgar', down to the use of homely biblical allusion to give authority to M.B.'s arguments.

Otherwise there is no real attempt to give substance to the Drapier's character. He may have been 'the perfect antagonist for William Wood', as he has been called,[41] but he is not a rhetorical device in the sense that the Hack, or Gulliver, or even the Modest Proposer, is, for the simple reason that Swift does not set out to parody the style of his own persona. Instead, the use of M.B. allows Swift to combine elements of the polemical strategy of the Bickerstaff papers with the force of such pamphlets as *The Conduct of the Allies.* Just as Bickerstaff is the foil for the astrologer Partridge, so M.B. is the ideal adversary for hardwareman Wood. But whenever Swift needs to address an audience on a level unsuitable to the character of a draper, the style and air of the narrator is noticeably different. Thus the third *Drapier's Letter* is addressed 'To the Nobility and Gentry of the Kingdom of Ireland', the fifth to Viscount Molesworth, and the unpublished sixth to Lord Chancellor Midleton. When the Drapier is clearly out of his supposed sphere, as he is self-consciously so in the third *Letter*, Swift is forced to equivocate. At such times the advantages of the alleged persona conspicuously do not outweigh the disadvantages.

But the more polemical *Drapier's Letters* have much in common with Swift's pamphlets on behalf of the Oxford ministry. Not only is Wood given a symbolic identity, just as Swift targets a number of key 'adversaries' in his earlier publications, but we have the same mixture of selected facts and distorted interpretation which is such a feature of *The Conduct of the Allies*, the same hint of a conspiracy – this time not to defraud the wealth of the landed man, but the entire wealth of a kingdom – and the same insistence (at least in the first *Letter*) on giving 'the *plain Story of the Fact*' (the *Conduct* proceeded by 'plain Matters of Fact').[42] Edward W. Rosenheim's distinction between satire and polemic can be usefully applied to Swift's method in both *The Drapier's Letters* and *The*

Conduct of the Allies. If his rhetorical devices succeed, 'it is because the rhetorician "brings off" his falsehood and is rhetorically successful precisely because the audience has accepted fiction for truth.'[43] Dr Johnson observed that the *Conduct's* 'efficacy was supplied by the passions of its readers'.[44] The same could truly be said of *The Drapier's Letters.* As Oliver W. Ferguson pertinently remarks, Swift 'wilfully manipulated "passion and argument" to serve his ends',[45] just as he had done over a decade earlier in his pamphlets on the question of peace.

Printed copies of the report of the committee of the Privy Council on Wood's halfpence reached Dublin on 18 August 1724. In *Some Observations Upon a Paper, Call'd, The Report of the Committee* – the third *Drapier's Letter*, published around the end of August or the beginning of September – Swift examined the report as if it were a pamphlet which required answering. In one sense it did. Openly availing himself of the opportunity of treating it as he did the publications of Partridge or Steele in questioning the validity of the paper – 'a Contrivance to *Fright* us; or a *Project* of some *Printer*, who hath a mind to make a Penny' – and insinuating that the 'whole is indeed written with the Turn and Air of a Pamphlet', Swift meted out to Wood the same sort of punishment previously inflicted upon those little scribblers who had roused his anger. He retained the pseudonym of M.B., Drapier, but the style is reminiscent of *The Importance of the Guardian Considered,* as Swift enquires into the origins of 'this *Wood*', who 'has the Honour to have a whole Kingdom at his Mercy, for almost two Years together'.[46]

However, the third *Drapier's Letter* opened up the whole question of Irish dependency on England, at once illustrating the inappropriateness of the persona of M.B., and the underlying issues at stake. It is not the Drapier, but Swift himself who asks:

> WERE not the People of *Ireland* born as *free* as those of England? How have they forfeited their Freedom? Is not their *Parliament* as fair a *Representative* of the *People*, as that of *England?* And hath not their Privy Council as great, or a greater Share in the Administration of publick Affairs? Are

240

they not Subjects of the same King? Does not the same *Sun* shine over them? And have they not the same *God* for their Protector? Am I a *Free-man* in *England*, and do I become a *Slave* in six Hours, by crossing the Channel?[47]

In this crucial passage Swift characterises his opposition to English oppression of Ireland. Certainly there is a personal element involved, but it shows how much the Irish tracts are politically of a piece with his statements on liberty and property since his first political pamphlet. Such attitudes are quintessentially 'Country' or 'Old Whig' in content, in inspiration, and in expression. It is in this sense that 'Fair LIBERTY was all his Cry'. The question really was 'whether People ought to be Slaves or no'. Instead of being treated as freemen with rights and privileges including a voice in the affairs of the kingdom, the Irish were being denied their birthright as subjects of the king. That was what provoked Swift's rage and resentment.

Although the third *Drapier's Letter* dealt with many other aspects of the committee's report, this was the all-important one, and Swift had drawn attention to it in a particularly dangerous and outspoken manner. No wonder one observer thought that even though many of the comments were 'very proper', the pamphlet 'may give offence'.[48] Only now were the real issues surrounding the granting of Wood's patent being openly discussed, and stands being made. The Commissioners of the Revenue were not alone in their refusal to accept Wood's halfpence. On 15 August Dublin bankers signed a resolution to that effect, and many other declarations followed their lead, including one allegedly from the 'Beggars, Lame and Blind, Halt and Maimed, both Male and Female, in and about the City of Dublin'.[49] With the situation getting out of hand Walpole finally responded to its seriousness by sending Carteret to Ireland with all speed.

Carteret arrived in Dublin on 22 October 1724 to be greeted by the fourth and most famous *Drapier's Letter. A Letter to the Whole People of Ireland* called Walpole's bluff. 'Cordials must be frequently applied to weak Constitutions,' Swift observed, '*Political* as well as *Natural*.' The question of Ireland's dependency on England was now in the forefront of

241

affairs. Considering the 'Slander spread by *Wood* and his Emissaries', M.B. noted 'how the publick Weal of two Kingdoms, is involved in his private Interest':

> First, all those who refuse to take his Coin *are Papists*; for he tells us, that *none but Papists are associated against him.*
> Secondly, *they dispute the King's Prerogative.* Thirdly, they *are ripe for Rebellion.* And Fourthly, they are going to *shake off their Dependance upon the Crown of* England; that is to say, *they are going to chuse another King*: For there can be no other Meaning in this Expression, however some may pretend to strain it.[50]

Once again Swift's voice has merged with the Drapier's, as he explains 'another Point, which hath often *swelled in my Breast*', that of whether or not '*Ireland* is a *depending Kingdom*'. According to Swift, this 'is a *modern Term of Art*; unknown, as I have heard, to all antient *Civilians,* and *Writers upon Government.*' Denying the very concept of dependency, he disputed the validity of the 'Power of binding this Kingdom' assumed by England 'by Laws enacted there'. 'For in *Reason*', he concluded, 'all *Government* without the Consent of the *Governed,* is the *very Definition of Slavery.*'[51]

At last Swift has spelled out the issue closest to his own heart. He has substituted direct statement for euphemism. But he did not rest content there. In a wonderfully ironic inversion of Wood's insinuation that opposition to this patent meant disaffection to the monarchy of George I, Swift, resuming the character of M.B., declared his conditions *sine qua non*:

> I declare, next under God, I *depend* only on the King my Sovereign, and on the Laws of my own Country, And I am so far from *depending* upon the People of *England,* that, if they should ever *rebel* against my Sovereign (which GOD forbid) I would be ready at the first Command from his Majesty to take Arms against them; as some of *my* Countrymen did against *theirs* at *Preston.* And, if such a Rebellion should prove so successful as to fix the *Pretender* on the Throne of *England*; I would venture to transgress that

Statute so far, as to lose every Drop of my Blood, to hinder him from being *King* of *Ireland*.[52]

Swift had gone too far. Talk of rebellion, however well-intentioned – and Swift was far from being well-intentioned towards the Court and government of England – was seditious. It was illegal for the King of Ireland to be other than the King of England. That was one of the consequences of dependency. At an Irish Privy Council meeting on 27 October Carteret made it clear that he regarded the *Letter* as treasonous, and he read 'some few of the many exceptionable passages', including the one I have just quoted.[53] A majority voted to arrest Harding the printer and to issue a proclamation against 'several seditious and scandalous paragraphs' in the *Letter*, offering a reward of £300 for information leading to the discovery of the Drapier's identity.

This was scarcely likely to be made. Thomas Tickell observed the 'great endeavours ... to get Dr Swift the freedom of the City [of Dublin] in a Gold-Box', and noted that a verse of scripture (I Samuel xiv, 45) had been 'got by rote, by men, women, and children, and ... takes wonderfully':

And the people said unto Saul, shall Jonathan die, who hath wrought this great salvation in Israel? God forbid: as the Lord liveth, there shall not one hair of his head fall to the ground, for he hath wrought with God this day. So the people rescued Jonathan, that he died not.[54]

Although Swift's responsibility for *The Drapier's Letters* was common knowledge throughout the kingdom, his authorship was never publicly acknowledged. ''Tis the general opinion here that Doctor Swift is the author of the pamphlet', Carteret wrote on 31 October, 'and yet nobody thinks it can be proved upon him; tho' many believe he will be spirited up to own it.'[55]

Carteret was not far from the mark. Swift had already started work on a *Letter to the Lord Chancellor Middleton* in his own name. The so-called sixth *Drapier's Letter*, dated 'Deanry House, Oct. 26, 1724', was first published in 1735 in the fourth volume of Swift's *Works*, with the note that the writer 'thought it more prudent to keep the Paper in his Cabinet'.[56] This was only sound sense in the present situation. Harding the printer was taken into custody on 7 November. Four days later Swift penned *Seasonable Advice to the Grand-Jury, concerning the Bill preparing against the Printer,* which assured any prospective jury that judgment against the fourth *Drapier's Letter* would also be a judgment 'in Favour of *Wood*'s Coin'.[57] Carteret was, apparently, more angered by this paper than by the *Letter to the Whole People of Ireland.* It was 'of so scandalous and seditious a nature' that he pressed for the Grand Jury to consider it before turning to Harding's case. But on 21 November a presentment of *Seasonable Advice* was turned down. Whitshed proceeded to discharge the jury and summon a fresh one, but when the paper was brought before them once more on the last day of Michaelmas term, they again failed to return a verdict in favour of the Irish government. Instead, as one contemporary put it, they brought in 'a presentment, a thorough one indeed, against Woods and all his "accomplices", who by fraud or any other means should attempt to vent those halfpence in that kingdom, &c.'. 'I am told Jonathan's picture is put up by the magistrates in the town hall at Dublin,' he added.[58]

Whether or not, in insisting on proceeding first with the presentment of *Seasonable Advice,* Carteret had deliberately tried to avoid exposing Swift is difficult to say,[59] but Harding was released at the end of Michaelmas term without having been brought to trial. The Dean of St Patrick's seemed to be orchestrating the whole clamour of Irish voices raised in outcry against English oppression. *The Presentment of the Grand-Jury of the County of the City of Dublin,* 'with all just Gratitude, acknowledge[d] the Services of all such *Patriots,* as have been eminently *zealous* for the Interest of his Majesty, and this Country, in detecting the fraudulent Impositions of the said *Wood,* and preventing the passing his base Coin'.[60] The Hibernian Patriot was even composing his own encomium. Whitshed was indicted of malpractice that was 'arbitrary, illegal, destructive to publick Justice, a manifest Violation of his Oath, and … a Means to subvert the Fundamental Laws of this Kingdom'.[61] Once again we can recognise a Swiftian concern for legal monarchy, and he published an extract of a collection of Commons' debates, with resolutions taken by the English House in 1680, in order to point up the issue at stake – the 'Fundamental Laws' not of England, but of Ireland.

Swift, then, had seen Walpole's new attempt to browbeat the Irish into accepting Wood's halfpence headed off. Victory was within his grasp. The fifth *Drapier's Letter – A Letter to the Right Honourable the Lord Viscount Molesworth* – was published on 31 December 1724, and in it M.B. surveyed the campaign he had fought so far without adding any new arguments. It was 'made only from the *Shreds and Remnants of the Wool employed*' in his previous pamphlets. But the metaphor was carefully chosen, for the Irish woollen industry had been at the heart of Swift's proposals for the country's economy from the very beginning. Deliberately drawing attention to the contentiousness of the *Letter to the Whole People of Ireland,* M.B. mentioned the 'Offence' taken at his 'discourse upon *Ireland*'s being a *Dependant Kingdom*'. 'WHETHER I were mistaken, or WENT TOO FAR in examining the *Dependency*', he continued, 'must be left to the impartial Judgment of the World, as well as to the Courts of Judicature.'[62]

This conscious acknowledgement of the defeat sustained by the Irish executive was followed by a passage in which Swift offered a transparent identification of himself as M.B., Drapier:

> I WILL now venture to tell your Lordship a Secret, wherein I fear you are too deeply concerned. You will therefore please to know, that this Habit of Writing and Discoursing, wherein I unfortunately differ from *almost* the whole Kingdom, and am apt to grate the Ears of more than I could wish; was acquired during my Apprenticeship in *London*, and a long Residence there after I had set up for my self. Upon my Return and Settlement here, I thought I had only *changed one Country of Freedom for another.* I had been long conversing with the Writings of your Lordship, Mr. *Locke*, Mr. *Molineaux*, Colonel *Sidney,* and other dangerous Authors, who talk of *Liberty as a Blessing, to which the whole Race of Mankind hath an Original Title; whereof nothing but unlawful Force can divest them.* I knew a good deal of the

several *Gothick* Institutions in *Europe*; and by what Incidents
and Events they came to be destroyed: And I ever thought
it the most uncontrolled and universally agreed Maxim,
that *Freedom consists in a People being governed by Laws made
with their own Consent; and Slavery in the Contrary.* I have been
likewise told, and believe it to be true; that *Liberty* and
Property, are Words of known Use and Signification in this
Kingdom; and that the very Lawyers pretend to understand, and have them often in their Mouths. These were
the Errors which have misled me; and to which alone I
must impute the severe Treatment I have received.[63]

This is not the Drapier speaking; this is Swift himself, listing
his own fundamental political beliefs, and imputing all he
has suffered since first joining forces with the Whigs in 1701
to 'Errors which have misled me'. It is not merely a
commentary on his Irish tracts, but on his political writings
tout court.

Molesworth was an Irish Commonwealthman, author of *An
Account of Denmark,* published in 1693, which was used to show
how 'corruption' could quickly lead to the loss of the rights
and privileges of mankind. Locke's *Two Treatises of Civil
Government* postulated a society formed through a contract
between King and people based on consent and trust. Swift
confessed himself to be 'of th[e] party' of 'those who thought
that there was an original contract between the kings and the
people of England'.[64] William Molyneux's *The Case of Ireland,*
as I have already noted, was the basis of many of Swift's
arguments in his Irish pamphlets. Algernon Sydney's *Discourses
concerning Government,* published in 1698, expounded a theory
of mixed monarchy, with the King's prerogative limited by
laws of the subject's own making, so that liberty and property
were safeguarded. It is important, I believe, to an understanding of Swift's ideas to realise how much he was influenced by
books published in the 1690s in the Commonwealth or
'neo-Harringtonian' tradition. Although he admired Thomas
Hobbes, and seems to have subscribed to the Hobbesian view
of human nature, Swift was certain that a single error led to
'all the political Mistakes' in Hobbes' system: 'he perpetually
confounds the *Executive* with the *Legislative* Power; though all

well-instituted States have ever placed them in different Hands'.[65] Yet once more the question of Swift's opinions on the constitution lead us straight to the heart of the dispute over Irish dependency.

Although Swift expressed his attitudes publicly in 1724 through the character of M.B. Drapier, he had provided an extended account of them in private in 1721 in the so-called *Letter From Dr. Swift to Mr Pope.* The consistency of principles is worth remarking. Supplying a *résumé* of his activities in Ireland since 1714, including the reaction to *A Proposal For the universal Use Of Irish Manufactures,* Swift proceeded to outline 'what my Political principles were in the time of her late glorious Majesty, which I never contradicted by any action, writing or discourse.'[66] These included belief in the Revolution Principle, in the Protestant Succession, in annual parliaments, and opposition to any measures which threatened the liberty and property of the subject, such as standing armies in peacetime and the suspension of the law. Not only do such attitudes throw light on Swift's motives in championing the cause of Ireland, they can be seen to correspond with what we know of his mature views since the year he first entered the political arena in publishing *A Discourse of the Contests and Dissensions between the Nobles and the Commons in Athens and Rome.*

Not only, then, was it true for Swift to say, in the guise of the Drapier, that he had acquired 'this Habit of Writing and Discoursing ... during [his] Apprenticeship in *London*', but he was justified, as far as we can tell, in assuring Pope that his 'Political principles' had never been 'contradicted by any action, writing or discourse'. Of course Swift was attacking the English Whigs in his Irish tracts. Of course he was personally as well as publicly motivated. Of course Wood's halfpence and even the Irish woollen industry were only symbols in a wider political debate. Through metonymy, that habitual Swiftian satirical device, Swift was criticising the gamut of political behaviour in the early eighteenth century as practised throughout the three kingdoms. But it is crucial to grasp the extent to which his Irish pamphlets were simply an extension of his English ones. The same themes, the same concerns, the same arguments recur, newly framed perhaps, but still recognisably Swiftian. Merely the circumstances had changed. The cry remained the same.

At the same time that Swift was urging the revocation of Wood's patent in public, Carteret was offering Walpole identical advice in private. In January 1725 Swift waited on the Lord-Lieutenant for the first time since his arrival in Ireland. Despite their official differences over the *Letter to the Whole People of Ireland* and the *Seasonable Advice,* they almost certainly saw eye to eye on the matter. Swift thanked Carteret for the 'great Civilityes' he had been shown in Dublin Castle.[67] Clearly they had renewed the close friendship that had been established in London. Swift was still working on more pamphlets to embarrass Wood and the Walpole ministry at Quilca during the summer, while he was revising and transcribing *Gulliver's Travels* in the company of the ladies. But his diligence was rendered redundant when Carteret received notification that Wood had surrendered his patent. On 26 August the news was proclaimed in Dublin. 'The work is done', Swift wrote five days later, 'and there is no more need of the Drapier.'[68] Plans to publish *An humble Address to both Houses of Parliament* 'just when the Parliament meets' on 7 September were shelved.[69] The Drapier had won.

And yet, such is the way of the world, nothing was done to relieve the sufferings of the Irish people. The victory over Wood's halfpence, like the conflict itself, proved symbolic, nothing more. Swift had made the Irish people aware of the difficulties facing the economy. He had given their grievances form, and that was all. In the process, he quite deservedly acquired enormous popularity within Ireland itself, especially with the common people of Dublin. He had stood out against the English government, risking personal injury. He could say, with truth, that in the cause of liberty he had 'oft expos'd his own'. It is less true to say that 'he boldly stood alone.'[70] He had been given sterling support by Archbishop King in particular. Nor were *The Drapier's Letters* solely Swift's responsibility. The *Humble Address* was concocted between Sheridan, John Worrall, John Grattan and Swift himself. As Herbert Davis remarks, 'This suggests that most of the letters were well edited by his friends before they were printed.'[71] Perhaps this was a reflection of Swift's ill health throughout the campaign against Wood's halfpence.

The Drapier's Letters none the less express Swift's own peculiar slant on events, even on Irish events. As he put it in the fifth *Letter,* his thoughts on such matters differed 'from *almost* the whole Kingdom'. When he returned to consideration of Irish affairs in 1728 and 1729, the public was to be treated to a further taste of his 'uncommon Way of Thinking'. But for the present his energies were being focused on wider aspects of human vice and folly than those apparent in the conflict over English oppression of Ireland. Since 1721 Swift had been concentrating on 'writing a History of my Travells, which will be a large Volume, and gives Account of Countryes hitherto unknown'. Even though they went on slowly 'for want of Health and Humor', by 19 January 1724 he had 'left the Country of Horses, and [was] in the flying Island, where I shall not stay long, and my two last Journyes will be soon over'.[72] He was interrupted by the requirements of *The Drapier's Letters,* and did not manage to find time to complete them until he stayed at Quilca in the summer of 1725. 'I have finished my Travells, and I am now transcribing them,' he told Ford on 14 August, 'they are admirable Things, and will wonderfully mend the World.'[73] The critical eye of the Hibernian Patriot was turned farther afield, as he indicted the entire civilisation of his own day.

12
Swift and Walpole

It has been suggested that although the struggle over the copper coinage was ostensibly between William Wood, Hardware-Man, and M.B., Drapier, the 'actual combatants were Walpole and Swift'.[1] There is truth in this. To Swift, Wood was a fictional character rather than a living person and the facts of his life were largely irrelevant. It was what Wood represented that mattered. Increasingly, from the *Letter to the Shop-keepers* to the *Letter to the Whole People of Ireland*, the attack on Wood's patent became submerged beneath the wider implications of Swift's condemnation of the English Court and government. At the head of the ministry stood Robert Walpole. As Swift's offensive gained momentum, Walpole, not Wood, was more and more the subject of his anger and abuse.

In the fourth *Drapier's Letter*, Swift referred to the threat that 'Mr. *Walpole will cram his Brass down our Throats*'. Whose brass? Wood's or Walpole's? Presumably Wood's, but the syntax is ambiguous. 'I will now demonstrate, beyond all Contradiction', the *Letter* concluded:

> that Mr. *Walpole* is against this Project of Mr. *Wood*; and is an entire Friend to *Ireland*; only by this one invincible Argument, That he has the Universal Opinion of being a wise Man, an able Minister, and in all his Proceedings, pursuing the *True Interest* of the *King his Master*: And that, as his *Integrity* is above all *Corruption*, so is his *Fortune* above all *Temptation*. I reckon therefore, we are perfectly safe from that *Corner*; and shall never be under the Necessity of Contending with so *Formidable a Power*; but be left to possess

250

our *Brogues* and *Potatoes* in *Peace,* as *Remote from Thunder as we are from Jupiter.*[2]

Despite the ironic inversion, Swift's implication is unmistakable: Walpole is behind the attempt to impose Wood's copper coinage on the people of Ireland. His cupidity was legendary. It hardly needed the italics ('his *Integrity* is above all *Corruption*') to point up the fact that, in his mock eulogy of the 'Great Man', Swift was employing the tactic of blame by praise.

In the light of *Gulliver's Travels,* it might be interesting to note the polemical strategy that Swift adopts in dealing first with Wood, and then with Walpole, for the latter is portrayed just as figuratively as the 'diminutive, insignificant Mechanick'.[3] Wood is consistently demeaned; described either as a rat or an insect, he is clearly Lilliputian. Walpole, on the other hand, is always viewed in Brobdingnagian proportions. He is the 'Great Man', 'That honest Statesman *BOB*', the *'brazen* Politician'.[4] His names are many, but the controlling metaphors refer either to his size – he was over twenty stones in weight – or to his appetite, or to his corruption. Allusions to his 'greatness' or 'honesty' were always subject to ironic reversal. In Fielding's *Tom Thumb* or *Jonathan Wild,* 'greatness' implies its opposite. To be great is to be mean or petty or (in the case of Tom Thumb) physically tiny. After *Gulliver's Travels,* the use of proportional paradox was commonplace.

In the hands of his opponents, then, the character of Walpole, too, is merely a fictional projection. The picture they paint of him is sufficiently suggestive to be recognisable as the living politician, but it is stylised, distorted for polemical purposes. The resulting fictional creation acted 'as a strong magnifying glass with which one can render visible a general but creeping calamity which it is otherwise hard to get hold of.'[5] *The Dunciad* best conveys the truth of such a statement, but Swift's writings from 1724 onwards similarly reflect a preoccupation with the 'Robinocracy' and all it stood for. They are incomprehensible without an awareness of the threat that Walpole posed for Swift, Pope and their circle, as they professed to witness 'the worst times and Peoples, and Oppressions that History can shew in either Kingdom'.[6]

Robert Walpole was of the third generation of Whig

politicians. Born in 1676, he was an infant at the time of the exclusion crisis when the first Whigs emerged under the leadership of the first Earl of Shaftesbury. When the Revolution of 1688 took place he was a boy of twelve. His whole adult life, therefore, was lived in the post-Revolution world. This at once set him apart ideologically from older men like Oxford and Swift. Not only did Walpole have no recollection of political events prior to the reign of William III, when Whigs began to be accommodated with places at Court, but his entry into Parliament in 1701 coincided with the hardening of party lines and the renewal of the party struggle between Whig and Tory which characterised the reign of Queen Anne. When the Whigs returned to office, Walpole returned with them, taking over from Henry St John as Secretary-at-War in February 1708. It was a curious coincidence, for Walpole and Bolingbroke were to be the great rivals of the new generation of English politicians.

Walpole learned to hate and fear the Tories, but he had no understanding of 'Old Whig' or 'Country Whig' attitudes of independence or permanent opposition to the executive. A tremendously ambitious man, his priority was to gain office and to hold it to the exclusion of all Tories whatsoever. In this he was the exact counterpart of St John. Walpole became the leader of the Whigs in the House of Commons, but in January 1712 he was found guilty of corruption as Secretary-at-War and sent to the Tower. The mould of future hatred between Walpole and the supporters of Oxford had been set. With the accession of George I, he was given the opportunity to repair his fortunes when appointed Paymaster-General. By 1717, with the deaths of Halifax, Wharton and Somers, the third generation of Whigs had the game all in their own hands. The Tories were powerless. Even Nottingham, the sole Tory in George I's first ministry, had resigned over the treatment meted out to the leaders of the Fifteen.

Power created jealousy between the young Whig lions. In April 1717, after a trial of strength, Walpole's brother-in-law and political ally, Charles, second Viscount Townshend, was dismissed from the post of Lord-Lieutenant of Ireland. The next day Walpole himself resigned, to be joined in opposition by Orford, William Pulteney and a number of close associates.

Whig fighting Whig was something new to Walpole. He had been apprenticed in the party conflict of Anne's reign, when the question of the Protestant Succession dominated politics. Throughout his career, Jacobitism remained his chief political preoccupation, and the only way to ensure that a Jacobite restoration did not take place, he thought, was to exclude the Tories from government. Walpole consistently blackened all Tories as Jacobites without exception. It is more difficult to decide whether or not he believed his own propaganda. But the ploy was most effective.[7]

However, Walpole was an opportunist. Not only did he want a Whig government, but he wanted a Whig government which included himself, preferably as Prime Minister. In opposition he quite brazenly joined with Tories, openly opposing measures he had championed when in office. Such shameless disregard for even the appearance of principle was remarkable, and helped to form Walpole's reputation as unscrupulous. 'I am no saint', he admitted, 'no spartan, no reformer.'[8] But he was an exceptionally able financial administrator. The South Sea Bubble enabled him to claw his way to the top. After engineering a spurious reconciliation between George I and his son, the Prince of Wales, Walpole was once more appointed Paymaster-General. Then, in 1720, the Bubble inflated to a monstrous size and burst.

In that year the Directors of the South Sea Company proposed to convert some £31,000,000 of the national debt in the form of annuities into company stock. In order to reduce the amount required to do this, they sought to push up the price of South Sea stock so that they would need to advance not the actual par value of the stock, but only the market value. At the beginning of the year £100 of South Sea stock was worth £128. Between the end of April and the end of June 1720, it had shot up from just over £130 to more than £745. In July the market peaked at over £1000 for £100 of South Sea stock, but by then shrewd investors were starting to pull out. The inevitable crash occurred, and fortunes were lost.[9] 'I cannot understand the South-Sea Mystery,' Swift had written to Ford on 4 April, 'perhaps the Frolick may go round, and every Nation (except this which is no Nation) have it's Missisippi.'[10]

But even Ireland felt the backlash of the Bubble. 'Conversation is full of nothing but South-sea', Swift wrote on 15 October, 'and the Ruin of the Kingdom, and scarcity of money.'[11] *The Bubble*, a broadside in verse published in several editions in Dublin and London in 1721, reveals his characteristic mistrust of projectors, and suggests that the South Sea cheat supplied some of the animus evident in his satire on the Academy of Lagado in *Gulliver's Travels.*[12]

> Ye wise Philosophers explain
> What Magick makes our Money rise
> When dropt into the Southern Main,
> Or do these Juglers cheat our Eyes?

Swift was convinced, with reason, that the stockjobbers and the directors of the new joint stock companies that flourished at the height of the craze for investment were simply knaves and rogues:

> While some build Castles in the Air,
> *Directors* build 'em in the Seas;
> *Subscribers* plainly see 'um there,
> For Fools will see as Wise Men please.

The reality was rather different: it was all a sham, a con, or, in the contemporary phrase, a bubble:

> The Nation t[hen] too late will find
> Computing all th[eir] Cost and Trouble,
> *Directors* Promi[ses] but Wind,
> South-Sea at best [a m]ighty BUBBLE.[13]

This was self-evident by 1721, and the public bayed for the blood of the South Sea Directors as confidence in credit collapsed. The political consequences of such a catastrophe could have been immense. There was even talk of bringing Oxford out of retirement to deal with the crisis. A Jacobite restoration was the worst Whig fear. Instead Walpole stepped into the breach. Thanks to J.H. Plumb, the myth that he wisely avoided speculating in South Sea stock himself, having seen through the bubble from the outset, has long been dispelled.[14] But his role in repairing the country's finances is less clear-cut. According to Professor Plumb, the finances 'repaired themselves'. P.G.M. Dickson, on the other hand, thinks that there can be 'little doubt that Walpole was the main architect' of the proposals that were put forward in 1721 in the Act to Restore Public Credit.[15]

Whatever the truth of the matter, there can be no question that Walpole made political capital out of the Bubble, using the aftermath to ingratiate himself with the King and his Court. Hitherto he had been unpopular, but by lowering a screen on investigations into the ministry's part in the affair, he successfully prevented any of George I's immediate circle being implicated (as they most certainly would have been). He courted unpopularity in the country at large and won for himself another nickname, that of the 'Skreenmaster-General', but Walpole had gained the King's confidence and, politically, that was what counted. He was appointed First Lord of the Treasury – where he had wanted to be all the time – and Chancellor of the Exchequer. With the deaths of Stanhope in 1721 and Sunderland in April 1722, the last obstacles to Walpole's premiership were removed. Three months later, as we know, Wood was granted a patent to mint £100,800-worth of copper coinage for Ireland.

Wood's patent was not the only grievance Swift had against Robert Walpole. When Sunderland died, his papers were speedily seized upon by the Secretaries of State. A fortnight later rumours of a Jacobite plot began to circulate, and Francis Atterbury, Bishop of Rochester, was implicated. That Swift's friend had Jacobite leanings cannot be disputed, nor can the fact that he was actively working for the restoration of the Pretender, but the charges brought against him were trumped up by Walpole. In *Gulliver's Travels*, in a passage which was, significantly, omitted from the first edition, Swift satirised Walpole's reasons for inventing the details of such a plot:

> ... in the Kingdom of *Tribnia,* by the Natives called
> *Langden* ... the Bulk of the People consisted wholly of
> Discoverers, Witnesses, Informers, Accusers, Prosecutors,
> Evidences, Swearers; together with their several subservient

and subaltern Instruments; all under the Colours, the
Conduct, and pay of Ministers and their Deputies. The
Plots in that Kingdom are usually the Workmanship of
those Persons who desire to raise their own Characters of
profound Politicians; to restore new Vigour to a crazy
Administration; to stifle or divert general Discontents; to
fill their Coffers with Forfeitures; and raise or sink the
Opinion of publick Credit, as either shall best answer their
private Advantage.[16]

'Walpole's exploitation of the most successful political scare
in the eighteenth century' angered Swift.[17] The Atterbury
trial did indeed divert attention away from the unpleasant
effects of the Bubble, and served to reaffirm the distinction
between Whig and Tory as one between Hanoverian and
Jacobite. What could be more effective than to draw attention away from the recent domestic credit crisis and Whiggish
incompetence and focus it in the direction of the safety of the
Protestant Succession?

Gulliver's Travels exposes, among many, many other things,
the behaviour of Walpole over the Atterbury affair, and the
way in which correspondence could be deciphered so that it
allegedly meant almost anything. 'So for Example', Swift
writes as Gulliver, 'if I should say in a Letter to a Friend, *Our
Brother* Tom *has just got the Piles*; a Man of Skill in this Art
would discover how the same Letters which compose that
Sentence, may be analysed into the following Words; *Resist,
—a Plot is brought home – The Tour.*'[18] In Atterbury's case, 'the
Anagrammatick Method' was scarcely necessary. The mere
fact that he had cover-names was sufficient. That Walpole
was unable to come up with anything concrete against him
was irrelevant. On his return from a four-month 'Summer
Expedition ... on Account of health' in 1723, Swift found a
letter waiting for him from Pope and Bolingbroke, informing
him of Atterbury's banishment. He noted his 'Infelicity in
being so Strongly attached to Traytors (as they call them) and
Exiles, and State Criminalls', and explained that he was
'every day perswading my self that a Dagger is at my Throat,
a halter about my Neck, or Chains at my Feet, all prepared
by those in Power'.[19]

The stage was set for a confrontation between Swift and
Walpole. The voices calling Swift to England were strong.
Oxford was ailing, and Swift wanted to see him before he
died. Bolingbroke had returned from the continent, having
received a pardon. Pope was staying with the Earl of
Peterborough. Rochester's exile was a further reminder of
Swift's English past. He was at work on *Gulliver's Travels,* and
ready to return once more to London life. *The Drapier's Letters*
delayed his crossing in more ways than one. He made up his
mind to leave at the end of March 1725, but was dissuaded
on account of his personal safety.[20] With the conclusion of the
affair of the halfpence, there was no practical reason to hinder
him from the journey. In fact Stella's continuing ill health
may well have contributed to his decision to set out early in
March 1726, and by the middle of that month he was
ensconced in 'Bury Street, next door to the Royal Chair', near
where he stayed over fifteen years earlier in the autumn of
1710.[21]

Ostensibly Swift was visiting England 'to see old friends'
and to transact some 'business' with 'two of them'.[22] Oxford
had died on 21 May 1724. This gave Swift the idea of writing
his life. 'And such a Work most properly belongs to me', he
assured his son, 'who loved and respected him above all Men,
and had the Honor to know him better than any other of my
Level did.' He proposed to make 'severall Alterations and
Additions' to the *History of the Four Last Years of the Queen,*
which 'by some Accidents was not printed'.[23] The new Earl of
Oxford proved to be as sceptical of Swift's schemes as the old.
Swift was still trying to find the opportunity to discuss the
matter with him in August, as he was preparing to return to
Ireland. *Gulliver's Travels* was similarly neglected, and steps
taken to secure its publication only at the last minute before
Swift was about to set out for home. The only other 'literary'
business he might have been engaged in was perhaps the
projecting of the volume of Pope-Swift *Miscellanies* which
appeared the following year.

Swift spent much more of his time 'rambling' with Pope
and Gay. Within a month, during which he had been 'picking
up the Remnants of [his] old Acquaintance, and descending
to take new ones',[24] he had met up with Arbuthnot in

London, and had stayed with Bolingbroke at Dawley and with Pope at Twickenham. Arbuthnot introduced him to Lord Chesterfield as well as to that important opposition politician, William Pulteney. Having been invited to meet the Princess of Wales, he had finally ventured to go to Leicester House. Even the Whigs were 'very civil' to him, and he dined with Walpole, entertaining hopes of persuading the Prime Minister to alter his attitude towards Ireland. Then, in May, he left for Pope's house at Twickenham once more. For the next two months Swift remained in the country in the company of friends such as Gay, Bolingbroke and the Earl of Bathurst. Sometimes he went wandering 'for a Fortnight together'.[25]

During his social round, however, he had managed to transact one piece of business. Through the offices of his old ally, the Earl of Peterborough, Swift had arranged a personal audience with Walpole. Attending the 'Great Man' 'at eight o'clock in the morning' of 27 April, he had 'somewhat more than an hour's conversation with him'. 'I had no other design', he assured Peterborough, 'than to represent the affairs of *Ireland* to him in a true light.' Swift's political naiveté is astounding. Did he really think a quiet word in Walpole's ear would serve to rectify the misunderstandings of the past few years and, at a stroke, reverse his Irish policy? Yet that was what Swift claimed to have been trying to do. Understandably enough, Walpole refused to regard Ireland in any other light than that of a dependency. 'I failed very much in my design', Swift conceded, 'for, I saw, he had conceived opinions from the examples and practices of the present and some former governors, which I could not reconcile to the notions I had of liberty, a possession always understood by the *British* nation to be the inheritance of a human creature.'[26]

The disagreement between Swift and Walpole was funda-mental. To Swift, the Revolution had restored the equili-brium of the 'ancient constitution' of King, Lords and Commons, re-establishing the balance between the three elements crucial to the Gothic concept of mixed monarchy. In common with other 'Country' thinkers, Swift argued that, far from endorsing the effects of the Revolution, Whig politicians had pursued the further corruption of the constitution to the situation which obtained in 1726. Walpole and 'upstart monied men' like him, having 'ousted the traditional rulers' – the 'natural aristocracy' which 'governed in the national interest' – 'governed entirely for their own self-interest'.[27] Swift dated the onset of this process at 1688. 'We are Slaves already', he told Sheridan in 1733, 'and from my Youth onwards.'[28] Similarly the 'grievances' of Ireland had been 'brought upon that kingdom since the Revolution'.[29] They were only the prelude to the subjection of England itself to a corrupt and rapacious regime. This was the invisible and creeping menace which he saw attacking liberty and property throughout the three kingdoms.

Walpole's attitude was rather different. He believed that the Revolution of 1688, far from restoring an ancient constitution, had established a mixed monarchy for the first time, removing the threat of absolutism posed by successive Stuart kings. These gains had to be consolidated at all costs, and so his main energies were devoted to defending the achievements of 1688 from the, largely imaginary, Jacobite threat. He was unable to appreciate Swift's concern for the rights and privileges of the Irish, or his fears for the Englishman's liberty and property. His main political objective was to achieve stability so that a Stuart restoration would be impossible. Far from endangering liberty, Walpole believed he was safeguarding it, even in Ireland, from the threat posed by Popery and the Pretender. His own position as Prime Minister confirmed the security of the Protestant Succession.

In July 1726 Swift had two more meetings with Walpole, 'the first time by invitation, and the second at my desire for an hour, wherein we differed in every point.'[30] As has been suggested, this was hardly surprising. 'I am weary of being among Ministers whom I cannot govern,' he wrote, 'who are all Rank Toryes in Government, and worse than Whigs in Church: whereas I was the first Man who taught and practiced the direct contrary Principle.'[31] Such a bald statement of political belief merits examination. Just what did Swift mean by being a Tory 'in Church' and a Whig 'in Government'? He believed in the protection of liberty and property, and championed the rights and privileges of the individual against the oppression of either a king or a ministry. He stood out against arbitrary monarchy and the abuse of prerogative. As such, he concurred with Walpole and the Whigs in denying hereditary title to the Crown. 'As the law stands, none has title to the crown but the present possessor,' he told Chetwode in 1721. 'I think I could defend myself by all the duty of a Christian to take oath to any prince in possession.'[32] He believed that 'whoever neither offends the Laws of God, or the Country he liveth in commiteth no Sin.'[33]

These were opinions more readily associated with Low Churchmen, like Bishop Burnet or Bishop Hoadly, than with a man who was fervent in his support for the rights of the Established Church. But Swift was a Whig 'in Government'. His concern was that 'all things' were 'tending towards absolute Power' under Walpole. 'I fear I might outlive liberty in *England*', he wrote in 1735. 'It hath continued longer than in any other monarchy.'[34] This is what he meant when he said that the ministers were 'all Rank Toryes in Government' – they seemed to be indifferent or oblivious to the threat that was being posed to liberty and property. At the same time they were failing to support the rights of the Church of England. Hence they were 'worse than Whigs in Church', caring little for its temporal and spiritual maintenance. No wonder Swift boasted that he was 'the first Man who taught and practiced the direct contrary Principle'. He 'split tickets' on questions of Church and State.[35]

Having quarrelled with Walpole a second and a third time, there was little he could do but return to Ireland. If, as gossip had it, he had been seeking preferment for himself in England (and there is no indication that he had), he failed dismally to secure it. True, he had renewed his contact both with those in the mainstream of London life and with those, like Pope, who were outside it. He had met influential opposition politicians like Pulteney, his correspondent of the future, as well as the Princess of Wales, and had formed a close friendship with the King's mistress, the charming Henrietta Howard. But he had not swayed Walpole. He set out for Ireland on 15 August 1726, and by the twenty-fifth he was back in Dublin.

Swift's 'business' with Walpole was not quite over. He had carried the manuscript of *Gulliver's Travels* with him to

London, and in the final weeks of his stay he had made arrangements for it to be published 'by Christmas at furthest'.[36] Everything was transacted by intermediaries. Not only was Swift fond of mystery, but *Gulliver's Travels* was politically dangerous. By the time it appeared on 28 October 1726, Swift was back in Ireland. The similarities to the way he published his other 'hot' books, the *Discourse* in 1701, and the *Tale* in 1704, is striking. With no prospect of bringing Walpole to an understanding through personal intercession, Swift had had no alternative but to unleash 'one of the most remarkable and virulent satires ever to be written against' his regime.[37]

13

Gulliver's Travels

Although Swift first mentions his 'Travels' in a letter of 15 April 1721, it was only in August 1725 that he admitted that he had 'finished' and was 'now transcribing them'.[1] In the intervening period much material of a topical nature had been added, particularly to the miscellaneous third voyage. It was another year before he took steps to secure the book's publication. Then, in a letter to Benjamin Motte, copied out by Gay, signed 'Richard Sympson', and dated 8 August 1726, Swift offered his 'Cousin' Lemuel Gulliver's history of his travels for publication, and demanded £200 as 'the least Summ I will receive on his account'. Motte offered 'punctually [to] pay the money' within six months 'if the Success will allow it'. A single-sentence rejoinder from 'Richard Sympson', dated 13 August 1726, authorised the publication, stipulating that 'both Volumes' should 'come out together', and 'by Christmas at furthest'.[2] Two days later Swift left for Ireland.

Gulliver's Travels was published on 28 October 1726. Soon it was 'the conversation of the whole town', and the entire first impression was 'sold in a week'.[3] Arbuthnot expected it to have 'as great a Run as John Bunian'.[4] Motte published three 'editions' in 1726, and, in addition, it began to be serialised, and translated into French and Dutch. Other publications, including keys and continuations, attempted to cash in on its tremendous success. And yet Swift was dissatisfied with the way in which his masterpiece had been treated. Within a month of the appearance of the original edition, he was complaining that 'in the second volume ... several passages ... appear to be patched and altered, and the style of a different sort.' 'Let me add', he concluded, 'that if I were

262

Gulliver's friend, I would desire all my acquaintance to give out that his copy was basely mangled, and abused, and added to, and blotted out by the printer; for so to me it seems, in the second volume particularly.'[5]

Now Swift was fond of playing games. *A Tale of a Tub,* replete with mock defects and hiatuses in the manuscript, was supposedly published without the author's knowledge and tampered with by the printer.[6] Was the accusation that Motte had censored and altered the text of *Gulliver's Travels* simply a further instance of Swift's playfulness? Apparently not, for there is abundant evidence that he was genuinely dissatisfied with the printer's performance. Swift told Chetwode that the book was 'mangled in the press, for in some parts it doth not seem of a piece', and Chetwode was scarcely in a position to assist in any joke at the printer's expense.[7] Charles Ford sent Motte a list of corrections to be inserted in the second edition with the explanation that the book 'abounds with many gross Errors of the Press'.[8] Motte's 'corrected' edition of May 1727 adopted almost all of Ford's suggestions.

The authenticity of these emendations can hardly be doubted. When Faulkner was preparing to publish *Gulliver's Travels* as the third volume of his edition of Swift's *Works,* Swift wrote to Ford:

> Now, you may please to remember how much I complained of Motts suffering some friend of his ... not onely to blot out some things that he thought might give offence, but to insert a good deal of trash contrary to the Author's manner and Style, and Intention. I think you had a Gulliver interleaved and set right in those mangled and murdered Pages ... I wish you would please to let me know, whether You have such an interleaved Gulliver; and where and how I could get [it]; For to say the truth, I cannot with patience endure that mingld and mangled manner, as it came from Mottes hands ...[9]

Ford's 'interleaved' copy of *Gulliver's Travels,* which Swift proposed to use as the basis of his corrections for Faulkner's edition, is preserved in the Victoria and Albert Museum.[10]

we must take seriously the author's allegations that
st edition did not consistently follow his own intentions.
for this reason that modern editions, despite the
arguments of Arthur E. Case and, more recently, F. P. Lock, in
favour of the earliest text,[11] usually use Faulkner's edition of
1735 as their copy-text. Not only did Faulkner make the
retrospective claim that Swift 'was so kind as to correct the
whole work, ready for printing', but a comparison of the
two texts bears out Swift's statement that 'several passages'
seemed to be 'patched and altered' in the 'second volume'.[12]

The fact is of some importance to the interpretation of
Swift's satire in *Gulliver's Travels*. According to Deane Swift,
the book was 'a direct, plain and bitter satire against the
innumerable follies and corruptions in law, politicks, learning, morals and religion'.[13] What was direct and plain in 1755
has now been encompassed by massive problems relating to
the role of Gulliver, the role of the reader, and the role of
topical political allusion in the overall satiric structure. A
whole critical industry has been built up around the vexed
question of the meaning of 'A Voyage to the Houyhnhnms',
and rival schools of 'hard' and 'soft' interpretation have
thrashed out the implications for mankind of the rational
ideal which is apparently offered. Whereas the fourth voyage
was used by earlier critics as evidence of the rampant
misanthropy of the 'mad Dean', modern critics have exposed
the flaws in any simple analysis which seeks to identify men
as they are with the Yahoos and men as they should be with
the Houyhnhnms. And yet we are no nearer to a consensus of
opinion on the meaning of the fourth voyage, let alone the
meaning of the *Travels* as a whole.

In his letter to Benjamin Motte, Richard Sympson noted
that the account of his Cousin Gulliver's travels 'may be
thought in one or two places to be a little Satyrical'. Whether
it was this, or merely a question of copy-editing, which caused
the printer to modify Swift's text, there can be little doubt
that many contemporaries were uneasy at the savageness of
the satire. According to Pope, some thought it 'rather too
bold, and too general a Satire', although 'none that I hear of
accuse it of particular reflections'. 'The Politicians to a
man agree, that it is free from particular reflections,' Gay

concurred, 'but that the Satire on general societies of men is too severe.' Arbuthnot appears to have been virtually alone in his sanguine view that 'Gulliver is a happy man that at his age can write such a merry work.'[14] There were good reasons, it seems, for Swift to take care that his authorship, though widely suspected, could not be proved.

Swift had intended to publish *Gulliver's Travels* 'when the world shall deserve them, or rather when a Printer shall be found brave enough to venture his Eares'. He wrote the book, he claimed, for the same reason that he wrote all his works – 'to vex the world rather then divert it'. Walpole's persistent disregard for not only the liberty and property of the individual, but for public morals, had provided the final spur for Swift to give his book to the world. But he wanted to 'compass that designe without hurting [his] own person or Fortune'. This could only be achieved, he thought, by protecting his anonymity, and although Pope remarked that he 'needed not to have been so secret upon this head', Swift's recent experience over his Irish pamphlets advocated caution.[15] He acknowledged that the 'whole Building' of the *Travels* was 'erected' upon a 'great foundation of Misanthropy', and yet he argued that he did not 'hate Mankind': 'it is vous autres who hate them', he explained to Pope, 'because you would have them reasonable Animals, and are Angry for being disappointed.'[16]

We must be careful to compensate for Swift's ironic tone in his letters to his friends before we can safely use his own statements as evidence of his intentions in *Gulliver's Travels*. And yet when he says that he has 'always rejected' the textbook definition of man as *animal rationale*, it is worth taking note. Instead he argued that the correct definition should be 'only *rationis capax*'.[17] It is an important distinction, even if, as Bolingbroke pointed out, it does not stand up. Man is an animal who is capable of reason, but it is the human predicament that, as *A Meditation upon a Broom-Stick* puts it, 'His Animal Faculties [are] perpetually mounted on his Rational'.[18] A constant struggle is taking place in the human breast between mind and body, reason and emotion. Swift recognised this as much as any man ever has, and it informs his various writing from the early odes onwards. In *A Tale of a*

Tub he stressed the conjunction between spiritual ecstasy and carnal pleasure. In *Gulliver's Travels* he is engaged once more in stripping man of his pretensions, exposing the gaping discrepancy between actual and ideal, between how things are and how they should be. Far from man being a rational animal – the ideal which the textbooks of logic stress in their definition – Swift suggests that he is merely an animal capable of reason but dominated, more often than not, by his passions. In this sense, *Gulliver's Travels* remains 'a direct, plain and bitter satire'.

The first thing the contemporary reader would have noticed on picking up the two volumes would have been the title-page: 'Travels into several Remote Nations of the World. In Four Parts. By Lemuel Gulliver, First a Surgeon, and then a Captain of several Ships'. Ostensibly, the work is a travel-book, and it purports to be genuine. Not only is there no indication of the wonders about to unfold, it appears to be just another volume of travellers' tales. Travel-writing was in vogue in the early eighteenth century. Defoe had exploited its popularity not only in *Robinson Crusoe*, but in more conventional travel-books. His fictitious accounts had their authentic counterparts. Swift was fond of travel literature. In 1720 he annotated *A Relation of some Yeares Travaile into Africa and Greater Asia* (1634) by Thomas Herbert. 'If this Book were stript of its Impertinence, Conceitedness and tedious Digressions', he wrote, 'it would be almost worth reading, and would then be two thirds smaller than it is.'[19] It was in the following year that he announced to Ford that he was 'now writing a History of my Travells, which will be a large Volume, and gives Account of Countryes hitherto unknown'.[20]

It would be reasonable to assume, then, that *Gulliver's Travels* started out as a parody of 'tedious' travel-books. During the summer of 1722 at Loughall, Swift read 'through abundance of Trash', including 'I know not how many diverting Books of History and Travells.'[21] But he wrote to 'vex the world rather then divert it', and although *Gulliver's Travels* performed the latter function, it also served to challenge and provoke. More than likely it owed something to the meetings of the Scriblerus Club. Pope noted that 'Dr Swift took his first hints for Gulliver' from *The Memoirs of Martinus Scriblerus,* a work of collaboration which satirised false learning and scholarly pedantry. Martin, too, visits 'the ancient Pygmaean Empire' before 'the Land of the Giants, now the most humane people in the world', as well as the 'Kingdom of Philosophers, who govern by Mathematicks', concluding with an account of how the traveller 'discovered a Vein of Melancholy proceeding almost to a Disgust of his Species'.[22]

Although Swift wrote his satire on travel literature in the first half of the 1720s, it is useful to think of it as an extension of Scriblerian activities. It is, in the first place, a spoof. It proffers information about 'Remote Nations of the World', and proceeds to test the credulity of the reader with accounts not only of pigmies and giants, but of men alternately six inches and sixty feet high, as well as flying islands, spirits, men who were immortal, and, to cap it all, talking horses. Swift himself told the story of an Irish bishop who said 'that Book was full of improbable lies, and for his part, he hardly believed a word of it'.[23] This oft-quoted anecdote nevertheless draws attention to the credulity of eighteen-century audiences. People turned to travel literature for wonderful tales and amazing adventures. Just how far could the writer go before their willing suspension of disbelief was shattered? Swift deliberately went too far, of course, but we should be aware of what he was testing.

His first task, then, was one common to all writers of fiction. He had to entrap the reader, to persuade him to suspend his disbelief. Only then could he begin to manipulate him to achieve his satiric end. And so *Gulliver's Travels* opens with all the paraphernalia of the travel-book, including an account of Lemuel Gulliver signed 'Richard Sympson' to establish authenticity and the provenance of the manuscript. The narrative, too, is straightforward enough at first, as it supplies the history of the putative author, and how he came to be shipwrecked on the shore of Lilliput. A simple comparison of the first few pages of *Gulliver's Travels* and *Robinson Crusoe* will amply demonstrate that, although Swift's account is compressed, omitting any reference to religious matters, they run along similar lines. 'Richard Sympson' is careful to assure the reader that Gulliver's account 'would have been at least twice as large, if I had not made bold to strike out innumerable Passages relating to the Winds and Tides, as well as to the Variations and Bearings in the several Voyages; together with the minute Descriptions of the Management of the Ship in Storms, in the Style of Sailors.'[24] Swift's exposition is at once an imitation and a gentle satire of the crude attempts of travel-writers to provide verisimilitude through the rehearsal of maritime jargon.

Swift also has to establish Gulliver's credentials, for the character of the narrator is the device through which the reader will be manipulated. Gulliver is by far Swift's most fully rounded persona, more of a character than the Hack, more of an individual than Isaac Bickerstaff or M.B., Drapier, more developed than the Modest Proposer. As Gulliver is telling his own story, he is subject to the conditions that apply to all first-person narrators. Are we to sympathise with him, or feel alienated from him? Should we believe what he says implicitly, or are we justified in questioning his judgment and motivation? Is he, in fact, a reliable or an unreliable narrator? The same initial problems which beset a reading of, say, *Moll Flanders*, also affect *Gulliver's Travels*. It is principally a reflection of our awareness of twentieth-century fictive techniques which leads us to accept that Gulliver is as much a butt as he is an agent of Swift's satire. Earlier critics were virtually unanimous in their identification of Swift as Gulliver, and in Gulliver's misanthropy they saw evidence of Swift's own.

And yet there are sufficiently obvious ironic pointers to resist any attempt to link Gulliver and Swift too closely. It is made clear almost from the outset that the narrator is a figure of fun. We are in effect introduced to him inauspiciously on the shore of Lilliput, flat on his back, bound and persecuted by numerous, insect-like individuals. Soon he is making water. Worse is to come. Chained like a dog, Gulliver is 'extremely pressed by the Necessities of Nature':

> I was under great Difficulties between Urgency and Shame [he explains]. The best Expedient I could think on, was to creep into my House, which I accordingly did; and shutting the Gate after me, I went as far as the Length of

my Chain would suffer; and discharged my Body of that
uneasy Load. But his was the only Time I was ever guilty of
so uncleanly an Action ...(p. 29)

Yet another example of Swift's cloacal obsession? Perhaps. But
there are rhetorical reasons for his concentration on Gulliver's
toilet habits at this early stage in the narrative. Not only does it
serve as a satiric reminder of what the travel-books leave
out – despite the excessive detail we are offered in *Robinson
Crusoe*, we are never told this one – it provides signal insight
into, not Swift's character, but Gulliver's, who supplies a full
account of how 'due Care was taken every Morning before
Company came, that the offensive Matter should be carried off
in Wheel-barrows'. 'I would not have dwelt so long upon such a
Circumstance', he explains, 'if I had not thought it necessary to
justify my Character in Point of Cleanliness to the World;
which I am told, some of my Maligners have been pleased,
upon this and other Occasions, to call in Question' (p. 29).

Already, before his adventures have really begun, we have
been given details of Gulliver's bowel movements. What sort
of a man is it who feels he has to justify his 'Character ... to
the World' in such a manner? This is not the only occasion on
which Gulliver's paranoia makes itself felt through his
eagerness to vindicate his conduct. Subsequently he explains
at great length how the Treasurer of Lilliput's wife conceived
'a violent Affection' for him. Seemingly oblivious of the ludicrousness of the proportional discrepancy between them, he
feels 'obliged' to vindicate her 'Reputation'. True, she visited
him at his lodgings, and was pleased to treat him 'with all
innocent Marks of Freedom and Friendship'. 'I have passed
many an Afternoon very agreeably in these Conversations,' he
admits, and denies that anything illicit ever took place:

> But I defy the Treasurer, or his two Informers. (I will name
> them, and let them make their best of it) *Clustril* and
> *Drunlo*, to prove that any Person ever came to me *incognito*,
> except the Secretary *Reldresal* ... I should not have dwelt so
> long upon this Particular, if it had not been a Point
> wherein the Reputation of a great Lady is so nearly
> concerned; to say nothing of my own ... (p. 65)

'I should not have dwelt so long' – it is a familiar formula. It is not so much that we feel Gulliver protests too much, more that we are uncertain why he dwells on such absurd details at all. The effect is comic, of course, and *Gulliver's Travels* is a marvellously funny book. But Swift's humour is rarely without a purpose. Now this passage could conceivably be said to satirise fashionable society, with the mores of the privileged classes of England being aped by a people no more than six inches high. More importantly, it works against Gulliver, and makes us less likely to trust his judgment. By informing us of his mental instability, he is unwittingly, as it were, preparing us for the time that he is pictured happily conversing with horses in his stable at Redriff.

Gulliver's naiveté is a principal ingredient of Swift's satiric platter. In Lilliput he is dazzled by the prospect of greatness. 'I had the Honour to be a *Nardac*, which the Treasurer himself is not,' he observes, 'for all the World knows he is only a *Clumglum*, a Title inferior by one Degree, as that of a Marquess is to a Duke in *England*' (pp. 65-6). He is undismayed by the irony of inversions of size, and willingly prostrates himself at the feet of the Emperor on being given his liberty. 'But he commanded me to rise', he relates, 'and after many gracious Expressions, which, to avoid the Censure of Vanity, I shall not repeat; he added, that he hoped I should prove a useful Servant, and well deserve all the Favours he had already conferred upon me' (p. 44). Instead of grinding the ridiculous insect beneath his heel, Gulliver immediately assumes an attitude of subservience, and is proud to flaunt the distinctions he receives from this diminutive majesty before the world. Even when he has been informed of his imminent blinding, a concessionary sentence for his great 'crime' won for him by 'the great Friendship of the Secretary', Reldresal, Gulliver confesses that, 'having never been designed for a Courtier, either by my Birth or Education, I was so ill a Judge of Things, that I could not discover the *Lenity* and Favour of this Sentence; but conceived it (perhaps erroneously) rather to be rigorous than gentle' (pp. 71-2). Blinkered by his customary deference to authority, in whatever form, Gulliver is prepared to submit to the opinions of others because he is 'so ill a Judge of Things'.

He is often an ill judge of things. He does, after all, possess 'a Pair of Spectacles (which I sometimes use for the Weakness of mine Eyes)' (p. 37). And yet he very rarely makes use of them. Does this mean that, generally, he is myopic?[25] If so, we should be wary of what he says. For instance, in supplying an impression of proportion in Lilliput, he observes that this is exact in 'Animals, as well as Plants and Trees':

> ... the tallest Horses and Oxen are between four and five Inches in Height, the sheep an Inch and a half, more or less; their Geese about the Bigness of a Sparrow; and so the several Gradations downwards, till you come to the smallest, which, to my Sight, were almost invisible ... (p. 57)

These are either tiny sheep, or enormous geese![26] If this is meant to be an example of the keenness of Gulliver's observation, then we would do well to treat his remarks with caution. Similarly, when he says that he 'with great Ease drew fifty of the Enemy's largest Men of War' after him during his descent on the coast of Blefuscu (p. 52), we would do well to reflect on the size of these ships. The Emperor of Lilliput's 'largest Men of War', we have already been told, 'are Nine Foot long' (p. 26). And yet Gulliver claims to have swum across the channel between Lilliput and Blefuscu pulling fifty of these craft behind him.

By his own admission, Swift published 'fifty-thousand Lies' in *Gulliver's Travels*. Gulliver is *'Splendide Mendax'* – the unreliable narrator *par excellence*.[27] His unreliability is rhetorical as much as it is comic. For Swift's purpose, the reader's confidence in the narrator must be undermined. We must learn to question what he says. This is why, in the first voyage, we see him defecating, urinating on the royal palace, denying that he has committed adultery with a lady less than six inches in height. He is progressively belittled in 'A Voyage to Brobdingnag', humiliated by the predicaments into which he is brought by his size. He is put in leading strings and treated as if he were, consecutively, a doll, a baby, or a household pet. The maids of honour dandle him on their nipples and use him as a dildo, surely one of the 'many other Tricks, wherein the Reader will excuse me for not being over

271

particular' (p. 119). He contributes to his own downfall through his unquenchable desire to show off. Attempting to leap over a cow pat to show his worth, he lands in the middle 'up to my Knees', and has to be wiped clean with a footman's handkerchief (p. 124)!

His experiences in Houyhnhnmland are prefigured by his kidnapping by a monkey who takes him 'for a young one of his own Species' (p. 122). The same thing happens when a young female Yahoo embraces him 'after a most fulsome Manner' when he is washing himself in a stream, 'inflamed by Desire' at the sight of his naked body (pp. 266-7). 'THIS was Matter of Diversion to my Master and his Family', Gulliver remarks, 'as well as of Mortification to my self.' The more he seeks to retain his dignity, the more he finds himself in embarrassing situations that are beyond his control. These humiliations serve a number of purposes. Firstly they are comic, and Swift succeeds in making the most of his hero's misfortunes. In addition they are often used to point up some local satiric angle, in this case the similarity between Gulliver and the Yahoos once his pretensions – his clothes – have been stripped from him. Above all they remind us of his character, his absurd pride, and his unhappy knack of getting into ridiculous scrapes. At such times he may be seen as Everyman, if Swift had not created a recognisable individual. It is Gulliver, not Everyman, who ends up conversing with his horses 'at least four Hours every Day' (p. 290).

However, it would be stretching the evidence too far to suggest that Gulliver is a consistent, three-dimensional character. He is functional – a device used by Swift to make satirical points. These points are by no means always obvious. Having warned the reader against placing too much faith in Gulliver's judgment, Swift forbears offering a positive ideal. He requires the reader to work out this idea for himself. 'I shall say nothing of those remote Nations where *Yahoos* preside; amongst which the least corrupted are the *Brobdingnagians,* whose wise Maxims in Morality and Government, it would be our Happiness to observe', Gulliver is made to say in conclusion. 'But I forbear descanting further, and rather leave the judicious Reader to his own Remarks and Applications'

(p. 292). At such points Gulliver's functional character is very much to the fore, as he serves as Swift's mouthpiece.

Swift refuses to apply his own lessons. He leaves these to 'the judicious Reader'. It is a key phrase. Swift's reticence is at once the most compelling feature of his satirical method, and the most infuriating. It is the reason that Swift, like Shakespeare, attracts so many diverse interpretations, some ingenious, some fanciful, some preposterous. And yet, with nothing issuing from the author's mouth to gainsay them, they continue to proliferate. We must seek Swift's meaning through an awareness of his over-riding literary concerns, and an appreciation of his rhetorical strategy. Only then can we begin to approach his meaning with a measure of confidence. For Swift's positive is almost always an implied positive, and we will search the surface of his work for it in vain. Having supplied the text, he challenges the reader to interpret his signs. It is in the task of interpretation that, to Swift, the reformative process lies. Satire is indeed too often 'a sort of *Glass*, wherein Beholders do generally discover every body's Face but their Own',[28] and the inferior satirist, in spelling out his moral, connives with complacency.

Swift's answer is to offer *apparent* morals which do not necessarily stand up to close examination. His satire involves the reader to such an extent that it is much less likely, though by no means impossible, that he will fail to recognise his own face in the glass which is being held up. 'Once you have thought of big men and little men', said Dr Johnson, 'it is very easy to do all the rest.'[29] *Gulliver's Travels* does more than merely work through a simple manipulation of perspective. True, in the first two voyages, the satiric glasses are alternately convex and concave, but they are subject to the distortion of Gulliver's own lenses. Nor does Dr Johnson's glib remark take into account the fascination of the Houyhnhnms, in which questions of proportion are submerged beneath more fundamental issues of morality. Beyond the problem of *meaning*, is that of *significance*. Almost inevitably, *Gulliver's Travels* offers insight into matters that cannot have exercised Swift. His satiric method allows us to derive messages for twentieth-century man from his text that were no part of his own, paternalistic concerns. In this sense it is the Academy of

Lagado and the cold, rational manner of the Houyhnhnms which offer instruction to the age of mutually assured destruction. It is a mark of the greatness of *Gulliver's Travels* that it is capable of bearing such a burden.

Deane Swift thought that both the 'Voyage to Lilliput' and the 'Voyage to Brobdingnag' were 'intirely political'.[30] In one sense they are. Irvin Ehrenpreis notes that 'if we must lay down a single, distinctive proposition as supporting all Swift's turns of doctrine, it might be this: the belief that morality, religion, and politics are inseparable'.[31] In the Lilliputian episodes, man's social behaviour is placed in perspective, his pettiness emphasised. 'A Voyage to Brobdingnag', on the other hand, magnifies man's faults and imperfections along with his bodily proportions. But local satiric points are constantly being made, and it is difficult to fit them into an overall satiric scheme. When Gulliver observes that the Lilliputian 'Manner of Writing is very peculiar; being ... aslant from one Corner of the Paper to the other, like Ladies in *England*' (p. 57), Swift succeeds in making an incidental comment on the waywardness of contemporary female handwriting which is only tenuously related to the principal satiric thrust of *Gulliver's Travels*. The work is coherent, but not necessarily uniform. Thus we are told that ingratitude is a 'capital Crime' among the Lilliputians, and yet they are singularly ungrateful to Gulliver after he has secured them from the threat of a Blefuscudian invasion (pp. 60, 69). The former tells us about Swift's own attitude towards ingratitude, the latter about the Lilliputians themselves. However much they manage to impress Gulliver, we might be more inclined to apply to them the wise King of Brobdingnag's judgment on British society: 'I cannot but conclude the Bulk of your Natives, to be the most pernicious Race of little odious Vermin that Nature ever suffered to crawl upon the Surface of the Earth' (p. 132). This, we may be sure, is not a conclusion Gulliver would have reached.

In comparing and contrasting other, imaginary societies with his own, Swift tries to force the reader into viewing afresh the basic assumptions he makes about British society. The first two voyages concentrate on the discrepancy between profession and practice. Neither Lilliput nor Brobdingnag represents England, but they both have important similarities to England in the early eighteenth century. In other ways they are revealingly different. Once again Swift is using the strategy of parallel history. Lilliputian and Brobdingnagian history may be fictitious, but it is analogous to that of England, as much as the early history of Athens and Rome is analogous to the state of England outlined in the *Discourse* in 1701. The method is not identical, to be sure, for *Gulliver's Travels*, as a satire, makes its point through humour, whereas the *Discourse* proceeds by scholarly argument. The polemical strategy, however, is the same.

Only the most obvious parallels between Lilliput and England can be noted here, but the comparison is not merely one of size. There are two 'struggling Parties' in Lilliput, known as '*Tramecksan*, and *Slamecksan*, from the high and low Heels on their Shoes, by which they distinguish themselves' (p. 48). The analogy with the Tory and Whig parties, which were also known as the High Church and Low Church parties, is sufficiently obvious to require no elaboration. Although the High-Heels are more numerous, the Low-Heels have all the power, just as in the England of 1726, in which, despite a natural Tory majority in the kingdom, the government was entirely in the hands of the Whigs. George I was an enemy of the Tories, but his son, the Prince of Wales, less obviously so. The Emperor of Lilliput's heels were 'lower at least by a *Drurr* than any of his Court', but 'the Heir to the Crown' was thought to 'have some Tendency towards the High-Heels' (p. 48). In this way England and Lilliput can be seen to have certain significant similarities.

By representing familiar things in an unusual light, Swift's satiric mirror invites us to examine our own prejudices. The conflict between Catholic and Protestant is reduced to a debate over whether one should break one's egg on the bigger or the smaller end. 'Many hundred large Volumes have been published upon this Controversy', Gulliver informs us, 'It is computed, that eleven Thousand Persons have, at several Times, suffered Death, rather than submit to break their Eggs at the smaller End.' These 'civil Commotions' including 'six Rebellions raised on that Account,' are 'constantly fomented by the Monarchs of *Blefuscu*; and when they were quelled, the Exiles always fled for Refuge to that Empire' (p. 49). In this way, Swift deliberately invites us to compare the situation in Lilliput and that in England. France becomes analogous to Blefuscu, the supporters of the Old Pretender to the Big-Endian exiles, and so on. The contemporary application is there to be made, as well as the universal significance to be derived from recognising the pettiness of the disputes from which confrontations develop.

The recent controversy over the topicality of the political allusions in *Gulliver's Travels* stems from the question of whether or not Blefuscu *represents* France, or whether or not the quaintly named Lilliputian characters are meant to suggest contemporary political figures.[32] The rope-dancers, for instance, provide a ready metaphor for those who wish to gain and keep political office. The passage retains a universal significance. Dancing on figurative ropes can be seen to be the customary practice of aspiring ministers. But when Gulliver states that '*Flimnap*, the Treasurer, is allowed to cut a Caper on the strait Rope, at least an Inch higher than any other Lord in the whole Empire' (p. 38), Flimnap is openly compared to Walpole, the Prime Minister, who is also Lord Treasurer of England. It would be pointless to say that Flimnap *is* Walpole, for the characterisation is never developed, although the identification is readily made. It is even more futile to speculate upon whether or not Skyresh Bolgolam is the Earl of Nottingham or the Duke of Marlborough, because Swift's allusions are seldom sufficiently specific.[33]

'A Voyage to Lilliput' none the less comments on the state of the nation under the Walpole ministry. This is readily apparent when that other Lilliputian 'Diversion' of leaping over or creeping under a stick is taken into account. In 1725 George I revived the Order of the Bath. Swift satirised the event in verse:

Quoth King Robin, our Ribbands I see are too few
    of St Andrew's the Green, and St George's the Blue
I must have another of Colour more gay
That will make all my Subjects with pride to obey.

Thus 'he who will leap over a Stick for the King/Is qualified best for a Dog in a String.'³⁴ This 'Ceremony' is described in detail in 'A Voyage to Lilliput':

> The Emperor holds a Stick in his Hands, both Ends parallel to the Horizon, while the Candidates advancing one by one, sometimes leap over the Stick, sometimes creep under it backwards and forwards several times, according as the Stick is advanced or depressed. Sometimes the Emperor holds one End of the Stick, and his first Minister the other; sometimes the Minister has it entirely to himself. Whoever performs his Part with most Agility, and holds out the longest in *leaping* and *creeping*, is rewarded with the Blue-coloured Silk; the Red is given to the next, and the Green to the third.... (p. 39)

Through comparing the English nobility's pursuit of empty honours with the undignified antics of the Lilliputians, Swift satirises Walpole's creation of 'jobs for the boys,' and exposes the tactics of the Robinocracy to buy off potential opposition – a policy which is connived at by George I himself.

Swift employs different satiric techniques when dealing with the laws, customs and education of the Lilliputians. 'THERE are some Laws and Customs in this Empire very peculiar,' Gulliver remarks, 'and if they were not so directly contrary to those of my own dear Country, I should be tempted to say a little in their Justification' (p. 58). The strange practices he proceeds to enumerate are all eminently sensible, and they coincide with what we know to have been Swift's own views on certain subjects. These, too, have contemporary applications as well as universal significance. For instance, in the wake of the Atterbury trial, the Lilliputian law relating to informers is of interest:

> All Crimes against the State, are punished here with the utmost Severity; but if the Person accused make his Innocence plainly to appear upon his Tryal, the Accuser is immediately put to an ignominious Death; and out of his Goods or Lands, the innocent Person is quadruply recompensed.... (p. 58)

277

So is the view that fraud is 'a greater Crime than Theft,' especially with regard to the recent South Sea Bubble.

In these instances, Swift is exposing the shortcomings of British society by comparing it with a Lilliputian ideal which, it must be said, the Lilliputians also patently fail to live up to. They are his habitual objects of concern. In Lilliput, for example, 'Males of Noble or Eminent Birth ... are bred up in the Principles of Honour, Justice, Courage, Modesty, Clemency, Religion, and Love of their Country' (p. 61), whereas his constant complaint about post-Restoration England is that the lines of once-virtuous families have degenerated sadly, to the inestimable loss of the nation. It is the decay of this natural aristocracy which has allowed upstarts like Walpole to dominate affairs. This is the theme developed in 'A Voyage to Brobdingnag' in Gulliver's conversations with the King, for they constitute the heart of the matter of this book.

'NOTHING but an extreme Love of Truth could have hindered me from concealing this Part of my Story,' Gulliver admits. 'It was in vain to discover my Resentments, which were always turned into Ridicule: And I was forced to rest with Patience, while my noble and most beloved Country was so injuriously treated.' And yet he 'gave to every Point a more favourable turn by many Degrees than the strictness of Truth would allow' (p. 133). The sagacious reader once again perceives that Gulliver protests too much. To try to retrieve the situation and win the King of Brobdingnag's admiration for the achievements of his own society, Gulliver offers to give him the secret of making gunpowder, but he is amazed at his reaction. 'THE King was struck with Horror at the Description I had given of those terrible Engines, and the Proposal I had made', he recalls. 'A STRANGE *Effect of narrow Principles* and *short Views!*' He finds it incomprehensible

that a Prince possessed of every Quality which procures Veneration, Love and Esteem; of strong Parts, great Wisdom and profound Learning; endued with admirable Talents for Government, and almost adored by his Subjects; should from a *nice unnecessary Scruple*, whereof in *Europe* we can have no Conception, let slip an Opportunity

278

put into his Hands, that would have made him absolute
Master of the Lives, the Liberties, and the Fortunes of his
People. (pp. 134-5)

The *leitmotif* of Swift's political writings sounds once more,
as *Gulliver's Travels* brings into focus the question of the royal
prerogative and the rights and privileges of the people. The
King of Brobdingnag is 'almost adored' by his subjects
precisely because he is a paternalistic Prince who respects the
liberty and property of his dependants. The contrast with
George I is marked. Gulliver's question-and-answer sessions
with the benevolent King are a serious indictment of the state
of the nation under Walpole. Gulliver's descriptions of the
House of Lords – 'the Ornament and Bulwark of the Kingdom; worthy Followers of their most renowned Ancestors,
whose Honour had been the Reward of their Virtue; from
which their Posterity were never once known to degenerate' – the House of Commons – 'all principal Gentlemen, *freely*
picked and culled out by the People themselves, for their
great Abilities, and Love of their Country' – the laws, religion,
customs and history of England 'for about an hundred Years
past,' provoke searching queries:

He asked, what Methods were used to cultivate the Minds
and Bodies of our young Nobility; and in what kind of
Business they commonly spent the first and teachable Part
of their Lives. What Course was taken to supply that
Assembly, when any noble Family became extinct. What
Qualifications were necessary in those who are to be
created new Lords: Whether the Humour of the Prince, a
Sum of Money to a Court-Lady, or a Prime Minister; or a
Design of strengthening a Party opposite to the publick
Interest, ever happened to be Motives in those Advance-
ments....
    HE then desired to know, what Arts were practised in
electing those whom I called Commoners. Whether, a
Stranger with a strong Purse might not influence the vulgar
Voters to chuse him before their own Landlord, or the most
considerable Gentleman in the Neighbourhood. How it
came to pass, that People were so violently bent upon

279

getting into this Assembly, which I allowed to be a
great Trouble and Expence, often to the Ruin of
their Families, without any Salary or Pension: Because
this appeared such an exalted Strain of Virtue
and publick Spirit, that his Majesty seemed to
doubt it might possibly not be always sincere....
(pp. 129-30)

The King of Brobdingnag's queries express Swift's own
views on English government and society. By presenting them
in this manner, he avoids any possible confusion that might
have resulted from using Gulliver as his mouthpiece. It is not
Gulliver, but the King of Brobdingnag, who suggests that
MPs might consider 'sacrificing the publick Good to the
Designs of a weak and vicious Prince, in Conjunction with a
corrupted Ministry' (p. 130). The naive Gulliver is exerting
his puny eloquence in *defence* of the system of Walpole, blind
to the pertinence of his royal adversary's observations.
Brobdingnag is a sort of England in pristine condition.
Instead of permitting the ancient constitution to fall into a
state of disrepair, the King of Brobdingnag actively promotes
the fulfilment of the paternalistic duties advocated so stren-
uously by Swift. It is for that reason that, in conclusion, the
'least corrupted' society is held to be that of the Brobdingnagians, 'whose wise Maxims in Morality and Government, it
would be our Happiness to observe' (p. 292). Given man's
fallen condition, it would be the most he could hope for – and
Swift did, fervently.

'A Voyage to Laputa' also celebrates Swift's ideal. In
Glubbdubdrib Gulliver summons 'some *English* Yeomen of
the old Stamp,' and is suitably impressed by what he sees.
These pillars of English society of old – 'so famous for the
Simplicity of their Manners, Dyet and Dress; for Justice in
their Dealings; for their true Spirit of Liberty; for their Valour
and Love of their Country' – compare favourably with their
grandchildren, 'who in selling their Votes, and managing at
Elections have acquired every Vice and Corruption that can
possibly be learned in a Court' (p. 202). Lord Munodi
similarly represents the old values, and reveals Swift's nostalgic yearning for the Golden Age (pp. 175-8). His estate

presented a 'delightful Prospect' to Gulliver, with 'Farmers Houses at small Distances, neatly built, the Fields enclosed, containing Vineyards, Corngrounds and Meadows' – a veritable paternalist's ideal.

Neither the old-fashioned yeoman nor the old-fashioned landowner has any place in new schemes of things, Swift suggests, and Munodi's downfall is laid at the door of the projectors, scientific charlatans who destroy when they cannot build, and make worse what they have no means of improving. Swift was not antipathetic to science *per se*, or even new scientific methods. He had read and approved of Francis Bacon's *The Advancement of Learning*.[35] But he abhorred misguided and dangerous experiment. He would have agreed wholeheartedly with the King of Brobdingnag, who 'gave it for his Opinion; that whoever could make two Ears of Corn, or two Blades of Grass to grow upon a Spot of Ground where only one grew before; would deserve better of Mankind, and do more essential Service to his Country, than the whole Race of Politicians put together' (pp. 135-6). This the projectors and virtuosi were, in Swift's opinion, patently failing to accomplish. Instead, like the pathetic inhabitants of the Academy of Lagado, they wasted time and effort upon impossibilities, like some scientific Aeolists worshipping a god of their own imagining.

The third voyage contains much incidental satire on morality and government – the Struldbruggs, say, or the comic exposure of the Atterbury trial. Although placed third, 'A Voyage to Laputa' was written last, and bears all the marks of a fragmentary conception. It is the least coherent of Gulliver's travels, not least because he does not confine himself to one land, but moves from one island to another. And yet the flying-island episode in particular contributes to the unity of the work. It is no accident that there are four parts to *Gulliver's Travels*, and 'A Voyage to the Houyhnhnms' is balanced by 'A Voyage to Laputa' in much the same way as 'A Voyage to Lilliput' is by 'A Voyage to Brobdingnag.' Whereas the first two voyages were more concerned with man in society, the two latter are preoccupied with human nature itself.

'The design of GULLIVER in his voyage to *Laputa*.'

according to Dean Swift, 'is to ridicule the vain pretensions of chymists, mathematicians, projectors, and the rest of that speculative tribe, who spend their time in aerial studies.'[36] Certainly, in the aftermath of the South Sea Bubble and the controversy over Wood's halfpence, 'the vain pretensions' of projectors of one sort or another are soundly rapped,[37] and the behaviour of the Laputians warns what might happen should an excess of reason lead to irrationality. Gulliver had never 'till then seen a Race of Mortals so singular in their Shapes, Habits, and Countenances. Their Heads were all reclined either to the Right, or the Left; one of their Eyes turned inward, and the other directly up to the Zenith' (p. 159). Even the bodily functions of the Laputians are impaired by their speculative natures so that they have to be flapped with a kind of bladder on the mouth in order to speak, on the ear in order to hear, and on the eyes in order to see.

The Laputian episodes illustrate the ways in which reason can be perverted. Instead of improving the quality of life, excessive use of reason can worsen it, and thus the houses of the Laputians 'are very ill built' because of 'the Contempt they bear for practical Geometry' (p. 163). They are so wrapped up in theoretical considerations that they neglect the realities of existence. When Gulliver is measured for a suit, the calculation is made along theoretical lines, so that his clothes are 'very ill made, and quite out of Shape, by happening to mistake a Figure in the Calculation' (p. 162). Such incidents contribute to the satire on abstract reasoning, but they also relate to the subsequent concerns of 'A Voyage to the Houyhnhnms,' in which we are presented with animals resembling human beings who are devoid of reason, and animals resembling horses who appear perfectly rational. If the Laputians are tainted with false reason taken to extremes, the Yahoos portray the other extreme – no reason at all.

The Yahoos and the Houyhnhnms serve to promote an investigation into the nature of man. The logic textbooks define man as *animal rationale*. By this definition, the Yahoos cannot be human, and Swift offers us a picture of a land in which animals who are patently not human none the less possess reason, which also contradicts the traditional manuals of logic: *Si simia non sit irrationalis, est homo* – if it is not irrational, it is man.[38] The Houyhnhnms are not man either. Further, *equus* was usually given as one of the most obvious examples of *animal irrationale*. Swift plays on this paradox in *On Poetry*: *A Rapsody*:

> A founder'd *Horse* will oft debate,
> Before he tries a five-barr'd Gate....[39]

How can a horse 'debate' if it is *animal irrationale*? In *Gulliver's Travels*, Swift questions the very basis of human assumptions about mankind. 'A Voyage to the Houyhnhnms' invites us, nay, challenges us, to re-assess our view of human nature, firstly by portraying an animal which, although rational, is not human, and, more importantly, by comparing human nature with Houyhnhnm nature, and asking us to choose which is more attractive or acceptable.

Swift is once again showing us the discrepancy between how things are, and how they should be. Unlike the Houyhnhnms, man clearly fails to live according to the dictates of reason, and yet he pretends to be a rational animal. He says the thing which is not – in other words, he tells lies. This fundamental perversion of reason leads to all the other perversions outlined in Gulliver's conversations with his Houyhnhnm master. These conversations fulfil the same basic purpose as Gulliver's earlier conversations with the King of Brobdingnag. They reveal the shortcomings of British society, and demonstrate how far practice falls short of the ideal projected by that society. Gulliver loses himself completely in admiration for the Houyhnhnms, whose name signifies 'in its Etymology, *the Perfection of Nature*' (p. 235), and, understandably, he contrasts the two societies. 'I enjoyed perfect Health of Body, and Tranquility of Mind' among the Houyhnhnms, he explains:

> I did not feel the Treachery or Inconstancy of a Friend, nor the Injuries of a secret or open Enemy, I had no Occasion of bribing, flattering or pimping, to procure the Favour of any great Man, or of his Minion. I wanted no Fence against Fraud or Oppression: Here was neither Physician to destroy my Body, nor Lawyer to ruin my Fortune: No

Informer to watch my Words and Actions, or forge
Accusations against me for Hire: Here were no Gibers,
Censurers, Backbiters, Pick-pockets, Highwaymen, House-
breakers, Attorneys, Bawds, Buffoons, Gamesters, Politi-
cians, Wits, Spleneticks, tedious Talkers, Controversists,
Ravishers, Murderers, Robbers, Virtuoso's; no Leaders or
Followers of Party and Faction; no Encouragers to Vice, by
Seducement or Examples: No Dungeon, Axes, Gibbets,
Whipping-posts, or Pillories; No cheating Shopkeepers or
Mechanicks: No Pride, Vanity or Affectation: No Fops,
Bullies, Drunkards, strolling Whores, or Poxes: No ranting,
lewd, expensive Wives: No stupid, proud Pedants: No
importunate, over-bearing, quarrelsome, noisy, roaring,
empty, conceited, swearing Companions: No Scoundrels
raised from the Dust upon the Merit of their Vices; or
Nobility thrown into it on account of their Virtues: No
Lords, Fidlers, Judges or Dancing-masters. (pp. 276-7)

Gulliver's list graphically captures the unattractive face of
society under Walpole, and of course it has universal significance. It illustrates perfectly the way in which Swift's social
satire is ultimately political, because this indictment of the
Robinocracy is closely linked to morality. But are the
Houyhnhnms the ideal *Gulliver* believes them to be? Clearly
the meaning of the last voyage, if not *Gulliver's Travels* as a
whole, hinges on the question of what the Houyhnhnms stand
for. 'I have got Materials Towards a Treatis proving the
falsity of that Definition *animal rationale*,' Swift wrote to Pope,
'and to show it should be only *rationis capax*.' He explained
that the 'whole building of my Travells is erected ... Upon this
great foundation of Misanthropy.'[40] In conclusion, *Gulliver's
Travels* insists that we compare the social behaviour of men and
Houyhnhnms. 'For, who can read of the Virtues I have
mentioned in the glorious *Houyhnhnms*, without being ashamed of his own Vices,' writes Gulliver, 'when he considers himself
as the reasoning, governing Animal of his Country' (p. 292)?

The 'grand Maxim' of the Houyhnhnms is 'to cultivate
Reason, and to be wholly governed by it' (p. 267). The same
might be said of the Laputians. But there is a vast difference
between the consequences of the Houyhnhnms' pursuit of

reason, and those of the Laputians.' In Houyhnhnmland, the dictates of reason and the dictates of nature are mutually compatible. Not so, it seems, in human societies. Should men, therefore, try to be more like the Houyhnhnms? Once again we come up against the problem of definition, for the Houyhnhnms are not men, and their way of life is not necessarily the ideal way of life for human beings. True, they emphasise the virtues of friendship and benevolence – qualities which Swift greatly admired – but in all other respects they resemble nothing so much as the Stoics. They have no faith, nor do they feel the need for religion. Death is neither welcomed nor feared, 'nor does the dying Person discover the least Regret that he is leaving the World' (p. 274). And although '*Nature* teaches them to love the whole Species,' their conception of such a feeling seems tenuous. 'They have no Fondness for their Colts or Foles,' explains Gulliver, 'the Care they take in educating them proceedeth entirely from the Dictates of Reason.' Nor are their marriages transacted 'upon the Account of *Love*, but to preserve the Race from degenerating' (pp. 268-9).

It is all too easy, of course, to allow twentieth-century prejudice to colour our interpretation of Swift's meaning. The cold, unemotional Houyhnhnms may be unattractive to us, and smack of the sort of dispassionate thinkers who formulate final solutions. But would this have been Swift's attitude? Now Stoicism is one of the vulgar errors of which he is elsewhere bitingly critical. 'The Stoical Scheme of supplying our Wants, by lopping off our Desires,' he wrote in his *Thoughts on Various Subjects*, 'is like cutting off our Feet when we want Shoes.'[41] In his sermons he was also ready enough to point out that Stoicism presented 'an impossible way of life and a false conception of human psychology.' As Louis A. Landa puts it, 'The Stoic rationalistic ideal, the man without passion, is exposed as being in sharp contrast to the Christian ideal which, however much it condemned the bad passions, still stressed the compassionate nature of man.'[42]

The Houyhnhnm ideal, then, goes against Christianity. In using reason to remove the problems which beset society, the Houyhnhnms have also done away with the supreme virtue of love. Benevolence is not enough. There is even a hint that, like the Stoics, they have not succeeded in anything more than lopping off desire. Gulliver tells the anecdote of a female Houyhnhnm who was delayed in a visit to his master because she had been widowed late that morning. 'I observed she behaved herself at our House, as cheerfully as the rest,' he relates, gratuitously adding the rider, 'She died about three months after' (p. 275). Could it be she died of that irrational condition, a broken heart? If the Houyhnhnms merely *repress* their feelings, then they are no better than the Stoics. They may have taken their control of the passions further through a superior exercise of 'reason,' but that is all. They are no ideal for man to follow.

The Houyhnhnms, like the Stoics, provide a false ideal which contradicts human nature, and therefore offers nothing more than an impossibility. True, they successfully show up man's shortcomings as a 'reasonable, governing Animal,' as Swift exploits the satiric discrepancy between appearance and reality, but man has to find another way of regulating his behaviour. Certainly this involves reason, as man has to learn to keep a tighter check on his passions. Otherwise he might end up behaving more like the Yahoos, who have surrendered all control over their senses, and have abandoned themselves to a lifestyle which ignores reason entirely. To be fair, the Yahoos cannot reason – they have lost that faculty. They have degenerated, this is Swift's point, from their original condition. They are fallen men – fallen to a situation beyond that of eighteenth-century civilisation through the abuse of reason. According to Swift, man is *rationis capax*, but, as Gulliver's Houyhnhnm master puts it, he makes 'no other Use' of this 'small Pittance of *Reason* ... than by its Assistance to aggravate *natural* Corruptions, and to acquire new ones which Nature had not given us' (p. 259).

If the Houyhnhnms represent one broad error – that of Stoicism – the Yahoos appear to portray the popular contemporary conception of Epicureanism as an abandoned sensuality. Their reason having decayed from generation to generation, they now have no way at all of regulating their behaviour. They are no longer *rationis capax*, they are *animal irrationalis*. But because man *is rationis capax*, he has the capacity to remedy his condition, if only he would choose to exercise his reason. Swift's positive is an implied positive, but in the persons of the King of Brobdingnag, Lord Munodi, and Pedro de Mendez, the wise, benevolent, humanitarian sea-captain who rescues and rehabilitates Gulliver after he has left Houyhnhnmland, we have an example to be followed which is not only worth following; it is attainable. 'I shall say nothing of those remote Nations where *Yahoos* preside; amongst which the least corrupted are the *Brobdingnagians*, whose wise Maxims in Morality and Government, it would be our Happiness to observe', *Gulliver's Travels* concludes. 'But I forbear descanting further, and rather leave the judicious Reader to his own Remarks and Applications' (p. 292).

I shall 'descant' just a little further before leaving the reader to his own remarks and applications. Swift, in *Gulliver's Travels*, seeks to rupture the reader's complacency about man and society by exploding the myth that his 'civilised' social behaviour approaches the ideal of Christianity. Man is not perfect. He has degenerated, along with his political institutions, from a pristine state, and is in danger of decaying still further. This is Swift's fear. The human predicament is one of two conflicting impulses, reason and passion, which, more often than not, threaten to tear him apart. Regulation is needed; a balance must be achieved in which emotion is regulated by the mind. Swift was fond of comparing the human body and the body politic. Just as he advocated a balance in the state, so he urged a balance in the human breast, so that neither mind nor flesh would predominate. Once this was achieved, the effects of moral health on government could hardly fail to follow. In offering the Brobdingnagians as the 'least corrupted' of men, Swift not only succeeds in condemning the system of Walpole, he shows yet again how closely concepts of morality and government were linked in his mind.

14
Swift, the Opposition and Ireland

Whether or not *Gulliver's Travels* was intentional opposition propaganda, there can be no doubt that is soon began to be regarded as such. 'Far from being received merely as an inoffensive romance, the potential of *Gulliver's Travels* as partisan propaganda was recognised, exploited, and attacked in the first five years of its history', writes Bertrand A. Goldgar, 'by both its "particular reflections" and its "general" satire it could easily be viewed as a contribution to the campaign of the Bolingbroke-Pulteney Opposition.'[1] Swift was more than willing to involve himself in the production of propaganda condemning the conduct of Walpole and his ministry. Despite the rapturous welcome he received on his return to Ireland in August 1726, he had already made up his mind to visit England once more the following year. Ostensibly his journey was 'made ... necessary' by 'the ommission of some matters last summer, by the absence of certain people',[2] but he was concerned with more than the ill-fated *History of the Four Last Years*, 'Pray tell Sr Robert Walpole', he wrote to Mrs Howard, 'that if he does not use me better next Summer than he did the last, I will study revenge, and it shall be *vengeance Eclesistique*'.[3]

In cultivating Mrs Howard, Swift hoped to influence the Prince and Princess of Wales. The Princess had 'commanded' that whenever he came to England, he 'should wait on her'.[4] He affected reluctance, but was soon a regular visitor not only to Mrs Howard's villa at Marble Hill, where she was a neighbour of Pope, but also to Richmond Lodge, one of the Prince's Houses. True, he did not meet the Prince in 1726. He took the opportunity, however, to improve his acquaintance with the Princess through the offices of Mrs Howard. He sent her a gift of Irish plaid, which was appropriated by the Princess herself. The present 'pleas'd extremely', and Swift was encouraged to hope for great things from the heir-apparent. The Prince's Court was perfectly aware of the political burden of *Gulliver's Travels*. Mrs Howard advised Swift of the Princess's thought that he 'can not in Com̃on Dencency [*sic*] appear in heels', having alluded to the Prince of Wales in the character of the Emperor of Lilliput's son, as having 'a Hobble in his Gait' because 'one of his Heels [was] higher than the other'.[5] The Dean of St Patrick's was unabashed. 'I desire you will order her Royal Highness to go to Richmond as soon as she can this Summer', he wrote to Mrs Howard on 1 February 1727, 'because she will have the Pleasure of my Neighborhood, for I hope to be in London about the middle of March.'[6]

After 'preparing a hundred little affairs which must be dispatched before I go',[7] including settling the ladies in the deanery for the summer, Swift set out for England on or around 9 April. Arriving at Pope's house at Twickenham via Goodrich and Oxford a fortnight later, he was soon commenting on the 'strange Situation' in England – 'a firm, settled Resolution to assault the present Administration, and break it if possible'.[8] Although 1725 had been Walpole's *annus mirabilis,* the alliance of his two most potent political opponents the following summer threatened the security of his premiership. Since returning from exile in 1723, Bolingbroke had been working to gain a full pardon. In 1726 he finally had to settle for the restoration of his estates and money, and nothing more. Excluded from the House of Lords, he was unable to resume his political life on an official basis. William Pulteney, Walpole's sometime friend and close political ally, had never been offered the important ministerial position his talents deserved, despite the fact that he had resigned in solidarity with him in 1717, and had been appointed to the lucrative if not very powerful position of Cofferer of the Household on his return to power in 1723. In 1725 Pulteney spoke out against Walpole's management of the Treasury and accused him of corruption. While Swift was visiting his old friends in England in 1726, Bolingbroke and Pulteney were closeted together at Dawley, hatching schemes to secure Walpole's downfall.

Soon after the publication of *Gulliver's Travels,* an opposition paper called *The Craftsman* began to appear. It was the organ of the Bolingbroke-Pulteney alliance, and *Gulliver's Travels* was linked with its outspoken criticism of the regime of Walpole. By 13 May 1727 Swift had 'twice' seen the Princess of Wales 'by her own Commands'. They discussed *Gulliver's Travels.* 'I told her how angry the Ministry were', he wrote to Sheridan, 'but she assures me that both she and the P[rince] were very well pleased with every Particular.' This was indeed encouraging. 'You will wonder to find me say so much of Politicks,' he concluded, 'but I keep very bad Company, who are full of nothing else.'⁹ Having thrown in his lot with the opposition, he was collaborating with Bolingbroke on *A Letter to the Writer of the Occasional Paper,* an attack on 'a great minister in the fulness of his power'.¹⁰ Opposition plans were rendered redundant when news of the death of George I *en route* to Hanover reached London on 15 June. Swift had previously assured Mrs Howard that the King was 'too tough a person for me to value any reversion of favor after him'.¹¹ Now the situation had altered dramatically.

Swift had been on the point of travelling to Aix-la-Chappelle on account of his health – a journey he had often thought of making – when George I died. Bolingbroke reminded him that he at last had 'the opportunity of quitting Ireland for England'.¹² Swift himself explained that he was 'with great Vehemence dissuaded from [leaving for Aix-la-Chappelle] by certain Persons whom I could not disobey'. Subsequently, he was peevish enough to blame Mrs Howard for this wrong counsel. He claimed to have been told not only that he would be made 'easy' in England, but that the new Queen would 'do all good offices in her power for this miserable and most loyall Kingdom'.¹³ Swift's bitterness was largely unwarranted. He had been backing the wrong horse. 'Not even the brightest sparks could expect favour if they courted Mrs Howard,' notes J. H. Plumb, 'she exercised not a scrap of influence.'¹⁴ She had offered Swift the best advice in her power, and it proved unfounded. But Swift built it up in his own chagrin to a studied attempt to mislead.

This was not how it appeared in 1727. He was 'so extreamly busy' in this 'strange World' that he was 'all in a Hurry, with Millions of Schemes'. He put off kissing the hands of the new King and Queen 'till the third Day', but then he was instrumental in persuading a 'Dozen' of his friends to 'go in a Line' to perform the ceremony. 'The Talk is now for a moderating Scheme, wherein no-body shall be used the Worse or Better for being call'd Whig or Tory', he noted, 'and the King hath received both with great Equality; shewing Civilities to several who are openly known to be the latter.' 'We have made our Offers,' he explained. 'If otherwise, we are as we were. It is agreed the Ministry will be changed, but the others will have a soft Fall; although the K[ing] must be excessive generous if he forgives the Treatment of some People.'[15] Yet again Swift was out of touch with events. Even while he was writing in this optimistic vein, it was 'common knowledge that George II had asked Walpole to continue' in office. The opposition had failed to dislodge the 'Great Man'. 'As the summer of 1727 turned to autumn', writes J.H. Plumb, the King 'grew to respect Walpole, then to like him; within a year he had become one of the necessities of his existence, a friend without whom the burden of governing would be intolerable.'[16]

And what of the opposition? Its weakness was displayed for all to see in the General Election which took place in July and August 1727. 'They settled for another seven years in the wilderness; the opposition, carried on with such panache in newspapers and ballads, had ended dismally.'[17] Bolingbroke and Pulteney continued to orchestrate a medley of complaints about the Robinocracy, largely through the columns of *The Craftsman*. Trying to impose a coherence on the disparate grievances of Whigs and Tory through the judicious application of Country theory, they sought to interweave them so that they became merely themes in the general symphony of opposition clamour against the ministry. In this task they were joined by Pope, Gay and Swift. Whereas Pulteney and Bolingbroke championed Country ideology in pursuit of the organisation of an effective opposition to Walpole, however, Swift was simply rehearsing opinions he had held at least since the beginning of the eighteenth century. Bolingbroke has, quite rightly, been taken to task for the insincerity of his new political stance.[18] Swift's opposition to Walpole was carried on for ideological reasons.

But for the time being Swift was unable to contribute anything to the common cause. Early in August 1727 he was visited with his old sickness on returning from a three-week ramble to Cambridge with Pope. Deafness, followed by giddiness and nausea, made his stay at Twickenham a torment to him. He hated being ill, more especially when in company. He felt a burden to those he had to impose himself upon, and sought relief in isolation. 'I want to be at home', he told Sheridan, 'where I can turn you out, or let you in, as I think best.' In this sad condition he was troubled still further by news of Stella's health. He postponed his return to Ireland, and asked his housekeeper, Mrs Brent, to take care that his old friend did not die 'in domi decanus'. Then he moved to London, to leave Pope in peace.[19]

Still he remained unsettled. At last he could stand it no longer. Setting out on 18 September, he determined, 'since I have a home in Dublin', to return 'before my health and the weather grow worse'.[20] Arriving in Chester by the 21st, he pressed on to Holyhead, where he was tormented by adverse winds. Tortured by thoughts of what he had had to turn his back upon yet again, and the bitter disappointment of the accession of George II, he was doomed to live out his life in Ireland, unless he chose to be 'a greater Rascal than happened to Suit with my Temper'.[21] Further, he was troubled by the knowledge that Stella's health was giving increasing cause for alarm. The 'Holyhead Journal' documents his basic insecurity. He refused to comment 'upon the suspense I am in about my dearest friend', but the old, familiar fears make themselves felt, as he languished in a strange place in which, were he to die, 'there is no[t] a welch house curr, that would not have more care taken of him than I and whose loss would not be more lamented'.[22] Holyhead took on a symbolic character as far as Swift was concerned. It was the gateway to the life in England he had coveted so long. As the final, supreme irony he expressed his desire to be buried there.[23]

Thus ended Swift's last sorry visit to England. Landing in

Ireland on 2 October, he found Stella lingering on. His own
illness recurred in December 1727 to torment him 'to a very
great degree'.[24] His absence was lamented by his English
friends. Pope complained not only about his leaving them,
but about the manner in which he had departed, and the
'kind letter' Swift left for him with Gay 'affected [him] so
much, that it made [him] like a girl'. 'I can't tell what to say
to you,' he wrote. 'I only feel that I wish you well in every
circumstance of life: that 'tis almost as good to be hated, as to
be loved, considering the pain it is to minds of any tender
turn, to find themselves so utterly impotent to do any good, or
give any ease to those who deserve most from us.'[25] In reply,
Swift offered an explanation of the circumstances which had
led him to forsake his friends. 'If it pleases God to restore me
to my health, I shall readily make a third journey,' he wrote,
'if not, we must part as all human creatures have parted. You
are the best and kindest friend in the world, and I know no
body alive or dead to whom I am so much obliged; and if ever
you made me angry, it was for your too much care about me.'[26]

Swift did not return to England. As time passed, its
attractions diminished. 'Except absence from friends, I
confess freely that I have no discontent at living here', he
assured Pope the following year, 'besides what arises from a
silly spirit of Liberty, which as it neither sowers my drink, nor
hurts my meat, nor spoils my stomach farther than in
imagination, so I resolve to throw it off.'[27] This was something
he was never able to do. His rage and resentment precluded
his 'having done' with either English or Irish politics, as he
often threatened. 'I will come in person to England, if I am
provoked', he told Bolingbroke, 'and send for the Dictator
from the plough.'[28] Walpole continued to act as a magnet for
his anger, as he began to think 'that Corruption, like avarice,
hath no bounds'. But Bolingbroke and Pope – 'the two best
companions and friends I ever had' – 'utterly disqualifyed
themselves for [his] conversation, and [his] way of living': 'the
former is too much a Philosopher; he dines at six in the
evening, after studying all the morning till after noon; and
when he hath dined; to his Studyes again ... Mr Pope can
neither eat nor drink; loves to be alone, and hath always some
poetical Scheme in his head.'[29]

Increasingly Swift was concerned with his own conduct, as he constantly rehearsed the past in his mind and his correspondence, asserting the rectitude of the Oxford ministry in 'the worst of times', and justifying his own relations with Mrs Howard and Queen Caroline. 'If you imagined me to have any favour at Court you were much mistaken or misinformed', he told Chetwode. 'It is quite otherwise, at least among the Ministry. Neither did I ever go to Court, except when I was sent for and not always then.'[30] Raking over old scores, Swift re-wrote history to suit his own version of things, and repeated his views over and over again, as if repetition would confer authority. As a result, he gradually fell out with those who refused to agree with his own distorted recollection of what had happened, and learned to rely on those who humoured his moods. Exaggerating his poverty, his loneliness and his inability to write, he offered spurious reasons for failing to cross over the Irish Sea.

In the autumn of 1727, then, Swift resumed the 'life of a monk' in Dublin. Particularly susceptible to the symptoms of Ménière's disease at this time, he was uncomfortable if he were 'above an hour distant from home' in case he were 'caught by a deafness and giddiness out of [his] own precincts'.[31] He was confined to the deanery for more than ten weeks from December 1727. Thus it was that the news was brought to him at 'about eight o'clock at night' on 28 January 1728 that Hester Johnson had died in the same house at 'about six in the evening'. Three hours later he put pen to paper 'for [his] own satisfaction' to write an account of her life and character. This was his usual way of throwing up barriers against the pain and grief that death could bring.[32] Seeking consolation for an irreparable loss in a change of scene, he accompanied Sheridan in a tour of the south-east of Ireland 'for [his] Health', and threatened to return to England. Instead he left Dublin in June 1728 for Market Hill near Armagh, on the first of three annual summer visits to the country seat of Sir Arthur Acheson. He did not return to Dublin until February 1729.

Swift's part in the opposition campaign to discredit Walpole in these years was minimal. 'I now compound if I can get an equall time of being well and ill', he explained to

Ford in March 1729, 'this disorder and my Monastick life takes off all invention.'[33] But he continued to take an interest in what was happening in England. Having been offered the totally inappropriate position of Gentleman-Usher to the two-years-old Princess Louisa – 'one of the cruellest actions I ever knew', Swift wrote, 'even in a minister of state, these thirty years past'[34] – Gay refused the employment and contemplated revenge. *The Beggar's Opera* began playing to packed audiences at the theatre in Lincoln's Inn Fields on 29 January 1728. The satire on the 'Great Man' and the corruption of the nation's manners had a prodigious run, and captured the capital's imagination. 'Does W[alpole] think you intended an affront to him in your opera,' Swift asked. 'Pray God he may, for he has held the longest hand at hazard that ever fell to any Sharpers Share and keepe his run when the dice are changed.'[35]

When *The Beggar's Opera* had 'done its task', Swift was impatient for the appearance of *The Dunciad*, which was finally published on 28 May 1728. 'I had reason to put Mr. *Pope* on writing the Poem, called the *Dunciad*,' he claimed, with some justice.[36] During the summer of 1727, Pope was working on 'The Progress of Dulness' and Swift was supplying hints. Pope offered to tell the world 'how much that poem is yours ... since certainly without you it had never been'.[37] Clearly he deserved the inscription:

> O thou! whatever Title please thine ear,
> Dean, Drapier, Bickerstaff, or Gulliver!
> Whether thou chuse Cervantes' serious air,
> Or laugh and shake in Rab'lais' easy Chair,
> Or praise the Court, or magnify Mankind,
> Or thy griev'd Country's copper chains unbind;
> From thy Baeotia tho' Her Pow'r retires,
> Grieve not at ought our sister realm acquires:
> Here pleas'd behold her mighty wings out-spread,
> To hatch a new Saturnian age of Lead.[38]

'Our Miscellany is now quite printed', Pope had enthusiastically informed Swift early in 1727. 'I am prodigiously pleas'd with this joint-volume, in which methinks we look like friends, side by side, serious and merry by turns, conversing interchangeably, and walking down hand in hand to posterity.'[39] The first two volumes of the Pope-Swift *Miscellanies* were published in June 1727 when Swift was in England, but the third volume, consisting solely of verses, not until the following year. Originally *Cadenus and Vanessa* was to open the collection, and *The Dunciad* ('The Progress of Dulness') to close it. These plans were shelved when Pope's satire outgrew such a scheme.

Swift and Pope shared a common world view, as outlined in *The Dunciad*. Failing to patronise writers of real merit who sought to correct the nation's manners, the Court was engaged in preferring 'no better writers than Cibber and the British Journalist'.[40] In 1730 Colley Cibber, a comic actor of some talent and a playwright of average ability, was appointed Poet Laureate. In 1743 Pope recast *The Dunciad* with Cibber as King Dunce. The *British Journal,* on the other hand, was Walpole's chief vehicle of propaganda at the time. Pope's poem was built around the concept of Dulness, and Walpole was given the role of 'the first who brings/The Smithfield Muses to the Ear of Kings', while

> Gay dies un-pension'd with a hundred Friends,
> Hibernian Politicks, O Swift, thy doom,
> And Pope's, translating three whole years with Broome.

But *The Dunciad* was not merely a personal plea of injustice. The Scriblerian satirists looked back to the Golden Age. In their view, Walpole was bent on instituting an 'Saturnian Age of Lead', the very opposite of a Golden Age. Dulness 'rul'd, in native Anarchy, the mind', and the Goddess was urged to proceed "till Learning fly the shore'. Swift and Pope perceived that Walpole not only posed a threat to English culture. Dulness led to moral blindness, a stupefying narcosis which eventually would facilitate the gradual erosion of constitutional safeguards and the surrender of rights and privileges. The perversion of literary and artistic taste was only one way in which the manners of the people were being debauched. Once their liberty and property were gone, then they really would be slaves. This was dulness in action, as 'the Goddess bade Britannia Sleep,/And pour'd her Spirit o'er the Land and deep'.[41]

All this time, Swift contributed little to the common fund of opposition propaganda. A poor *Account of the Court and Empire of Japan* – a transparent allegory which attacked Walpole as 'Lelop-Aw' – remained unfinished and unpublished.[42] It was in the columns of *The Intelligencer,* a Dublin journal which he launched in conjunction with Sheridan on 11 May 1728, that Swift offered his support to Gay and Pope. The third number (Swift's second contribution), as well as offering significant insight into his view of satire, is an important defence of *The Beggar's Opera.* Drawing attention to Gay's exposure of 'the whole System of that Common-wealth, or that *Imperium in Imperio* of Iniquity, established among us, by which neither our Lives nor our Properties are secure', Swift justifies his reflections 'upon *Courtiers* and *Statesmen*'. *Intelligencer* no. IX, on the other hand, returns to one of Swift's pet subjects, the deleterious effects of an effete nobility. As we have seen, he had the example of the Irish landlords before him as a prime instance of aristocratic self-interestedness as opposed to paternalistic duty. In the *Intelligencer,* Swift returned to the consideration of the plight of his native land.[43]

Intelligencer no. XV was a reprint of a pamphlet he had published earlier in the year as *A Short View of the State of Ireland.* This straightforward essay lists fourteen 'true Causes of any Countries flourishing and growing rich', and then compares the situation in Ireland with the intention of proving that only the first could be said to apply – 'the Fruitfulness of the Soil, to produce the Necessaries and Conveniences of Life'. Lyon noted that Swift 'often spoke with pleasure of [Ireland's] excellent soil, fine climate[,] Harbours & many other natural advantages'.[44] But the combination of external restraints and domestic folly kept the country in a perpetual state of poverty. Those who should have provided national leadership were especially culpable. As he put it in *An Answer to a Paper, Called A Memorial,* published in March 1728, 'neither are the *'Squires* and *Landlords* to be excused; for to them is owing the depopulating of the *Country*, the vast Number of *Beggars* and the Ruin of those few sorry Improvements we had.'[45] Twenty months later he was to offer a proposal to the world that would have effectively disposed once and for all of the problem of the beggars.

It was appropriate that the state of Ireland provoked a return of Swift's great satiric gift. Throughout 1729 he had been commenting on the grave condition of the country in his letters to his English friends. He wrote thus to Pope on 11 August:

> As to this country, there have been three terrible years dearth of corn, and every place strowed with beggars, but dearths are common in better climates, and our evils here lie much deeper. Imagine a nation the two-thirds of whose revenues are spent out of it, and who are not permitted to trade with the other third, and where the pride of the women will not suffer them to wear their own manufactures even where they excel what come from abroad: This is the true state of Ireland in a very few words. These evils operate more every day, and the kingdom is absolutely undone, as I have been telling it often in print these ten years past.[46]

Now the beggars were a symptom of the Irish disease; they were not its cause. But towards the end of October 1729 a pamphlet appeared which suggested a remedy for these unsightly sores on the national body. The author was so confident of the reception of his scheme that he hinted optimistically that his statue should be set up 'for a Preserver of the Nation'.[47] The essay was called *A Modest Proposal for Preventing the Children of poor People in Ireland, from being a Burden to their Parents or Country; and for making them beneficial to the Publick.*

'IT is a melancholy Object to those, who walk through this great Town, or travel in the Country', the *Modest Proposal* opens, 'when they see the *Streets*, the *Roads*, the *Cabbin-doors* crowded with *Beggars* of the Female Sex, followed by three, four, or six Children, *all in Rags,* and importuning every Passenger for an Alms' (p. 109). Swift had drawn attention in the past to this melancholy object. Truly, 'whoever could find out a fair, cheap, and easy Method of making these Children sound and useful Members of the Commonwealth', would indeed deserve the nation's thanks. But this 'modest' proposal offered to go further, and 'take in the whole Number of Infants at a certain Age, who are born of Parents, in effect as little able to support them, as those who demand our Charity in the Streets' (p. 110). Instead of them remaining 'a Charge upon their *Parents*, or the *Parish*', this projector suggested means by which they would 'on the contrary, contribute to the Feeding, and partly to the Cloathing, of many Thousands'.

Hitherto the Modest Proposer's credentials seem impeccable. Having spent 'many Years' brooding 'upon this important Subject', and having 'maturely weighed the several *Schemes of other Projectors*', we can be confident that his ideas are not half-baked. Above all, his motives appear to be founded on humanitarian principles. His project 'will prevent those *voluntary Abortions*, and that horrid Practice of *Women murdering their Bastard Children*; alas! too frequent among us'. Concern for 'the *poor innocent Babes*' moves his great mind to seek a solution to the nation's ills, as it 'would move Tears and Pity in the most Savage and inhuman Breast' (p. 110). Surely given the '*present deplorable State of the Kingdom*', his anxiety about the people's welfare is highly commendable.

At last he unveils his 'own Thoughts; which [he] hope[s] will not be liable to the least Objection':

> I HAVE been assured by a very knowing *American* of my Acquaintance in *London*; that a young healthy Child, well nursed, is, at a Year old, a most delicious, nourishing, and wholesome Food; whether *Stewed, Roasted, Baked*, or *Boiled*; and, I make no doubt, that it will equally serve in a *Fricasie*, or *Ragoust*. (p. 111)

Now we begin to understand how these children will 'contribute to the Feeding, and partly to the Cloathing, of many Thousands', as the scheme involves the use of human skin, 'artificially dressed', to 'make admirable *Gloves for Ladies,* and *Summer Boots for fine Gentlemen*' (p. 112). The reader has been hoodwinked, and the Modest Proposer suggests the erection of shambles 'in the most convenient Parts' of Dublin for the butchering of the children, adding the rider, 'Butchers we may be assured will not be wanting'! Even this gruesome idea admits of refinement in Swift's hands, as he recommends 'buying the Children alive, and dressing them hot from the Knife, as we do *roasting Pigs'* (p. 113).

The Modest Proposer is merely one more in Swift's long line of personae. He is a projector, and his cold, dispassionate exposition of his scheme resembles the cold, dispassionate exposition of final solutions and economic plans to which modern man has grown accustomed. There are, after all, sufficient ironic pointers to suggest that the author's attitude towards the beggars does not coincide with his persona's. Animal imagery is employed throughout, and the terms of animal husbandry seem horrifically inappropriate when applied to human beings. Perhaps our first real indication that irony is at work is when the Proposer admits that 'a Child, *just dropt from its Dam,* may be supported by her Milk, for a Solar Year with little other Nourishment' (p. 110). Here three ironic pointers can be seen operating together. *'Just dropt from its Dam'* is a curiously inapposite phrase to describe a new-born baby, especially when supposedly written by a humane man. Notice also that the crucial ironic phrase is italicised – an habitual Swiftian trait. Finally the ludicrousness of projecting terminology is exposed by the absurd insistence on 'a Solar Year' – what other sort is there?

Once the fact that Swift is employing irony in *A Modest Proposal* has been established, many other ironic meanings can be found which contribute to the pamphlet's black humour. 'I HAVE reckoned upon a Medium, that a Child just born will weight Twelve Pounds', the Modest Proposer glibly announces (p. 112). Like Lilliputian geese, these are impossibly large babies, especially for a people suffering from extreme poverty. The rest of the Proposer's figures and schemes, I would suggest, can carry very little weight after this example of his careful thinking. *A Modest Proposal* is a parody of the pamphlets of projectors, in the same way that *Gulliver's Travels* exposes 'the writings of Travellers, by publishing a collection of the most palpable *falshoods, absurdities,* and *contradictions,* in a grave and serious manner, with the same solemn Grimace and repeated professions of *truth* and *simplicity'*.[48] This is precisely the method employed by Swift to expose the chimerical schemes of projectors in *A Modest*

Proposal, and the speaker, like Captain Gulliver, is the butt of
the satire as well as its agent.

It has been pointed out that *A Modest Proposal* exploits the
contemporary belief that people are the riches of a nation.[49] A
further instance of Swift's ability to give new meaning to
figurative language through the assertion of its literalness can
be found in his insistence that 'this Food will be somewhat
dear, and therefore very *proper for Landlords*; who, as they have
already devoured most of the Parents, seem to have the best
Title to the Children' (p. 112). In suggesting that the Irish
landlords should actually consume the children of the people
they have ruined, Swift simply removes the metaphor. Once
again the irresponsibility of the very men who should be
setting an example to the lower orders is stressed, and there
can be little doubt that at this point Swift emerges from
behind the mask of the Modest Proposer. For an instant, the
dispassionate tone of the narrator gives way to genuine anger.
Whether or not Swift has actually allowed his feelings to get
the better of him, we simply cannot say. We have no means of
knowing for certain. In fact the careful structure of the tract
would suggest otherwise. But at least Swift judges it to be
rhetorically important that his wrath should *appear* to boil
over at this point.

For *A Modest Proposal,* above all, is a masterpiece of polemical strategy, a brilliant exercise in the manipulation of the
reader. It does not depend simply on the shock tactics of
cannibalism. It is often suggested that the beggars themselves
are the subject of the pamphlet. This is not so. As Swift told
Pope, 'our evils here lie much deeper.' His sermon, *Causes of
the Wretched Condition of Ireland,* had put forward harsh
solutions to the problem of the beggars.[50] Admittedly this had
been written before the dearth of the summers of 1727, 1728
and 1729, but in *A Modest Proposal,* too, the plight of the
beggars was used by Swift primarily to bring home the
severity of the economic disadvantages that Ireland laboured
under. Even in a Christian kingdom, a 'vast Number of poor
People, who are Aged, Diseased, or Maimed' were 'every Day
dying, and *rotting,* by *Cold* and *Famine,* and *Filth,* and *Vermin,* as
fast as can be reasonably expected' (p. 114). The inappropriateness of the term *reason* to describe such a situation is yet

301

another example of Swift's talent for satiric wordplay, 'I CAN think of no one Objection, that will possibly be raised against this Proposal', the pamphlet concluded, 'unless it should be urged, that the Number of People will be thereby much lessened in the Kingdom.' This seemed to be flying in the face of contemporary population theory, that the larger the number of people, the better off the nation. However the reader was asked to observe that this remedy was calculated *'for this one individual Kingdom of* IRELAND, *and for no other that ever was, is or I think ever can be upon Earth'* (p. 116).

In the closing paragraphs of *A Modest Proposal*, Swift turns back once again to the real evils of the Irish situation, its dependence on England, and the follies of its own inhabitants – with a difference. He had employed irony before in discussing the Irish economy, particularly in *A Proposal for the universal Use Of Irish Manufacture*. But then he had also been putting forward a genuine proposal. The sustained irony of *A Modest Proposal* appears to rule out such practical measures. There was only one conceivable remedy for the Kingdom's ills, Swift suggested, 'Therefore, let no man talk to me of other Expedients' (p. 116). Here he proceeds to trot out the ideas he and others had been putting forward for the past decade and more: taxing absentee landlords; using Irish manufactures; voluntarily imposing import controls; abolishing rack-renting, and so on. Now these were to be avoided as useless contrivances until there was 'at least, a Glimpse of Hope, that there will ever be some hearty and sincere Attempt to put *them in Practice*' (p. 117).

What was Swift's intention? Did he really despair of finding a solution to the wretched condition of Ireland? Does *A Modest Proposal* not even suggest an implied positive, such as we find in his other ironic satires? In the antepenultimate paragraph, Swift once more appears to let the mask drop so that, although irony can still be detected, it is as if he is addressing the reader 'directly', and not through a persona:

BUT, as to my self; having been wearied out for so many Years with offering vain, idle, visionary Thoughts; and at length utterly despairing of Success, I fortunately fell upon this Proposal; which, as it is wholly new, so it hath

something *solid* and *real,* of no Expence, and little Trouble,
full in our own Power; and whereby we can incur no
Danger in *disobliging* ENGLAND: For, this Kind of Com-
modity will not bear Exportation; the Flesh being of too
tender a Consistence, to admit a long Continuance in Salt;
although, perhaps, I could name a Country, which would be glad to
eat up our whole Nation without it. (p. 117)

Ireland's dependence on England is the true subject of *A*
Modest Proposal, just as it had been the true subject of *The*
Drapier's Letters. Swift's *cri de coeur* was the most terrible
indictment of the Court and ministry of England.

In this sense, the beggars were incidental to Swift's purpose.
They were simply the most obvious manifestation of Ireland's
poverty. How else, *A Modest Proposal* asked, will it be possible
'to find Food and Raiment, for a Hundred Thousand useless
Mouths and Backs?' He was not seriously advocating the
eating of babies, but if he was challenging the reader to come
up with a solution to the problem, he did not appear to hold
out much hope of success. What would be the response, he
asked, if the parents of these sad children were canvassed
'Whether they would not, at this Day, think it a great
Happiness to have been sold for Food at a Year old, in the
Manner I prescribe; and thereby have avoided such a
perpetual Scene of Misfortunes, as they have since gone
through' (p. 117)? Unless practical measures were taken to
remedy the situation, he asserted, then the only answer is to
eat babies. Otherwise even the most down-to-earth suggestion
was no better than idle and visionary. 'I hope to mend a
little', Swift wrote to Pope early in 1730, 'being cured of Irish
Politicks by despair.'[51]

A Modest Proposal is as much an opposition pamphlet as it
is an essay on the state of Ireland. In Swift's mind the politics
of the two countries had always been inextricably interlinked.
He represented his efforts in these years as 'engaging with a
Ministry to prevent if possible, the Evils that have over-run
the Nation, and my foolish Zeal in endeavouring to save this
wretched Island.'[52] If, as Herbert Davis remarks, *A Modest*
Proposal was 'really Swift's last word on the state of Ireland',[53]
it did not prevent him from constantly 'writing bad prose, or

303

worse verses, either of rage or raillery, whereof some few escape to give offence, or mirth, and the rest are burnt'.[54] Many of these were pieces concerning Ireland, and they continued to offer practical advice about the Irish economy, as well as other internal matters. But in one sense *A Modest Proposal* was his final word. It reveals Swift plumbing the depths of despair, but it also shows that he touched the bottom only to re-surface on a wave of fury, resentful of the indifference of the English and the folly of the Irish alike.

His rage and resentment continued to simmer, and increasingly they found an outlet not in prose, but in verse. While poems like *A Libel on D— D—, An Epistle to a Lady* and *On Poetry: A Rapsody* expressed Swift's growing contempt for the system of Walpole, others, such as *The Legion Club,* testify to his habitual bitterness towards his own countrymen. He turned his satire on mankind in general, examining his animal side, and deflating the romantic ideal. And finally he looked inward, and analysed himself. Swift's imperiousness was becoming intolerable, as, with the tediousness of old age, he was finding fault with everybody and everything. A lonely old man in his sixties, he was peevish and dispirited, and increasingly pessimistic about the future. Above all, he hated the thought of dying in Ireland 'in a rage, like a poisoned rat in a hole'.[55] In response, he produced his most memorable verse in a final burst of creative activity.

15
A Man of Rhimes

It is only recently that a genuine critical interest has been taken in Swift's poetry. In the nineteenth century, when even Pope's poetry was judged to be prosaic, Swift's verse was sadly neglected. 'We cannot claim for any of his verses the qualities of real poetry,' wrote Henry Craik. 'We find in them no flights of imagination: no grandeur either of emotion or of form: and even the deftness of his rhythmical skill never attains to the harmony of poetic utterance.'[1] There is some sort of justification for such a view to be found in Swift's own words on the subject.

> In POPE, I cannot read a Line,
> But with a Sigh, I wish it mine:
> When he can in one Couplet fix
> More Sense than I can do in Six:
> It gives me such a jealous Fit,
> I cry, Pox take him, and his Wit.[2]

What was said in a spirit of raillery in *Verses on the Death of Dr. Swift* is corroborated in Swift's confession to a casual correspondent: 'I have been only a Man of Rhimes, and that upon Trifles, never having written serious Couplets in my Life; yet never without a moral View.'[3]

But as a balanced assessment of Swift's poetic achievement, Craik's comment simply will not do. He chooses to measure Swift's verse against a set definition of what poetry must and must not do, and finds it lacking. Instead, it is more fruitful to ask what it is that Swift accomplishes in his metrical compositions. The satisfaction to be derived from his poetry is of a different kind from that sought by Craik. The power of Swift's imagination is to be found not in elevated language or metaphorical virtuosity, but in his extraordinary phonetic awareness allied to economy of expression and a moral purpose. When he lamented that Pope could fix more sense in a single couplet than he could do in six, Swift was merely versifying a common complaint about his own failing powers. 'Proper Words in proper Places, makes the true Definition of a Stile' is Swift's own, oft-quoted maxim. It is a pity he never did find time to supply the 'ample Disquisition' he said it would require to elucidate his meaning.[4] As it stands, it is a trite enough remark, but surely he is referring to the potential of language to convey meaning efficiently and eloquently. When he told Bolingbroke that 'I can now express in a hundred words what would formerly have cost me ten',[5] he is advocating economy.

Like Johnson's, Swift's prose is replete with the mechanisms of balance and symmetry in expression, parallelisms and antitheses, doublets and triplets. Take the opening sentence of *A Modest Proposal*:

> IT is a melancholly Object to those, who *walk* through this great *Town*, or *travel* in the *Country*; when they see the *Streets*, the *Roads,* and *Cabbin-doors* crowded with Beggars of the Female Sex, followed by *three, four,* or *six* Children ... (My italics.)

Such patterns are pleasing to the eye and soothing to the ear. However, prose rhythm does not have the resources of metre to assist in the exploitation of patterning. By setting up a pattern of stress which the ear comes to expect or anticipate, verse can make use of those features of metrical composition, unexpected stress and stress failure. And for a man who had no knowledge of music, Swift had a remarkably good rhythmic sense. Allied to this is his skilful manipulation of words. Through distortion, colloquialism and slang, comic rhyme and pararhyme, Swift explores the full potential of language in verse. When, in 1734, he satirised a member of the Irish House of Commons, Sergeant-at-law Richard Bettesworth, he adopted a characteristic method:

Thus at the Bar that Booby *Bettesworth*,
Tho' Half a Crown o'er-pays his Sweat's Worth ... 6

Swift was known to be responsible for this particular couplet,
because Bettesworth suspected, quite rightly, that the 'two
words that rhymed to his name ... could come from none but'
the pen of the Dean of St Patrick's![7] Swift may have been 'a
Man of Rhimes', but there remained a crucial originality even
in his employment of such a stock resource of verse.

Swift's poetry, then, relies for its effect on phonetic devices,
and quite often these involve the distortion of the natural sound
of the words themselves. The use of comic rhyme, with two
monosyllables balancing a single word of two syllables, is one of
his best-known characteristics. A short poem of 1731, *The Place
of the Damned*, illustrates others:

ALL Folks who pretend to *Religion* and *Grace*,
Allow there's a *HELL*, but dispute of the Place;
But if *HELL* by *Logical* Rules be defin'd,
The Place of the *Damn'd*, – I'll tell you my Mind.
   Wherever the Damn'd do Chiefly abound,
Most certainly there is *HELL* to be found,
Damn'd *Poets*, Damn'd *Criticks*, Damn'd *Block-Heads*,
   Damn'd *Knaves*,
Damn'd *Senators* brib'd, Damn'd prostitute *Slaves*;
Damn'd *Lawyers* and *Judges*, Damn'd *Lords* and Damn'd
   Squires,
Damn'd *Spies* and *Informers*, Damn'd *Friends* and Damn'd
   Lyars;
Damn'd *Villains*, Corrupted in every *Station*,
Damn'd *Time-Serving Priests* all over the *Nation*;
And into the Bargain, I'll readily give you,
Damn'd Ignorant *Prelates*, and *Councellors Privy*.
Then let us no longer by *Parsons* be Flam'd,
For We know by these *Marks*, the place of the Damn'd;
And *HELL* to be sure is at *Paris* or *Rome*,
How happy for *Us*, that it is not at *Home*.[8]

The lines are quintessentially Swiftian, not only in their
overriding moral and political concerns, but in their expression.

This is not merely a case of rhyme, although the 'give you,/Privy' rhyme is similar to *'Bettesworth,/* Sweat's Worth', while the unusual coupling of *'Squires'* and *'Lyars'* is especially effective. The first seventeen lines are subordinated to the ironic reversal of the final line: 'How happy for *Us*, that it is not at *Home*'. Once again we see Swift exploiting the cumulative effect of the list, just as he had done in *Gulliver's Travels.* This takes the place of more conventional imagery. Instead, we have the almost hypnotic repetition of the single word, 'Damn'd', which is at once literal and expletive, as if the entire poem were built around one, powerful figure.

The rhythm, too, works with the final line in mind. Ostensibly the couplets are anapaestic tetrameters, with an unstressed syllable missing from the initial foot of each line. But at times it is as if Swift has forsaken metre altogether in favour of T. S. Eliot's four stresses to the line. Although subtle changes of rhythm chop the anapaestic beat to great effect, four emphases are constant, however many syllables Swift chooses to put in the line. The dexterity is reminiscent of the closing lines of *A Description of a City Shower,* in which Swift moves for two-and-a-half lines from a dual to triple rhythm, before returning to the original iambic pulse. Similarly, Swift's experiments with lines of many syllables – as many as nineteen in *The Humble Petition of Frances Harris* – meant that he was accustomed to playing with verse rhythms. Henry Craik was right to respond to 'the deftness of his rhythmical skill', although it is impossible to evaluate the precise effect of Swift's ability to manipulate words. It is a question of personal enjoyment, and it takes a good ear to appreciate the nuances of his diction and rhythm. In *The Place of the Damned,* however, there is a measurable intent. The exigencies of metre allow Swift to stress, quite deliberately, the ironic meaning of the poem at the expense of the apparent one. For in the final line it is not the negative which is emphasised, but the positive. The words tell us that the place of the damned is *not* at home while the entire phonetic structure is devoted to assuring us that it *is!*

In addition to reliance on phonetic devices, Swift's mature poetry exploits familiar rhetorical features. In prose, Swift tends to probe the weaknesses of existing works through parody. The frustration of conventional expectation is not far removed, in principle, from stress failure, and in poetry Swift often debunks traditional forms, particularly the pastoral. True, in the scatological poems, hardly anything other than the names – Corinna, Strephon, Celia and Chloe – suggests the pastoral. But even these tenuous links serve to manipulate conventional attitudes to women, love and marriage, as Swift undercuts the mode's romantic idyllicism through wit and humour. The aim is satirical. And yet much has been made of Swift's 'excremental vision'. Middleton Murry pointed out that the subject 'cannot be burked by any honest critic of Swift', and he found ridiculous the 'conventional excuses' made for 'the strange and disquieting combination of his horror at the fact of human evacuation with a peculiar physical loathing of women'.[9] Before we rush to accuse him of misogynism on the one hand, or of some sexual perversion on the other, it is salutary to remind ourselves that, *pace* would-be psycho-analysts, 'Swift was following faithfully an ancient tradition.' Obscenity is reductive. As Matthew Hodgart remarks, whatever pretensions man may have to spirituality are debunked in the act of reminding him that he is no more than 'a mammal that feeds, defecates, menstruates, ruts, gives birth and catches unpleasant diseases'.[10] Instead of Swift's scatological poems necessarily revealing something unstable or unsavoury about his character, they may be merely an extension of his satire on human behaviour.

The satirist is constantly seeking to expose the discrepancy between how men like to view themselves, and how they appear in reality. There are many ways of holding the satiric glass up to nature, but they have one thing in common: a desire to make the reader look at society in a fresh light. In the scatological poems Swift dwells on the seedy side of life. It is impossible to decide whether or not this is indicative of an anal fixation. But what the strategy achieves is not in doubt: the poems succeed in differentiating quite strikingly between illusion and reality, and while this may not contribute to an ideal portrait of mankind, it fulfils perfectly the brief of the satirist. In *Strephon and Chloe*, the heroine's graceful *Mein*, her Shape, and Face,/Confest her of no mortal Race'. The story is rather different, however, after twelve cups of tea and a pea supper. Then the pissing, farting nymph convinces her swain that she is 'As *mortal* as himself at least'.[11] This is the key phrase. Far from celebrating man's achievements, Swift, as a satirist, is concerned with his failures. Reminders of his mortality are prime ways of attaining this end.

Instead of Chloe being portrayed as a goddess, then, she is captured performing one of her most human activities:

> *STREPHON* who heard the fuming Rill
> As from a mossy Cliff distill;
> Cry'd out, ye Gods, what Sound is this?
> Can *Chloe*, heav'nly *Chloe* —?

The absurd inappropriateness of the diction serves merely to point up the discrepancy between the romantic ideal which poetry, in particular, has fostered about woman, and the physical actuality. Thus another Strephon is invited 'To see [Celia] from her Pillow rise/All reeking in a cloudy Steam', rather than after 'four important Hours' during which she is transformed into 'the Wonder of her Sex'. Were he to view her in the morning, *The Progress of Beauty* suggests, with 'Crackt Lips, foul Teeth, and gummy Eyes,/Poor Strephon, how would he blaspheme!' Swift wishes to puncture the illusion of the goddess, woman. We may recall the wise words he offered on the subject at the ripe, old age of twenty-four: 'among all the young gentlemen that I have known to have Ruind them selves by marrying (which I assure you is a great number) I have made this general Rule that they are ... young, raw & ignorant Scholars, who for want of knowing company, believe every silk petticoat includes an angell.'[12]

If nothing else, Swift's reductive satire in the scatological poems exposes this sort of human complacency. It is only the logical conclusion of the drift of the argument of *The Progress of Beauty* to picture woman defecating and micturating. This need not be misogyny nor an excremental vision, but simply a means of stressing man's mortality. When 'Disgusted *Strephon*' steals away from his peephole in *The Lady's Dressing Room* 'Repeating in his amorous Fits,/Oh! *Celia, Celia, Celia* shits!', or when the naive Cambridge undergraduate Cassinus loses his wits, and echoes the refrain, this surely reflects not on Swift's mentality, but on man's. And while poems like *The Lady's Dressing Room, Strephon and Chloe* and *Cassinus and Peter* take their theme thus far and no further, others, like *Phillis, Or, the Progress of Love* or *A Beautiful Young Nymph Going to Bed,* lay bare not only man's physicality, but the hollowness of his wonted spirituality.[13]

If the need to excrete is one, inescapable sign of man's animal nature, the need to copulate in order to propagate the species is another. But man has endowed the sex act with a spiritual significance. Marriage is a Christian sacrament, and intercourse a Christian duty. In *Phillis, Or, the Progress of Love,* however, the heroine is forced to break her marriage vows

> In kindness to maintain her Spouse;
> Till Swains unwholsome spoyld the Trade,
> For now the Surgeon must be paid;
> To whom those Perquisites are gone
> In Christian Justice due to John.[14]

In ironically suggesting that the proceeds of Phillis' prostitution should, 'In Christian Justice', have gone to her husband, Swift brings the whole question of the relationship between sex, love and marriage under the satirist's lens. He delves towards the heart of the matter of religion and morality, condemning society by reference to the ideal of Christian love and Christian marriage.

This might be best viewed at work in *A Beautiful Young Nymph Going to Bed,* a poem which has suffered from a marked reluctance to peer below the surface comedy. '*CORINNA, Pride of Drury-Lane*' is a prostitute 'For whom no Shepherd sighs in vain'. Once again, the preposterousness of the mock-pastoral setting is crucial for the humour through which the satire operates. But Swift has a serious purpose. As Blake makes clear in 'London', the prostitute, by her very existence, indicts a society which is supposedly Christian, 'And blights with plagues the marriage hearse'. The poem begins humorously enough, to be sure, as Corinna, seated 'on

311

a three-legg'd Chair', proceeds to pull herself apart – the literal application of reductive satire:

> Now dextrously her Plumpers draws,
> That serve to fill her hollow Jaws.
> Untwists a Wire; and from her Gums
> A Set of Teeth completely comes.
> Pulls out the Rags contriv'd to prop
> Her flabby Dugs and down they drop.
> Proceeding on, the lovely Goddess
> Unlaces next her Steel-Rib'd Bodice ... [15]

The technique hitherto is not very different from that employed in, say, *The Lady's Dressing Room*. In stripping Corinna of her cosmetic accoutrements, Swift is also stripping her of her pretensions. This is pointed up brilliantly by the simple inclusion of the phrase, 'the lovely Goddess'. Here the ploy adopted in *Strephon and Chloe* is used to even greater effect.

What is often missed is the change of tone upon which the satiric meaning of the poem turns. In *A Beautiful Young Nymph Going to Bed* the humour gradually subsides, and feelings of comic revulsion give way to pathos. This is achieved by the introduction of the element of pain. There is not only physical pain, although Corinna 'explores/Her Shankers, Issues, running Sores', and 'to each applies a Plaister'. Swift explores his subject's mind.

> She takes a *Bolus* e'er she sleeps;
> And then between two Blankets creeps.
> With Pains of Love tormented lies;
> Or if she chance to close her Eyes,
> Of *Brideswell* and the *Compter* dreams,
> And feels the Lash, and faintly screams ...

Like Phillis, in *Phillis, Or, the Progress of Love*, Corinna has venereal disease. These are the 'Pains of Love' with which she 'tormented lies'. The ideal of love is mocked by comparison with its antithesis – illicit sexual liaison. The falsity of applying such a term to the sex act is emphasised by the satiric reminder that copulation leads to the catching of nauseating diseases.

It is not simply that, as Geoffrey Hill has written, 'the superior intelligence can assert itself only by extravagant gestures of revulsion.'[16] That is neither a true assessment of Swift's character, nor an adequate analysis of his satiric strategy. Swift employs obscenity to reveal the depths of the human predicament. *A Beautiful Young Nymph Going to Bed*, despite the surface appearance, *is* concerned with love in its ideal state. While she writhes in bed as a result of the physical condition that copulation, the mockery of spiritual union, has brought her to, Corinna is nevertheless troubled about the loneliness of her existence:

> Or to *Jamaica* seems transported,
> Alone, and by no Planter courted. . . .

The poem is not merely a satire on prostitution. It goes much deeper than that. Like the beggars, the prostitute is a symptom of what is wrong with society. It is society which permits Corinna to get into such a 'mangled Plight'.

In this sense even the scatological poems could be said to be political. Given Swift's views on the connection between morality, religion and government, they can be seen as an indictment of a system which does nothing to prevent the corruption of manners. 'Religious Clubs' do nothing to relieve Corinna's hardships nor to put a stop to prostitution, 'Because she pays 'em all in Kind.' Swift exposes and censures the hypocrisy of those in positions of authority. It is not Corinna who is the principal satiric butt of this poem, perhaps, but the nation's leaders. In fact there is a sneaking admiration for this derelict who, every morning, has to 'recollect [her] scatter'd Parts', and get on with the job of living. She is a fictional projection of those Dublin down-and-outs whom the Dean of St Patrick's is known to have befriended – Cancerina, Stumpa-Nympha and Pullagowna[17] – although it is significant that Corinna is located in Drury Lane in London. In the scatological poems Swift does not make 'extravagant gestures of revulsion'. He condemns the deceitfulness of a loveless society which perpetrates violence on its members in the name of a God of Love. That is why Corinna 'With Pains of Love tormented lies'. *A Beautiful Young Nymph Going to Bed* is a prime example of Swift's 'hum'rous biting Way', as it mixes comedy with serious intent in an explicit condemnation of society. Its obscenity is satirical.

At the same time that he was writing the scatological poems and other poems critical of man and society such as *The Place of the Damned* and *The Day of Judgment*, Swift was turning his hand to more explicit political verse satire. Early in 1730, in *A Libel on D— D—*. *And a Certain Great Lord*, he launched a vitriolic attack on 'True *Politicians*'. He thought it the 'best thing I writt', and certainly it was one of his most outspoken attacks on corruption, well deserving of the name of libel. Politicians did not reward literary merit or sound scholarship, he points out, merely 'solid Work' in the sense of propaganda. This cynical view of the system of patronage was one to which Swift would return, and of course it had been orchestrated into a massive symphony of discontent in *The Dunciad*. In exploring the reasons for Lord-Lieutenant Carteret's failure to prefer Delany, Swift observed his submission 'To W[alpole]'s more than R[oyal] Will', and offered an explanation of his Irish policy:

> He comes to *drain* a *Beggar's Purse*:
> He comes to tye our Chains on faster,
> And shew us, *E[ngland]* is our Master:
> Caressing Knaves and Dunces wooing,
> To make them work their own undoing.[18]

Although Swift stressed that he was critical of Carteret 'the *Vice-Roy*', and not of Carteret 'the Man',[19] there can be little doubt that *A Libel on D— D—* was a particularly dangerous poem. It indicted the King's representative in Ireland of corruption, and openly suggested that he was merely following orders from England. Swift pictured himself as someone

> ... in *Politicks* grown old,
> Whose Thoughts are of a diff'rent Mold,
> Who, from my Soul, sincerely hate
> Both [Kings] and *Ministers* of *State*,
> Who look on *Courts* with stricter Eyes,
> To see the Seeds of *Vice* arise....

It would be difficult to find a clearer statement of Swift's anachronistic political ideas, or one which links politics and morals so closely. It explains to a very great degree his opposition to the system of Walpole. In *A Vindication Of His Excellency the Lord C[artere]t*, published in the wake of *A Libel on D— D—*, he drew attention to the political situation in Ireland, and the fact that 'many *Whigs* in this Kingdom of the *old fashioned Stamp*', were being abused 'under the Names of *Tories, Jacobites, Papists, Libellers, Rebels*, and the like'.[20]

We would be justified in regarding this as a private plea, as it had been Swift's constant complaint since 1713. Since then Whig propagandists had sought to taint all Tories with Jacobitism. In *The Intelligencer*, Swift had published scurrilous verses on the rabid Whig, Richard Tighe, who was obsessed with Jacobitism. Tighe had reported to Carteret Sheridan's mistake in preaching, on the anniversary of the accession of George I, a sermon on the text: 'Sufficient unto the day is the evil thereof'. In *Mad Mullinix and Timothy*, 'the only Tory now remaining, who dares own himself to be so' accosts Tighe (as Timothy) thus:

> ... prithee *Tim*, why all this Clutter?
> Why ever in these raging Fits,
> Damning to Hell the *Jacobits?*
> When, if you search the Kingdom round,
> There's hardly twenty to be found....[21]

After the publication of *A Libel on D— D—*, Swift was once again publicly accused of Jacobitism. This time it was Lord Allen who, in a Privy Council meeting, called him 'a Jacobite Libeller &c. and ... brought the same affair into the H. of Lords, that the Printer &c may be prosecuted'.[22]

The matter was never prosecuted, but it sharpened Swift's resolve to deal with his enemies in Ireland and England. *Traulus*, a poem in two parts, claimed that Allen was mad:

> SAY, *Robin*, what can *Traulus* mean
> By bell'wing thus against the D—?
> Why does he call him paultry Scribler,
> *Papist*, and *Jacobite*, and *Lib'ller?*

Yet cannot prove a single Fact.

Forgive him, *Tom*, his Head is crackt.[23]

A Vindication of Carteret ridiculed 'one or two principal Patriots', at the head of which was Tighe (as *'Pistorides'*). Allen was, by implication, another. Swift continued to vilify the so-called patriots who did nothing to preserve their country:

> YE paultry underlings of state,
> Ye s[enato]rs, who love to prate;
> Ye r[asca]ls of inferior note,
> Who, for a dinner, sell a vote;
> Ye pack of pensionary P[ee]rs,
> Whose fingers itch for poets ears....[24]

Virtually impervious to any proceedings that could be taken against him in Ireland, Swift responded to what he considered the malice and folly of his compatriots in verse notable principally for the ingenuity and anger of its abuse. The culmination of this line of attack was *The Legion Club*, which administered a sound lashing to all his Irish adversaries, including Allen, 'a Queer,/ Brainsick Brute, they call a Peer', and Tighe and Bettesworth, *'Dick Fitz-Baker, Dick* the Player':

> Tye them Keeper in a Tether,
> Let them stare and stink together;
> Both are apt to be unruly,
> Lash them daily, lash them duly,
> Though 'tis hopeless to reclaim them,
> Scorpion Rods perhaps may tame them.[25]

From Ireland, Swift turned his attention to England. In *To Mr. Gay, On Mr. P[ultene]y being put out of the Council*, and *The Character of Sir Robert Walpole* (this last evidently included in a letter of 26 October 1731 to Mrs Howard, now Countess of Suffolk), Swift resumed his pursuit of the *'brazen* Minister of State'. Although the first two were not published until 1735, while the *Character* remained unpublished in Swift's lifetime, the depth of his anger and hatred of the Prime Minister can

can hardly be questioned. True, he was by now becoming a peevish old man, discontented with anything and everything except the memory of his glorious past, but in his celebration of 'Bob', 'the Poet's Foe,' Swift's wrath knew no bounds. In *To Mr. Gay*, Walpole was portrayed as

> A bloated *M[iniste]r* in all his Geer,
> With shameless Visage, and perfidious Leer,
> Two Rows of Teeth arm each devouring Jaw;
> And, *Ostrich*-like, his all-digesting Maw ...
> Of loud un-meaning Sounds, a rapid Flood
> Rolls from his Mouth in plenteous Streams of Mud;
> With these, the Court and Senate-House he plies,
> Made up of Noise, and Impudence, and Lies.

His downfall was predicted in *On Mr. P—y*, upon which he would 'be mawl'd, fly where thou wil't.' He was advised to be careful, at that time, of his 'Corps.' And the *Character* succinctly expressed Swift's view of 'the Cur dog of Brittain,' whose conduct consisted of 'oppressing true merit exalting the base/ and selling his Country to purchase his peace.'[26]

As yet Swift's spleen was only being vented in private. Finally his conception of Walpole's abuse of government led him to publish two poems, *An Epistle to a Lady* and *On Poetry: A Rapsody*, which stung the Prime Minister to meditate revenge. Both poems were published towards the end of 1733, the *Epistle* in November, and *On Poetry* on 31 December. Early in 1734 steps were taken to arrest those involved in the appearance of the two poems. Needless to say, Swift was suspected of authorship. According to Sheridan, Walpole was 'exasperated to the highest degree' by the poems, and ordered a warrant for Swift's arrest, only to be told that he would need an army of ten thousand men to bring this about.[27] The story may well be apocryphal, but in the event Swift's minions in the matter, Matthew Pilkington and Mrs Barber, were released together with the printer and bookseller. Evidently there was nothing in the poems that could be adjudged libellous.

Perhaps Swift had been sufficiently careful not to include offensive material that could not be taken at least two ways. But when, in *An Epistle to a Lady*, he admits that

> All the Vices of a Court,
> Do but serve to make me Sport.
> Shou'd a Monkey wear a Crown,
> Must I tremble at his Frown?
> Could I not, thro' all his Ermin,
> Spy the strutting chatt'ring Vermin?
> Safely write a smart Lampoon,
> To expose the brisk Baboon?

his clear reference to the monarchy could hardly have been misconstrued. Certainly, the conditional element in the lines ('Shou'd ... Must ... Could') serves to render the satire slightly less direct, but the implication that George II might be likened to a monkey cannot be missed. Thus, when the poem turns specifically to ironic comment at Walpole's expense:

> WHEN my Muse officious ventures
> On the Nation's Representers;
> Teaching by what *Golden* Rules
> Into Knaves they turn their Fools:
> How the Helm is rul'd by [Walpole]
> At whose Oars, like Slaves, they all pull....

the audacity of Swift's attack on the Court becomes readily apparent, so that the response

> DEUCE is in you, Mr. DEAN;
> What can all this Passion mean?
> Mention Courts, you'll ne'er be quiet;
> On Corruptions running Riot.[28]

is a perfectly reasonable one.

An Epistle to a Lady is of interest on a number of counts: as evidence of the lengths to which Swift was prepared to go to censure the corruption of manners under Walpole; and as an indication of Swift's own view of his achievements and capabilities in verse, his 'Rocket ... Muse' unable to scale the heights of Parnassus. But it is not a polished performance, and its unity suffers from the intrusion of political material, as one of the pieces of Market Hill raillery becomes the vehicle for his satire on Walpole and the Court of George II. This cannot be said of *On Poetry: A Rapsody*, however, which might be called Swift's *Dunciad*. Once again the state of letters in the kingdom is offered as symptomatic of a much deeper social malaise. The poem is a 'rapsody' not so much because it is an ecstatic, free-form celebration of its subject, but because it is a round attack on the pitiful condition of contemporary literature. For this reason, those well-meaning editors who insist on correcting Swift's spelling mislead when they refer to his *rhapsody* on poetry. A rap is a short, sharp blow – precisely what Swift administers. It is also, in eighteenth-century usage, both a counterfeit coin (as Swift himself explained in *The Drapier's Letters*) and, according to Fielding, a 'cant word, meaning to swear, or rather to perjure yourself'.[29] Thus Swift's *rapsody* on poetry is an attack on, not a celebration of, contemporary poetry, which suggests that it is a sham product, unworthy of the name, and that to offer a supposed *rhapsody* on such a subject would, indeed, be for Swift to perjure himself.

On Poetry: A Rapsody is a fine satirical exposure of contemporary 'literary' practices in the Britain of 1733, in which Colley Cibber's monopoly of royal patronage is 'For ever fixt by Right Divine,/ (A Monarch's Right) on *Grubstreet* Line'. Swift offers ironic advice to would-be poetasters – how 'In modern Wit all printed Trash, is/ Set off with num'rous *Breaks*— and *Dashes*—', say, or if 'To Statesmen wou'd you give a Wipe,/ You print it in *Italick Type*'. This recalls the counsel offered previously in *A Tale of a Tub* or *Directions for a Birth-day Song*. Swift's strategy is blame by praise. Like Pope's *Peri Bathous: Or, The Art of Sinking in Poetry, On Poetry: A Rapsody* is concerned not with questions of greatness, but of poorness – 'who can reach the Worst of all?'

> For, tho' in Nature Depth and Height
> Are equally held infinite,
> In Poetry the Height we know;
> 'Tis only infinite below.[30]

Playing with the concept of profundity, Swift ironically

condemns the 'achievements' of modern verse.

But his censure of contemporary letters is subordinate to his criticism of contemporary manners. Having prepared the reader for the ironic inversion of values, so that bad poetry is celebrated as if it were sublime, Swift introduces the royal family, and invites us to apply the same ironic criteria to his apparent panegyric on their alleged virtues. From the King himself

> Fair *Britain* in thy Monarch blest,
> Whose Virtues bear the strictest Test;
> Whom never *Faction* cou'd bespatter,
> Nor *Minister*, nor *Poet* flatter.
> What Justice in rewarding Merit?
> What Magnanimity of Spirit?

through Queen Caroline

> The *Consort* of his Throne and Bed,
> A perfect Goddess born and bred.
> Appointed sov'reign Judge to sit
> On Learning, Eloquence and Wit.

to George's heir, his son, Frederick Louis, the Prince of Wales,

> Our eldest Hope, divine *Iülus*,
> (Late, very late, O, may he rule us.)

the Hanoverians are subjected to Swift's withering sarcasm. And finally the focus is turned once more on the symbolic figure of Walpole, the 'great Viceregent of the King.'

> In all Affairs thou sole Director,
> Of Wit and Learning chief Protector;
> Tho' small the Time thou hast to spare,
> The Church is thy peculiar Care.
> Of pious Prelates what a Stock
> You chuse to rule the Sable-flock.
> You raise the Honour of the Peerage,
> Proud to attend you at the Steerage,

> You dignify the noble Race,
> Content yourself with humbler Place.
> Now Learning, Valour, Virtue, Sense,
> To Titles give the sole Pretence.

Throughout, Swift's strategy of blame by praise is consistently applied, down to the ironic denunciation of the entire political system.

> Say, Poet, in what other Nation,
> Shone ever such a Constellation.[31]

The conclusion is a damning one, as Swift follows the advice of his own earlier *Directions for a Birth-day Poem*: 'Thus your Encomiums, to be strong,/ Must be apply'd directly wrong', he explained:

> A Tyrant for his Mercy praise,
> And crown a Royal Dunce with Bays:
> A squinting Monkey load with charms;
> And paint a Coward fierce in arms.[32]

The difference is that in *On Poetry: A Rapsody* his raillery remained unexplained. It was up to the reader to apply it properly.

The converse of blame by praise is, of course, praise by blame. In these years Swift turned his raillery upon himself. In 1730, in pursuit of his self-appointed role as 'an improver of Irony on the subject of Satyr and praise', he had penned an attack in the 'style & manner' of his literary enemies, choosing 'to abuse myself with the direct reverse of my character'.[33] Most probably, this was *An Answer to Dr. D[elan]y's Fable of the Pheasant and the Lark*, with which Swift perhaps sought to draw the sting of the poetasters who were still making free with Delany's character for his sycophantic *Epistle to Carteret*.[34] But towards the end of the summer of 1731 he decided to offer the world a genuine portrait of what he regarded as his own character. Although this would operate initially through raillery, with Swift humorously suggesting 'what my friends and enemyes will say on me after I am dead',

321

ultimately the poem would supply what purported to be an 'impartial' character, drawn by 'One quite indiff'rent in the Cause'.[35]

Verses on the Death of Dr. Swift, D.S.P.D. Occasioned by reading a Maxim in Rochefoulcault cannot be ignored by the biographer. It is an extraordinary poem, not so much for the view of human nature drawn from Rochefoucauld – 'Dans l'adversité de nos meilleurs amis nous trouvons quelque chose, qui ne nous deplaist pas' – which Swift translated as

> In all Distresses of our Friends
> We first consult our private Ends,
> While Nature kindly bent to ease us,
> Points out some Circumstance to please us.[36]

as for the difficulties it presents to those who wish to interpret *Swift's* character. Admittedly, this 'Maxim more than all the rest/ Is thought too base for human Breast', but it was fully in accordance with his repeated insistence that one should not expect too much from human nature. Rochefoucauld was Swift's 'Favorite because I found my whole character in him'.[37] But Swift had his tongue in his cheek in choosing this particular maxim as the ostensible subject of his poem, because one of its chief themes – if not the chief – is friendship, and in *Verses on the Death of Dr. Swift*, he is concerned with exposing the discrepancy between genuine and feigned affection.

Thus Swift's real friends are subjected to apparent criticism:

> In POPE, I cannot read a Line,
> But with a Sigh, I wish it mine....
>   WHY must I be outdone by GAY,
> In my own hum'rous biting Way?
>   ARBUTHNOT is no more my Friend,
> Who dares to Irony pretend;
> Which I was born to introduce,
> Refin'd it first, and shew'd its Use.

This is just one more splendid example of 'That Irony which

turns to Praise.'[38] In the 'Proem' to *Verses on the Death*, Swift praises friendship and celebrates his true friends through raillery. Similarly, when, in the 'Poem' proper, he singles out Pope, Gay and Arbuthnot (along with Bolingbroke) as those who will genuinely regret his passing:

> Poor POPE will grieve a Month; and GAY
> A Week; and ARBUTHNOTT a Day.

we should not treat as serious the relative duration of mourning allotted to these true friends. Instead we should concentrate on the attitude of the remainder of mankind as depicted by Swift:

> The rest will give a Shrug and cry,
> I'm sorry; but we all must dye.
> Indifference clad in Wisdom's Guise,
> All Fortitude of Mind supplies:
> For how can stony Bowels melt,
> In those who never Pity felt....[39]

Given the Scriblerians' great emphasis on true friendship, Swift's theme was a choice one.

Encouraged by Pope to pursue his 'design upon Rochefoucault's maxim',[40] Swift predicted the reaction to his death to great comic effect, paying off old scores at the expense of Court friends he thought had let him down, and undercutting his own significance at the same time, first in his own circle

> MY female Friends, whose tender Hearts
> Have better learn'd to set their Parts.
> Receive the News in *doleful Dumps*,
> 'The Dean is dead, (*and what is Trumps?*)

and then, a year hence, with the booksellers

> Some Country Squire to *Lintot* goes,
> Enquires for SWIFT in Verse and Prose:
> Says *Lintot*, 'I have heard the Name:
> He dy'd a Year ago.' The same.

323

He searcheth all his Shop in vain. . . .

Thus far, the poem is humorous and uncontroversial. It is a further example of Swift's happy knack of approaching familiar subjects in a novel and inventive way as 'an improver of Irony on the subject of Satyr and praise'.

But the conclusion to *Verses on the Death* troubled Pope, and has exercised critics' minds ever since, as Swift offers posterity a character-sketch of himself supposedly drawn by 'One quite indiff'rent in the Cause.' Is this meant to be taken ironically? When Swift's 'Works in Verse and Prose' are represented 'As with a moral View design'd/ To cure the Vices of Mankind', this coincides with his own private claim in a letter of the same year that his verse has 'a moral View'. Similarly the statement that he 'Expos'd the Fool, and lash'd the Knave' can be paralleled by his hope that 'charitable People will suppose I had a Design to laugh the Follies of Mankind out of Countenance, and as often to lash the Vices out of Practice.'[41] There are sufficient indications that Swift meant his lines to be taken seriously, not ironically.

If this is so, *Verses on the Death* is a singularly revealing poem, in which Swift makes a number of curious claims.

> PERHAPS I may allow, the Dean
> Had too much Satyr in his Vein;
> And seem'd determin'd not to starve it,
> Because no Age could more deserve it.
> Yet, Malice never was his Aim;
> He lash'd the Vice, but spar'd the Name.
> No Individual could resent,
> Where Thousands equally were meant.

With *Verses on the Death* itself, Swift has patently done the very opposite of what he here alleges. Several of his 'enemies' are mentioned by name – Lady Suffolk, Queen Caroline and Walpole, as well as those consistent targets of his personal satire, Charteris, Cibber and Stephen Duck. Surely this is meant to be taken ironically? Swift even suggested that he 'put Mr. *Pope* on writing the … *Dunciad* … to hale [i.e. haul] those Scoundrels out of their Obscurity by telling their Names at Length.'[42]

Even though within the context of the poem itself, this seems to be an ironic comment, Swift's intent appears to have been different. The 'impartial' eulogist brings up certain anxieties which are gnawing at the sixty-four-year-old Dean of St Patrick's. He had always wished to *appear* disinterested in his satire, whether or not he had achieved the aim, and so he emphasised his objectivity, his lack of malice. Similarly from the *Tale of a Tub* onwards he had jealously guarded the originality of his wit, and therefore the couplet:

> To steal a Hint was never known,
> But what he writ was all his own.

was particularly apposite, whether or not it was true. He was proud of his invention. In view of Swift's increasing morbidity, the claim that he 'Was chearful to his dying Day' seems ludicrous. This is not the disposition suggested by the available evidence, for his correspondence stresses his growing despondency. Why then does the eulogist draw attention to Swift's hopefulness?

Although it is probable that no completely convincing reading of *Verses on the Death of Dr. Swift* will be forthcoming, certain facets of Swift's personality can be confidently illustrated from its lines. Probably, as James Woolley suggests, the eulogist must be distinguished from Swift *in propria persona*: 'Where the eulogist's character fades into the author's own voice, as it often does, it is a sign that Swift has found his character unable to serve as his biographer (he doesn't know enough) and inadequate to perform a friend's office – to say for Swift what he cannot with propriety say for himself.'[43] Hence, not only can the strange claim that he retained his cheerfulness to the end be explained, but Pope's (and the reader's) uneasiness about the fulsomeness of the praise written by Swift about himself, albeit in another voice, can be accommodated. There *is* distance between Swift and his persona, through which, at times, irony can operate. At the same time, *Verses on the Death* provides signal insight into Swift's own ideal view of his character – the character that is drawn is how, in many instances, he would like to think of himself. As Professor Woolley puts it, 'the eulogist's statements ... more nearly express hopes or intentions than facts'.[44]

Verses on the Death of Dr. Swift poses the same sort of problems as all of Swift's great ironic works. How can we interpret correctly what Swift is saying when we can never be sure of our ground? The only resource we have is rhetorical analysis, and for that we need contextual awareness. The poem was written at a particularly difficult time in his life. For years he had been brooding on the past, regretting the many missed opportunities of his life, and regarding the future with increasing anxiety. He desperately wanted the comfort of knowing that his conduct would be accurately recorded for posterity. He wanted, in short, someone to do for himself what he had offered to do for Oxford. He hinted to Pope that he would have liked more addressed to him than merely *The Dunciad*, but Pope never wrote a moral essay to the Dean of St Patrick's. And so Swift was forced to perform for himself an office more suited to a friend. 'Swift threw up ramparts against pain and loss', observes W. B. Carnochan. 'His satire murdered – not only to dissect but, ironically, to heal the wound of life itself.'[45] In *Verses on the Death*, Swift prepared for his greatest defeat. And he did so with the usual weapons of an ironist: wit, raillery and humour. So that while he was unable to resist the temptation to put forward an ideal view of himself:

> Fair LIBERTY was all his Cry;
> For her he stood prepar'd to die;
> For her he boldly stood alone;
> For her he oft expos'd his own.

he was still prepared to undercut his own eulogy:

> That Kingdom he has left his Debtor,
> I wish it soon may have a Better.

16

A Driv'ler and a Show?

Swift had been living in the past ever since the death of Queen Anne, his ambition and his hopes prematurely curtailed. Despite his spirited defence of Ireland, despite his continuing opposition to the regime of Walpole, despite the success of *Gulliver's Travels*, he regarded his life in exile as merely the prolonged epilogue to his years of greatness. 'As to Mortality,' he wrote in 1733, tracing the onset of his morbidity from the Hanoverian Succession, 'it hath never been out of my head eighteen minutes these eighteen years.'[1] The death of Hester Johnson in 1728 had simply aggravated this tendency, and had contributed to his increasing tetchiness. 'I am daily harder to please,' he confessed. 'I dine alone or only with my House keeper. I go to my Closet immediately after dinner[,] there sit till eleven and then to bed. The best company here grows hardly tolerable, and those who were formerly tolerable, are now insupportable. This is my life five nights in Seven.'[2]

Although Swift habitually exaggerated his loneliness in his correspondence, it was true that he now socialised on only two nights a week. Delany kept open house at Delville, a northern suburb of Dublin, and for several years Swift repaired there on Thursdays. On Sundays he was himself at home at the deanery, when his guests could look forward to plain fare of excellent quality and exceptional wine. Until just before his death in 1738, Sheridan continued to act as Swift's 'Viceroy Trifler', and *la bagatelle* diverted the Dean during the long evenings alone in his closet, when almost all thoughts of genuine literary pursuits were at an end. 'I have done with everything & of every kind that requires writing',

327

he wrote in 1734, 'except now & then a Letter, or, like a true old Man scribbling trifles only fit for children or Schoolboys.' He interested himself to a degree in the publication of Faulkner's edition of his *Works*, the first three volumes of which were ready for subscribers on 27 November 1734,[3] but by the following year his 'rhyming' had 'fled with [his] health', so that even his 'vein of satire upon ladies [was] lost'.[4] Only the *Legion Club* roused him for a final, brief burst of angry creativity. Thereafter he had to content himself with fiddling additions to *Polite Conversation* and *Directions to Servants* (which remained unfinished), and revisions to his various memoirs of the reign of Queen Anne, as he continued to re-write the past.

What we know of Swift's circle in the early 1730s tends to bear out his claim that although he could 'walk the streets in peace, without being justled, nor ever without a thousand blessings from my friends the Vulgar', although he had 'a set of easy people whom I entertain when I have a mind', he did not 'converse with one creature of Station or Title'.[5] Before he was given the Freedom of the City of Dublin in 1730, the Irish Privy Council sent for the Mayor and accused him of 'squander[ing] away the public money, in giving a gold box to a fellow who hath libelled the government'. Swift meted out his own punishment to the man who had been behind this malicious suggestion, Joshua, Lord Allen, and he continued to act the part of an absolute prince in his *imperium in imperio*, the Liberty of St Patrick's. 'I am Lord Mayor of 120 houses,' he explained to Pope. 'I am absolute Lord of the greatest Cathedral in the Kingdom: am at peace with the neighboring Princes, the Lord Mayor of the City, and the A. Bp. of Dublin, only the latter, like the K. of France sometimes attempts encroachments on my Dominions.'[6]

Despite his acknowledgment that he was using 'railery,' and his confession that, in 'Seriousness ... these advantages contribute to my ease, & therefore I value them', Swift's behaviour as Dean of St Patrick's was increasingly extravagant, and it could hardly fail to attract the attention of those in authority. His outspokenness often gave offence, and made him appear 'more mad and absurd than ever'. In 1737, when a proclamation regulating the value of gold coinage was issued, he put out a black flag of mourning and had the Cathedral bells rung accordingly. Such actions were viewed with growing dismay by men of rank. 'The Dean of St. Patrick's involves himself sometimes in such strange, improper, insignificant oppositions to matters of a public nature', one contemporary explained, 'that, by hanging out black flags and putting his bells in mourning, he makes it impossible for one in my station to converse much with him.'[7] Also in 1737 he returned the parchment and silver box sent by the borough of Cork giving him the Freedom of the City, because they had neglected to offer any reason for conferring the honour. But none of this altered the great regard in which he was held by the common people, particularly of Dublin, who lit bonfires and rang bells in annual celebration of his birthday.

After Stella's death, Swift's circle altered considerably. In the three summers of 1728, 1729 and 1730 he made lengthy visits to Market Hill, near Armagh, where he was received by Sir Arthur Acheson, 'a man of Sense, and a scholar', and his wife, who was 'perfectly well bred, and desirous to improve her understanding'. Lady Acheson filled at least part of the vacuum left by Hester Johnson. 'She was my pupil [at Market Hill]', Swift explained to Pope, 'with that, and walking and making twenty little amusing improvements, and writing family verses of mirth by way of libels on my Lady, my time past very well.'[8] Swift's visits to Armagh ended abruptly in 1730, but he continued to see Lady Acheson in Dublin, and at her mother's at the Grange, just outside the city. In addition, he made periodic visits to the Grattans at Belcamp, and Lord and Lady Howth at Howth Castle. However, his treks around Ireland were virtually over. True, as late as the summer of 1738 he was alleging that, 'if it were not for this cruel deafness, I would ride through the kingdom, and half through England', but his last journey of any significance was his visit to Sheridan's school at Cavan in the autumn of 1735. Soon after Stella's death he began to 'hate the thoughts of London, where I am not rich enough to live otherwise than by shifting'. Having tied up the larger part of his fortune in 'mortgages on lands, and other the like securities', he affected to be short of ready money, and practised ruthless economies in his own lifestyle, despite a combined income (from St Patrick's and Laracor) of not less than £800 a year. 'I chuse to be a freeman among slaves', he wrote to Pope in support of his decision not to return to England, 'rather than a slave among freemen.'[9]

For a time he maintained close contact with his English friends through the medium of correspondence, until gradually the links corroded. Gay died in 1732 and Arbuthnot in 1735. In that year Bolingbroke, thwarted in his schemes for dislodging Walpole, retired to the continent once more. The entertaining exchange of letters between Swift and Lord Bathurst ceased in 1737, as did the extensive correspondence which had been kept up between Swift and Lady Betty Germain. Only the association with Pope endured. Although it was once fashionable to question Pope's motives in prolonging his relationship with Swift, to examine his sincerity, and to pose disconcerting queries about his involvement in the publication of the third volume of *Miscellanies* in 1732, and the Pope-Swift *Correspondence* almost a decade later, there is no firm evidence to suggest deliberate under-handedness on Pope's part. Correspondence between the two men remained unbroken until Swift's loss of memory forced it to end in 1740. 'I have no body now left but you', Swift wrote to Pope in 1736, alarmed and distressed at the gradual but inexorable contraction of the circle of friends in whom he set so much store. 'Pray be so kind to out-live me, and then die as soon as you please, but without pain, and let us meet in a better place.'[10] Whether or not his faith was misplaced, Swift's trust in Pope was absolute.

By 1733 Swift had discovered that 'all things except friendship and conversation' were worthless, and he had 'become perfectly indifferent' to them.[11] Nevertheless he attempted to alleviate the afflictions of old age through exercise and diet. 'I do not value long life', he explained, 'but while it continueth, I endeavour to make it tolerable by Temperance.' This, allied to his obsession with strenuous physical exercise – he would walk for miles given the opportunity; and, if prevented by the weather, he would run up and down the stairs of the deanery for hours on end – drastically reduced his natural stoutness. His complexion darkened, giving his face 'a hard look'.[12] He became too lean to ride a horse with comfort. 'I have not an ounce of Flesh about me', he admitted in 1736. His deafness still pestered him, and his memory began to fail, leaving him 'sickly, weak, lean, forgetful, peevish, spiritless'.[13] 'What vexes me most,' he confessed, 'is, that my female friends ... have now forsaken me.'[14]

The loss of his 'set of easy people' was a sore blow to Swift. He graphically captured his own condition in the lines, *Written by the Reverend Dr. Swift. On his own Deafness*:

> DEAF, giddy, helpless, left alone,
> To all my Friends a Burthen grown,
> No more I hear my Church's Bell,
> Than if it rang out for my Knell:
> At Thunder now no more I start,
> Than at the Rumbling of a Cart:
> Nay, what's incredible, alack!
> I hardly hear a Woman's Clack.[15]

Even in the early 1730s he had had a well-established coterie of friends and admirers upon whom he could rely. In addition to Sheridan and Delany, there were the Rev. John Worrall and his wife, who had long been friends of Hester Johnson and Rebecca Dingley. When Swift was ill for several months towards the end of 1733, he 'let no Company see [him] except Mr Worrall and his wife', and it was at Worrall's house in January 1734 that Bettesworth threatened Swift on account of his ridiculing him in print. Of Swift's new acquaintances in these years the most significant was perhaps John Boyle, the fifth Earl of Orrery, who Swift thought in 'every way a most deserving Person, a good Scholar, with much wit, manners and modesty'. 'I have not known for his age a more valuable Person', Swift assured Pope in 1733, but his judgment was not always sound. Orrery was later to exalt his own intelligence at Swift's expense, rewarding the Dean's good words with a number of uncharitable comments in his unreliable *Remarks on the Life and Character of Dr. Jonathan Swift*.[16]

Swift's assessment of the characters of Matthew and Laetitia Pilkington was even more shaky. After supplying them with glowing testimonials to their uprightness, and involving Pilkington in the arrangements for the publication of some of his works, Swift finally discovered him to be 'the falsest Rogue, and she the most profligate whore in either Kingdom'.[17] He was similarly misled in his estimate of, if not the morals, then at least the mediocre poetical talents of Mrs Mary Barber. He himself penned the preface to her *Poems on Several Occasions* (1734), and recommended the collection enthusiastically to his friends in London. He patronised other female pretenders to letters such as Mrs Constantia Grierson and Mrs Sican, and other ladies of position continued to respond to the great Dean's humour. Anne Donnellan, Mrs Mary Pendarves (who was later to marry Delany), and Frances Kelly all bear witness to the loyalty Swift could inspire in women, even in his old age.

Without a moderating influence on his over-inflated sense of his own importance, Swift was susceptible to flattery. While his connexions with the past severed one by one, he began to be 'beset', as one contemporary observer noted, 'with odd persons who command every thing that he says, writes, or does, and every letter or paper that he has'. 'This fact is certainly so,' the second Earl of Oxford was assured in 1738.[18] By then Mrs Brent, Swift's long-serving housekeeper whom he liked to call Sir Robert (after Walpole), was dead. In 1735 she had been replaced by her daughter Mrs Ridgeway. Sheridan died on 10 October 1738 after an enigmatic breach with Swift about which little is known. The Dean was becoming increasingly dependent on his cousin, Mrs Martha Whiteway. Delany accused her of excessive interference in Swift's affairs, particularly in a self-appointed role of intermediary between Swift and his old friends. But Swift himself regarded her as 'a very worthy, rational, and judicious Cousin', and, as he put it in 1738, 'the only relation whose visits I can suffer'.[19] She remained loyal to him and to his memory, and friendly with Sheridan, Orrery, Pope and Deane Swift, Swift's nephew and biographer, who married her daughter.

None the less, 1738 does mark the period at which Swift's active involvement in public affairs began to wane. Until then, his interest in English and Irish politics had continued unabated, as he viewed with horror 'all things tending towards absolute Power'. Although he claimed to 'have utterly waved intermeddling ... out of perfect despair', he could never sit idly by and watch what he believed to be projects for the subjugation of the people's liberty advancing unchecked. 'The publick Corruptions in both Kingdoms allow me no Peace or Quiet of Mind,' he told John Barber in 1737, and in the same year he portrayed himself as 'modestly standing up for preserving some poor Remaindr in the Constitution of Church and State.'[20] No doubt by this time he was really tilting at windmills, as his ill-considered, almost paranoid response to regulation of the coinage in 1737 suggests strongly. But his persistent opposition to projects for the repeal of the Test Act, his constant advocacy of the Irish woollen manufacture, and his never-failing astonishment at the conduct of the Irish leaders themselves bear witness to the well-laid lines along which his political principles had run. By 1738 he was simply responding as if automatically to the battle cries he had answered wholeheartedly over the years. The spark of anger and indignation was still there, but the consuming passion and energy had failed.

Swift's last, great outburst of invective was written in 1736, when the Irish House of Commons refused to uphold the Church of Ireland's claim to the tithe of pasturage commonly known as 'agistment'. Instead they supported a petition of gentlemen and freeholders which complained about this alleged 'new Kind of Tythe'. Once more, this touched a raw chord in Swift's mind, and he reacted as one would have expected from a great champion of the temporal rights of the Church. *A Character, Panegyric, and Description of the Legion Club* mercilessly assaulted the credibility of the nation's elected representatives in Parliament. It is now fashionable to bestow high praise on Swift's tirade. True, it displays energy and anger to a degree which is unusual, even for the Dean of St Patrick's. As John Irwin Fischer succinctly puts it, in *The Legion Club*, 'Swift takes his contemporaries, members of the Irish Parliament, and transplants them as demons and madmen within a fantastic and allusive landscape that is part modern madhouse, part classical Hades, and part Christian hell.'[21] But there is surely little that is original in calling one's adversary fool and knave, madman or devil. To claim, as Peter J. Schakel does, that 'Swift brilliantly fused madness with damnation and the classical with the Christian', and that it is this which makes *The Legion Club* 'his finest prophetic indictment in verse' is to mistake the strength of abuse for the strength of poetry.[22] Swift's libel is remarkable more for its testimony to the depth of his feeling in his sixty-ninth year than as an example of his continuing power as a poet.

In *Verses on the Death of Dr. Swift*, Swift had referred to his intention to leave 'the little Wealth he had,/ To build a House for Fools and Mad'. He once more mentioned the scheme in *The Legion Club*, suggesting that the members of the club should 'have Right to dwell/ Each within his proper Cell' in the hospital for 'Lunatics and Fools'.[23] By 1735 Swift's thoughts were, he professed, 'wholly taken up in considering ... how to dispose my poor fortune for the best publick Charity'. He purchased land at Oxmantown Green in Dublin, with the intention 'to build a convenient house at his own expense for the reception of lunatics.'[24] Swift had always feared madness. The Hack in *A Tale of a Tub* proved to be acquainted with Bedlam, the London madhouse to which Swift was appointed a governor early in 1714. At the end of his travels, Gulliver's hold on his sanity is shown to be rather precarious, as he happily converses for hours on end with the horses in his stable. The Irish leaders were continually being indicted of lunacy by the Dean of St Patrick's, while Dick Tighe, perhaps the most outrageous madman of them all, was captured talking to Mad Mullinix. With his knack of confounding the literal and the figurative, Swift developed the idea of political madness. It was only appropriate that, in the end, he would remove the metaphor from his persistent suggestion that it was all madness, and frankly accuse the members of the Irish Parliament of insanity.

Swift's satire involves the reader. He, too, is implicated in the mad conspiracy to corrupt the people's manners. Swift demands that the reader shoulder his own share of responsibility for the failure to live up to the Christian ideal, so that he is also weighed down by the tremendous burden of guilt which oppresses the Dean of St Patrick's. However, Swift's madness runs deeper. Only a raving lunatic could possess the clarity of vision and the necessary courage to tell what he sees to a deluded public. Like Yeats's Crazy Jane, Swift functions as a perverse seer, disturbing the complacency of a besotted society. Now Swift was faced with the genuine prospect of, if not insanity, then at least senile decay. As his memory worsened, his hold on reality became more tenuous, and his confusion increased. By 1738 his condition had deteriorated sufficiently to give him serious trouble when he tried to attend to business.

In that year he had been making strenuous efforts to revise the *History of the Four Last Years*, having corrected *Some Free Thoughts on the Present State of Affairs* and sent 'a Fair Copy ... to be printed in England' in June 1737.[25] But his English friends persisted in their strenuous attempts to dissuade Swift from publishing the *History*, just as they had done almost twenty-five years earlier. While Swift fretted 'at universall publick Mismanagement', and viewed the telling of the 'true' facts of the four last years of Anne's reign as his contribution to the opposition to the Whig oligarchy, his English associates thought differently. Erasmus Lewis, prompted by the second Earl of Oxford, asked the Dean to consider 'that three and twenty years, for so long it is since the death of Queen Anne, have made a great alteration in the world, and that what was sense and reason then, is not so now'. 'It is now too late to publish a pamphlet', Lewis reasoned, 'and too early to publish a history.'[26] In the end Swift allowed himself to be over-ruled. The *History* was, indeed , historical propaganda rather than a genuine attempt at objective reality; a pamphlet, not a history. It remained unpublished in Swift's lifetime, along with the *Memoirs* and the *Enquiry*. Of his retrospective writings on the Oxford ministry, only *Some Free Thoughts*, published in 1741, saw the light of day.

Two other projects from Queen Anne's reign occupied Swift in these years, *Polite Conversation* and *Directions to Servants*, both of which appear to have originated around 1704. Although the latter also remained unfinished, and was published only on his death, *Polite Conversation* came out in London in 1738, and was included the same year in Volume VI of Faulkner's edition of Swift's *Works*. At the same time that he had been tidying up the *History*, Swift had sent Mrs

Barber a copy of *Polite Conversation* to be published in London, and had given her the rights to the proceeds of the work. He also corrected the proofs of Faulkner's edition.[27]

Polite Conversation and *Directions to Servants* both stemmed from Swift's inordinate interest in language and the manner in which words are used. They lose nothing by the fact that they had lain in Swift's hands for thirty years and more. He collected new sayings to add to his stock all the time. *Polite Conversation* is in the form of a dialogue, and resembles the clichéd exchanges of Restoration comedy, as Swift satirises the hackneyed speech of polite society. The piece was acted by Sheridan's pupils in 1738, and can still be staged today. Compared with Swift's other satires, it is light-hearted, but it offers incisive comment on the shallowness of contemporary conversation, reinforcing his other ironic remarks on the abuse of language. *Directions to Servants*, on the other hand, chronicles the speech, not of polite society, but of society below stairs. Instead of using the form of a dialogue, Swift chooses his more familiar first-person narrator as an 'old Practitioner' in all the arts of abusing masters and mistresses reveals the secrets of his trade, and offers sound advice to novices in service.

Clearly Swift's material was drawn from his own experiences. He had moved extensively within contemporary society on both sides of the Irish Sea, and had heard many a would-be wit utter the most appalling platitudes in imitation of a smart exchange:

> *Miss.* Manners is a fine Thing truly.
> *Col.* Faith Miss, depend upon it, I'll give you as good as you bring. What? if you give a Jest, you must take a Jest.
> *Lady Sm.* Well, Mr. *Neverout*, you'll never have done 'till you break that Knife, and then the Man won't take it again.
> *Miss.* Why Madam, Fools will be meddling; I wish he may cut his Fingers: I hope, you can see your own Blood without fainting?
> *Nev.* Why, Miss you shine this Morning like a sh—Barn-Door; you'll never hold out at this Rate; pray save a little Wit for To-morrow.[28]

Similarly he had suffered both the anguish of losing good servants like Mrs Brent and Sanders (Alexander McGee,) 'the best servant in the world',[29] and the indignities to which a master might be put by rogues like Patrick of the *Journal to Stella. Directions to Servants* suggested the ways in which servants might wilfully infuriate their masters:

> When you have done a Fault, be always pert and insolent, and behave your self as if you were the injured Person; this will immediately put your Master or Lady off their Mettle.[30]

This humorous inventory of the tricks played by servants is extended wonderfully by the fertility of Swift's own inventive imagination.

By 1739 Swift's memory was so bad that he could not remember where had left the manuscript of *Directions to Servants*. Although, according to Orrery, he was 'in excellent Health and Spirits', his memory was 'quite gone', and he was forced to ask Faulkner if he knew what had become of it.[31] It is doubtful if he ever worked on it, or anything else, again. The following year he was 'as good as can be expected', as Mrs Whiteway assured Pope, 'free from all the tortures of old age', but *Directions to Servants*, the one 'treatise [still] in his own keeping,' was no nearer completion. 'A few years ago he burnt most of his writings unprinted', Mrs Whiteway explained, evidently in response to Pope's question about further publishable Swiftiana, 'except a few loose papers, which are in my possession, and which I promise you (if I out-live him) shall never be made publick without your approbation.'[32]

Swift, then, had done with writing. His disabilities were preventing him from taking much part in public affairs, and even the office of Dean was becoming too much for him. He had signed his will on 3 May 1740, taking especial care over the provisions governing the erection and foundation of his hospital. Thereafter, although he made entries in his account books as late as 1742, he chose not to put pen to paper. Mrs Whiteway had already remarked on his 'indolence' in writing.[33] It was for these reasons, presumably, that he had appointed John Wynne Sub-Dean of St Patrick's on 30 April 1739. Finally, on 28 January 1742, Swift confirmed Wynne's powers, because the 'infirmities of age and ill-health' had prevented him attending Chapter meetings. He exhorted his Chapter to help him not only 'to preserve the dignity of my station, and the honour of my Chapter', but to 'show who and what the Dean and Chapter of St. Patrick's are.'[34] Just over six months later, on 12 August, Swift was officially found 'incapable of transacting any business, or managing, conducting, or taking care either of his estate or person', by a commission *de lunatico inquirendo*.

The commission dated his incapability from 20 May 1742, although he had 'for these nine months past been gradually failing in his memory and understanding.'[35] The question of Swift's mental state had been rendered urgent by an incident which occurred on 14 June 1742. For some years Swift had been friendly with Dr Francis Wilson, Prebendary of Kilmactolway in the Cathedral of St Patrick's. Whether or not Wilson tried to influence Swift unjustly whilst the balance of his mind was gradually being eroded, or whether, in an outburst of madness, Swift turned on Wilson, the fact is that an altercation took place after the two men had gone out for a ride together. Wilson claimed that the Dean 'of a sudden' called him 'the devil and bid him go to Hell', and proceeded to strike him 'several times on the Face[,] s[c]ratched him, and tore of[f] his Wig ... untill he thrust his Fingers into ... Wilsons Eyes'. Swift's servant, Richard Brennan, on the other hand, swore that Wilson had abused the Dean in order to try to get himself made Sub-Dean. When words ensued, Wilson had climbed out of the coach, calling Swift 'a stupid old Blockhead & an old Rascall'. He was so angry that Brennan had had to restrain him to prevent him offering Swift physical violence.

Swift was placed in the care of the Rev. John Lyon, who tended him until his death. His intellect speedily declined, and soon he was unable to recognise those around him. 'I was the last person whom he knew', Mrs Whiteway wrote to Orrery on 22 November 1742:

> and when that part of his memory failed, he was so
> outragious at seeing any body, that I was forced to leave
> him, nor could he rest for a night or two after seeing any
> person: so that all the attendance which I could pay him

was calling twice a week to enquire after his health, and to observe that proper care was taken of him, and durst only look at him while his back was towards me, fearing to discompose him. He walked ten hours a day, would not eat or drink if his servant stayed in the room.[36]

Once this fit of 'outrageousness' passed, Swift was plagued by boils and a swelling of the eye which has since been diagnosed as orbital cellulitis.[37] Thereafter he subsided into a state of tranquil senility, began to put on weight, and his health generally improved.

As early as 1744 Deane Swift observed that a 'thousand stories' had been 'invented' about the great Dean once he had been declared incapable. These have been 'imposed upon the world' ever since. What is known for certain about his last years is as slight as what is known about his first. Irvin Ehrenpreis has painstakingly assembled the available evidence to dismiss many of the legends that have grown up around the 'mad Dean'. Swift's condition was one of motor aphasia, not of mental instability. 'All authorities are agreed', writes Ehrenpreis, 'that motor aphasia has nothing to do with psychosis, madness, insanity, or imbecility.'[38] The tradition of Swift's madness, like other traditions such as the one that he was shown by his servants to a curious public for a shilling a time, must now be discounted.[39]

In reality, Swift was seen by very few people in his final years. Neither Orrery nor Delany, his first biographers, were allowed in the deanery in these years, so their accounts are necessarily second-hand at best. Deane Swift did visit his cousin, and offered Orrery an account of his health on 4 April 1744. A few days previously Swift had tried 'several times to speak to his servant'; 'at last, not finding words to express what he would be at, after some uneasiness, he said "I am a fool".'[40] These are the last words for which we have authority. Swift died on 19 October 1745 in his seventy-eighth year. For three days (in accordance with his will) he lay unburied, as people thronged to see his body. Finally he was interred 'as privately as possible' in St Patrick's Cathedral 'at Twelve o'Clock at night'. On these points his instructions were quite clear. Seven feet from the ground, fixed to a wall, a black tablet of marble was erected, in which the following inscription in large letters was deeply cut and strongly gilded:

> HIC DEPOSITUM EST CORPUS *JONATHAN SWIFT*, S.T.D. HUJUS ECCLESIAE CATHEDRALIS DECANI, UBI SAEVA INDIGNATIO ULTERIUS COR LACER-ARE NEQUIT. ABI VIATOR, ET IMITARE, SI POTER-IS, STRENUUM PRO VIRILI LIBERTATIS VINDICA-TOREM. OBIIT ANNO (1745) MENSIS (OCTOBRIS) DIE (19) AETATIS ANNO (78).

Swift's 'fierce indignation' was at an end. The man 'who strove his utmost to champion liberty' was dead.

Appendix I:
Swift's Reputed
Marriage to Stella

The tradition of Swift's marriage to Hester Johnson is a long one. Orrery first committed it to print in 1752 in his *Remarks on the Life and Writings of Dr. Jonathan Swift*:

> during ... SWIFT's residence with Sir WILLIAM TEMPLE he became intimately acquainted with a Lady ... he married her ... in the year seventeen hundred and sixteen, by Dr. ASHE then bishop of CLOGHER ... yet ... she never could prevail upon Dr. SWIFT to acknowledge her openly as his wife. A great genius must tread in unbeaten paths, and deviate from the common road of life ... They lived in separate houses; he remaining at the deanery, she, in lodgings at a distance from him, and on the other side of the river *Liffy* ... the general voice of fame was willing to make them both the natural children of Sir WILLIAM TEMPLE ... Inward anxiety affected by degrees the calmness of her mind, and the strength of her body ... She died towards the end of *January*, seventeen hundred and twenty-seven, or eight, absolutely destroyed by the peculiarity of her fate....[1]

Observations might be made about Orrery's tone, and about his intention in treating Swift in this way, particularly as he never met Stella, nor was acquainted with Swift during her lifetime. But in his *Observations upon Lord Orrery's Remarks*, Delany chose not to contradict Orrery. 'Your account of [Swift's] marriage, is, I am satisfied, true,' he wrote.[2] In addition, there is the admittedly hostile testimony of Bishop Evans of Meath, who supplies the most pertinent contemporary evidence in a letter of 27 July 1723 to Archbishop Wake. Writing of Vanessa's death, Evans reports that 'In April last she discovered the D[ean] was married to Mrs. Johnson (a n[atura]ll daughter of Sir W. Temple, a very good woman.'[3]

Although subsequent writers elaborated upon the theme of Swift's marriage to Stella, these are the relevant pieces of evidence. Even when they claim to derive from different sources, later accounts were clearly influenced by the existing printed tradition, and generally

341

they seek merely to offer tenuous corroborating evidence which is, at best, second-hand.[4] The attractiveness of the story of a clandestine marriage is that it serves to explain the peculiarly intimate relationship between Swift and Stella, and the legitimacy of both partners is called into question to suggest a reason for the failure to consummate the union. If they were both the natural children of Sir William Temple, then any sexual liaison would have been incestuous. In this way, some writers have chosen to account for the mad Dean's misanthropy: his tragedy was that the woman with whom he was in love was a close blood relation.

Firstly, it must be said that there is no evidence whatsoever to suggest that Swift was the son of anyone other than Jonathan Swift senior.[5] Secondly, Orrery's curious story of Stella's decline should be set against the very different account offered around 1730 by Sir John Percival, according to which Swift

> took to him Mrs. Johnson ... hoping the World would esteem her his wife, though not own'd by him as such. He thought his humour being confessedly odd, they would pass over this part of his conduct what ever they imagined, *but marry'd he was not*, for when a little before her Sickness he propos'd it to her, she declined it, telling her acquaintance that she perceived him every year to grow more bizarre, and she did not know how he might use her when so much in his power.[6]

Finally, John Lyon, Swift's guardian during his closing years, concurs with the view that 'marry'd he was not'. 'Notwithstanding Dr *Delany*'s Sentiments of *Swift*'s Marriage, & notwithstanding all that Ld *Or[rery]* and others have said about it', he wrote, 'there is no Author[ity] for it, but a Hear say story, & that very ill founded.'[7]

Lyon's argument is a convincing one. There is no *first-hand* evidence to suggest that a marriage took place. Yet there is very weighty evidence indeed to point to Hester Johnson dying a spinster. She consistently subscribed herself so in legal documents. In 1718 an agreement was drawn up 'Between Esther Johnson of the City of Dublin Spinster of the one part and the Reverend Jonathan Swift Dr in Divinity Dean of the Cathedrall of St Patrick's Dublin of ye other pt.'[8] This was two years *after* the reputed marriage ceremony. And in her will, Stella obstinately signed herself 'I, Esther Johnson, of the City of Dublin, *spinster*'.[9] Would the God-fearing Stella have signed her name thus if she had been married? Would Jonathan Swift, Dean of St Patrick's, Dublin, have let her describe herself as a spinster in a legal transaction in which he was concerned? I think not. Therefore in the body of this study I have studiously avoided any mention of the wedding which supposedly took place in 1716 in the garden of the deanery at Clogher. 'There is of course, no decisive proof of the marriage', wrote Middleton Murry, 'but it seems to us that the weight of the evidence makes it overwhelmingly probable.'[10] I can do no better than repeat John Lyon's eminently sensible words: notwithstanding what has been said about it, there is no authority for it, but a hearsay story, and that very ill-founded.

Appendix II:
Swift's Alleged
Jacobitism

From the death of Queen Anne onwards, Swift was periodically accused of being a Jacobite. The interception of his correspondence in 1715 was expected to bring to light his involvement in treasonable activities, and as late as 1730 he was publicly indicted as 'a Jacobite Libeller &c.' on account of *A Libel on D— D—.*[1] The claim has been repeated from time to time down to our own day, and certainly if guilt could be established by association, then Swift's loyalty to the Hanoverian regime would be in grave doubt. Many of his friends and acquaintances were active Jacobites. Bolingbroke, Ormond and Ford had fled to the Court of the Pretender during 1715, while Knightley Chetwoode was, with reason, under constant suspicion in Ireland, and Atterbury was found guilty of conspiring to restore the House of Stuart and banished in 1723 for his Jacobite sympathies.

Instead of damning Swift because of the political conduct of his associates, it is surely more pertinent to examine his own statements on the question of the succession, and investigate any evidence (as opposed to rumour or assertion) which might serve to suggest that he was, indeed, a Jacobite.[2] In the 'Letter' to Pope of January 1721 in which he outlined his own political principles, Swift emphasised that 'I always declared my self against a Popish Successor to the Crown, whatever Title he might have by the proximity of blood.' He went on to explain that he did not 'regard the right line except upon two accounts, first as it was establish'd by law; and secondly, as it hath much weight in the opinions of the people'.[3] As the Old Pretender was a Roman Catholic, and as the Hanoverian line was established by law, this statement would appear to rule out Jacobitism as far as Swift was concerned.

But can such an unequivocal account of Swift's beliefs be trusted for, after all, what were his motives in penning the curious 'Letter'? Surely it was meant to remove any lingering doubts about his loyalty to George I. However, on another occasion, when the question of the succession was not at issue, Swift observed that 'whoever neither offends the Laws of God, or the Country he liveth in, commiteth no Sin'.[4] Once again we have this emphasis on the legal nature of man's conduct in society. As the Hanoverians were the lawful monarchs after 1714, presumably Swift, or anyone else who chose to offend against British or Irish law by supporting the claims of the Pretender, would be committing a sin. He had explained the situation in 1721 to his Jacobite friend, Chetwode. 'I think I could defend myself by all the duty of a Christian to take oath to any prince in possession', he wrote, 'as the law stands, none has title to the crown but the present possessor', in other words, George I.[5] On this particular issue, Swift was perfectly consistent.

Was he then an oath-swearing Jacobite? Did he choose to pay lip-service to the Hanoverians, while secretly hoping for a Stuart Restoration? There is of course no way of knowing for certain. Had James III chosen to renounce his Popery, and had the law relating to the succession been altered, or had it been clear that 'the people' desired a divergence from the Hanoverian line, then it would still have been in keeping with Swift's stated principles to support the claims of the Pretender. But let there be no mistaking the grounds upon which Swift would have welcomed such a development. If a Stuart Restoration meant the re-institution of arbitrary monarchy, then he would have been vehemently opposed to it. Certainly he was disaffected under the Hanoverians. 'It is a great comfort to See how corruption and ill conduct are instrumental in uniting Virtuous Persons and lovers of their country of all denominations ... Whig and Tory high and low Church as Soon as they are left to think freely, all joyning in opinion', he wrote in 1731. 'If this be disaffection, pray God Send me allways among the disaffected.'[6] Certainly he satirised, perhaps he libelled, the Court of George II and the ministry of Sir Robert Walpole. Why? Not simply because he was a Jacobite, but because he was concerned 'to see all things tending towards absolute Power' under the Hanoverians.[7] He would not have wished to change one tyrant for another.

In the final analysis, evidence for Swift's Jacobitism appears non-existent. Nowhere does he state either in print, in his extant correspondence, or in his manuscript remains, that he supported the claims of the Pretender. In fact he says the exact opposite. It is quite likely that he burnt any incriminating documents that came his way, and he was scrupulously careful not to leave any of his own scribbles in case they implicated him in unsavoury transactions. In the absence of such materials, we have no alternative but to accept his own protestations that, however much he found to criticise under the Hanoverians, he was a 'true loyal Whig'.[8] Otherwise we must be prepared to contradict Swift's statements on the succession, and allow conjecture to take their place.

Abbreviations
used in the Notes

Add. MS	Additional Manuscript.
B.L.	British Library.
Corr.	*The Correspondence of Jonathan Swift,* ed. Harold Williams [and David Woolley] (Oxford, 1963, 1965, repr. corr. 1965, 1972), 5 vols.
C.U.L.	Cambridge University Library.
Deane Swift	*An Essay upon the Life, Writings, and Character of Dr. Jonathan Swift* (London, 1755).
Delany	[Patrick Delany,] *Observations upon Lord Orrery's Remarks on the Life and Writings of Dr. Jonathan Swift* (London, 1754).
Downie	J. A. Downie, *Robert Harley and the Press: Propaganda and Public Opinion in the Age of Swift and Defoe* (Cambridge, 1979).
Ehrenpreis	Irvin Ehrenpreis, *Swift: The Man, His Works, and the Age* (London, 1962-) 2 vols published.
Forster Coll.	Forster Collection, Victoria and Albert Museum Library, London.
Hawkesworth	John Hawkesworth, *The Life of the Revd. Jonathan Swift, D.D.* (London, 1755).
HMC	Reports of the Royal Historical Manuscripts Commission.
Lyon	Dr John Lyon's annotations to Hawkesworth, Forster Coll., no. 579 (MS. 48. D. 39).
Orrery	John Boyle, Earl of Orrery, *Remarks on the Life and Writings of Dr. Jonathan Swift* (London, 1752).
Poems	*The Poems of Jonathan Swift,* ed. Harold Williams (2nd edn., Oxford, 1958), 3 vols.

PW   *The Prose Writings of Jonathan Swift,* ed. Herbert Davis et al (Oxford, 1939-1975), 16 vols.

Sheridan   Thomas Sheridan, *The Life of Dr. Swift* (London, 1784).

Notes

Chapter 1   Infancy

1   *Corr.*, III, 132: Swift to the Earl of Peterborough, 28 Apr. 1726.
2   Orrery, p. 6.
3   Deane Swift, p. 26.
4   *Corr.*, IV, 229: Swift to Francis Grant, 23 Mar. 1734.
5   Hawkesworth, p. 7.
6   Ehrenpreis, I, 27.
7   *PW*, V, 191.
8   Deane Swift, p. 22.
9   *PW*, V, 192.
10   Ehrenpreis, I, 23; Hawkesworth, p. 11; cf. Orrery, p. 6.
11   *PW*, V, 192.
12   Lyon, p. 11; *PW*, V, 192.
13   Ibid.
14   Ehrenpreis, I, 32.
15   *PW*, V, 192.
16   Lyon, p. 10.
17   *Corr.*, IV, 229.
18   Orrery, p. 4.
19   *PW*, IX, 219.
20   Ibid., pp. 199-200.
21   *Corr.*, IV, 130: Swift to the Rev. Thomas Sheridan, 27 Mar. 1733.
22   *PW*, IX, 223; XII, 47.
23   Quoted by W. A. Speck, *Stability and Strife: England 1714-1760* (London, 1977), p. 224.
24   *Corr.*, III, 329: Swift to Viscount Bolingbroke and Alexander Pope, 5 Apr. 1729. On the importance of a belief in the Golden Age, see Speck, *Stability and Strife,* esp. pp. 224-6.
25   *Corr.*, IV, 230: Swift to Francis Grant, 23 Mar. 1734.
26   *PW*, IX, 220.
27   See Sir William Temple, *An Essay upon the Original and Nature of Government (1680),* intro. Robert C. Steensma (Augustan Reprint Society, reprint no. 109, Los Angeles, 1964), pp. 83-6.

348

28 Quoted by Christopher Hill, *The World Turned Upside Down: Radical Ideas During the English Revolution* (Harmondsworth, 1975), p. 60.
29 *PW*, IX, 220. Cf. ibid., I, 195-236 for Swift's *Discourse.*
30 *Britain after the Glorious Revolution 1689-1714*, ed. Geoffrey Holmes (London, 1969), p. 5.
31 *PW*, II, 16.
32 *Corr.*, V, 150: Swift to Alexander Pope, 28 Apr. 1739.
33 Deane Swift, Appendix, p. 35.
34 *Corr.*, I, 43-4: Swift to the Rev. William Tisdall, 3 Feb. 1704.
35 See ibid., V, 272-3.
36 The question of the authorship of *A Tale of a Tub* is dealt with infra, pp. 89–91.
37 *Corr.*, IV, 154: Swift to Alexander Pope, 1 May 1733. Cf. Lyon, p. 150: 'He never was avaricious'.
38 *Corr.*, III, 103: Swift to Alexander Pope, 29 Sept. 1725.
39 Ibid., p. 145: Swift to the Rev. James Stopford, 20 July 1726. See also ibid., p. 142: Swift to the Rev. John Worrall, 15 July 1726.
40 Ibid., I, 4-5: Swift to the Rev. John Kendall, 11 Feb. 1692.
41 Lyon, fol. 9 of the preliminaries. On Swift's voyages, see Irvin Ehrenpreis in *Modern Language Notes*, 65 (1950), 256-7.
42 See Lyon, fol. 9 of the preliminaries. Admittedly Lyon says she 'sometimes came to *Ireland*, to visit him after his settlement at Laracor', but as Swift was never settled at Laracor, only one visit can be confidently assumed. According to Lyon, on this occasion Swift was introduced to his mother's landlady, Mrs Brent, as her secret admirer. Swift joined in the joke, and 'smiled at his Mother's Humour'.
43 *PW*, V, 196.
44 Delany, p. 72. See also *Corr.*, III, 380: Swift to John Gay: 19 Mar. 1730: 'I pay an Annuity of 15ll per Ann: in Surrey'. Lyon says that Swift 'put on mourning' for his sister's death in 1738. Lyon, fol. 9 of the preliminaries.
45 See for example B. L. Add. MS 47119, fol. 100, quoted in Ehrenpreis, II, 770-1: '… nor is drunkenness his failing. Perhaps women is more so … '. According to another near-contemporary correspondent, Swift was unquestionably '*no good*'. C.U.L. Add. MS 7788, Box 14: J. C. Walker to Edward Berwick, 12 Dec. 1790 (copy).
46 Swift's own phrase. *Corr.*, I, 3: Swift to the Rev. John Kendall, 11 Feb. 1692. Examples of Swift's 'unconfin'd humour' are legion. Esther Vanhomrigh thought it impossible to guess Swift's thoughts, 'because never any one liveing thought like you'. Ibid., II, 364.
47 *PW*, IX, 87; *Corr.*, I, 36: Swift to Jane Waring, 4 May 1700.
48 For the phrase, see John Middleton Murry, *Jonathan Swift: A Critical Biography* (London, 1954), p. 432. The question of Swift's scatological satire is discussed infra, pp. 309–14.
49 The claim originated in Thomas Beddoes, *Hygeia: Or Essays Moral and Medical* (1803), III, 189 et seq.
50 *PW*, IX, 263.

51 Ibid., V, 227.
52 *Corr.*, III, 330-1: Swift to Viscount Bolingbroke and Alexander Pope, 5 Apr. 1729.

Chapter 2   Education

1 Ehrenpreis, I, 34.
2 Details of the curriculum of Kilkenny College are taken from Ehrenpreis, I, 40.
3 *Corr.*, I, 109: 12 Nov. 1708.
4 Ibid., III, 329: Swift to Viscount Bolingbroke and Alexander Pope, 5 Apr. 1729.
5 Lyon, pp. 12-13. For Swift's Anglo-Latin word-games, see George P. Mayhew, *Rage or Raillery: The Swift Manuscripts at the Huntington Library* (San Marino, California, 1967), pp. 131-55.
6 Ehrenpreis, I, 40.
7 *PW*, XV, 18.
8 Ehrenpreis, I, 43.
9 *PW*, V, 192.
10 *Corr.*, I, 12: Swift to William Swift, 29 Nov. 1692.
11 Orrery, p. 6.
12 Ehrenpreis, I, 64.
13 *PW*, IV, 282.
14 *Corr.*, IV, 85: 7 Nov. 1732.
15 Ibid., I, 11-12.
16 Lyon, p. 27; *Corr.*, I, 38: Mrs Jonathan Swift to Deane Swift, 10 Aug. 1703.
17 Ibid., p. 11. Cf. *Poems*, I, 27.
18 Orrery, p. 7.
19 Ehrenpreis, I, 61-2, 279.
20 *PW*, V, 192.
21 Ehrenpreis, I, 61.
22 Ibid.
23 Ibid., p. 68.
24 Ibid., p. 69.
25 See George P. Mayhew, 'Swift and the Tripos Tradition', *PQ*, 45, (1966), 85-101. Cf. Ehrenpreis, I, 66-7.
26 Ibid., pp. 69-70.
27 *Corr.*, I, 1: to Sir Robert Southwell, 29 May 1690. For the permissive, see John William Stubbs, *The History of the University of Dublin* (Dublin, 1889), p. 129.
28 J. G. Simms, *Jacobite Ireland, 1689-1691* (London, 1969), p. 12.
29 *PW*, IX, 262.
30 Ibid., II, 116.
31 See J. P. Kenyon, *The Popish Plot* (Harmondsworth, 1974), p. 3.
32 Quoted ibid., p. 96.

33 [Daniel Defoe?], *Tories and Tory Principles Ruinous to both Prince and People* (London, 1714), p. 19.

34 *Corr.*, IV, 230: Swift to Francis Grant, 23 Mar. 1734. See also ibid., p. 100: Swift to Lady Elizabeth Germain, 6 Jan. 1733.

35 *State Tracts of the Reign of William III* (London, 1706), II, 565. See *Corr.*, IV, 336: Swift to William Pulteney, 12 May 1735, for Swift's views on monarchies 'established by the *Goths*'.

36 Ibid.

37 *The Restored Monarchy 1660–1688*, ed. J. R. Jones (London, 1979), p. 18.

Chapter 3   Moor Park

1 *PW*, V, 193. George P. Mayhew suggests that Swift visited England in 1686-7, but this is based on a literal acceptance of Swift's dating of the onset of Ménière's disease 'before [he was] twenty years old'. See George P. Mayhew, *Rage or Raillery: The Swift Manuscripts at the Huntington Library* (San Marino, California, 1967), pp. 116-18; cf. Irvin Ehrenpreis, 'Swift's Voyages', *Modern Language Notes*, 55 (1950), 256-7; and *Corr.*, V, 37: Swift to William Richardson, 30 Apr. 1737. However, Swift dates the first attack quite specifically as October 1689. Infra, p. 34.

2 *Corr.*, III, 309: Swift to the Rev. John Worrall, 18 Jan. 1729.

3 Joseph Spence, *Observations, Anecdotes, and Characters of Books and Men*, ed. J. M. Osborn (Oxford, 1966), I, 52.

4 See *The London Gazette*, no. 2418: 10-14 Jan. 1689. I owe this reference to George P. Mayhew.

5 Recently, A. C. Elias, Jr, has questioned the validity of any interpretation which assumes that the relationship between Swift and Temple was in any sense a filial one. See *Swift at Moor Park: Problems in Biography and Criticism* (Philadelphia, 1982), passim. But in my view he does not dispose of the evidence on which such an interpretation is based.

6 See, for example, Orrery, p. 16.

7 *PW*, V, 193; *Corr.*, I, 2; Hawkesworth, p. 15.

8 *Corr.*, I, 2, 12, 16.

9 *PW*, V, 193.

10 Joseph August Du Cros, *A Letter from Monsieur de Cros … Being An Answer to Sir Wm Temple's Memoirs* (London, 1693), p. 2.

11 *PW*, I, 258.

12 T. B. Macaulay, 'Sir William Temple', *Edinburgh Review*, 68 (1838), 179.

13 *Corr.*, III, 125: Swift to Viscount Palmerston, 29 Jan. 1726.

14 Ibid., I, 1-2.

15 *PW*, V, 193.

16 *Corr.*, III, 232: Swift to Mrs Howard, 19 Aug. 1727.

17 *PW*, XVI, 564.

18 *Corr.*, IV, 257: Swift to Mrs Pendarves, 7 Oct. 1734.

19 *PW*, V, 193.

20 Ibid., pp. 193-4.

21 *Corr.*, I, 7: Swift to Thomas Swift.
22 *PW*, V, 194.
23 *Corr.*, I, 1-2.
24 On this point, see Louis G. Schwoerer, *The Declaration of Rights, 1689* (Baltimore and London, 1981), passim. For Swift's view on contract theory, see *PW,* V, 291, and infra, p. 246.
25 *PW*, IX, 31.
26 Ibid., Cf. *Corr.*, III, 384: Swift to Knightley Chetwode, 29 Apr. 1721.
27 Ibid., IV, 333-4: Swift to Alexander Pope, 12 May 1735.
28 *PW*, IX, 32.
29 *Cobbett's Parliamentary History of England* (London, 1806-1820), V, appendix, p. lxvi.
30 Downie, pp. 25 et seq.
31 *PW*, IX, 32.
32 J. G. A. Pocock, 'Machiavelli, Harrington, and English Political Ideologies in the Eighteenth Century', *William and Mary Quarterly*, 22 (1965), 571.
33 *PW*, II, 16.
34 Ibid., V, 193-4.
35 Ibid., IX, 31; XI, 131.
36 Pocock, op. cit., p. 563.
37 *Corr.*, IV, 230: Swift to Francis Grant, 23 Mar. 1734.
38 Ibid., III, 467: Knightley Chetwode to Swift, [May 1731].
39 See Downie, pp. 23-40, and infra, pp. 136–7.
40 See George P. Mayhew, op. cit., p. 117n.
41 *PW*, IX, 19.
42 *Corr.*, I, 5: Swift to the Athenian Society, 14 Feb. 1692: 'Being last year in Ireland (from whence I returned about half a year ago).'
43 Ibid., pp. 2-5: Swift to the Rev. John Kendall, 11 Feb. 1692.
44 Ibid., p. 11: 3 May 1692.
45 Ibid., p. 12: Swift to William Swift, 29 Nov. 1692. And yet, in later life, Swift claimed to have 'had the Honor to be *for some years* a Student at Oxford'! Such was his ability to distort the facts of his life. Ibid., IV, 274: Swift to the Rev. Henry Clarke, 12 Dec. 1734 (my italics).
46 Ibid., I, 12.
47 Ibid., pp. 1-2.
48 Ibid., p. 155: Swift to Lady Giffard, 10 Nov. 1709.
49 Ibid. Cf. *PW*, I, 255-71.
50 *Corr.*, I, 156.
51 [Jonathan Swift?], *An Answer To A Scurrilous Pamphlet, Lately Printed, Intituled, A Letter from Monsieur de Cros, to the Lord*—(London, 1693), p. 10; *Correspondence of the Family of Hatton*, ed. E. Maunde Thompson (London, 1878), II, 191: Charles Hatton to Viscount Hatton, 23 Feb. 1693. I owe this reference to George P. Mayhew.
52 Public Record Office, S.P. 105/50, fol. 92: DuCros to George Stepney, 20/30 May 1692. I owe this reference to George P. Mayhew.
53 *A Letter from Monsieur de Cros ... Which may serve for an Answer to the Impostures of Sir Wm Temple ...* (London, 1693), pp. [34-7].

54 Charles Hatton believed the *Answer* to be by Temple. See Homer E. Woodbridge, *Sir William Temple* (New York, 1940), pp. 224-8.
55 [Swift?], *An Answer*, p. 9.
56 *Corr.*, I, 10.
57 *An Answer*, p. 7.
58 *PW*, I, 269; *Answer*, p. 10.
59 *Corr.*, I, 156: Swift to Lady Giffard, 10 Nov. 1709.
60 Ibid., pp. 3-4.
61 *Poems*, I, 14.
62 For Dunton, see Stephen Parks, *John Dunton and the English Book Trade: A Study of His Career with a Checklist of his Publications* (New York and London, 1976).
63 *Poems*, I, 15, 17-18.
64 Ibid., p. 16.
65 Ibid., pp. 15, 19.
66 *Corr.*, I, 8.
67 Samuel Johnson, *Lives of the Poets*, ed. G. B. Hill (Oxford, 1905), III, 7.
68 *Corr.*, I, 9.
69 *PW*, II, 114; I, 158-9.
70 *Corr.*, I, 10.
71 When first published in 1745 in the *Miscellanies*, the *Ode to Temple* was said to have been 'Written at *Moorpark, June* 1689'. See *Poems*, I, 26. But Temple was at Sheen, not Moor Park, in June 1689.
72 John Irwin Fischer, *On Swift's Poetry* (Gainesville, Florida, 1978), p. 5.
73 *Poems*, I, 36.
74 See Emile Pons, *Swift, Les Années de jeunesse et le 'Counte du tonneau'* (Strasbourg, 1925), pp. 246-7, 325-6; *PW*, I, xvi.
75 *Poems*, II, 638.
76 *Corr.*, I, 8-9. Cf. E. W. Rosenheim, Jr., 'Swift's *Ode to Sancroft:* Another Look', *Modern Philology*, 73 (1976), S24-S39.
77 *Corr.*, I, 14: Swift to Thomas Swift, 6 Dec. 1693.
78 *Poems*, I, 48.
79 Ehrenpreis, I, 109; cf. *Corr.*, III, 410.
80 *Corr.*, I, 14.
81 It has been argued also that *A Description of Mother Ludwell's Cave* is Swift's. See *Poems*, III, 1068-9.
82 Ibid., I, 55.
83 *PW*, V, 193.
84 Ibid., p. 194.

Chapter 4   Swift and the Church

1 *Corr.*, I, 16.
2 Ibid., p. 17.
3 Ibid.
4 Ibid., p. 18.

5 See Louis A. Landa, *Swift and the Church of Ireland* (Oxford, 1954, repr. corr., 1965), p. 7.

6 *PW*, V, 194. For a discussion of who recommended Swift to Capel, see Landa, pp. 8-10.

7 Ibid., p. 8.

8 Ibid., p. 13.

9 Ibid.

10 Ibid.

11 Quoted by G. V. Bennett, 'Conflict in the Church', in *Britain after the Glorious Revolution 1689-1714*, ed. Geoffrey Holmes (London, 1969), p. 163.

12 Ibid., p. 154.

13. Quoted by Landa, p. 19.

14 *PW*, IX, 262.

15 Landa, pp. 16-17.

16 Quoted by Landa, p. 14.

17 Ibid., p. 11.

18 *Corr.*, I, 27: 1 Apr. 1698 (my italics).

19 Although there is a suggestion that there was glebeland in 'one of his three parishes'. See Landa, p. 22.

20 Quoted ibid.

21 Ehrenpreis, I, 159.

22 Landa, p. 15n.; *Corr.*, I, 31: Swift to the Rev. John Winder, 13 Jan. 1699.

23 Quoted by Landa, p. 20.

24 Ibid., p. 11.

25 *Corr.*, I, 28, 31.

26 Ibid., p. 21: Swift to Miss Jane Waring, 29 Apr. 1696.

27 Ibid.

28 Ibid., p. 4: Swift to the Rev. John Kendall, 11 Feb. 1692.

29 Ibid., pp. 25, 31, 28: Swift to the Rev. John Winder, 1 Apr. 1698 and 13 Jan. 1699.

30 Ibid., p. 33: Swift to Miss Jane Waring, 4 May 1700.

31 For the *Tale*, see infra, pp. 87–111.

32 *PW*, V, 194.

33 *Corr.*, I, 32: Miss Jane Swift to Deane Swift, 26 May 1699.

34 Ibid., p. 21.

35 Ibid., p. 26.

36 So did his son, Lord Spencer. See *PW*, XVI, 476.

37 *Corr.*, I, 26.

38 The question of Swift's salary at Moor Park has recently exercised A. C. Elias, Jr., in *Swift at Moor Park: Problems in Biography and Criticism* (Philadelphia, 1982), esp. pp. 140 et seq. Samuel Richardson quoted Temple's nephew as saying that Swift was hired 'at his first entrance into the world, to read to him, and sometimes to be his amanuensis, at the rate of 20 1. a year and his board'. But this does not shed light on Swift's salary, if he had one, in 1699, and originates at a source of dubious reliability. It is just as likely that Swift lived off the income of

Kilroot until Temple's death in 1699. At least, in the total absence of
evidence, there is little point in speculating about a possible income
from Temple.

39 For Thomas Swift at Moor Park, see Elias, *Swift at Moor Park,* pp. 50-66.
40 *Corr.,* I, 24.
41 Quoted by Ehrenpreis, I, 257.
42 Ibid., p. 256.
43 *PW,* XV, 183.
44 Ehrenpreis, I, 175.
45 Lyon, fol. 6 of the preliminaries; Ehrenpreis, I, 175.
46 *PW,* I, [xliii]. See also infra, pp. 87–8.
47 Lyon, p. 24.
48 Hawkesworth, p. 24.
49 *PW,* I, 2.
50 Lyon, fol. 6 of the preliminaries; cf. *PW,* V, 196, 198, 227.
51 *Corr.,* I, 32.
52 Quoted by Ehrenpreis, I, 260.
53 Victoria and Albert Museum, Forster Collection, no. 504.
54 *PW,* I, 244.
55 *Corr.,* I, 5.
56 *PW,* VIII, 120.
57 Ibid., V, 195: cf. *Corr.,* IV, 505: Swift to Charles Ford, 22 June 1736.
58 *PW,* V, 195.
59 Ibid.
60 Ibid.
61 Ibid.
62 Quoted by Landa, p. 30.
63 Lyon, p. 29.
64 Landa, p. 44.
65 *Corr.,* I, 34.

Chapter 5   Swift and the Whigs

1 *PW,* V, 11.
2 See Downie, p. 46.
3 *PW,* VIII, 119.
4 Ibid., I, 1.
5 Henry Craik, *The Life of Jonathan Swift* (London, 1882), p. 86.
6 Jonathan Swift, *A Discourse of the Contests and Dissensions between the Nobles
   and the Commons in Athens and Rome,* ed. Frank H. Ellis (Oxford, 1967), pp.
   156 et seq.
7 *PW,* I, 236, 301.
8 Ibid., p. 210.
9 See my essay, 'Swift's *Discourse*: Allegorical Satire or Parallel History?',
   forthcoming.
10 *PW,* I, 228.

11 Ibid., VIII, 119.
12 Ibid., V, 228.
13 Ehrenpreis, II, 73.
14 Margaret Toynbee, 'The Two Sir John Dingleys', *Notes and Queries*, 198 (1953), 417-20, 478-83; *Corr.*, V, 54-5 and n.
15 Ibid., p. 6: Swift to John Temple, [Feb.] 1737.
16 *PW*, V, 227, 228, 235.
17 Ibid., p. 227.
18 *Poems*, II, 735.
19 Quoted by Ehrenpeis, II, 771.
20 Lyon, fol. 14^v of the end leaves.
21 The question of Swift's relations with Stella is the subject of Appendix A.
22 Swift's own description of himself. *Corr.*, IV, 460.
23 See Swift, *A Discourse,* ed. Ellis, pp. 184-5.
24 *PW,* VIII, 119; cf. Ehrenpreis, II, 770.
25 *PW,* VIII, 120.
26 Their ways parted when Somers took office in 1693. See Angus McInnes, *Robert Harley, Puritan Politician* (London, 1970), p. 32.
27 *PW*, XV, 173.
28 On this point, see Frances Harris, 'Paper-Round: The Distribution of Whig Propaganda in 1710', *Factotum,* 9 (1980), 12-13.
29 *PW*, VIII, 119; XVI, 476.
30 Ibid., VIII, 120.
31 Ibid.
32 Ibid.; *Poems,* II, 566.
33 *Corr.,* I, 38: Swift to the Rev. William Tisdall, 16 Dec. 1703.
34 Ibid., pp. 38-9.
35 Ibid., pp. 39, 44.

Chapter 6   *A Tale of a Tub*

1 *PW*, I, [12]. Subsequent page-references are given in the body of the text within parentheses.
2 *The Anti-Nicene Fathers. Translations of the Writings of the Fathers down to A.D. 325,* ed. Alexander Roberts and James Donaldson (Edinburgh, 1885), I, 346.
3 Lucretius, *De Rerum Natura,* with an English trans. by W. H. Rouse (London, 1924), p. 69.
4 *Corr.,* I, 166: Swift to Benjamin Tooke, 29 June 1710.
5 Deane Swift, p. 31.
6 Lyon, p. 24.
7 *PW*, I, 279-81.
8 *Corr.*, I, 165-6.
9 *PW*, VIII, 119.
10 See his essays, 'Jonathan Swift, Thomas Swift, and the Authorship of *A*

Tale of a Tub', *Modern Philology*, 64(1967), 198-232, and 'In search of Baron Somers', in *Culture and Politics: from Puritanism to Enlightenment*, ed. Perez Zagorin (Berkeley and London, 1980), pp. 165-202 (esp. pp. 188 et seq.). Adams claims that Swift became acquainted with Somers at Moor Park, but Swift himself states quite clearly that he was not introduced to Somers until after the publication of his *Discourse* (ibid., p. 185; *PW*, VIII, 119).

11 Section X is not called a digression, but it is digressive, offering no contribution to the tale of the brothers and their coats. Even Section VIII, which deals with the Aeolists, is only marginally concerned with Jack's history.

12 Pat Rogers, *An Introduction to Pope* (London, 1975), p. 114.

13 Ronald Paulson, *Theme and Structure in Swift's 'Tale of a Tub'* (New Haven, 1960), p. 33.

14 Pat Rogers, 'Form in *A Tale of a Tub'*, *Essays in Criticism*, 22 (1972), 157.

15 *PW*, I, 107. It is interesting that this is the reading only of the first three editions of the *Tale*. In the fourth and fifth editions, this sentence was altered to read 'would *happily* be reduced' (ibid., p. 297, my italics). Evidently Swift felt that this particularly dangerous use of irony was too apt to be misunderstood to stand with safety.

16 See, among others, Robert C. Elliott, 'Swift's *Tale of a Tub*: an Essay in Problems of Structure', *Publications of the Modern Language Association*, 66 (1951), pp. 441-55. John M. Bullitt, *Jonathan Swift and the Anatomy of Satire* (Cambridge, Mass., 1953); William B. Ewald, *The Masks of Jonathan Swift* (Oxford, 1954); Edward W. Rosenheim, Jr., *Swift and the Satirist's Art* (Chicago, 1962).

17 John Traugott, '*A Tale of a Tub'*, in *Focus: Swift*, ed. C. J. Rawson (London, 1971), p. 76.

18 Ibid., p. 77.

19 For an extended treatment of the religious satire, see Phillip Harth, *Swift and Anglican Rationalism: The Religious Background of 'A Tale of a Tub'* (Chicago and London, 1961).

20 Frederik N. Smith, *Language and Reality in Swift's 'A Tale of a Tub'* (Columbus, Ohio, 1979), p. 21.

21 *Poems*, II, 579.

22 Although the Anglican Church is not Lutheran, it is clear that Martin stands for both Luther and the Church of England. His moderation is what Swift particularly admires.

23 *PW*, IX, 163.

24 Ibid., p. 168.

25 Harth, *Swift and Anglican Rationalism*, p. 59.

26 *PW*, IX, 262.

27 Ibid.

28 From 'A Satyr against Reason and Mankind' in *The Complete Poems of John Wilmot, Earl of Rochester*, ed. David Vieth (New Haven, 1968), p. 97.

29 Miriam K. Starkman, *Swift's Satire on Learning in 'A Tale of a Tub'* (Princeton, 1950), p. 45.

30 On this point, see Smith, *Language and Reality in Swift's 'A Tale of a Tub'*, pp. 27-43.

31 From *An Essay on Criticism* in *The Poems of Alexander Pope,* ed. John Butt et al. (London and New Haven, 1938-61), I, 249.

32 *Sir William Temple's Essays On Ancient & Modern Learning and On Poetry,* ed. J. E. Spingarn (Oxford, 1909), p. 32.

33 T.R., *An Essay Concerning Critical and Curious Learning* (London, 1698), p. 47.

34 Richard Foster Jones, 'The Background of *The Battle of the Books'* in *The Seventeenth Century: Studies in the History of English Thought and Literature from Bacon to Pope* (Stanford, California, 1951), p. 35.

35 *PW*, I, xvii-xviii, 139.

36 *Corr.,* IV, 53: Swift to Charles Wogan, July-2 Aug. 1732.

Chapter 7   Vicar of Laracor

1 *Corr.,* I, 56.

2 Ibid., pp. 41-2, 45: Swift to the Rev. William Tisdall, 3 Feb. and 20 Apr. 1704.

3 Ibid., p. 45.

4 Ibid., p. 46.

5 Landa, p. 38.

6 Victoria and Albert Museum, Forster Collection, no. 505, MS. 48. D. 34/I.

7 Landa, p. 37.

8 Quoted ibid.

9 *Corr.,* I, 46.

10 Ibid., p. 54: Swift to John Temple, 15 June 1706.

11 Ibid., p. 51: 22 Mar. 1705.

12 See Landa, pp. 50-2.

13 *PW*, I, [246].

14 See *Corr.,* IV, 31: Swift to Alexander Pope, 12 June 1732: 'I have a thing in prose, begun about twenty-eight years ago, and almost finished'.

15 Ehrenpreis, II, 190.

16 *PW*, IV, 264.

17 *Corr.,* I, 56-8: Swift to Archbishop King, 6 Dec. 1707.

18 Ibid., p. 58.

19 Ibid., pp. 68, 65.

20 Ibid., IV, 182: Swift to Bishop Stearne, July 1733. Cf. ibid., I, 67, 73, 76.

21 Ibid., pp. 80, 84.

22 Ibid., p. 114: Swift to Archbishop King, 30 Nov. 1708.

23 *Corr.,* I, 181. Cf. ibid., p. 137; *PW*, VIII, 121.

24 Landa, p. 56.

25 *Corr.,* I, 70: Swift to Archbishop King.

26 Ibid., pp. 120, 121: Swift to Robert Hunter, 12 Jan. 1709.

27 Ibid., p. 105.

28 *PW,* XV, 36; *Corr.,* I, 173. Cf. *PW,* VIII, 122.

29 HMC *Portland,* IV, 502.

30 See *Corr.,* I, 105: Swift to Archbishop King, 9 Nov. 1708.

31 Ibid., pp. 74, 91.

32 Ibid., p. 164; II, 298, 286.

33 Charles L. Batten, Jr., *Pleasurable Instruction: Form and Convention in Eighteenth-Century Travel Literature* (Berkeley and Los Angeles, 1978), p. 10.

34 *Corr.,* I, 142, 143, 144: Swift to Lord Halifax, 13 June 1709. Cf. ibid., IV, 344-5: Swift to Lady Elizabeth Germain, 8 June 1735.

35 *PW,* V, 258.

36 *Corr.,* I, 170: Swift to Joseph Addison, 22 Aug. 1710.

37 On this point see Ricardo Quintana, *The Mind and Art of Jonathan Swift* (Oxford, 1936), pp. 162-3.

38 See Downie, p. 10.

39 *PW,* II, xxv. Cf. Bertrand A. Goldgar, *The Curse of Party: Swift's Relations with Addison and Steele* (Lincoln, Nebraska, 1961), pp. 5-6.

40 On this point, see my 'Polemical Strategy and Swift's *The Conduct of the Allies', Prose Studies,* 4 (1981), 134-45, esp. pp. 135-7.

41 *PW,* II, x-xi.

42 Ibid., p. 145.

43 Ibid., p. [195]. Cf. ibid., XII, 34.

44 Ibid., II, 155, 154.

45 Ibid., p. [225].

46 Ibid., p. 162.

47 Quoted ibid., p. xxvii.

48 Ibid., p. 172.

49 Ibid., p. 173. Swift's contributions to *The Spectator* can scarcely have amounted to much. By March 1711 he was barely on speaking terms with Addison and Steele. See ibid., pp. xxxvi-xxxvii, 264-8.

50 Ibid., p. 172.

51 *Poems,* I, 124-5.

52 In particular, see Roger Savage, 'Swift's Fallen City: *A Description of the Morning',* in *The World of Jonathan Swift: Essays for the Tercentenary* (Oxford, 1968), pp. 171-94; David M. Vieth, '*Fiat Lux*: Logos versus Chaos in Swift's "A Description of the Morning" ', *Papers on Language and Literature,* 8 (1972), 302-7; and A. B. England, *Energy and Order in the Poetry of Swift* (London and Toronto, 1980), pp. 93-100.

53 *PW,* II, 172.

54 Ibid., I, 109.

55 On this point, see also infra, pp. 283–7.

56 *PW,* I, 3.

57 Ibid., II, 29.

58 Ibid., p. 27.

59 Thomas Hobbes, *Leviathan,* ed. C. B. Macpherson (Harmondsworth, 1968), p. 186.

60 *PW,* II, 27.

61 See infra, pp. 301–4, and David Nokes, 'Swift and the Beggars', *Essays in Criticism,* 26 (1976), 218-33. Cf. Claude Rawson, 'A Reading of *A Modest Proposal*', in *Augustan Worlds: Essays in Honour of A. R. Humphreys,* ed. J. C. Hilson, M. M. B. Jones, and J. R. Watson (Leicester and New York, 1978), pp. 29-50.

62 *PW,* II, 45, 57.

63 Ibid., IX, 262.

64 Ibid., p. 171: cf. p. 248.

65 *Corr.,* III, 87, 289.

66 Ibid., I, 114-15: Swift to Archbishop King, 30 Nov. 1708. Cf. ibid., p. 111: Archbishop King to Swift, 20 Nov. 1708.

67 *PW,* II, 114.

68 *The Letters of Joseph Addison,* ed. Walter Graham (Oxford, 1941), pp. 134-5.

69 Ibid.

70 The publication of *Memoirs III* was the occasion of disagreement between Swift and Lady Giffard. See *Corr.,* I, 154-7: Swift to Lady Giffard, 10 Nov. 1709.

71 *PW,* II, 130.

72 Ibid., p. 131.

73 Ibid., pp. 129, 132.

74 My view of the Sacheverell affair follows Geoffrey Holmes, *The Trial of Doctor Sacheverell* (London, 1972).

75 See Geoffrey Holmes, 'The Sacheverell Riots: The Crowd and the Church in early eighteenth-century London', *Past & Present,* no. 72 (1976), 55-85.

76 *Corr.,* I, 166: 29 June 1710.

77 Ibid., p. 167: 10 July 1710.

78 Ibid., p. 150: Lord Halifax to Swift, 6 Oct. 1709.

79 See Downie, passim.

Chapter 8 Swift and the Tories

1 *PW,* XV, 4.

2 Ibid., pp. 5-6.

3 Ibid., pp. 3, 6, 7-8.

4 Ibid., pp. 7, 13, 16; *Corr.,* I, 178.

5 See J. A. Downie, 'The Commission of Public Accounts and the formation of the Country Party', *English Historical Review,* 91 (1976), 33-51.

6 Quoted in Downie, p. 21.

7 HMC *Portland,* IV, 261: to Sir Robert Davers, 6 Oct. 1705.

8 Harley's phrase, as reported in *Cobbett's Parliamentary History of England* (London, 1806-1820), V, 830.

9 British Library, Loan 29/10.

10 Quoted in Downie, p. 120.
11 *Corr.*, IV, 100: Swift to Lady Elisabeth German, 8 Jan. 1733. Cf. infra, p. 315.
12 *PW*, XV, 44.
13 Ibid., VIII, 76.
14 Ibid., XV, 41, 46, 47, 36.
15 *Corr.*, I, 189-90: Swift to Archbishop King, 4 Nov. 1710.
16 According to Lyon, Swift made a list of 'Subjects for a Volume' in October 1708, including 'Apology for the &c'. The rest of the list comprises the contents for the planned *Miscellanies*. Lyon's dating cannot be considered unimpeachable. When printed, the 'Apology' was dated 3 June 1709. See *PW*, I, 11 and Ehrenpreis, II, 768-9.
17 *PW*, XV, 60.
18 *Poems*, I, 133.
19 Ibid., pp. 134, 135.
20 *PW*, XV, 59, 60.
21 Ibid., pp. 62, 74.
22 *Poems*, I, 137.
23 *PW*, XV, 50-1.
24 *Poems*, I, 138, 139.
25 See infra, pp. 119–20.
26 *PW*, III, 3, 14.
27 Ibid., VIII, 123.
28 See Downie, p. 127.
29 *PW*, III, 15.
30 Ibid., p. 12.
31 Ibid., p. 35.
32 Ibid., I, 1.
33 Ibid., XV, 146.
34 Ibid., pp. 107-8. My italics.
35 Ibid., pp. 19-24, 80-5, 24-9.
36 Ibid., p. 46.
37 Ibid., p. 12.
38 John Middleton Murry, *Jonathan Swift: A Critical Biography* (London, 1954), p. 171. Cf. *PW*, VIII, 124.
39 Ibid., XV, 85.
40 Ibid., p. 126.
41 Ibid., XVI, 589.
42 Ibid., XV, 230.
43 Orrery, pp. 29-30.
44 See *Corr.*, V, 228-9.
45 *PW*, XVI, 421, 603.
46 See Downie, pp. 162-70, for a detailed account.
47 *PW*, XV, 333-4.
48 He repeatedly referred to his efforts in later life. See *Corr.*, V, 45-6; *PW*, VIII, 76.

49 Orrery, pp. 29-30.
50 See J. A. Downie and David Woolley, 'Swift, Oxford, and the Composition of Queen's Speeches, 1710-1714', *British Library Journal,* 8 (1982), 122-3.
51 *PW*, XVI, 635.
52 HMC *Portland,* V, 464.
53 For the October Club, see H.T. Dickinson's essay in *Huntington Library Quarterly,* 33 (1969–1970), 155-73.
54 *PW*, XV, 195.
55 Ibid., p. 208.
56 Ibid., III, 87.
57 *PW*, XV, 178.
58 Ibid., p. 159.
59 Ibid., III, 109.
60 Ibid., VIII, 128.
61 Ibid., p. 245.
62 Ibid., p. 252.
63 Longleat House, Portland MSS, X, fol. 134: 'Heads for a Memoriall for the E[arl] of Oxford'. Cf. *PW*, VIII, 128.
64 Ibid., XV, 280, 291-2n.
65 W. A. Speck, '*The Examiner* Examined: Swift's Tory Pamphleteering', in *Focus: Swift*, ed. C. J. Rawson (London, 1971), 154.
66 *PW*, XV, 303.
67 Ibid., p. 208.
68 *Corr.,* II, 44.
69 Ibid., p. 182.
70 *PW*, XI, 196, for More's place in the *Sextumvirate* to which all the Ages of the World cannot add a Seventh'. Swift called More 'The only Man of true Virtue tha(t) ever Engld produced' (ibid., V, 247), but both More and Oxford are included in his list *Of Mean and Great Figures made by several Persons,* the former for his behaviour 'during his Imprisonment, and at his Execution', the latter both for his demeanour 'at his Tryall', and 'when he was stabbed by Guiscard' (ibid., p. 84).
    Swift's admiration for Charles XII is perhaps best seen in a letter he wrote to Ford on hearing of the King's death, in which he confessed to be 'personally concerned', 'I intended to have beggd my Bread at His Court', he explained, 'whenever our good Friends in Power thought fit to put me and my Brethren under the necessity of begging' (Corr., II, 311; cf. *PW*, V, 11).
71 Ibid., XV, 92.
72 Ibid., XVI, 401.
73 Ibid., XV, 343.
74 Ibid., III, 223, 222, 224.
75 Ibid., XV, 159.
76 Ibid., III, 87.
77 Ibid., XVI, 397.
78 Ibid., III, 5; cf. ibid., IX, 220.

79 Bodleian Library, MS Eng. Misc. e.180, fol. 4.
80 For the 'peace campaign', see Downie, pp. 139 et seq.
81 See A. D. MacLachlan, 'The Road to Peace 1710-13', in *Britain after the Glorious Revolution 1689-1714* (London, 1969), p. 209.
82 *PW*, VI, 15-16.
83 Ibid., p. 47.
84 Ibid., p. viii.
85 Samuel Johnson, *Lives of the Poets,* ed. G. B. Hill (Oxford, 1905), p. 19.
86 See J.A. Downie, '*The Conduct of the Allies*: The Question of Influence', in *The Art of Jonathan Swift,* ed. Clive T. Probyn (London, 1978), pp. 119-20.
87 See J. A. Downie and David Woolley, 'Swift, Oxford, and the Composition of Queen's Speeches', pp. 122–3.
88 *PW*, XVI, 441. Oxford bought 200 copies of Swift's pamphlet. See British Library, Loan 29/13/1.
89 *PW*, XVI, 480, 482.
90 Ibid., 430, 431.
91 *Poems*, I, 142-3.
92 See Maurice Quinlan, 'The Prosecution of Swift's *Public Spirit of the Whigs*', *Texas Studies in Literature and Language,* 9 (1967), 167-84.
93 *Journals of the House of Lords*, XIX, 339.
94 *PW*, XVI, 432, 433, 434, 435.
95 Ibid., p. 446. Cf. infra, pp. 180–1.
96 *PW,* XVI, 439, 435-6.
97 Ibid., VII, 73.
98 Ibid., XVI, 449.
99 Ibid., p. 452.
100 Ibid., p. 472.

Chapter 9   Dean of St Patrick's

1 See *PW*, XV, 272-3.
2 Ibid., p. 294.
3 Ibid., p. 303; *Corr.,* IV, 203: Charles Ford to Swift, 6 Nov. 1733.
4 *PW*, XV, 53-4, 140.
5 Ibid., pp. 207, 55; *Poems*, I, 137.
6 *PW,* XV, 51, 141.
7 Ibid., p. 250; XVI, 380; Forster Coll., no. 508. For Swift's lodgings in London, see *PW*, XV, 142n.
8 Ibid., pp. 86-7.
9 Ibid., pp. 204, 202.
10 Ibid., pp. 64n, 87, 179, 191; XVI, 333.
11 *Corr.,* I, 305: [1 Aug. 1712].
12 Ibid., p. 276: [18 Dec. 1711]; II, 393: 5 July 1721.
13 C.U.L. Add. MS 7788, Box 14: J. C. Walker to Edward Berwick, 12 Dec. 1790 (copy).

14 *Corr.*, I, 220: 10 Apr. 1711.
15 Ibid., p. 311: Swift to Miss Esther Vanhomrigh, 3 Sept. 1712.
16 *Poems*, II, 702-3.
17 Leslie Stephen, *Swift* (London, 1882), p. 128.
18 Peter J. Schakel, *The Poetry of Jonathan Swift: Allusion and the Development of a Poetic Style* (Madison, Wisconsin, 1978), p. 96.
19 *Poems*, II, 703, 708, 711.
20 John Irwin Fischer, *On Swift's Poetry* (Gainesville, Florida, 1978), pp. 110, 117, 118.
21 *Poems*, II, 707.
22 Ibid., p. 712.
23 Sheridan, p. 314.
24 *Corr.*, II, 392-3: 5 July 1721.
25 *Poems*, II, 691.
26 Ibid., p. 711.
27 Ibid., p. 725.
28 *PW*, XV, 303.
29 *Poems*, II, 684; cf. Schakel, op. cit., p. 82.
30 *Corr.*, III, 130, 137.
31 *PW*, XVI, 430, 519, 472. For a fuller account of Swift's role as the Oxford ministry's *chef de propagande*, see my *Harley and the Press*, pp. 162-70.
32 *PW*, XV, 320-1.
33 Ibid., p. 210. For Ford, see the introduction to *The Letters of Jonathan Swift to Charles Ford,* ed. D. Nichol Smith (Oxford, 1935).
34 *PW*, XVI, 553. For the Stamp Act, see Downie, pp. 149-61.
35 *PW*, II, 172.
36 G. M. Trevelyan, *England Under Queen Anne: The Peace and the Protestant Succession* (London, 1934), p. 208.
37 A. D. MacLachlan, 'The Road to Peace, 1710-13', in *Britain after the Glorious Revolution 1689-1714,* ed. Geoffrey Holmes (London, 1969), pp. 208, 207.
38 *PW,* XVI, 635.
39 Ibid.
40 *The Letters and Correspondence of Henry St John, Lord Viscount Bolingbroke,* ed. Gilbert Parke (London, 1798), II, 320-1.
41 *A Letter to Sir William Windham* (London, 1753), p. 31.
42 *PW*, XVI, 545.
43 H. T. Dickinson, *Bolingbroke* (London, 1970), p. 99.
44 *PW*, XVI, 604.
45 *Corr.*, V, 66: 4 Aug. 1737.
46 *PW*, XVI, 564, 664-5.
47 See J. A. Downie, 'Secret Service Payments to Daniel Defoe, 1710-1714', *Review of English Studies,* 30 (1979), 437-41.
48 *PW,* XVI, 669. As late as 1726, Swift was commenting on the £1000 he was owed by the Crown, and which he never received. See *Corr.*, III, 139: Swift to the Rev. Thomas Sheridan, 8 July 1726.
49 Ibid., I, 288; *PW,* XVI, 518.

50 See ibid., p. 530.
51 Ibid., p. 660: entry for 13 Apr. 1713.
52 Ibid., pp. 660-1.
53 *The Diary of Sir David Hamilton 1709-1714,* ed. Philip Roberts (Oxford, 1975), pp. 40, 41, 47, 54.
54 See B.L. Loan 29/415: 'State of the Case of the deanery of St Patrick's', MS notes in Oxford's hand.
55 *Corr.,* I, 345-6: 30 Apr. 1713.
56 Ibid., p. 371: Swift to Joshua Dawson, 29 June 1713.
57 Ibid., p. 373: Swift to Miss Esther Vanhomrigh, 8 July 1713.
58 See Geoffrey Holmes, 'Harley, St John and the Death of the Tory Party', in *Britain after the Glorious Revolution,* pp. 224-5.
59 *Corr.,* I, 374.
60 Ibid., p. 373.
61 Ibid., p. 378.
62 Ibid., p. 387n.
63 HMC *Portland,* V, 466.
64 Ibid., p. 660; cf. ibid., p. 300: Bolingbroke to Oxford, [June 1713].
65 Holmes, 'Harley, St John and the Death of the Tory Party', pp. 224-5.
66 *Corr.,* V, 45-6: Swift to the [second] Earl of Oxford, 14 June 1737.
67 *PW,* XV, 173, 68, 119, 180.
68 *Corr.,* II, 369: Swift to Alexander Pope, 10 Jan. 1721.
69 [Arthur Maynwaring], *Remarks On a False, Scandalous, and Seditious Libel, Entitled, The Conduct of the Allies* (London, 1711), p. 2.
70 Quoted by Harold Williams, *PW,* XVI, 573n.
71 Ibid., p. 572.
72 See ibid., p. 654.
73 *Corr.,* I, 347: 13 May 1713.
74 Ibid., pp. 355, 348.
75 Ibid., p. 351; Richard Steele to Swift, 19 May 1713; *PW,* VI, 165-78.
76 *Corr.,* I, 355; cf. *PW,* XVI, 637.
77 *Corr.,* I, 356; *The Guardian,* ed. John Calhoun Stephens (Lexington, Kentucky, 1983), p. 000.
78 Richard Steele, *Tracts and Pamphlets,* ed. Rae Blanchard (Baltimore, 1944), pp. 95-7.
79 *PW,* VIII, 4–6.
80 Ibid., p. 9.
81 Steele, *Tracts and Pamphlets,* ed. Blanchard, pp. 125-6.
82 *Poems,* I, 180. Samuel Buckley was a principal organiser of Whig propaganda. See Downie, p. 178.
83 Ehrenpreis, II, 702.
84 *PW,* VIII, 31, 34.
85 Ibid., pp. 43-4.
86 Ibid., p. 46.
87 Ibid., p. 65.
88 Ibid., p. 36.
89 See Downie, pp. 179-81.

90 *Corr.,* II, 22: Swift to the Earl of Peterborough, 18 May 1714.
91 [Abel Boyer], *The Political State of Great Britain* (1714), VII, 223.
92 *Corr.,* II, 12.
93 Ibid., p. 49.
94 Ehrenpreis, II, 301.
95 *PW*, XI, 292.
96 Ibid., II, 174.
97 Ibid., XV, 295.
98 Ibid., XVI, 532.
99 Ibid., IV, 5-6.
100 *Corr.,* V, 66; *PW*, XVI, 535.
101 Ibid., IV, 14, 13-14; *Corr.,* I, 301; Swift to Archbishop King, [26 June 1712].
102 *PW*, IV, 15.
103 Ibid., I, 2.
104 Ibid., IV, 14-15.
105 Frederik N. Smith, *Language and Reality in Swift's 'A Tale of a Tub'* (Columbus, Ohio, 1979), p. 21.
106 *PW*, XI, 199.
107 Ibid., IV, 61.
108 Ibid., pp. 57, 61-2.
109 *PW,* VIII, xix.
110 *Corr.,* II, 62.
111 *PW,* XV, 219-20.
112 *Corr.,* III, 3: 19 Jan. 1724; ibid., p. 104: Swift to Alexander Pope, 29 Sept. 1725.
113 *PW,* XVI, 597.
114 *Poems,* I, 186; *Corr.,* II, 42, 46.
115 *Corr.,* V, 46: Swift to the [second] Earl of Oxford, 14 June 1737.
116 HMC *Portland,* V, 466.
117 *Corr.,* I, 404-6.
118 See Angus McInnes, *Robert Harley, Puritan Politician* (London, 1970), p. 146; cf. Downie and Woolley, 'Swift, Oxford', p. 124.
119 B.L. Loan 29/138/5: Oxford to Harcourt, 15 Mar. 1714 (copy); Loan 29/10/10, 11.
120 *Corr.,* II, 41.
121 Quoted by Dickinson, *Bolingbroke,* p. 131.
122 *PW*, VIII, 132.
123 *Poems,* I, 173, 175.

Chapter 10 Exile

1 *Corr.,* II, 127: Swift to Charles Ford, Sept. [for Aug.] 1714.
2 Ibid.
3 Ibid., p. 126: Swift to the Earl of Oxford, 15 Aug. 1714.
4 Ibid., p. 132: Swift to Charles Ford, 27 Sept. 1714.
5 Ibid., p. 129: 14 Sept. 1714.

6   HMC *Portland*, V, 484 (draft).
7   Ibid., pp. 495-6.
8   *The History of Parliament: The House of Commons 1715-1754,* ed. Romney Sedgwick (London, 1970), I, 62.
9   *Memoirs and Correspondence of Francis Atterbury, Bishop of Rochester,* ed. R. F. Williams (London, 1869), I, 279.
10 See W. A. Speck, 'The General Election of 1715', *English Historical Review,* 90 (1975), 507-22.
11 *PW*, VIII, 107.
12 *Corr.,* II, 127: Swift to Charles Ford, Sept. [for Aug.] 1714.
13 Ibid., p. 131: Swift to Charles Ford, 27 Sept. 1714.
14 Ibid., pp. 138-9: Swift to Knightley Chetwode, 20 Oct. 1714.
15 Ibid., p. 127; ibid., p. 132.
16 *Poems,* I, 203-4.
17 *Corr.,* II, 132-3: 27 Sept. 1714.
18 *PW*, VIII, 107.
19 *Corr.,* II, 130.
20 Ibid., p. 135: Swift to Knightley Chetwode, 6 Oct. 1714.
21 Ibid., p. 130: Swift to Viscount Bolingbroke, 14 Sept. 1714.
22 The postmark of his letter of Aug. 1714 to Charles Ford shows that it was posted at Trim (ibid., p. 128).
23 Ibid., p. 130.
24 Ibid., p. 142: 5 Nov. 1714.
25 Ibid., pp. 149-50: [? 27 Dec. 1714].
26 Ibid., p. 150: 1714.
27 Ibid., I, 276: Swift to Esther Vanhomrigh, 18 Dec. 1711.
28 Ibid., II, 145: Swift to Archdeacon Walls, 23 Nov. [1714].
29 Ibid., p. 161: Swift to Knightley Chetwode.
30 For Swift's movements, see ibid., pp. 170-1: Swift to Archdeacon Walls, 22 May 1715. He wrote to Walls from Trim on 15 June, but was back in Dublin by the 21st when he wrote to Chetwode (ibid., p. 172).
31 H. T. Dickinson, *Bolingbroke,* p. 135.
32 *Corr.,* II, 140: 24 Oct. 1714.
33 Ibid., V, 232-3.
34 Ibid., pp. 231, 232; II, 167: 3 May 1715.
35 Ibid., V, 230.
36 See ibid., II, 171: Swift to Archdeacon Walls, 22 May 1715.
37 Ibid., p. 177: to Pope.
38 Ibid., p. 184: 2 Aug. 1715.
39 Ibid., p. 182: 19 July 1715.
40 Ibid., p. 176.
41 *PW*, VIII, 132.
42 Ibid., p. 141.
43 Ibid., p. 134.
44 Dickinson, *Bolingbroke,* p. 138.
45 Swift's alleged Jacobitism is discussed in Appendix II.

46 *Corr.*, II, 177.
47 Landa, *Swift and the Church of Ireland*, p. 68.
48 Ibid., p.69.
49 *Corr.*, I, 427: Swift to the Rev. John Worrall, 31 Dec. 1713.
50 HMC *Var. Coll.*, III, 262: to his wife, 28 Apr. [1713].
51 Quoted by Landa, p. 73.
52 *Corr.*, II, 152, 154.
53 Orrery, pp. 50-1.
54 *Corr.*, II, 133: to Knightley Chetwode.
55 See Landa, pp. 75-6.
56 *Corr.*, II, 279: 18 July 1717.
57 Ibid., p. 194: Swift to Bishop Atterbury, 24 Mar. 1716.
58 Ibid., p. 377: Swift to Dean Mossom, 14 Feb. 1721.
59 Ibid., p. 293: Swift to Knightley Chetwode, 2 Sept. 1718.
60 Ibid., p. 291: 29 May 1718.
61 Ibid., p. 307: Swift to Charles Ford, 20 Dec. 1718. For the verse-letters, see *Poems*, III, 966 et seq.
62 Ibid., I, 215. Cf. *Corr.*, II, 301-2.
63 Ibid., IV, 136: 30 Mar. 1733.
64 Ibid., p. 367; II, 334: Swift to Viscount Bolingbroke, 19 Dec. 1719.
65 James Woolley, 'Thomas Sheridan and Swift', *Studies in Eighteenth-Century Culture*, 9 (1979), 105, 93. For many of the details of Swift's relationship with Sheridan, I am indebted to Professor Woolley.
66 *PW*, V, 216-17; *Corr.*, IV, 310.
67 *Poems*, III, 1049.
68 Ibid., I, 313.
69 Ibid., pp. 215-16; *Corr.*, II, 301: Swift to the Rev. Patrick Delany, 10 Nov. 1718.
70 Quoted by James Woolley, 'Thomas Sheridan and Swift', p. 106.
71 *Corr.*, II, 333.
72 Ibid., p. 331: to Charles Ford.
73 Ibid., p. 322: Swift to Charles Ford, 3 May 1719.
74 Ibid., pp. 336, 341, 348, 330.
75 *Poems*, II, 721-2.
76 There are two versions of this poem, see ibid., pp. 744-52.
77 Peter J. Schakel, *The Poetry of Jonathan Swift: Allusion and the Development of a Poetic Style* (Madison, Wisconsin, 1978), p. 78.
78 John Irwin Fischer, *On Swift's Poetry* (Gainesville, Florida, 1978), p. 123.
79 *Poems*, II, 735.
80 Fischer, *On Swift's Poetry*, p. 125.
81 *Poems*, II, 734-6.
82 *Corr.*, II, 450; III, 47, 52.
83 *Poems*, II, 759.
84 *Corr.*, III, 52: to Charles Ford, 1 Mar. 1725.
85 *Ibid.*, p. 141.
86 *Poems*, II, 764.
87 *Corr.*, III, 141.

88 Ibid., p. 354. Swift was 47 in 1714, the year of Queen Anne's death.
89 Ibid., p. 142.
90 *Poems*, II, 766.
91 John Middleton Murry, *Jonathan Swift: A Critical Biography* (London, 1954), p. 276.
92 *Corr.*, II, 336: [1720?].
93 Ibid., pp. 334-5: [? 1719-20].
94 *The Correspondence of Jonathan Swift*, ed. F. Elrington Ball (London, 1910-14), III, 463.
95 Murry, p. 308.
96 *The Prose Works of Jonathan Swift*, ed. Temple Scott (London, 1897-1908), XII, 95. For Swift's reputed marriage to Stella, see Appendix I.
97 This is the version of the story given by Sheridan, pp. 330–1.
98 Lyon, p. 81.
99 *Prose Works*, ed. Temple Scott, XII, 95.
100 *Corr.*, II, 364.
101 Ibid., pp. 362-3.
102 Ibid., p. 364.
103 Ibid., p. 429: [June 1722].
104 Ibid., p. 325: 12 May 1719.
105 Ibid., III, 137-138: Swift to Thomas Tickell, 7 July 1726.
106 Delany, p. 58.
107 C.U.L. Add. MS 7788, Box 14: J. C. Walker to Edward Berwick, 12 Dec. 1790 (copy).
108 *Corr.*, II, 455-6: Swift to Robert Cope, 1 June 1723.

Chapter 11   Swift and Ireland

1 *Corr.*, II, 127: Swift to Charles Ford, Sept. [for Aug.] 1714. On this point, see also Angus Ross, 'The Hibernian Patriot's Apprenticeship', in *The Art of Jonathan Swift*, ed. Clive T. Probyn (London, 1978), pp. 83-107.
2 *PW*, IX, 5.
3 Ibid., II, 114.
4 *Corr.*, III, 289: 1 June 1728.
5 *PW*, IX, 199-200.
6 Ibid., pp. 208-9, 19.
7 Ibid., p. 200.
8 Ibid., XII, 18.
9 Ibid., IX, 200, 201.
10 Ibid., pp. 205-6.
11 *Corr.*, II, 342.
12 *PW*, IX, 21.
13 Ibid., pp. 15, 16.
14 Ibid., pp. 18-19.
15 Ibid., II, 114.
16 Ibid., IX, 18, 21, 16.

17 Ibid., pp. 16-17, 15, 21.
18 Oliver W. Ferguson, *Jonathan Swift and Ireland* (Urbana, Illinois, 1962), p. 57.
19 This is Swift's account of the prosecution, *PW*, IX, 26-7.
20 *Poems*, I, 237.
21 *Corr.*, II, 358: Swift to Sir Thomas Hanmer, 1 Oct. 1720. Hanmer was a close friend of the Duke of Grafton.
22 *PW*, IX, 26-7.
23 Ibid., pp. 21-2.
24 Ibid., pp. xxi, 306-7.
25 *Poems*, I, 275.
26 Quoted by A. Goodwin, 'Wood's Halfpence', *English Historical Review*, 51 (1936), 660 n.
27 *PW*, X, 11.
28 See Goodwin, 'Wood's Halfpence', p. 654.
29 *PW*, X, 16.
30 Ibid., p. 4.
31 Ferguson, *Swift and Ireland,* pp. 87-8.
32 *PW*, X, 7-8.
33 Quoted by Ferguson, p. 91.
34 *PW*, X, 4-5.
35 *Corr.*, III, 11-12; ibid., p. 17: Lord Carteret to Swift, 20 June 1724; *PW*, X, 189; Ferguson, p. 103.
36 *PW*, X, 15.
37 Ibid., pp. 18, 19-20.
38 On this point, see J. M. Treadwell, 'Swift, William Wood, and the Factual Basis of Satire', *Journal of British Studies*, 15 (1976), 76-91.
39 *Corr.*, III, 9, 12.
40 *PW*, X, 7.
41 Ferguson, p. 98.
42 *PW*, X, 4; VI, 15.
43 Edward W. Rosenheim, Jr., *Swift and the Satirist's Art* (Chicago, 1963), pp. 17-18, 23.
44 Samuel Johnson, *Lives of the Poets,* ed. G. B. Hill (Oxford, 1905), p. 19.
45 Ferguson, p. 84.
46 *PW*, X, 27, 28.
47 Ibid., p. 31.
48 Quoted by Ferguson, p. 108.
49 Ibid., p. 111.
50 *PW*, X, 53, 61.
51 Ibid., pp. 61-3.
52 Ibid., p. 62.
53 William Coxe, *Memoirs of the Life and Administration of Sir Robert Walpole, Earl of Oxford* (London, 1798), II, 396-7.
54 *PW*, X, xx.
55 Ibid.
56 Ibid., p. 97.

57 Ibid., p. 70.
58 HMC *Portland,* VII, 393: William Stratford to the Earl of Oxford, 12 Dec. 1724.
59 See Ferguson, p. 126.
60 *PW,* X, 75-6.
61 Ibid., p. 73.
62 Ibid., pp. 83, 84, 85.
63 Ibid., pp. 86-7.
64 Ibid., V, 291.
65 Ibid., II, 16.
66 Ibid., IX, 31.
67 *Corr.,* III, 57: 17 Apr. 1725.
68 Ibid., p. 93: Swift to the Rev. John Worrall, 31 Aug. 1725.
69 Ibid., p. 69: Swift to the Rev. Thomas Sheridan, 29 June 1725.
70 *Poems,* II, 566.
71 *PW,* X, xxvii.
72 *Corr.,* II, 381; III, 5.
73 Ibid., p. 87.

Chapter 12   Swift and Walpole

1 Oliver W. Ferguson, *Jonathan Swift and Ireland* (Urbana, Illinois, 1962), p. 98.
2 *PW,* X, 67, 68.
3 Ibid., p. 19. Cf. *Poems,* I, 350-2: *Wood, an Insect;* ibid., pp. 352-3: *On Wood the Iron-monger.* Swift is consistently concerned to belittle his adversary, while augmenting the threat he poses.
4 *An Ode for the New Year, Written by Colley Cibber, Esq; Poet Laureat,* n.d., broadside; *Poems,* I, 354; cf. II, 536.
5 Nietzsche's phrase, quoted by Isaac Kramnick, *Bolingbroke and his Circle: The Politics of Nostalgia in the Age of Walpole* (Oxford and Cambridge, Mass., 1968), pp. vii-viii.
6 *Corr.,* IV, 504: Swift to Charles Ford, 22 June 1736.
7 On this point, see T. N. Corns, W. A. Speck and J. A. Downie, 'Archetypal Mystification: Polemic and Reality in English Political Literature, 1640-1750', *Eighteenth-Century Life,* 7 (1982), 17–23.
8 Quoted by W. A. Speck, *Stability and Strife: England 1714-1760* (London, 1977), p. 228.
9 I have followed the brief account of the Bubble given in Speck, pp. 196 et seq.
10 *Corr.,* II, 342. France had suffered its own collapse of confidence in credit systems with the crash of John Law's Mississippi scheme in 1719, and this is what Swift is referring to.
11 Ibid., p. 361.
12 On this point, see Pat Rogers, 'Gulliver and the Engineers', *Modern Language Review,* 70 (1975), 260-70; J. M. Treadwell, 'Jonathan Swift:

The Satirist as Projector', *Texas Studies in Literature and Language,* 17 (1975), 439-60; and J. A. Downie, 'Political Characterization in *Gulliver's Travels'. Yearbook of English Studies,* 7 (1977), 108-21.

13 *Poems,* I, 250, 257, 259.

14 J. H. Plumb, *Sir Robert Walpole: Volume I: The Making of a Statesman* (London, 1956), pp. 293-328.

15 Ibid., p. 339; P. G. M. Dickson, *The Financial Revolution* (Oxford, 1967), p. 176.

16 *PW*, XI, 191. Cf. ibid., p. 311 for Ford's MS version.

17 G. V. Bennett, 'Jacobitism and the Rise of Walpole', in *Historical Perspectives: Studies in English Thought and Society in Honour of J. H. Plumb,* ed. Neil McKendrick (London, 1974), p. 71.

18 *PW*, XI, 191-2.

19 *Corr.,* II, 464, 465: Swift to Alexander Pope, 20 Sept. 1723.

20 See ibid., III, 52-3: Swift to Charles Ford, 11 Mar. 1725.

21 Ibid., p. 127n.

22 Ibid., pp. 130, 178, 211.

23 Ibid., III, 19, 39: Swift to the Earl of Oxford, 9 July and 27 Nov. 1724.

24 Ibid., p. 128: Swift to Thomas Tickell, 16 Apr. 1726.

25 Ibid., p. 137: the same to the same, 7 July 1726.

26 Ibid., pp. 131-2.

27 Speck, p. 225.

28 *Corr.,* IV, 130.

29 Ibid., III, 134-5: Swift to the Earl of Peterborough, 28 Apr. 1726.

30 Ibid., p. 144: Swift to the Rev. James Stopford, 20 July 1726.

31 Ibid., p. 138: Swift to Thomas Tickell, 7 July 1726.

32 Ibid., II, 384.

33 Ibid., IV, 493.

34 Ibid., pp. 333-4, 336.

35 W. A. Speck's phrase, see 'From Principles to Practice: Swift and Party Politics', in *The World of Jonathan Swift,* ed. Brian Vickers (London, 1968), p. 81.

36 *Corr.,* III, 166: 'Richard Sympson' to Benjamin Motte, 13 Aug. 1726.

37 J. H. Plumb, *Sir Robert Walpole: The King's Minister* (London, 1960), p. 104.

Chapter 13 *Gulliver's Travels*

1 *Corr.,* II, 381; III, 87.

2 Ibid., pp. 152-5.

3 Ibid., p. 182: John Gay to Swift, 17 Nov. 1726.

4 Ibid., p. 179: 5 Nov. 1726.

5 Ibid., pp. 189-90: Swift to Alexander Pope, [27] Nov. 1726.

6 See infra, pp. 87, 91-2.

7 *Corr.,* III, 198: 14 Feb. 1727.

8 Ibid., p. 194; Forster Coll. no. 561.

9   *Corr.*, IV, 197-8: 9 Oct. 1733.

10 Forster Coll., no. 8551.

11 Arthur E. Case, *Four Essays on Gulliver's Travels* (Princeton, 1945), pp. 1-49; F. P. Lock, *The Politics of Gulliver's Travels* (Oxford, 1980), pp. 66-88; F. P. Lock, 'The Text of *Gulliver's Travels*', *Modern Language Review*, 76 (1981), 513-33.

12 *The Dublin Journal*, 29 Sept.-2 Oct. 1744, quoted by Harold Williams, *PW*, XI, xxvii; *Corr.*, III, 189.

13 Deane Swift, p. 206.

14 *Corr.*, III, 153, 181, 182, 179.

15 Ibid., pp. 102, 181.

16 Ibid., pp. 103, 118.

17 Ibid., p. 103.

18 *PW*, I, 240.

19 Ibid., V, 243.

20 *Corr.*, II, 381.

21 Ibid., pp. 431, 430.

22 See *PW*, XI, xiii.

23 *Corr.*, III, 189.

24 *PW*, XI, 9. Subsequent page-references are given in the body of the text within parentheses.

25 On this point, see Pat Rogers, 'Gulliver's Glasses', in *The Art of Jonathan Swift*, ed. Clive T. Probyn (London, 1978), pp. 179-88.

26 On the illusion of verisimilitude in *Gulliver's Travels*, see Frank Brady, 'Vexations and Diversions: Three Problems in *Gulliver's Travels*', *Modern Philology*, 75 (1978), 346-67.

27 *Corr.*, III, 189. The frontispiece of Faulkner's edition of *Gulliver's Travels* is an engraving of Gulliver with an inscription, 'Splendide Mendax'. See *PW*, XI, plate facing p. [1].

28 Ibid., I, [140].

29 James Boswell, *Life of Johnson*, ed. G. B. Hill and L. F. Powell (Oxford, 1934), II, 319.

30 Deane Swift, p. 207.

31 Irvin Ehrenpreis, 'Jonathan Swift', *Proceedings of the British Academy*, 54 (1968), 150.

32 I have dealt with this problem at length in 'Political Characterization in *Gulliver's Travels*', *Yearbook of English Studies*, 7 (1977), 108-21. More recently, F. P. Lock, in *The Politics of Gulliver's Travels* (Oxford, 1980), has rejected the idea that Swift was 'referring to particular events and politicians' through 'specific allegories and allusions' (p. 89). But I see no reason to alter my own, earlier views on the topicality of *Gulliver's Travels*, although, as I have explained, Swift's method is one of allusion and analogy, rather than of allegory.

33 Downie, 'Political Characterization', pp. 112-14; Lock, pp. 115-16.

34 *Poems*, II, 389. In the first edition of *Gulliver's Travels*, the colours of the silks were given as purple, yellow and white, and although Ford included the correct colours in his list of necessary emendations in his

'interleaved' copy of the first edition (Forster Coll. 8551), these were retained in the so-called 'Second Edition Corrected' (see *PW*, XI, 303). Clearly Swift was upset at this attempt to generalise the political satire.

35 He owned a copy of Bacon's *Works*, which was marked by an asterisk in the sale catalogue of his library to indicate 'Remarks or Observations on them in the Hand of Dr. *Swift*'. See *A Catalogue of Books, The Library of the late Rev. Dr. Swift, Dean of St. Patrick's, Dublin. To be Sold by Auction* (Dublin, 1745), p. 15. According to Harold Williams, *Dean Swift's Library* (Cambridge, 1932), p. 48: 'The general character of Swift's closer reading is to be judged by those works marked with asterisks in the catalogue'.

36 Deane Swift, p. 177 [for 213].

37 See infra, p. 254.

38 Irvin Ehrenpreis, 'The Meaning of Gulliver's Last Voyage', *Review of English Literature*, 3 (1962), 23. See also R. S. Crane, 'The Houyhnhnms, the Yahoos, and the History of the Ideas', in *Reason and the Imagination: Studies in the History of Ideas, 1600-1800*, ed. J. A. Mazzeo (New York and London, 1962), pp. 231-53.

39 *Poems*, II, 640.

40 *Corr.*, III, 103.

41 *PW*, I, 244.

42 Ibid., IX, 114.

Chapter 14   Swift, the Opposition and Ireland

1 Bertrand A. Goldgar, *'Gulliver's Travels* and the Opposition to Walpole', in *The Augustan Milieu*, ed. Henry Knight Miller, Eric Rothstein and G. S. Rousseau (Oxford, 1970), p. 172.

2 *Corr.*, III, 198: Swift to Knightley Chetwode, 14 Feb. 1727.

3 Ibid., p. 196: 1 Feb. 1727.

4 Ibid., p. 144: Swift to the Rev. James Stopford, 20 July 1726.

5 Ibid., p. 185: Mrs Howard to Swift, [17 Nov. 1726]; *PW*, XI, 48.

6 *Corr.*, III, 195.

7 Ibid., p. 198.

8 Ibid., p. 207: Swift to the Rev. Thomas Sheridan, 13 May 1727.

9 Ibid., pp. 207-8.

10 *PW*, V, 97.

11 *Corr.*, III, 196: 1 Feb. 1727.

12 Ibid., p. 215.

13 Ibid., p. 219: Swift to the Rev. Thomas Sheridan, 24 June 1727; ibid., IV, 58: Swift to Gay and the Duchess of Queensberry, 12 Aug. 1732; ibid., III, 422-5: Swift to Mrs Howard, 21 Nov. 1730.

14 Plumb, *Walpole*, II, 175.

15 *Corr.*, III, 218-9: Swift to the Rev. Thomas Sheridan, 24 June 1727.

16 Plumb, *Walpole*, II, 167n, 161.

17 Ibid., p. 183.

18 See Quentin Skinner, 'The Principles and Practice of Opposition: The Case of Bolingbroke versus Walpole', in *Historical Perspectives*, pp. 93-128.

19 *Corr.*, III, 228-9; 237.

20 Ibid., p. 238.

21 Ibid., p. 421: Swift to John Gay and the Duchess of Queensberry, 19 Nov. 1730.

22 *PW*, V, 204, 205. The 'Holy head Journal' is an account of his days at Holyhead, waiting for the ship to set sail for Ireland.

23 *Corr.*, V, 35. He changed his will in 1740, directing that his body should be buried in the great aisle of St Patrick's Cathedral.

24 *Corr.*, III, 257: Swift to Benjamin Motte, 28 Dec. 1727.

25 Ibid., pp. 240-1.

26 Ibid., p. 242.

27 Ibid., p. 286.

28 Ibid., p. 383.

29 Ibid., IV, 184: Swift to Mrs Caesar, 30 July 1733.

30 Ibid., III, 248.

31 Ibid., p. 249: Swift to Knightley Chetwode, 23 Nov. 1727.

32 *PW*, V, 227.

33 *Corr.*, III, 320, 322.

34 Ibid., p. 260: Swift to Lord Carteret, 18 Jan. 1728.

35 Ibid., p. 267.

36 Ibid., IV, 53: Swift to Charles Wogan, [July]-2 Aug. 1732.

37 Ibid., III, 303.

38 *The Poems of Alexander Pope,* ed. John Butt et al. (London and New Haven, 1938-1961), V, 62-3.

39 *Corr.*, III, 201.

40 Ibid., p. 265.

41 *Poems of Alexander Pope,* V, 189-91, 63, 61, 191, 269.

42 *PW*, V, 99-107.

43 Ibid., XII, 32-7, 46-53.

44 Ibid., p. 5; Lyon, fol. 8 of the preliminaries.

45 *PW*, XII, 18.

46 *Corr.*, III, 341.

47 *PW*, XII, 109. Subsequent references to *A Modest Proposal* are given in the body of the text within parentheses.

48 *The Craftsman,* no. XIV: 20 Jan. 1727.

49 Louis A. Landa, 'A *Modest Proposal* and Populousness', *Modern Philology,* 40 (1942), 161-70.

50 *PW*, IX, 205-209. On this point, see David Nokes, 'Swift and the Beggars', *Essays in Criticism,* 26 (1976), 218-33.

51 *Corr.*, III, 375.

52 Ibid., IV, 53-4.

53 *PW*, XII, xxi.

54 *Corr.*, III, 382: Swift to Viscount Bolingbroke, 21 Mar. 1730.

55 Ibid., p. 383.

Chapter 15   A Man of Rhimes

1 Henry Craik, *The Life of Jonathan Swift* (London, 1882), p. 498.
2 *Poems,* II, 555.
3 *Corr.,* IV, 52: Swift to Charles Wogan, [July 1733].
4 *PW,* IX, 65.
5 *Corr.,* II, 333: Swift to Viscount Bolingbroke, 19 Dec. 1719.
6 *Poems,* III, 812.
7 *Corr.,* IV, 220: Swift to the Duke of Dorset, Jan. 1734. Bettesworth threatened Swift when he was visiting the Worralls, which led to the publication of a memorial signed by thirty-one of the inhabitants of the Liberty· of St Patrick's declaring their resolution to defend the Dean. See Sheridan, pp. 438-41.
8 *Poems,* II, 575-6.
9 John Middleton Murry, *Jonathan Swift: A Critical Biography* (London, 1954), p. 439.
10 Matthew Hodgart, *Satire* (London, 1969), pp. 30, 118.
11 *Poems,* II, 584, 589.
12 Ibid., I, 226-7; *Corr.,* I, 4.
13 *Poems,* II, 529, 597.
14 Ibid., I, 225.
15 Ibid., II, 581-2.
16 Geoffrey Hill, 'Swift: The Poetry of "Reaction" ', in *The World of Jonathan Swift,* ed. Brian Vickers (Oxford, 1968), p. 207.
17 See Delany, pp. 131-4; and *Corr.,* IV, 130: Swift to the Rev. Thomas Sheridan, 27 Mar. 1733: '*Cancerina* is dead'.
18 *Poems,* II, 483, 484; *Corr.,* IV, 83: Swift to Benjamin Motte, 4 Nov. 1732.
19 *Poems,* II, 485.
20 Ibid., p. 484; *PW,* XII, 156.
21 *Poems,* III, 772-3.
22 *Corr.,* III, 374: Swift to Alexander Pope, 26 Feb. 1730.
23 *Poems,* III, 795.
24 *PW,* XII, 155; *Poems,* II, 487.
25 Ibid., III, 837, 835-6.
26 Ibid., II, 536, 531, 532, 538-9, 540.
27 Sheridan, pp. 276-8.
28 *Poems,* II, 634-5.
29 Henry Fielding, *Amelia* (Everyman edn., London, 1962), I, 48n.
30 *Poems,* II, 642, 643, 653-4.
31 Ibid., pp. 655, 656.
32 Ibid., p. 464.
33 *Corr.,* III, 410-11: Swift to Lord Bathurst, [Oct. 1730].
34 There is considerable confusion about the identification of Swift's poem in the style and manner of his enemies, and until recently it was thought to have been *A Panegyric on the Reverend D-n S—t In Answer to the Libel on Dr. D—y, and a certain Great L—d* (see *Poems,* II, 491-2). However, Faulkner specifically attributed the *Panegyric* to James Arbuckle, and

essays by Aubrey L. Williams (' "A vile Encomium": That "Panegyric on the Reverend D—n S—t" ') and James Woolley ('Arbuckle's "Panegyric" and Swift's Scrub Libel: The Documentary Evidence') in *Contemporary Studies of Swift's Poetry,* ed. John Irwin Fischer and Donald C. Mell, Jr. (Newark, Delaware, 1981), pp. 178-90, 191-209, surely rule out Swift's authorship. Professor Woolley suggests that the *Answer to Dr. D—y's Fable* is the 'Scrub Libel' to which Swift was referring. See *Poems,* II, 514-15 for the character of 'The Worst of disaffected Deans'.

35 *Corr.,* III, 506: Swift to Gay and the Duke and Duchess of Queensberry, 1 Dec. 1731; *Poems,* II, 565. A problem surrounds the text of *Verses on the Death,* and the poem's relationship to *The Life and Character of Dean Swift. Upon a Maxim in Rochefoucault,* which was repudiated by Swift on its publication in 1733 (see *Poems,* II, 541-3). When they published the *Verses* in 1739, Pope and William King excised 'almost the whole of ll. 325-454' (ibid., p. 552) containing the major part of Swift's 'impartial' character, presumably because they felt it smacked of vanity on the Dean's part. They substituted 'over sixty lines' from the *Life and Character* to fill out the poem, and that is how it was printed in London. Faulkner's Dublin edition, however, 'showed the extent to which the poem had been cut down and altered', although until the publication of Harold Williams's edition of Swift's *Poems,* the 'text and notes of the "Verses" ha[d] never been fully or accurately printed' (ibid.). With regard to the pressure of space, I have decided to concentrate on the version of the *Verses* printed by Williams, and to omit consideration of the *Life and Character.* Middleton Murry thinks that the latter 'is, if not the better poem, at least the less incoherent and unequal one' (op. cit., p. 460), but *Verses on the Death* presents familiar Swiftian problems, and reveals more, in my view, of Swift the man.

36 *Poems,* II, 553-4.

37 *Corr.,* III, 118: Swift to Alexander Pope, 16 Nov. 1725.

38 *Poems,* II, 555; I, 216.

39 Ibid., II, 561.

40 *Corr.,* III, 510: Alexander Pope to Swift, 1 Dec. 1731.

41 Ibid., IV, 52-3: Swift to Charles Wogan, [July] 1733.

42 Ibid.

43 James Woolley, 'Friends and Enemies in *Verses on the Death of Dr. Swift*', in *Studies in Eighteenth-Century Culture,* ed. Roseann Runte (Madison, Wisconsin, 1979), VIII, 223.

44 James Woolley, 'Autobiography in Swift's Verses on his Death', in *Contemporary Studies of Swift's Poetry,* p. 119.

45 W. B. Carnochan, 'The Consolations of Satire', in *The Art of Jonathan Swift,* ed. Clive T. Probyn (London, 1978), p. 19.

Chapter 16   A Driv'ler and a Show?

1 *Corr.,* IV, 134: Swift to Alexander Pope, 30 Mar. 1733.

2 Ibid., III, 375: the same to the same, 29 Feb. 1730.
3 Ibid., IV, 262: the same to the same, 1 Nov. 1734; *PW*, XIII, xxxiii-xxxvi. Cf. *Corr.*, IV, 154, 169.
4 Ibid., p. 299: Swift to Mrs Pendarves, 22 Feb. 1735.
5 Ibid., p. 171; III, 289.
6 *PW*, XII, 141; *Corr.*, IV, 171. Cf. ibid., III, 471.
7 HMC *Stopford-Sackville*, I, 166: Lord George Sackville to the Duke of Dorset, 6 Oct. 1737; HMC *Portland*, VI, 68: J. Wainright to [the Earl of Oxford], 24 June 1738.
8 *Corr.*, III, 311.
9 Ibid., V, 118; IV, 171; V, 112; IV, 171. For Swift's loans at interest, see Forster Coll., no. 512. He was especially committed to his nephew, Deane Swift. See *Corr.*, IV, 139-40: Swift to Samuel Gerrard, 7 Apr. 1733. This explains the several references to Swift's being short of ready money and his 'embroylment' in an expensive and extended lawsuit (see, *inter alia*, ibid., p. 58).
10 Ibid., p. 457.
11 Ibid., p. 169.
12 Ibid., p. 505; John Middleton Murry, *Jonathan Swift: A Critical Biography* (London, 1954), pp. 465-6.
13 *Corr.*, IV, 536; cf. p. 545; ibid., p. 297.
14 Ibid., p. 458.
15 *Poems*, II, 673-4.
16 *Corr.*, IV, 197, 91, 169.
17 Ibid., V, 95: Swift to John Barber, 9 Mar. 1738.
18 HMC *Portland*, VI, 68.
19 *Corr.*, V, 120: Swift to Pope, 8 Aug. 1738.
20 Ibid., IV, 333-4, 346; V, 20, 3.
21 John Irwin Fischer, *On Swift's Poetry* (Gainesville, Florida, 1978), p. 200.
22 Peter J. Schakel, *The Poetry of Jonathan Swift: Allusion and the Development of a Poetic Style* (Madison, Wisconsin, 1978), p. 167.
23 *Poems*, II, 572; III, 830.
24 *Corr.*, IV, 381; National Library of Ireland, MS 2977; *Corr.*, IV 296 n.
25 Trinity College Library, Cambridge, Rothschild Coll., no. 2263.
26 *Corr.*, V, 23, 66.
27 *PW*, IV, 290-1.
28 Ibid., p. 149.
29 *Corr.*, II, 422: Swift to Knightley Chetwode, 13 Mar. 1722.
30 *PW*, XIII, 7.
31 *Corr.*, V, 168 n, 172.
32 Ibid., p. 188: 16 May 1740. Although he did respond to the publication of the Swift-Pope letters in a clandestine volume in 1740. See *The Correspondence of Alexander Pope*, ed. George Sherburn (Oxford, 1956), I, xviii: 'It is necessary to insist that in the summer of 1740 Swift, while not in good health, was perfectly able to revise and authorize the texts of his letters.'
33 Ibid., p. 142.
34 *PW*, XIII, 195-7.

35 *The Correspondence of Jonathan Swift,* ed. F. Elrington Ball (London, 1910-1914), VI, 184.
36 *Corr.,* V, 207.
37 See Irvin Ehrenpreis, *The Personality of Jonathan Swift* (London, 1958), pp. 120-1.
38 Ibid., p. 124.
39 See Elizabeth Duthie, ' "And *Swift* expires a Driv'ler and a Show" ', *Notes and Queries,* 222 (1977), 250.
40 *Corr.,* V, 215.

Appendix I Swift's Reputed Marriage to Stella

1 Orrery, pp. 14-17.
2 Delany, pp. 52-3.
3 Quoted by Murry, *Swift,* p. 278.
4 See, particularly, Sheridan, pp. 323 et seq.
5 See my letter to the *TLS,* 29 Oct. 1982, p. 1193.
6 Quoted by Ehrenpreis, II, 771.
7 Lyon, fol. 14 of the end leaves.
8 Trinity College Library, Dublin, MS 2051-2052.
9 The will is printed in W. R. Wilde, *The Closing Years of Dean Swift's Life: with Remarks on Stella, and on Some of his Writings Hitherto Unnoticed* (2nd edn, revised and enlarged, Dublin, 1849), pp. 97-101.
10 Murry, p. 505. Cf. Maxwell B. Gold, *Swift's Marriage to Stella* (Cambridge, Mass., 1937), passim.

Appendix II Swift's Alleged Jacobitism

1 Infra, pp. 207–8, 314–15.
2 The contrary practice has been unconvincingly adopted by Howard Erskine-Hill in the case of Pope (see 'Alexander Pope: The Political Poet in His Time', *Eighteenth-Century Studies,* 15 [1981-82], 123-48). In my view, it can be a particularly misleading approach.
3 *Corr.,* II, 372.
4 Ibid., IV, 493: Swift to Benjamin Motte, 25 May 1736.
5 Ibid., II, 384; 29 Apr. 1721.
6 Ibid., III, 506: Swift to John Gay and the Duke and Duchess of Queensberry, 1 Dec. 1731.
7 Ibid., IV, 333-334: Swift to Alexander Pope, 12 May 1735.
8 For this phrase, see ibid., p. 346: Swift to Lady Elizabeth Germain, 8 June 1735. Cf. ibid., III, 378: Alexander Pope to Swift, 4 Mar. 1730: 'tho' you are a Whig, as I am'.

Index

In general, works are listed under the name of the author. Extended discussions of individual works are indicated by boldface. Peers are usually listed under their best-known title.

Sheridan, Thomas, the elder, 16,
213-15, 218, 223, 233, 248, 259,
290, 292, 294, 297, 315, 327, 329,
331, 332, 336; *Ars Pun-ica*, 215
Sheridan, Thomas, the younger, 317
Shrewsbury, Charles Talbot, 1st
Duke of, 133, 196
Sican, Mrs, 332
Sidney, Sir Philip, 173; *Astrophil and
Stella*, 173
'Sixth of George I', 42, 228, 229-30,
234
Smith, Mr, Swift's curate, 114
Smith, Frederik N., 98
Snow, John, 185
Socrates, 193
Solomon, 193
Somers, John, Baron, 74, 75, 77, 81,
84, 85, 86, 91, 92, 118, 119, 120,
121, 132, 136, 137, 138, 183, 202,
252, 356, 357
Somerset, Elizabeth, Duchess of,
162
South, Dr Robert, 121
South Sea Bubble, 233, 253-5, 256,
278, 282
South Sea Company, 253
Southwell, Sir Robert, 30, 34, 35, 41,
42, 44
Span, Mr, 69
Speck, W.A., 152
Spectator, The, 121, 124, 189
Stamp Act, 175, 364
Stanhope, James, 207, 255
Starkman, Miriam, 102-3
Stearne, John, Bishop of Dromore,
69, 115, 118, 179
Steele, Richard, 120, 121, 122, 123-
4, 135, 183, 184-9, 193, 240;
Crisis, The, 187-9; *Importance of
Dunkirk Consider'd, The,* 185
Stella, *see under* Johnson, Hester
Stephen, Leslie, 169
Stratford, Francis, 16
'Stumpa-Nympha', 313
Sunderland, Charles Spencer, 3rd
Earl of, 81, 82, 84, 120, 132, 133,
202, 255, 354
Sunderland, Robert Spencer, 2nd
Earl of, 30, 34, 35, 41, 42, 44
Swift, Abigail, 3-5, 12-13, 16, 17, 18,
29, 31, 223, 349
Swift, Adam, Swift's uncle, 4

Swift, Deane, Swift's cousin, 18, 54
Swift, Deane, Swift's nephew, 10,
88-9, 264, 274, 274, 282, 332,
339, 378
Swift, Godwin, Swift's uncle, 4, 5,
12, 15, 17, 18, 30
Swift, Jane, Swift's sister, 3, 13, 18,
62, 115
Swift, Jonathan, the elder, Swift's
father, 3-4, 12-13, 28, 342
**Swift, Jonathan, the younger,
Dean of St Patrick's, Dublin:
biographical information:** 1667,
birth, 3; 1668-71, kidnapping,
4-5; 1674-82, Kilkenny School,
15-6; 1682-9, TCD, 16-21; 1689,
Leicester, 29; 1689, Sheen, 29-34;
1689-90, Moor Park, 33-5; 1690-
1, Ireland, 41-2; 1691-4, Moor
Park, 42-53; 1692, Oxford, 43;
1693, London, 45-6, 53; 1694-7,
Ireland, 54-62; 1695-8, Kilroot,
56-62; 1697-9, Moor Park, 62-8;
1699, London, 68, 245-6; 1699-
1701, Ireland, 68-70; 1700-1,
Laracor, 69-70; 1700-1, Dublin,
69-70; 1701, England, 73-9;
1701-2, Ireland, 79-80; 1702,
England, 80-5; 1703-4, England,
85-6, 112-13; 1704-7, Ireland,
112-7; 1707-19, England, 117-30;
1709-10, Ireland, 130-4; 1710-3,
London, 135-81; lodgings in
London, 166-8; visits to Windsor, 166, 168, 174, 197; 1713,
Ireland, 181-2; 1713-14, London,
182-95; 1714, Letcombe Bassett,
195-201; 1714-26, Ireland, 201-
57; 1726, England, 257-61; 1726-
7, Ireland, 288-9; 1727, England,
289-92; 1727-45, Ireland,
293-340

characteristics: ambitious, 14, 31,
33, 69, 118, 121, 138, 178-9;
anachronistic views, 41, 314-15;
appearance, 29, 73, 330-1; attitude to sex, 13-14, 172, 217,
309-14; attitude to women, 12-
14, 60, 67, 172, 217, 219-24,
309-11, 331, 349; belief in exercise, 73, 218, 330; 'born to disappointments', 16, 80, 181, 197,
219, 292; careful about money,

10-11, 70, 113, 114, 165-6, 178,
181, 201, 329-30, 349; charitable,
11, 115, 233, 313; depression,
152, 154, 203, 215, 219; fear of
emotional entanglements, 11-12,
113, 219-24; insecurity, 11-14,
18, 203, 219, 292, 323; morbidity, 219, 292, 325, 327, 334;
pretence to disinterestedness,
113, 178, 325; poor memory, 5-6,
34, 174, 330-1, 335, 337, 338,
352; prone to 'hero worship', 12,
153; proud, 35, 63, 66, 138, 139,
147, 151, 325, 332, 377; 'rage and
resentment', 225, 304, 333, 340;
tendency to embroider the truth,
3, 5-6, 68-9, 283, 294, 352; unfor-
giving, 17-18, 68-9, 290
opinions: absolutism, 27, 38, 260,
279, 345; 'ancient constitution',
6, 9, 27, 38-9, 144-5, 156, 157,
191, 241-2, 245-7, 258-9, 280, 296,
333; atheism, 6, 10, 25, 48, 127,
192-3; beggars, 227-8, 297-303;
Charles I, 6; Charles II, 6;
Church of England, 9, 10, 50, 67,
81, 84, 96, 99, 119, 126-30, 143,
180, 191, 259-60; Dissenters, 10,
57, 83, 96, 99-104, 108-11, 122-3,
127; duty, 227-8, 260, 280; English language, 191-2, 306, 336;
faith, 101, 104, 128; Golden Age,
6, 48, 129, 190-1, 280-1, 296;
'Gothic' monarchy, 27, 38, 245-7,
258, 351; Great Rebellion, 6-7,
76; history, 76, 192-4, 208, 294,
328; human institutions, 77-8,
96, 99, 104, 190, 245-7, 280, 287;
human nature, 11, 129, 131, 169-
70, 216, 228, 246, 265, 278, 280,
281-7, 304, 309-14, 322; Ireland,
3, 42, 114, 131-2, 201, 224, 225-
49, 253, 297-304, 314-16, 333;
Irish landlords, 226, 230, 235,
297, 301; law, 9, 234, 242-3, 244,
245-7, 260, 344; Liberty and
Property, 6, 27, 38, 39, 67, 84,
144-6, 156, 225-8, 229, 240-3,
245-7, 248, 258-60, 265, 279, 280,
293, 296, 333, 340; love, 67, 113,
128-9, 169-70, 172, 219, 284, 313-
14; manners, 144-5, 227, 230,
295, 296, 309, 313, 318, 320, 334;

marriage, 4, 12-13, 66-7, 113,
309, 311; monied interest, 156;
morals, 6-7, 144, 227, 230, 265,
274, 296, 305; nobility, 6-7, 144-
5, 278, 279, 297; old age, 66-7;
Parliament, 38-40, 84, 240, 247,
279; the 'people', 7, 9, 76, 228,
240, 279, 333, 344; philosophy,
19, 48, 254; political parties,
27, 67, 81-4, 119, 120, 126,
131, 137, 143, 144-6, 191, 240-1,
259-60, 291, 315, 345; politics,
27, 37-41, 67, 81-4, 119, 120,
131, 137, 143, 144-6, 156, 191-4,
208-9, 225-49, 250-1, 254, 255-6,
258-60, 274, 291, 303, 314-15,
333; projectors, 254, 281-2, 298-
304; Protestant Succession, 38,
82, 84, 157, 242-3, 247, 260,
344-5; reason, 101, 102, 242, 282-
6, 301-2; religion, 6, 25, 102, 104,
228, 274; Revolution Principles,
37, 82, 84, 144, 156, 242-3, 247,
258, 260; Roman Catholicism,
96, 97-99, 100; science, 281-2;
slavery, 6, 27, 225-8, 229, 240-3,
245-6, 296; standing armies, 40,
84, 191, 247; Test Act, 25, 83, 85,
119, 131, 333
with reference to: Anglo-Latin
word games, 16, 21, 116; art, 190;
Brothers' Club, 164-5; Church of
Ireland, 54-9, 68-70. 115-16, 117,
118-19, 130, 138-9, 210-13, 333,
337-8; 'excremental vision', 14, 309-
11; friendship, 11, 172-3, 217, 219,
292, 322; Historiographer-Royal,
194; irony, 90, 126-9, 214-15,
228-31, 242, 250-1, 268-74, 300,
302, 308, 320-1, 322, 324, 325-6,
357; letter-writing style, 14, 146-
7, 148, 165, 167, 222-3, 265, 328;
madness, 334-5, 338-9; Ménière's
syndrome, 34, 181, 215, 292, 294,
351; parallel history, 76, 192,
193-4, 275; parody, 96, 126-7,
239, 266, 300, 308; phonetic
awareness, 306-8; Pindaric odes,
46-51, 65, 265; raillery, 51, 53,
169, 173-4, 214-5, 221, 305, 321,
323, 328; rhetorical strategies,
76, 92-6, 98, 101, 122, 126-7, 141,
144-5, 158-60, 185-6, 188-9, 192,